The Canadian Writer's Market

Sixteenth Revised Edition

THE CANADIAN WRITER'S MARKET

Sixteenth Revised Edition

Sandra B. Tooze

National Library of Canada Cataloguing in Publication

The National Library of Canada has catalogued this publication as follows:

The Canadian writer's market

[1st ed.]– ISSN 1193-3305
ISBN 0-7710-8527-3 (16th edition)

1. Authorship – Handbooks, manuals, etc. 2. Publishers and publishing – Canada – Directories. 3. Canadian periodicals – Directories. 4. Advertising agencies – Canada – Directories. 5. Journalism – Study and teaching – Canada – Directories.

PN161.C3   070.5'2'02571   C92-032255-7

We acknowledge the financial support of the Government of Canada through the Book Publishing Industry Development Program for our publishing activities. We further acknowledge the support of the Canada Council for the Arts and the Ontario Arts Council for our publishing program.

Typeset in Plantin by M&S, Toronto
Printed and bound in Canada

McClelland & Stewart Ltd.
The Canadian Publishers
481 University Avenue
Toronto, Ontario
M5G 2E9
www.mcclelland.com

1 2 3 4 5   08 07 06 05 04

Contents

INTRODUCTION

You may write for your own enjoyment or for the challenge of it, but it's not until your work is published – made public – that you can truly call yourself a writer. Presumably, too, you write in the hopes of making some money. If, however, you have to begin by writing for publishers who can't afford to pay you, you will still gain valuable experience, compile a clipping file, and increase your confidence for more lucrative assignments to come.

The Canadian Writer's Market is designed to serve both the aspiring and the experienced freelance writer who wants to get his or her work published but needs some guidelines and/or accurate up-to-date listings of potential markets. Use this reference tool as a guide to prepare your manuscript, acquire a literary agent, approach an editor, evaluate a contract, choose a writing class, find style guides and how-to writing books, join a writers' organization, obtain funding, or enter a writers' competition. Refer to it also to determine which publishers to pursue and what they pay for freelance work.

This new, sixteenth edition of *The Canadian Writer's Market* includes the most current information available on market opportunities in Canadian publishing. It is an industry in flux and expansion, where data change with regularity, making it imperative that this reference book maintain the standard of accuracy freelance writers have come to depend upon. Back in the 1970s, when *The Canadian Writer's Market* was first published, the country sported a mere 100 consumer magazines, about 150 trade journals, two dozen or so farm publications, and 147 book publishers. Today there are over 1,600 Canadian magazines listed in *CARD* (Canadian Advertising Rates and Data) alone, and 300 to 400 English and French book publishers. *The Canadian Writer's Market* has always kept pace.

This edition lists only English-language publishers and publications, although some publishers are bilingual. Readers looking to sell their work in the French-language market in Canada should examine *CARD* for French-language magazines and *Quill & Quire*'s biannual guide, the *Canadian Publishers Directory*, for a full listing of French-language book publishers.

As in previous issues, *The Canadian Writer's Market* puts magazines into three groups: Consumer Magazines; Literary & Scholarly Publications; and Trade, Business, Farm, & Professional Publications. To facilitate your research to find a suitable market, or to recycle an article to other buyers, these groups have been broken down further, according to subject. Consumer magazines appear in fourteen sub-groups: arts and cultural; business; city and entertainment; the environment; feminist; general interest; home and hobby; lifestyle; news, opinions, and issues; special interest; sports and outdoors; travel and tourism; women's; and youth and children's. Trade publications are divided into twenty sub-sections according to the professions or trades they serve. A section of prominent business journals is included in Chapter 1 in order to describe in greater detail the market they offer, but many comparable business publications retain a simplified listing in Chapter 3.

Inevitably, however, these classifications are somewhat arbitrary and have a tendency to overlap. Even the distinction between consumer and trade publications is sometimes difficult to delineate. Some "trade" periodicals – the book industry's *Quill & Quire*, for instance – have such a general popularity that they are considered consumer magazines.

Manuscripts

As a freelance writer, your manuscript is your product, and it should have a professional, uncluttered appearance. That means it ought to be as grammatically correct as you can make it and without any spelling mistakes. The more editorial work the publisher has to do on your article or book, the more expensive and time-consuming it becomes to produce; consequently, the less attractive it becomes.

A manuscript should be presented on standard 8 1/2-by-11-inch, 20-pound, white bond paper. Your work should be computer generated so later it can be formatted from your electronic files. The font you select must be easily readable; italic or sans-serif typefaces should not be used as your primary font. The manuscript must be double-spaced and the margins at least one inch wide; this gives an editor space in which to write suggestions, queries, and editorial notations. The main body of text should be justified to the left-hand margins, and each page must be numbered.

The first page of your manuscript should prominently display the title of your work followed by your name. In one corner put your name again with your mailing address, telephone and fax numbers, and e-mail address. It is also a good idea (but not necessary) to include on this sheet a copyright notice (© Mary Smith) and the word count. To begin each chapter, start partway down the page with the chapter number and its title, if any.

A manuscript should not be bound or stapled; this impedes the editorial process. For a book-length manuscript, simply fasten it with elastic bands and support it between two sheets of cardboard, front and back, or better still, place it in a box. A magazine article can be secured with paper clips. Never send a publisher the only copy of your work.

If you are submitting your article in response to an editor's invitation or if you have signed a contract with a book publisher, it is likely they will ask for a copy of your work on disk as well. Inquire as to what program and format they require. Microsoft Word is usually a safe bet. They may want each article or chapter of a book in a separate file, but this varies from publisher to publisher.

Style

By style, most book and magazine editors mean the conventions of spelling, punctuation, and capitalization. There is, of course, no universally accepted manual for style because it varies from periodical to periodical, publishing house to publishing house, fiction to non-fiction, from genre to genre, and from discipline to discipline. Writers should remember, however, that style is an integral part of their craft, and by showing a blatant disregard for it, they can quite inadvertently prejudice an editor against their work.

Writers are expected to observe at least some of the basic house rules, and these should be obvious in what has already been published by those magazines and book-publishing houses for which they aspire to write. If they are not, the writer is always wise to find out as much as possible about what these rules are, and what stylistic traits – as idiosyncratic as many may appear to be – are preferred.

Canadian newspapers generally follow *The Canadian Press Stylebook* (which also contains some good tips on reporting), and magazines tend to develop their own standards and preferences from one authoritative source, or a compilation of several. Book publishers, however, usually adhere to well-known manuals. A selection of the best style and resource books is provided at the end of this book. Very often, a publishing house has compiled its own guide to house style, and the aspiring writer should never be afraid to ask for a copy of this.

Sending Out Queries and Submissions

It is crucial to research which magazine, newspaper, or book publisher is the best fit for your idea or manuscript. The listings in *The Canadian Writer's Market* are designed to help you determine the best publisher for your writing. In addition, read back issues of periodicals and newspapers, and study book publishers' catalogues to make sure you will not be wasting either your time or that of the editor. It's a mark of a professional to know what market in which to place your work.

Unless specifically told to do so, it is unwise to send queries or submissions by fax or e-mail. If e-mail is acceptable, resist the urge to become more informal or to take less care with your correspondence.

Of course, once you are ready to submit your writing, or even just send queries about it, you must maintain accurate records.

Keep a list of dates that manuscripts or query letters were sent out, what publishers they were sent to, the date the editor responded, his or her comments, whether or not the work was sold, and, if you are fortunate, the payment particulars.

Simultaneous Submissions

There is nothing wrong with sending the same article, proposal, or book manuscript to more than one potential market at the same time. It is your work, after all, so you can do with it whatever you please. But unless you are sending off material simultaneously to magazines that are happy to buy second, third, or fourth rights (which we discuss later), you could run into problems.

The practice can sometimes be unethical. Busy magazines need at least a month to assess an idea or a manuscript properly, sometimes more. During this time, several people may be assigned to the job of writing an informed critique explaining to the writer and the senior editor how the manuscript or article is effective, how it isn't, and what revisions may be necessary.

In publishing houses, this work takes considerably longer and is correspondingly more expensive. Judging a promising book proposal or an intriguing manuscript of two or three hundred pages usually means that an editor must set aside present work. If the editor is busy, an assistant or an outside reader might be engaged to do this job instead. Readers may be hired for their specialized expertise, to judge whether a writer has covered his or her chosen subject, be it fact or fiction, well and accurately. If an idea or manuscript appears tempting, the publisher may recruit market researchers to assess its sales potential. By sending the same material to several houses, the writer may automatically involve them all in the expense of assessing something only one of them would eventually be able to acquire.

Indeed, to established writers, the idea of simultaneous submissions is distasteful. Knowing how overworked editors can be, they give them reasonable time to respond – about six weeks for a magazine and as long as three months for a publishing house. If after that they have heard nothing, they fire off a reminder, then turn immediately to other productive work. The publishing business is notorious for its slowness, and, unfortunately, this is something all writers have to accept.

Postage

All publishers are under pressure to reduce costs wherever possible. Postage rates have soared in recent years, and so for any business that relies heavily on our mail system, they represent a bigger expense than ever. It should now be taken for granted that if you want your manuscript returned, you must include a self-addressed, stamped envelope (SASE) so that it will not incur any cost to the publisher. Increasingly, publishers will assume that you do not want your material back if an SASE is not included, and will simply throw it away.

Magazine and book editors stress this point again and again, and writers ignore it at their peril. If submitting to U.S. publishers, enclose international postage coupons or keep a supply of American stamps. You can order them online at http://shop.usps.com.

Rejection

Authors must learn to cope with rejection. First-timers might draw comfort from the knowledge of how many great writers could have papered their walls with publishers' rejection letters received early in their careers. Faulkner's great work *The Sound and the Fury* was rejected thirteen times before finding a publisher, as, coincidentally, was William Kennedy's Pulitzer Prize–winning *Ironweed*. On an altogether different scale, big-selling English crime writer John Creasey is said to have received no fewer than 744 rejections during his career!

Since editors usually don't have time to issue more than a standard rejection note, take heart if the rejection is sugared with qualified praise or, better still, specific constructive criticism. Chances are the editor is not simply letting you down gently but genuinely sees value in your work. Be open to suggestions, and rework your manuscript according to the advice. Take note of the editor's name, and resubmit your improved work to the same person.

Copyright

Copyright means the sole right to reproduce – or allow others to reproduce – a literary or artistic work. If you own a copyright, you are solely responsible for ensuring it is not infringed, and if you use work that belongs to another, you must respect his or her copyright rights. Therefore, as a freelance writer, you must have at least a general understanding of this area of law.

Here are some of the most frequently posed questions about copyright, with general answers:

What types of work are protected by copyright law?

According to the Copyright Act, writing is protected by copyright law "if the author has used labour, skill, and ingenuity to arrange his or her ideas." It may include poetry, novels, non-fiction works, compilations of literary works, catalogues, tables, reports, translations of these works, computer programs, unpublished writing, letters, e-mail, speeches, and song lyrics. Photographs and artwork are also protected by copyright.

When does copyright protection begin?

It begins upon creation rather than on publication.

Is every piece of written work copyrighted?

No. In Canada, copyright on a work lasts for the life of the author plus fifty years. In the United States, it lasts for the life of the author plus seventy years. After that, the work falls into the public domain and may be legally copied at will.

How can I tell who the rightful owner of a copyright is?

In the first few pages of a book or magazine there is a copyright notice. Typically it will read, "Copyright Josephine Blow, 2004" or "© Joseph P. Blow & Sons, Publishers, 2004." In Canada, the use of the symbol "©" is not required to establish copyright, but it is recommended. If you hold the copyright, you may use this symbol even if you have not registered your work with the Copyright Office.

The publisher's address will usually be printed above or below the copyright notice. Even if the copyright is held in the author's name, it is generally the publisher who has the right by contract to authorize reprints of excerpts. If, however, the author has retained these rights exclusively, which may sometimes be the case, he or she can be contacted through the publisher.

If you have difficulty contacting the copyright owner, try searching the Copyright Register at the Canadian Copyright Office (http://stategis.ic.gc.ca/cipo/copyrights/jsp/search.jsp). Sometimes copyright is held by collectives who administer the copyrights for their clients. A list of these collectives is available at www.cb-cda.gc.ca/societies/index-e.html.

How does copyright infringement occur?

Usually through carelessness or ignorance. Few writers deliberately set out to steal something that doesn't belong to them. They either quote too much of someone else's work without first seeking permission to do so, or use previously written words without making a sufficient effort to rework them.

What is too much of someone else's work?

The answer to this isn't easy. It depends on several factors, principally the quantity and quality of the portion taken and whether its use will detract from the impact and/or the marketability of the original. No one minds if a writer uses a line or two from a book and attributes its source; to reproduce three or four key paragraphs without permission, however – even with attribution – could lead to problems.

Some book publishers have established a guideline whereby permission is applied for if 100 or more words are borrowed from a single source. But, as previously stated, this is not a hard and fast rule. If the material is a key component of the original, permission may be necessary for far fewer words. Permission is required for the use of even one line of a song lyric or two lines from a short poem.

When it is determined that permission is necessary, the writer should contact the copyright holder to ask for the right to reproduce the work, quoting the extract(s) he or she wants to use in full, giving a true indication of context, details of the format (a magazine article, script, or book), size of audience or print run, the territory in which the periodical or book will be published, and the price of the publication. A neophyte writer wanting to use 100 words for publication in a small magazine probably will not be charged what a name writer would be expected to pay for a similar-sized extract in an article for one of the big players.

How can I copyright my work?

According to the Copyright Act of Canada, the act of creating the work is enough to establish copyright.

If, however, you feel there is a chance that one day the ownership of your manuscript may be in dispute or you want to be extra cautious, you may register it for a fee with Industry Canada. If your work is registered in this way, you would be in a much stronger position if the case ever went to court. It would be up to the other party to prove that you are not the creator of your work.

You can also mail a copy of your manuscript to yourself in a registered package containing the date of creation. This will provide you with a dated receipt. Store the unopened package and its receipt in a safe place in case the manuscript's rightful ownership ever becomes a legal issue.

Does a Canadian copyright protect me worldwide?

Yes, throughout most of the world, in those countries that are signatories of the Berne Copyright Convention or the Universal Copyright Convention, which are most nations.

Can an idea be copyrighted?

No, ideas are considered part of the public domain. If, however, you worked on developing a central character and the plot of a novel, you are considered a co-author of that work even if you did not actually write it.

Can news items or real-life events be protected under copyright?

No, they are similar to ideas in that no one has exclusive rights to them; they are part of the public domain. It is the *presentation* of those facts, however, that is covered by copyright.

If I work for a newspaper or magazine, who owns the copyright on my work?

Usually, if you are employed by a company, it automatically owns the copyright of everything that is published by it in the course of your work. The article cannot be reproduced or re-sold in any form without permission first being obtained. Often, newspapers generously allow articles, or portions of them, to be reprinted without charge.

Can a magazine editor steal the idea contained in my story proposal and assign it to someone else to write?

Yes, because ideas are in the public domain and cannot be protected by copyright law. For this reason, it is useless to write "copyright" on your proposal. But reputable magazines and publishing houses won't take your idea. They stay in business because their editors are ethical.

What does "fair dealing" mean in regard to copyright?

The Copyright Act allows for quotes to be used without permission for purposes of criticism, review, and private, unpublished study or research. There are no limits stipulated on the number of words that can be used without permission; the courts are the only arbiter.

Should I copyright the book I have been contracted to write before sending it to the publisher?

No. All publishers will copyright your work for you, under either their name or yours, depending on the terms of the contract you have signed. They will also register it for you at the National Library in Ottawa as an original Canadian work.

Does copyright still apply when work is reproduced on the Internet?

Yes, although this can be very difficult to monitor. It is suggested that you put a copyright notice on all your work that appears on the Internet. If you use a quotation taken from a web site, you will need permission if it is a significant part of the entire piece.

For specific information on copyright as it applies to periodical publishing, see Chapter 1.

Libel

Defamation is an untrue statement about a person that harms his or her reputation. A person's reputation is deemed to be his or her property, which he or she has the right to protect. It is considered to have been harmed if as a result of a statement, that person is now hated, disrespected, or held in low esteem. If the defamation is spoken, it is slander; if it is written, it is libel. Someone who defames another may be sued in civil court.

Libel does not have to be malicious or intended in order to be proven. Negligence on behalf of the author is no defence. But if a damaging statement is proven to be true, whether the subject's reputation was sullied or not, it is not libellous. In English Canada, only the living can sue for libel; in Quebec, an action can be brought by a descendant if the libel defamed him or her.

Writers should understand enough about Canadian libel law to protect both themselves and their publishers against court action. This is absolutely necessary since nearly all publishers' contracts provide for indemnification for the publisher in cases where a person maligned in a manuscript resorts to a lawsuit.

Many writers hold the mistaken belief that the use of fictitious names, or a statement saying that any resemblance between the characters in the book and living persons is purely coincidental, will automatically protect them from the possibility of a libel suit. This assumption is wrong. If the average reader associates a character described in a manuscript with an actual person, and the description reflects unfavourably on that person's reputation or integrity, there is always the danger of libel. The apparent intention to libel a person, even in fiction, could be interpreted by legal minds as a personal attack and could possibly lead to an action.

Fair and honest statements on matters of public interest, as long as they are true, are permitted. An author who comments on current affairs or writes a biography is allowed to express honest opinions or fair criticism of someone's works or accomplishments because this is usually in the public interest and serves to promote a useful purpose. Fair comment extends to criticism of books, magazines, articles, plays, and films.

In a situation where a libel suit is possible, newspapers and magazines have a distinct advantage over book publishers due to their frequency of publishing. Sometimes a timely retraction is enough to avert a court case, or at least lower damages.

Taxes

In Canada, the Income Tax Act is good to writers, allowing you to deduct legitimate work expenses from your taxable income. In return, you are trusted to show all your earnings, particularly fees that are unsupported by T4, T4a, or T5 slips from magazines and publishing houses that have printed your work.

Basically, writers come under three classifications:

- Salaried employees who supplement their incomes by earning a little extra money as occasional freelance writers.
- Part-time writers whose major income comes from another job that will almost certainly be cast aside the moment writing becomes more profitable.
- Totally self-employed, full-time writers not on any payroll who are expected to file honest returns mindful that no income taxes have been deducted at source.

Writers with other jobs need only attach to their income tax returns a statement summarizing writing income and expenses, and to show whether this extra work resulted in a profit or a loss. Any profit must be added to that taxable income earned from the other job. Losses, however, may be used to reduce it.

Writers living entirely from their craft must keep many more details: a list of all income and its sources, and receipts and vouchers to support expenses. Maintaining proper financial records not only serves as a reminder of cash that has flowed both in and out, but also helps to reduce problems that might be encountered should a tax return be audited.

Legitimate business expenses are allowable deductions from a freelance writer's gross income. Letterhead, envelopes, manuscript paper, labels, file folders, and other office supplies, including pens, pencils, erasers, and paperclips, can be deducted. The price of photocopying, copyright costs, reference books, other research materials, subscriptions to magazines and newspapers, union dues, dues in writers' organizations, bank charges (if you maintain a separate account for your writing business), the cost of secretarial help, and any payment for research assistance are also deductible. Business telephone, fax, and Internet costs can be written off, as can postage and courier expenses. If you take a course related to your writing or attend up to two professional conventions per year, they are also allowable deductions.

The purchase price of a computer, printer, and other expensive office equipment can not be deducted all in one year; rather, the Canada Revenue Agency (CRA) stipulates at what rate each item can be written off. But related expenses, such as computer paper, manuals, ink cartridges, software, and equipment repairs are permitted deductions in the year they are purchased, as are the cost of other essential devices used in your work; for example, a tape recorder and tapes with which to record interviews.

An area of tax deduction often overlooked is the depreciation of office furniture and equipment. Both may be written off according to a fixed percentage determined by the income tax regulations. A computer or typewriter can be depreciated by 20 per cent of the total cost each year for five years. The same tax saving may be applied to printers, modems, fax machines, cameras, tape recorders, filing cabinets, desks, chairs, and telephone answering machines. It is permissible to defer depreciation deductions to a future year when the business will be more profitable.

Travel is also an allowable expense, whether it is to visit a publisher or to gather research for an article, be it by bus, subway, car, or plane. The non-fiction writer may have to interview people in a different town or find other resource information there; the cost of hotels, transportation, and generally 50 per cent of the price of meals and entertainment are deductible.

Keep track of how much time you use your vehicle for business and the distance you travel, for this is a legitimate write-off, as are payments for gas, oil, insurance, lease fees, interest on a car loan, maintenance, and repairs. CRA also allows you to claim depreciation on your vehicle.

If you are a freelance writer working in a commercial office space, you may claim its rent as an expense. If you work from an office in your home, you are permitted to write off a reasonable portion of your living space. A writer using one room as an office in a four-room apartment, for example, may claim one-quarter of the rent or mortgage interest, property taxes, home insurance, maintenance and repairs, and utilities. You can deduct 100 per cent of telephone expenses if it's a separate business line.

For more complete information on income tax and the freelance writer, obtain a copy of the *Business and Professional Income Tax Guide*, a manual published by CRA.

If you have your own business, you must also be aware of the Goods and Services Tax (GST), or Harmonized Sales Tax (HST) in Newfoundland and Labrador, Nova Scotia, and New Brunswick. When your taxable sales of goods or services exceed $30,000 per year, you must register to file GST/HST returns. An option for some businesses with total sales under $200,000 is to use the "quick method" to calculate the amount owing as a percentage of total sales, instead of tracking the actual GST/HST paid out and collected throughout the year. A guide is available at www.ccra-adrc.gc.ca or at local CRA Tax Services offices.

Writers' Organizations

Writing is an isolating occupation, so it is good for morale as well as immensely practical to tap into one or more of the many writers' groups that exist in your community (a list of associations is provided in Chapter 10).

For professional writers with at least one published book behind them, valuable support is available from the Writers' Union of Canada, which offers members an impressive array of resources, including assistance with contracts and dealing with grievances with publishers, a manuscript evaluation service, your own web page on their web site, a newsletter seven times a year, and a range of practical publications free of charge. The professional guides that may be ordered from the union by non-members for a small cost are *Anthology Rates and Contracts, Income Tax Guide for Writers, Author and Editor, Author and Literary Agent, From Page to Screen, Writers' Guide to Canadian Publishers, Incorporation for Writers, Glossary of Publishing Terms,* and *Ghost Writing.* At a higher cost, their *Contracts Self-Help Package* includes a model trade-book contract, *Help Yourself to a Better Contract,* and *Writers' Guide to Electronic Publishing Rights.* Above all, the Writers' Union of Canada gives its members the opportunity to share their concerns and experiences with fellow writers, providing a forum for collective action to support their interests.

Many of these services are also available to members of the Canadian Authors Association, which has branches across the country. Founded in Montreal in 1921, the CAA has represented the interests of Canadian writers on many fronts, from championing improved copyright protection and the Public Lending Right to helping individual writers improve their contracts with publishers. (The Public Lending Right provides published writers with income from books held in libraries by compensating them according to how often their books are borrowed. As of 2004, 13,889 authors received a total of $9.4 million.) The CAA publishes *The Canadian Writer's Guide*, a handbook for freelance writers, it administers several major literary awards (see Chapter 7), and local branches hold writing classes and workshops.

The Writers' Trust of Canada is another national non-profit service organization mandated to advance and nurture Canadian writers and writing. Since 1976, working with an ever-changing pool of corporate partners, it has done just that in a number of practical and creative ways. It sponsors several major writing awards (see Chapter 7), supports the Woodcock Fund to provide bridge funding for established writers facing financial crises, and celebrates the importance of Canadian literature through the annual Politics and the Pen gala and the Great Literary Dinner Party.

Specialist writers' organizations, too, offer resources and support to writers in their field. The Canadian Society of Children's Authors, Illustrators and Performers (CANSCAIP), through its newsletter, regular meetings, and other organized activities, offers practical advice, moral support, and useful contacts to writers of children's books. Members are listed on their web site and in an annual directory. The Canadian Children's Book Centre also provides writers and illustrators of children's books with a range of resources and services. The centre has a comprehensive reference library of children's books, and promotes children's writers and titles through author tours, book readings, publications such as the quarterly magazine *Canadian Children's Book News*, and the annual TD Canadian Children's Book Week.

For freelancers who write for magazines, an excellent way to keep abreast of changes and developments in the industry is to join the Periodical Writers Association of Canada. PWAC membership entitles you to a subscription to their informative quarterly newsletter, *PWAContact*, and the electronic *PWAC Bulletin*; a comprehensive listing in their database, sent to editors and publishers nationwide; a copyright information kit; a mentoring program; and the opportunity to exchange market information and make important contacts with other writers. PWAC also sells several books, including *The PWAC Guide to Roughing It in the Market* ($24.60 for non-members).

American Markets

The English-speaking Canadian who has begun to sell with some consistency in this country should not ignore the colossal market in the United States.

The American annual *Writer's Market* (see Chapter 11, Resources) lists more than 3,000 magazine and book publishers in the United States. It also gives the names and addresses of editors, and sets out their requirements: what they expect from a manuscript in content and length, and how long it takes them to report back to a writer with a decision on whether or not they will publish.

Two U.S. monthly magazines are also indispensable to Canadian writers seeking new markets south of the border: *Writer's Digest* (the publisher of the *Writer's Market*), for practical-minded freelancers, and *The Writer*, for those with more literary tastes. These journals not only keep readers informed about markets and trends, but provide both a stimulus and a constant flow of fresh ideas. By the way, Writer's Digest Books publishes an astonishing array of practical books for writers, from guides to writing genre fiction to manuals on magazine-article writing.

Remember that just as you have to research magazines or book publishers in Canada before you send out a query letter or manuscript, it is imperative that you study the American market as well. Nearly all publishers have their own special character and narrow, specific needs.

But the enormous selection of American publishers in no way diminishes the difficulty of breaking into their huge market. Ask yourself why a U.S. publisher would be interested in your story, unless it is on a theme that has broad appeal to both nations. If it is specifically a Canadian story, there must be a compelling reason why Americans should care. Some Canadian stories will, of course, have an obvious, natural tie-in with American events. A perceptive article on NAFTA from a Canadian perspective might attract the interest of a U.S. business magazine. As a Canadian writer, you will have to work hard to penetrate the American market, especially with ideas for their consumer magazines.

Most Canadians who have consistently sold their writing in the United States do so thanks to the opportunities provided by the vast collection of American trade publications. Canada is closely related to the United States through common trade channels and by having similar concerns about world politics and business. The moment American equipment and/or expertise is brought to bear on a Canadian building site, for example, there could legitimately be the makings of a story for an American trade or professional magazine. Sometimes there may also be a story in how Canada sees, or deals with, problems specific to both countries.

But there is yet another hurdle to cross. Many American trade magazines are staff-written. This means that a staff writer will travel to Canada to cover an American story rooted here, so a manuscript from a Canadian freelancer must be exceptionally strong to win a place. The odds can be beaten, though. After accepting a few manuscripts from a Canadian contributor, the editor of an American trade magazine might be willing to publish a monthly feature written by a Canadian on the Canadian viewpoint: what his or her country thinks about mutual problems and issues, and what solutions it can offer.

It is well worth trying to secure a foothold in the American market for purely economic reasons. After all, it is still extremely difficult for Canadians to make a satisfactory living by writing exclusively for magazines and publishing houses in their own country, which explains why most writers combine the crafting of poetry, novels, magazine articles, and non-fiction with other work. The situation may change, though. Writing opportunities for Canada's writers have certainly increased since this book first appeared, and let's hope the trend continues. As it does, *The Canadian Writer's Market* will be there to guide and inform you with a richer list of resources than ever.

1

CONSUMER MAGAZINES

Writing for magazines can be both lucrative and fulfilling for the freelance writer. As you will see in the list below, pay rates vary widely, from a top figure of $1 per word down to zero. It can be argued, however, that even if you receive no payment for your work, just being published is an important step in the development and growth of your career.

In order to be a valuable marketing tool, *The Canadian Writer's Market* provides thumbnail sketches for each consumer magazine to briefly explain what types of articles it publishes. This is useful because so many magazines have names that give little indication of what they really are, who reads them, and, consequently, the kinds of articles or stories they buy. No one would ever guess, for instance, that a bimonthly Nova Scotia magazine called *Our Times* is a forum for workers' rights. Or that, far from being a farm publication, as one might first suspect, *Grain* is a spunky little literary publication that has been produced quarterly in Regina since 1973.

The term *publication* is often used throughout this book because, strictly speaking, many of its listings are not really magazines as we have come to know them. Some are tabloid newspapers, some simple, one-colour, staple-bound periodicals that feed the needs, sometimes sporadically, of a small group of loyal readers, some are even e-zines (electronic magazines). Others, however, are magazines in the truest sense: glossy, highly professional consumer or

18

trade journals that boast respectable circulations. The word *publication*, then, seems to safely cover all listings, both large and small.

Much more important to the freelance writer is that many of these publications provide opportunities both for established freelancers wanting to break fresh ground and for neophyte writers seeking to have their work published. Each one listed accepts outside contributions with varying frequency and for equally varying fees.

When writing for magazines, it is usual to present the idea for an article to the editor before you have completed the piece. Of course, you should do some initial research on the story so that you can decide on its focus and direction, and are able to write a compelling pitch to the magazine in your query letter. Large magazines plan their editorial content up to a year in advance. Therefore, if you have an article idea relating to a specific holiday, season, event, or anniversary, you must query the editor this far ahead.

Try to expand one article idea into several. Be alert as to how you can use the research for one story to provide the bases for other different but related pieces. For instance, background information for an article on city gardens for a general-interest consumer magazine could be utilized for a story on the gardening-centre phenomenon sold to a business journal or used for a more technical piece aimed at a trade publication.

For feature articles, editors tend to call on freelancers they have worked with before and know to be accurate and reliable. To break into this somewhat closed system, you may have to start by writing smaller pieces for a particular publication, then, after proving yourself, work your way up to the major stories. Along the way, try to establish relationships with the editors to whom you sell your work.

Researching Target Magazines

It is a waste of everyone's time to send a query letter to a business periodical if you are proposing to write about a religious pilgrimage to Mecca. By using the list below, research what magazines publish the type of article you are proposing. Get the name of the editor or contact person. Note the frequency of publication; those magazines that publish more often require the most articles.

Read copies of the publications that are likely candidates for your story, and become familiar with their content and focus. It may be helpful to look at a magazine from the editor's point of view. His or her focus is to keep the readers resubscribing and keep them buying the advertisers' products. From this perspective, it's obvious that your article must appeal to the reader that the publication targets through its editorial and advertising focus. Use this information to either adjust the slant of your article or to determine that this is or is not a magazine to approach with your idea.

Another way to ascertain what magazines to query is to look at their mastheads and compare personnel names with the names of those who wrote each article. You may discover that a staff writer always pens the type of article or column you are intending to write. In these circumstances, it is unlikely that the editor will hire an outsider for these stories.

Find out if your target magazine has an editorial calendar or if it runs special or theme issues for which you could write a piece. The *CARD* directory and its annual supplement, *Publication Profiles*, sometimes list these. Also check a periodical's web site for information about forthcoming issues.

Once you understand what a magazine requires in terms of content, you must determine what its editor wants regarding format. Check the web site for guidelines or request them before you send a query letter, and follow them exactly. For example, it would be a waste of effort to offer an editor a 3,000-word article if the publication never publishes more than 2,000.

Payment Policy

Check the following listings to determine if payment for articles is due on acceptance or on publication, and always confirm this before reaching an agreement. Although you may be delighted to be published either way, you should understand the two schedules of compensation.

While payment on acceptance is much less common, it is preferable for the writer because even if the magazine decides not to publish your article or goes out of business, you will still receive the amount owing. By waiting until after the publication of your work to receive compensation, you run the risk of long delays or even the return of your work due to policy changes, a turnover of editorial staff, or a business setback.

The Query Letter

The query letter is usually the vehicle for a freelancer's initial contact with a magazine, as most editors prefer not to receive unsolicited articles. Query by phone only if the article you are proposing is time sensitive or if a magazine specifically invites telephone queries. It has been estimated that in order to sell one article, you must be prepared to send out ten queries.

No matter how ingenious your article (or idea) may be, if your query letter to an editor is not equally compelling, your work likely will not see the published page. It must be professional, well written, and convincing. As it's often the only means by which you can break into a new market, the query letter is a key factor in becoming a successful freelance writer.

Choose unadorned, business-like stationery on which you have included your name, address, telephone and fax numbers, and e-mail address. Address your letter to a specific person, using Mr. or Ms. Your correspondence must be typed, using an easily read font, and single-spaced. Mail your query (do not fax or e-mail it unless a magazine indicates otherwise) and enclose an SASE.

Since the query letter may be the only opportunity an editor has had to see your writing, it is crucial that the style of your letter attracts his or her attention and indicates you are a proficient journalist. Begin with an attention-grabbing intro and write in the style of your proposed article. If, for example, you want to write a humorous piece, your query must reflect that, leaving the editor in no doubt that you are up to the job.

Keep your letter to one page in length. In it you must provide a captivating, but brief, synopsis of the article you are proposing. Include your research plans and indicate what section of the magazine it would be most appropriate for. Then inform the editor why you are the person best suited to write this piece. Mention any first-hand knowledge or special interest you might have in the subject area you wish to write about. Indicate your publishing background and include the clippings most relevant to the magazine you are targeting.

Tell the editor what rights you are offering and if the article has appeared elsewhere. Provide the most accurate word count you can and the approximate delivery date. Also, mention any photos you can provide to accompany the piece (but do not send them at this time). Remember to check your spelling and grammar carefully before you send the letter.

Photographs

Photographs are another means by which you can increase the saleability of your article and earn extra money as well. By reviewing previous issues of your target publications, you will know whether they publish colour or black-and-white photos, or if they accept photos at all.

Describe in your query letter the photos you can provide. If interested, the editor will tell you the specifications the magazine requires. Before mailing off any pictures, make sure you have duplicates and print your name, address, and copyright notice on each slide or print. Captions may be typed and attached to photos individually, or several captions could be printed on a page and numbered to correspond to each image. Alternatively, your editor may prefer scanned photos and captions sent by e-mail.

Sidebars

Sidebars can be a means to help sell your article and boost your income. Also called boxes or bars, and often shaded to set them off from the rest of the text, these supplemental information bytes contain information germane to, but not intrinsically part of, the primary article. For example, if you are writing about the recording business in Canada, a sidebar might highlight the experiences of one specific record company; alternatively, a sidebar accompanying a piece about the challenges faced by XYZ Recording Company could give a broad overview of the entire industry.

Discuss the possibility of one or more sidebars with the editor; if accepted, they should earn you extra money. When preparing your manuscript, make sure sidebars are clearly marked so an editor knows they are not part of the main text.

Copyright and Contracts

Understanding how rights to published works are categorized is an important factor in making a living as a freelance writer. Before signing a contract or making a verbal agreement with a magazine or newspaper editor, you may wish to contact a lawyer specializing in this field. Nevertheless, you should still have a basic knowledge of what obligations and opportunities exist when you sell the rights to your work.

1) All rights: When you sell all rights to an article, it can be sold only once. You can, however, reuse the idea for the original work, as long as you completely rewrite and restructure the article and make it significantly different from the original by, for example, using new data, fresh quotes, a different focus, and by arriving at a contradictory conclusion.

2) First rights: First rights allow the periodical to publish your work once. After it has appeared in print, you are permitted to resell that same article as many times as you wish.

3) Second (or reprint) rights: These are the rights you are permitted to sell after your article has appeared in the publication that bought the first rights.

4) North American rights: This gives the publication the right to publish an article to be read by an audience across the continent.

5) Canadian rights: With these rights, the magazine has permission to publish a work that will be read only within the country.

6) Serial rights: This gives the publication the right to publish a work in a sister publication without having to pay extra for it.

In addition to specifying which of the above rights you are selling, the magazine or newspaper should inform you which electronic rights are included in the sale. If not, you could receive a hard lesson by discovering your work on the Internet, on a commercial database, or on a CD-ROM without compensation.

When buying first rights, some companies now insist on acquiring second rights and electronic rights for no additional fee or for a small payment at best. Do not sign away additional rights without consulting a legal specialist; you may lose a lucrative source of income. Always aim to retain as many rights as possible. Contact the Canadian Authors Association, the Periodical Writers Association of Canada, or the Writers' Union of Canada for more information.

Online Publications

When you are considering what publications to target, don't forget that publishing opportunities now exist in cyberspace. E-zines are proliferating on the Internet due in part to the lower costs of production. In addition, writers are required for online press releases, newsletters, and the larger web sites. While many electronic publishers do not pay writers, their sites may provide a good starting point to get your work in print.

As with hard-copy magazines, a query letter should be your first introduction to the editor. For this format, an e-mail query is required. Resist the urge toward informality; as is the case when you write to regular publications, you should correspond in a professional manner, showing the editor your best work.

The electronic medium fosters impatience in its users, so tailor the writing style of your article accordingly. Use shorter paragraphs and consider using subheads and sidebars. Long, dense articles appear daunting and tedious on a computer screen.

Arts & Cultural

Applied Arts
18 Wynford Drive, Suite 411, Toronto, ON M3C 3S2
Phone: (416) 510-0909 Fax: (416) 510-0913
E-mail: editor@appliedartsmag.com
Web site: www.appliedartsmag.com
Contact: Sara Curtis, editor
Circulation: 12,000
Published bimonthly

Canada's leading graphic arts magazine, targeting visual communicators (designers, photographers, illustrators, art directors) who work in traditional and new media. Spotlights the work of graphic design, advertising, photography, and illustration professionals, featuring outstanding examples of their work. Pays 40¢ to 60¢/word on acceptance for articles of 800 to 1,500 words. Guidelines available. "Please be familiar with the magazine before submitting queries. Knowledge of design, photography, and/or illustration is an asset."

Artichoke: Writings about the Visual Arts
901 Jervis Street, Unit 208, Vancouver, BC V6E 2B6
Phone: (604) 683-1941 Fax: (604) 683-1941
E-mail: editor@artichoke.ca
Web site: www.artichoke.ca
Contact: Paula Gustafson, editor
Circulation: 1,500
Published 3 times a year

The only nationally distributed magazine consistently presenting and discussing the visual arts in Western Canada. Also features articles and reviews about national and international artists and exhibitions, analysis of current and critical issues, and stories connected with the visual arts. Preferred length for features 1,500 to 2,000 words, reviews 1,000 to 1,500 words, book reviews and ArtSeen column 500 to 750 words. Pays on publication: $125 for features and reviews, less for shorter pieces. "*Artichoke* does not publish academic jargon or artspeak. Articles written with clarity, precision, and a knowledge of art are welcomed." Guidelines available on web site.

ArtsAtlantic

P.O. Box 36007, RPO Spring Garden Road, Halifax, NS B3J 3S9
Phone: (902) 420-5045 Fax: (902) 491-8624
E-mail: arts.atlantic@smu.ca
Web site: www.artsatlantic.ca
Contact: Mimi Fautley, editor
Circulation: 2,500
Published 3 times a year

Award-winning arts magazine carrying features, reviews, and essays on Atlantic Canada's visual arts. Reviews are 700 words, feature articles 2,500 to 3,500 words. Pays a flat rate of $100/review, $250 for features, on publication.

Azure

460 Richmond Street W., Suite 601, Toronto, ON M5V 1Y1
Phone: (416) 203-9674 Fax: (416) 203-9842
E-mail: azure@azureonline.com
Web site: www.azureonline.com
Contact: Nelda Rodger, editor
Circulation: 20,000
Published bimonthly

A design review covering graphic, interior and industrial design, architecture, landscape architecture, and contemporary art in Canada and abroad. Directed toward designers, architects, and the visually aware. Design projects and products are selected with an eye to technical and design innovation, aesthetics, and functionality. Pay varies depending on department and is paid on publication. Unsolicited submissions not encouraged. Guidelines available.

B.C. BookWorld

3516 West 13th Avenue, Vancouver, BC V6R 2S3
Phone: (604) 736-4011 Fax: (604) 736-4011
E-mail: bookworld@telus.net
Contact: David Lester, editor
Circulation: 100,000
Published quarterly

Covers books written by B.C. authors and books about B.C. Circulated by more than 700 distributors. Preferred length 500 to 750 words. Pay rates vary depending on project, but most writing is in-house, so phone or write first. This is not a trade publication or a review periodical; it's a populist, tabloid-format newspaper.

Blackflash

12 – 23rd Street E., Saskatoon, SK S7K 0H5
Phone: (306) 374-5115 Fax: (306) 665-6568
E-mail: editor@blackflash.ca or blackflash@quadrant.net
Web site: www.blackflash.com
Contacts: Theo Sims and Carrie Horachek, managing editors
Circulation: 1,800
Published 3 times a year

Focuses on critical writing about photo-based and new-media art production. Pays $150 to $300 on publication for 1,000 to 2,500 words. Accepts proposals/outlines only. Guidelines available on web site.

Border Crossings

70 Arthur Street, Suite 500, Winnipeg, MB R3B 1G7
Phone: (204) 942-5778 Fax: (204) 949-0793
E-mail: bordercrossings@mts.net
Web site: www.bordercrossingsmag.com
Contact: Meeka Walsh, editor
Circulation: 5,500
Published quarterly

An interdisciplinary arts review with an educated national and international audience, featuring articles, book reviews, artist profiles, and interviews covering the full range of the contemporary arts in Canada and beyond. Subjects include architecture, dance, fiction, film, painting, photography, poetry, politics, and theatre. Pays a negotiated fee on publication. Use the magazine as your guide when formulating submissions, but query first by letter or phone.

Broken Pencil

P.O. Box 203, Stn. P, Toronto, ON M5S 2S7
E-mail: editor@brokenpencil.com
Web site: www.brokenpencil.com
Contact: Emily Schultz, editor
Circulation: 3,000
Published 3 times a year

The guide to underground publishing and independent culture in Canada, including zines, politics, art, film, music, and general zaniness from an alternative perspective. Pays $50 to $400 on publication for articles and fiction 500 to 4,000 words. "Read the magazine first! Only the knowledgeable and unconventional need apply."

Canadian Art
51 Front Street E., Suite 210, Toronto, ON M5E 1B3
Phone: (416) 368-8854, ext. 384 Fax: (416) 368-6135
E-mail: info@canadianart.ca
Contact: Richard Rhodes, editor
Circulation: 20,000
Published quarterly
Covers visual arts in Canada in a lively and opinionated way. Includes articles on painting, sculpture, film, photography, and video, with critical profiles of new artists and assessments of established art-world figures. Reviews are 500 words and features 2,000 to 3,000 words. Pays $200 for 500 words, up to $1,500 for 3,000 words, on publication. Query first. No unsolicited submissions.

Canadian Musician
23 Hannover Drive, Unit 7, St. Catharines, ON L2W 1A3
Phone: (905) 641-1512 Fax: (905) 641-1648
Web site: www.canadianmusician.com
Contact: Jeff MacKay, editor
Published bimonthly
A magazine for professional and amateur musicians, as well as serious music enthusiasts and industry personnel. Most articles (2,000 to 3,000 words) are assigned and fees are negotiable. Pays on acceptance. All writers must be technically and musically literate. Guidelines available.

Canadian Notes & Queries
c/o The Porcupine's Quill, 68 Main Street, Erin, ON N0B 1T0
Phone: (519) 833-9158 Fax: (519) 833-9845
E-mail: pql@sentex.net
Web site: www.sentex.net/~pql
Contact: Elke Inkster, general manager

Circulation: 600
Published twice a year
Publishes articles, essays, memoirs, reviews, and other material for those interested in Canadian studies. It is a forum in which writers, scholars, historians, and genealogists seek answers to research questions and share their own original discoveries with others. Articles 1,000 to 10,000 words. Pays $100 per article on publication.

Canadian Screenwriter
366 Adelaide Street W., Suite 401, Toronto, ON M5V 1R9
Phone: (416) 979-7907 Fax: (416) 979-9273
E-mail: writers@moscovitch.com
Web site: www.wgc.ca/magazine
Contact: Philip Moscovitch, editor
Circulation: 8,000
Published quarterly
A magazine for professionals in the Canadian film and television industry and for those who want to break in to those fields. "Make sure your pitch focuses on writers and writing." Articles 800 to 3,000 words. Pays 50¢/word on acceptance. Guidelines available.

Canadian Theatre Review
School of English and Theatre Studies, Massey Hall, University of
    Guelph, Guelph, ON N1G 2W1
Phone: (519) 824-4120, ext. 53882 Fax: (519) 824-0560
E-mail: preynen@utpjournals.com
Web site: www.utpjournals.com
Contact: editorial committee
Circulation: 850
Published quarterly
Publishes playscripts, essays of interest to theatre professionals, and interviews with playwrights, actors, directors, and designers. Issues are thematic. Preferred article length 1,500 to 3,000 words. Pay scale and guidelines available on request.

Canadian Writer's Journal
P.O. Box 1178, New Liskeard, ON P0J 1P0
Phone: (705) 647-5424 or 1-800-258-5451 Fax: (705) 647-8366

E-mail: cwj@cwj.ca
Web site: www.cwj.ca
Contact: Deborah Ranchuk, editor
Circulation: 400
Published bimonthly

A digest-size quarterly that is a useful source of ideas on professional, motivational, and marketing aspects of the profession of writing. Emphasis on short how-to articles for both apprentice and professional writers. Also opinion pieces, book reviews, and short poems. Pays on publication $7.50/page (approximately 450 words). Contributor copies sent for each item published. "Queries or complete manuscripts welcome. Writers should present specifics rather than generalities, and avoid overworked subjects such as overcoming writer's block, handling rejection, etc." Read guidelines.

Chart Magazine

41 Britain Street, Suite 200, Toronto, ON M5A 1R7
Phone: (416) 363-3101   Fax: (416) 363-3109
E-mail: chart@chartattack.com
Web site: www.chartattack.com
Contact: Nada Laskovski, co-publisher
Circulation: 40,000
Published monthly

Covers new music for a high school/university audience, including Canadian bands, independent/alternative music, campus radio, pop-culture reviews, and articles. Pays on publication; rates vary depending on project. Guidelines available. "Generally ideas are worked through with editor(s). We rarely accept/publish completed articles as is."

Coda, Journal of Jazz and Improvised Music

161 Frederick Street, Toronto, ON M5A 4P3
Phone: (416) 596-1480   Fax: (416) 596-9793
E-mail: broomer@sprynet.com
Contact: Stuart Broomer, editor
Circulation: 3,000
Published bimonthly

Specializing in jazz for over 45 years. Publishes articles on historical subjects as well as current music. "It takes jazz very seriously." Fees negotiated and paid on publication. "The magazine requires genuine expertise in the area of jazz/improvised music under discussion."

The Dance Current
55 Mill Street, Suite 312, Toronto, ON M5A 3C4
Phone: (416) 588-0850
E-mail: editor@thedancecurrent.com
Web site: www.thedancecurrent.com
Contact: Megan Andrews, publisher/founding editor
Circulation: 1,000
Published 9 times a year
  Provides insight into professional dance, art, and culture for artists, dance professionals, students, and the general public. Articles 500 to 1,800 words. Fees are honoraria, paid on publication, and vary depending on the project. Guidelines available.

Dance International
677 Davie Street, Level 6, Vancouver, BC V6B 2G6
Phone: (604) 681-1525 Fax: (604) 681-7732
E-mail: danceint@direct.ca
Web site: www.danceinternational.org
Contact: Maureen Riches, managing editor
Circulation: 4,000
Published quarterly
  Provides a forum for lively and critical commentary on the best in national and international dance, classical and contemporary, including features, reviews, reports, and commentaries. Preferred length 1,000 to 1,500 words. Pays on publication $100 to $150 for features, $65 to $80 for commentaries, $40 to $60 for reviews, and $60 to $75 for notebook. Guidelines available.

Espace
4888 St-Denis, Montreal, QC H2J 2L6
Phone: (514) 844-9858 Fax: (514) 844-3661
E-mail: espace@espace-sculpture.com
Web site: www.espace-sculpture.com
Contact: Serge Fisette, editor
Circulation: 1,400
Published quarterly

A magazine devoted to contemporary sculpture. Preferred length for articles is 1,000 to 2,000 words. Pays $50/page on publication.

Exclaim!

7B Pleasant Boulevard, Suite 966, Toronto, ON M4T 1K2
Phone: (416) 535-9735 Fax: (416) 535-0566
E-mail: exclaim@exclaim.ca
Web site: www.exclaim.ca
Contact: James Keast, editor-in-chief
Circulation: 100,000
Published 11 times a year

A music and popular culture magazine focusing on the best unheard music worldwide with a Canadian slant. Freelance writers must be knowledgeable music fans. Articles 300 to 3,000 words. Pays 10¢/word on publication, although rates can vary. Guidelines available.

Fuse Magazine

401 Richmond Street W., Suite 454, Toronto, ON M5V 3A8
Phone: (416) 340-8026 Fax: (416) 340-0494
E-mail: content@fusemagazine.org
Web site: www.fusemagazine.com
Contact: Michael Maranda, associate publisher
Circulation: 3,000
Published quarterly

Addresses all aspects of contemporary art production, both nationally and internationally. Provides thorough coverage of art and its cultural climate, with a special emphasis on issues relating to cultural differences in terms of class, race, and gender. Reviews cover visual arts (including film, video, performance, and related books) to media coverage of the arts. Regularly features artist pages. Articles 1,500 to 3,000 words. No fiction. Pays 10¢/word on publication; $100 for art and book reviews. Guidelines on web site.

Inuit Art Quarterly

2081 Merivale Road, Ottawa, ON K2G 1G9
Phone: (613) 224-8189 Fax: (613) 224-2907
E-mail: iaq@inuitart.org

Web site: www.inuitart.org
Contact: Sheila Sturk-Green, managing editor
Circulation: 3,800
Published quarterly

Devoted exclusively to Inuit art and directed toward art specialists, artists, historians, teachers, and all interested readers with the purpose of giving Inuit artists a voice. Carries feature articles, profiles, interviews, news and reviews, and reader commentary. Most features (2,000 to 4,000 words) pay $500 to $1,000 (no fixed rate). Pays on acceptance. A knowledge of Inuit art and culture essential. Query editor first. Guidelines available.

Legacy

9667 – 87 Avenue, Edmonton, AB T6C 1K5
Phone: (780) 439-0705 Fax: (780) 439-0549
E-mail: legacy@compusmart.ab.ca
Web site: www.legacymagazine.ab.ca
Contact: Barbara Dacks, publisher
Circulation: 7,300
Published quarterly

Contains stories about the ways in which Albertans create, celebrate, and preserve their cultural heritage, past and present. Includes articles on events, art, architecture, music, poetry, crafts, destinations, and challenging ideas, as well as recipes, book reviews, and profiles. Does not respond to telephone inquiries. Send a query letter and brief résumé by mail or e-mail. Articles generally 300 to 700 words; features from 1,200 to 2,200 words. Pays $150 to $750 and a complimentary 1-year subscription. Guidelines available on web site.

Masthead

1606 Sedlescomb Drive, Suite 8, Mississauga, ON L4X 1M6
Phone: (905) 625-7070 Fax: (905) 625-4856
E-mail: wshields@masthead.ca
Web site: www.mastheadonline.com
Contact: William Shields, editor
Circulation: 4,400
Published 10 times a year

Offers news and feature coverage of Canada's periodical publishing industry. Fees are negotiable and paid on publication for articles of 150 to 2,500 words. "If you've got insight into Canada's periodical publishing industry, let's get writing!" Guidelines available.

Mix: A Declaration of Creative Independence
401 Richmond Street W., Suite 446, Toronto, ON M5V 3A8
Phone: (416) 506-1012 Fax: (416) 506-0141
E-mail: mix@web.net
Web site: www.mixmagazine.com
Contact: Claudia McKoy, editor
Circulation: 4,000
Published quarterly
A national magazine that covers the work of younger and emerging Canadian artists, including painting, sculpture, installations, video, performance art, radio and television, dance, and new media. Articles 1,000 to 2,500 words. Pays on publication 20¢/word. Contact editor with article ideas.

Montage
1 Eglinton Avenue E., Suite 604, Toronto, ON M4P 3A1
Phone: (416) 482-6640 Fax: (416) 482-6639
E-mail: editor@dgcmontage.com
Web site: www.dgcmontage.com
Contact: Marc Glassman, editor
Circulation: 11,000
Published quarterly
Profiles people and issues in the film and television industries. Articles 1,500 to 2,500 words. Pay varies and is paid on acceptance. "All inquiries should be made to the editor by e-mail. No phone calls or faxes, please."

Musicworks: Explorations in Sound
401 Richmond Street W., Suite 358, Toronto, ON M5V 3A8
Phone: (416) 977-3546
E-mail: sound@musicworks.ca
Web site: www.musicworks.ca
Contact: Gayle Young, editor

Circulation: 3,000
Published 3 times a year
Distributed with an audio component – cassettes or CDs – to illustrate articles and interviews covering a broad range of contemporary classical and experimental music. Also ethnic music and sound related to dance and visual art. Features are 1,000 to 3,500 words. Fees depend on length, complexity, and other factors. Pays on publication. Welcomes inquiries. Guidelines available.

On Site Review

1326 – 11 Avenue S.E., Calgary, AB T2G 0Z5
Phone: (403) 266-5827
E-mail: editor@onsitereview.ca
Web site: www.onsitereview.ca
Contact: Stephanie White, editor
Circulation: 500
Published twice a year
A magazine devoted to architecture created by, written about, and photographed by young Canadian architects. Readers include practising architects, students, and interested lay people. Letters 200 to 500 words; real places, photo collages, and articles 800 words; and building studies 1,000 words. Articles accepted in English or French. Cannot pay but welcomes submission inquiries. "Wants sophisticated ideas in accessible language. Architectural or design training useful." Guidelines available.

On Spec

P.O. Box 4727, Edmonton, AB T6E 5G6
Phone: (403) 413-0215
E-mail: onspec@onspec.ca
Web site: www.onspec.ca
Contact: Diane Walton, general editor
Circulation: 1,500
Published quarterly
Specializes in science fiction, fantasy, and horror. Publishes short stories and poetry. Payment on acceptance: stories less than 3,000 words earn $100; longer stories pay $180; poetry $20 to $50. "We do not read e-mailed or faxed submissions, and we do not

buy stories or poetry that have appeared in print or on the Internet. Non-fiction and artwork by commission only. Send an SASE for guidelines."

Opera Canada

366 Adelaide Street E., Suite 244, Toronto, ON M5A 3X9
Phone: (416) 363-0395 Fax: (416) 363-0396
E-mail: suewhite922@sympatico.ca
Contact: Sue White, executive director
Circulation: 4,000
Published quarterly

Devoted for 40 years to Canadian opera. Reviews international performances, interviews Canada's best singers, and addresses opera-related cultural issues. Reviews up to 300 words; features 1,200 to 1,500 words. Accepts submissions and submission inquiries. Pays $300 on publication for 1,500 words; reviews $25 to $75.

Parachute

4060 St. Laurent Boulevard, Suite 501, Montreal, QC H2W 1Y9
Phone: (514) 842-9805 Fax: (514) 842-9319
E-mail: info@parachute.ca
Web site: www.parachute.ca
Contact: Chantal Pontbriand, editor
Circulation: 4,000
Published quarterly

A bilingual magazine offering readers in-depth articles on the theory and practice of art today: interviews with artists and articles on music, cinema, photography, theatre, dance, and video. Each issue is thematic. Pays about $100 for reviews and issues column (to a maximum of 1,000 words), up to $500 for articles and interviews (3,000 to 5,000 words), on publication. Guidelines available.

Performing Arts & Entertainment in Canada

565 Avenue Road, Suite 206, Toronto, ON M4V 2J9
Phone: (416) 925-2649 Fax: (416) 925-3918
E-mail: cadmus@interlog.com
Contact: Sarah Hood, editor
Circulation: 44,000
Published quarterly

Explores the issues and trends affecting performing arts in Canada, primarily theatre, dance, opera, television, and film. Also carries profiles on individual performers, companies, and troupes. Prefers articles of 600 to 1,500 words, which earn $50 to $150, paid on publication. Query first.

Quill & Quire
70 The Esplanade, Suite 210, Toronto, ON M5E 1R2
Phone: (416) 360-0044 Fax: (416) 955-0794
E-mail: info@quillandquire.com
Web site: www.quillandquire.com
Contact: Scott Anderson, editor
Circulation: 6,000
Published monthly
The news journal of the Canadian book trade for booksellers, librarians, educators, publishers, and writers. Prints news, reviews, lists of recently published and upcoming books, and profiles of authors and publishing houses. Includes the biannual supplement *Canadian Publishers Directory*. (Also publishes the compendious sourcebook of the publishing industry, *The Book Trade in Canada*.) Pays 45¢/word for news and feature articles, $90 for reviews of 300 to 500 words, on acceptance. "We do not accept unsolicited articles. Query by phone or fax."

Storyteller: Canada's Short Story Magazine
858 Wingate Drive, Ottawa, ON K1G 1S5
Phone: (613) 521-9570
E-mail: info@storytellermagazine.com
Web site: www.storytellermagazine.com
Contact: Terry Tyo, publisher
Circulation: 2,000
Published quarterly
Features popular fiction of all types that focuses on entertainment value and literary merit. "Our market is avid readers who prefer fiction with a Canadian flavour. They especially enjoy humour, mystery, science fiction, and historical and other genres." Stories 2,000 to 6,000 words. Rates vary and are paid on publication. "Our stories have won awards, nominations, and honourable mentions in diverse genres. Our concern is quality entertainment.

We look for interesting characters doing interesting things."
Guidelines available.

Take One
128 Danforth Avenue, Suite 252, Toronto, ON M4K INI
Phone: (416) 944-1096 Fax: (416) 465-4356
E-mail: takeone@interlog.com
Web site: www.takeonemagazine.ca
Contact: Wyndham Wise, editor-in-chief
Circulation: 5,000
Published quarterly
   Canada's only film magazine devoted entirely to Canadian film
and television. Pays 12¢/word on publication for articles 2,500 to
3,000 words. "Must have a working knowledge of the Canadian
film and television industry." Guidelines available.

Tribe Magazine
P.O. Box 65053, 358 Danforth Avenue, Toronto, ON M4K 3Z2
Phone: (416) 778-4115 Fax: (416) 406-9473
E-mail editor@tribe.ca
Web site: www.tribe.ca
Contact: Alex D., publisher/editor
Circulation: 94,000
Published 10 times a year
   Canada's national after-dark entertainment monthly, focusing
on new music, nightclub culture, new fashion, urban gossip, and
news. Looking for "articles and features that are relevant to 18- to
28-year-old readers living in urban Canada. Fresh perspectives, raw
humour, edgy writing. No PR-company crap, please." Articles 600
to 1,200 words. Cannot pay but welcomes submission inquiries.

Vallum Magazine
P.O. Box 48003, Montreal, QC H2V 4S8
E-mail vallumadmin@bellnet.ca
Web site: www.vallummag.com
Contacts: Joshua Auerback and Eleni Zisimatos Auerbach, editors
Circulation: 2,300
Published twice a year

Established 2000. Publishes poetry that's fresh and edgy, something that reflects contemporary experience and is also well crafted (about 45 poems/issue). Open to diverse styles. Publishes leading Canadian and international English-language poets, as well as the most exciting new voices that come its way. Also interested in quality essays on poetry, interviews, reviews, and visual texts. Submit 5 to 8 poems at a time. No previously published poetry or simultaneous submissions. Do not submit by e-mail or fax. Cover letter is preferred, with an SASE or IRC. Sometimes will comment on rejected poems. Accepts less than 1% of poetry received. Pays an honorarium and 1-year subscription. Reviews of poetry should be 400 to 900 words. Send material for consideration. Guidelines and upcoming themes available on web site.

Writer's Block: The Canadian Web Magazine for the Writing Trade

30 Murray Street, Suite 300, Ottawa, ON KIN 5M4
Phone: (613) 737-6000, ext. 307 Fax: (613) 737-5868
E-mail: dgoldberger@niva.com
Web site: www.writersblock.ca
Contact: Dalya Goldberger, managing editor
Circulation: 1,500
Published quarterly

"The only Canadian web magazine that explores ideas that matter most to Canadians in the writing trade. Each issue offers information, insights, and opinions that help define the environment in which we work, learn, and create." Articles 1,500 to 2,500 words. "Please read our contribution guidelines before submitting material. We also accept fiction and poetry." Guidelines available.

Business

Atlantic Business Magazine

P.O. Box 2356, Stn. C, St. John's, NL AIC 6E7
Phone: (709) 726-9300 Fax: (709) 726-3013
E-mail: dchafe@atlanticbusinessmagazine.com
Web site: www.atlanticbusinessmagazine.com

Contact: Dawn Chafe, editor
Circulation: 30,000
Published bimonthly

Publishes stories about business activities unique to or specifically focused on Atlantic Canada. "We have a positive mandate to highlight the character and determination of Atlantic Canadians and the success of their economic initiatives in the global marketplace." Pays on publication 25¢/word for 1,200- to 2,500-word articles printed in magazine with an additional 5¢/word for online publication. "View recent copies online for sample of our style. Also, when pitching a story, writers new to us should reference previous published material." Guidelines available.

Backbone Magazine

300 Beaver Road, Suite 200, North Vancouver, BC V7N 3H6
Phone: (604) 986-5352 Fax: (604) 986-5309
E-mail: info@backbonemag.com
Web site: www.backbonemag.com
Contact: Peter Wolchak, editor
Circulation: 105,000
Published bimonthly

A national magazine that publishes articles on business, technology, and lifestyle. It delivers in-depth analysis and insight into the real benefits of e-commerce, online revenue strategies, and technological innovations that affect the way we live and do business. Articles from 300 to 2,000 words. Pays on publication 50¢/word. Guidelines available.

BCBusiness

4180 Lougheed Highway, 4th Floor, Burnaby, BC V5C 6A7
Phone: (604) 473-0348 Fax: (604) 299-9188
E-mail: birving@canadawide.com
Contact: Bonnie Irving, editor
Circulation: 26,000
Published monthly

A regional business publication covering real estate, telecommunications, personal finance, management trends and technology, and lifestyle. Directed toward business owners, managers, entrepreneurs, and professionals. Pays 50¢ to 60¢/word two weeks before publication for features of 1,500 to 4,000 words, 40¢/word for advertising features. "No industry overviews, please. Read at least 6 back issues before querying." Query by e-mail. Guidelines available.

Business Examiner
818 Broughton Street, Victoria, BC V8W 1E4
Phone: (250) 381-3926 Fax: (250) 381-5606
E-mail: be@busex.bc.ca
Web site: www.businessexaminer.net
Contact: Lyle Jenish, editor
Circulation: 14,000
Published twice a month
   Provides news, features, and columns with a strong business angle. Pays $50 to $150 on publication for 300 to 600 words. Fees are negotiated. Submit story ideas first. Vancouver Island and Victoria region subjects and hard news get preference. Guidelines available.

Business London
P.O. Box 7400, London, ON N5Y 4X3
Phone: (519) 472-7601 Fax: (519) 473-7859
E-mail: editorial@businesslondon.ca
Web site: www.businesslondon.ca
Contact: Gord Delamont, publisher/editor
Circulation: 12,000
Published monthly
   Profiles business success stories, trends, and issues with a London connection. Pays on publication $125 to $600 for articles of 400 to 1,800 words. Rates depend on kind of story, number of sources, and writer's experience. "The pages of *Business London* are dedicated to the local business community. All stories must have a London connection." Guidelines available.

Canadian MoneySaver
P.O. Box 370, Bath, ON K0H 1G0
Phone: (613) 352-7448 Fax: (613) 352-7700
E-mail: moneyinfo@canadianmoneysaver.ca
Web site: www.canadianmoneysaver.ca
Contact: Dale Ennis, publisher/editor-in-chief

Circulation: 34,400

Published 10 times a year

A national consumer finance magazine offering articles (800 to 1,500 words) on such current topics as personal finance, tax, investment techniques, retirement planning, consumer purchases, small business practices, and discount services. "Contributors have the opportunity to participate in national and offshore conferences, and propose other writing projects." Rates are negotiated. Guidelines available. An online edition is also published.

Contact Magazine

145 Wellington Street W., Suite 610, Toronto, ON M5J 1H8

Phone: (416) 408-2685 or 1-800-267-2772 Fax: (416) 408-2684

E-mail: bruffell@cpsa.com

Web site: www.cpsa.com

Contact: Brett Ruffell, publications co-ordinator

Circulation: 37,000

Published bimonthly

The number-one source for sales and marketing professionals in Canada. Provides up-to-date information on what's new and important in sales and marketing. Articles 700 to 1,200 words. Some articles are unpaid; others receive approximately 70¢/word on acceptance. Guidelines available.

The Far North Oil & Gas Review

4920 – 52 Street, Suite 800, Yellowknife, NT X1A 3T1

Phone: (867) 920-4343 Fax: (867) 873-2844

E-mail: sunny@uphere.ca

Web site: www.uphere.ca

Contact: Sunny Munroe, editor

Circulation: 10,000

Published quarterly

Covers news, politics, business, and other issues related to northern oil and gas development. Reaches a northern audience of Aboriginals and non-Aboriginals, the Canadian oil and gas industry in Calgary, and the related corporate offices in Houston, Dallas, and Toronto. The magazine deals with issues specific to the north and some general information issues. "Freelancers should be knowledgeable about northern issues and Aboriginal issues as they pertain to the north. Freelancers should also have a basic understanding of the Canadian oil patch and related technical issues. Copies of the magazine available upon request." Articles 2,500 to 4,000 words. Pays a minimum of 25¢/word on publication. Fees are negotiated.

Home Business Report

2625A Alliance Street, Abbotsford, BC V2S 3J9
Phone: (604) 854-5530   Fax: (604) 854-3087
E-mail: info@homebusinessreport.com
Web site: www.homebusinessreport.com
Contact: B. Mowat, vice president
Circulation: 50,000
Published quarterly

A magazine to link home-based businesses across the country, providing a network for sharing experiences, including advice for launching new businesses and support for those that are struggling. Articles 800 to 2,000 words. Pay rates depend on assignment: sometimes cannot pay, sometimes pays on publication from 10¢/word to $250 to $400 for a 1,200-word feature. Very interested in successful rural and small-town, home-based businesses offering an unusual product or service. Guidelines available.

Ivey Business Journal

179 John Street, Suite 501, Toronto, ON M5T 1X4
Phone: (416) 598-1741   Fax: (416) 598-0669
E-mail: sbernhut@ivey.uwo.ca
Web site: www.ivey.uwo.ca/ibj
Contact: Stephen Bernnut, editor
Circulation: 9,000
Published bimonthly

A long-established business journal, now published online only, that is directed toward senior managers, with a mission to improve the practice of management. Features about 3,000 words; shorter pieces 1,500 to 2,000 words. Contributors are unpaid. Inquiries welcome. Guidelines available on web site.

KidScreen

366 Adelaide Street W., Suite 500, Toronto, ON M5V 1R9
Phone: (416) 408-2300   Fax: (416) 408-0870
E-mail: mmaddever@brunico.com
Web site: www.realscreen.com
Contact: Mary Maddever, editorial director
Circulation: 11,500
Published 10 times a year

An international publication about the business of international, non-fiction film and children's entertainment. Written for producers, distributors, broadcasters, and suppliers, and those involved in consumer products, marketing, and retail. "We need everything from 50-word news stories to 3,000-word special reports." Fees (paid on acceptance) vary depending on project. Writers must have previous experience writing for this industry.

Pet Commerce

530 Century Street, Suite 225, Winnipeg, MB R3H 0Y4
Phone: 1-888-573-1136   Fax: (866) 957-0217
E-mail: r.naud@august.ca
Web site: www.petcommerce.ca
Contact: Rache Naud, editor
Circulation: 8,400
Published bimonthly

Circulated to 8,000 specialty pet-supply retail outlets, veterinarians, pet stores, and pet-supply managers of major chains. "*Pet Commerce* offers a full product showcase, pet wellness features, merchandising opportunities, and informative articles on current issues in the retail pet industry." Articles 1,200 to 2,000 words. Fee paid on publication and varies according to project. Guidelines available.

Profit: Your Guide to Business Success

1 Mount Pleasant Road, Toronto, ON M4Y 2Y5
Phone: (416) 764-1402   Fax: (416) 764-1404
E-mail: profit@profit.rogers.com
Web site: www.profitguide.com
Contact: Ian Portsmouth, editor
Circulation: 100,000
Published bimonthly

Canada's only national magazine that delivers hands-on management advice to business owner/managers of small- to medium-sized businesses. Features regular columns and departments along with articles on management topics and other issues of interest. Offers insights and practical advice in the areas of marketing, technology, finance, innovators and trends, and personnel management. Pays about 75¢/word on acceptance for stories of 600 to 2,000 words. "You must know something about business and be prepared to rewrite." Guidelines available.

RealScreen

366 Adelaide Street W., Suite 500, Toronto, ON M5V 1R9
Phone: (416) 408-2300 Fax: (416) 408-0870
E-mail: mmaddever@brunico.com
Web site: www.realscreen.com
Contact: Mary Maddever, editorial director
Circulation: 7,500
Published 10 times a year

An international publication about the business of international, non-fiction film and television. Written for producers, distributors, broadcasters, and suppliers. "We need everything from 50-word news stories to 3,000-word special reports." Fees, paid on acceptance, vary depending on project. Writers must have previous experience writing for this industry.

Saskatchewan Business

2213B Hanselman Court, Saskatoon, SK S7L 6A8
Phone: (306) 244-5668 Fax: (306) 244-5679
E-mail: news@sunrisepublish.com
Contact: Keith Moen, editor
Circulation: 10,000
Published 8 times a year

Has a mandate to promote positive news stories within the Saskatchewan business community. Articles 300 to 1,200 words. Pays on publication 20¢/word based upon the final, printed version of the submission. "It's recommended that you submit a brief outline of a story idea." Guidelines available.

Summit: Canada's Magazine on Public Sector Purchasing
180 Elgin Street, Suite 800, Ottawa, ON K2P 2K3
Phone: (613) 688-0762 Fax: (613) 688-0767
E-mail: info@summitconnects.com
Web site: www.summitconnects.com
Contact: Anne Phillips, editor
Circulation: 20,000
Published 8 times a year

For public-sector purchasers at the decision-making and policy levels of all municipal and provincial governments and the federal government. Stories on policy matters and how-to articles. Articles 1,000 to 1,500 words. Pays on publication 75¢/published word (20% of the proposed published word count is the kill fee). "Please confirm the potential for publication before submitting your article by calling or e-mailing the contact listed." Guidelines available.

Trade & Commerce
1700 Church Avenue, Winnipeg, MB R2X 3A2
Phone: (204) 632-2606 Fax: (204) 694-3040
E-mail: wpgsun@wpgsun.com
Contact: Laura Jean Stewart, editor
Circulation: 10,000
Published quarterly

Profiles companies and communities with an emphasis on their contribution to the economy or economic-development activity. Pays 25¢ to 40¢/word on acceptance for 1,500 to 2,500 words. Works with freelance writers all over Canada and the United States. Guidelines available.

City & Entertainment

Avenue
1902K – 11th Street S.E., Calgary, AB T2N 3G2
Phone: (403) 232-7703
E-mail: info@avenuemagazine.ca
Web site: www.avenuemagazine.ca
Contact: Janice Paskey, editor

Circulation: 45,000
Published 10 times a year
The city magazine for Calgary. Articles 750 to 3,000 words. Pays
about 40¢/word on acceptance, although rates can vary.

City Life: Life North of the City
60 Winges Road, Unit 1, Woodbridge, ON L4L 6B1
Phone: (905) 264-6789 Fax: (905) 264-3787
E-mail: editor@dolcemag.com
Web site: www.dolcemag.com
Contact: Michelle Zerillo-Sosa, editor-in-chief
Circulation: 45,000
Published 10 times a year
A magazine for communities north of Toronto, including
Woodbridge, Vaughan, and Richmond Hill. Provides readers with
news and insight into their neighbourhoods, and includes a restau-
rant guide and stories on health, food, sports, home décor, fashion,
and more. Articles 800 to 3,000 words. Rates vary depending on
project and are paid on publication. "Please call to get a copy of our
writer's guidelines."

The Coast: Halifax's Weekly
5435 Portland Place, Halifax, NS B3K 6R7
Phone: (902) 422-6278 Fax: (902) 425-0013
E-mail: lp@thecoast.ns.ca
Web site: www.thecoast.ns.ca
Contact: Lynne Patterson, managing editor
Circulation: 20,000
An alternative newspaper serving Metro Halifax that publishes
short news stories and arts profiles as well as magazine-style fea-
tures. Pays 10¢ to 20¢/word on acceptance for 500 to 3,000 words.
Rate depends on complexity of topic and is negotiated up front.
Expenses may be covered. "Our freelancers know they may not get
high pay, but they can count on a level of editing and care for their
pieces comparable to the best in Canada. We've heard time and
again that that balances the pay scale to make writing for *The Coast*
a valuable experience." Guidelines available.

Destination: Centre-Ville
1470 Peel Street, Tour A, Suite 252, Montreal, QC H3A 1T1
Phone: (514) 844-2377 Fax: (514) 844-1988
E-mail: info@lcrpub.com
Web site: www.lcrpub.com
Contact: Nathalie Gascon, associate publisher
Circulation: 55,000
    Published on behalf of the Downtown Montreal Commercial Development Association. Showcases downtown businesses, featuring their activities, attractions, events, restaurants, and more. Articles 500 to 1,200 words. Fees negotiated and paid on acceptance.

eye Weekly
70 Peter Street, Toronto, ON M5V 2G5
Phone: (416) 596-4393 Fax: (416) 504-4348
Web site: www.eye.net
Contact: Catherine Tunnacliffe, managing editor
Circulation: 110,000
Published weekly
    Toronto's definitive source of alternative cultural commentary, with extensive arts and entertainment coverage, and listings. "We welcome submissions, particularly 700-word op-ed pieces, but are not responsible for unsolicited material." Pay rates vary and are paid on publication.

Famous
102 Atlantic Avenue, Suite 100, Toronto, ON M6K 1X9
Phone: (416) 539-8800 Fax: (416) 539-8511
E-mail: mweisz@fpmedia.ca
Contact: Marni Weisz, editor
Circulation: 500,000
Published monthly
    An in-theatre magazine for Famous Players Theatres. Content focuses on movies, music, books, video games, and DVDs. Articles 600 to 1,400 words. Pays 50¢/word.

Feature Magazine
12100 St. Catherine Street W., 2nd Floor, Montreal, QC H3H 2T3
Phone: (514) 939-5024

E-mail: editor@feature.ca
Contact: David Sherman, managing editor
Circulation: 850,000
Published monthly
   A guide and entertainment magazine for Pay-TV subscribers.
Articles 250 to 500 words. Pays 50¢/word on publication.

Hamilton Magazine

1074 Cooke Boulevard, Burlington, ON L7T 4A8
Phone: (905) 522-6117 Fax: (905) 634-7661
E-mail: info@townmedia.ca
Web site: www.townmedia.ca
Contact: David Young, editor
Circulation: 40,000
Published bimonthly
   A general-interest magazine for Hamilton and its suburbs, focus-
ing on city living – the people, places, and events that shape the com-
munity. The emphasis is on lifestyle, covering food, fashion, the arts,
and interior design. Features focus on ideas, issues, and social trends.
Feature length 3,000 to 8,000 words. Phone or write with ideas.
"Make sure article ideas focus on Hamilton and surrounding region."
Fees are negotiated and paid on publication. Guidelines available.

Kingston Life Magazine

P.O. Box 1352, Kingston, ON K7L 5C6
Phone: (613) 549-8442 Fax: (613) 549-4333
E-mail: editorial@kingstonpublications.com
Web site: www.visitkingston.com
Contact: Mary Owens, associate editor
Circulation: 15,000
Published quarterly
   Reflects the personalities, passions, successes, hobbies, and
leisure pursuits of Kingstonians. Articles assigned by publisher.
Résumés welcome. Pay rates vary and are paid on publication.

London City Life

1147 Gainsborough Road, London, ON N6H 5L9
Phone: (519) 473-0010 Fax: (519) 473-7859
E-mail: janed@bowesnet.com

Contact: Jane Dupere, publisher
Circulation: 30,000
Published bimonthly

A lifestyle magazine pertaining to London and a sourcebook of events, restaurants, etc. Features 1,500 words. Pays $600 to $650 on publication.

Marquee
1325 Burnhamthorpe Road E., Mississauga, ON L4Y 3V8
Phone: (905) 274-7174 Fax: (905) 274-9799
E-mail: marquee@marquee.ca
Contact: Alexandra Lenhoff, editor
Circulation: 334,000
Published 5 times a year

Distributed in university and college newspapers across Canada, *Marquee* carries feature stories, previews, and profiles of upcoming movies and personalities. Editorial has expanded to include coverage of new product releases for DVDs, music, games, and gadgets. Given the magazine's advance deadline, writers need access to on-set and on-location interview opportunities. Articles 300 to 1,500 words. Pays on publication. Fees vary.

Montreal Mirror
465 McGill Street, 3rd Floor, Montreal, QC H2Y 4B4
Phone: (514) 393-1010 Fax: (514) 393-3173
E-mail: asutherland@mtl-mirror.com
Contact: Alastair Sutherland, editor-in-chief
Circulation: 80,000
Published weekly

An alternative tabloid featuring articles on major issues written from a local perspective. Also reviews and previews music releases and concerts, films, art shows, books, and theatre. Features are 1,300 to 2,000 words. Fees are negotiated and paid on publication.

Niagara Life
20 South Drive, St. Catharines, ON L2R 4T8
Phone: (905) 641-1984 Fax: (905) 641-0682
E-mail: niagaralifemag@cogeco.ca
Web site: www.niagaralifemag.com

Contact: Sharon DeMarko Gordon, executive editor
Circulation: 100,000
Published 5 times a year in Niagara, 3 times a year for Toronto-
  Burlington
A guide to the Niagara region, covering such topics as cultural
heritage, political and economic issues, culinary arts, and current
events, and featuring Niagara's only authentic dining guide. Named
"Niagara's premier magazine" by the *Buffalo News*. Articles 500 to
850 words. Pays on publication from $300 for cover story to $60 for
neighbourhood profiles and $50 for music, book, and play reviews.
Fees are negotiated for photography and art. Guidelines available
from the editor.

North of the City
P.O. Box 236, 580B Steven Court, Newmarket, ON L3Y 4X1
Phone: (905) 853-8888 Fax: (905) 853-5379
E-mail: dkelly@yrng.com
Web site: www.yorkregion.com
Contact: Debora Kelly, editor
Circulation: 40,000
Published 5 times a year
A glossy lifestyle magazine highlighting the best of living in York
Region, including home trends, fashion, fitness, entertainment, and
health. Distributed to upscale homes. Articles 1,000 to 1,600
words. Must be relevant to York Region readers and include local
sources. Pays about 15¢/word on acceptance.

NOW Magazine
189 Church Street, Toronto, ON M5B 1Y7
Phone: (416) 364-1300 Fax: (416) 364-1166
E-mail: publishers@nowtoronto.com
Web site: www.nowtoronto.com
Contacts: Ellie Kirzner (ellie@nowtoronto.com), associate editor
  (for news); Susan Cole (susan@nowtoronto.com), entertain-
  ment editor (for entertainment)
Circulation: 108,000
Published weekly
A news, entertainment, and listings magazine covering Toronto-
region news, music, film, theatre, fashion, and the arts. Story length

from 400 to 2,000 words. Most work is assigned. Uses very few
out-of-town writers. Toronto-region news submissions with an
alternative perspective have best chance. Rates vary. Pays on publication. All fees negotiable. Inquiries welcome.

Ottawa City Magazine
226 Argyle Avenue, Ottawa, ON K2P 1B9
Phone: (613) 230-0333 Fax: (613) 230-9169
E-mail: ottawacity@capitalpublishers.com
Web site: www.capitalpublishers.com
Contact: Rosa Harris-Adler, editor
Circulation: 40,000
Published bimonthly
Targeted toward upwardly mobile Ottawans between the ages of
35 and 50. Pays 50¢/word on acceptance for articles 800 to 3,500
words.

Ottawa City Woman Magazine
226 Argyle Avenue, Ottawa, ON K2P 1B9
Phone: (613) 230-0333 Fax: (613) 230-9169
E-mail: sarah@capitalpublishers.com
Web site: www.citywomanmagazine.com
Contact: Sarah Brown, editor
Circulation: 30,000
Published quarterly
Articles 1,000 to 2,500 words. Pays about 50¢/word on acceptance.

Planet S Magazine
220 – 3rd Avenue S., Suite 308, Saskatoon, SK S7K 1M1
Phone: (306) 651-3423 Fax: (306) 351-3428
E-mail: reception@planetsmag.com
Contact: David Shield, managing editor
Circulation: 16,000
Published biweekly
An alternative urban news and entertainment magazine. Affili-
ated with *prairie dog Magazine* in Regina. Articles 500 to 2,000
words. Pay varies depending on assignment, up to 15¢/word.
Welcomes submission inquiries.

prairie dog Magazine
1834 Scarth Street, 2nd Floor, Regina, SK S4P 2G9
Phone: (306) 757-4366 Fax: (306) 352-9686
E-mail: reception@prairiedogmag.com
Web site: http://prairiedog.inregina.com
Contact: Stephen Whitworth, managing editor
Circulation: 16,000
Published biweekly

An alternative urban news and entertainment magazine. Affiliated with *Planet S Magazine* in Saskatoon. Articles 500 to 2,000 words. Pay varies depending on assignment, up to 15¢/word. Welcomes submission inquiries.

Toronto Life
59 Front Street E., 3rd Floor, Toronto, ON M5E 1B3
Phone: (416) 364-3333 Fax: (416) 955-4982
E-mail: editorial@torontolife.com
Contact: John Macfarlane, editor
Circulation: 91,000
Published monthly

Established 1966. A city magazine that tells readers how Toronto works, lives, and plays. Examines city politics, society, business, entertainment, sports, food and restaurants, and shopping in a unique mix of reporting and service journalism. Also publishes city guides. Draws on a stable of experienced writers and rarely accepts outside submissions. Pays on acceptance between $500 and $5,000 for 100 to 6,000 words, depending on assignment. "Submissions should have a strong Toronto orientation. Story suggestions should be submitted in writing in the form of a 1-page proposal." Guidelines available.

TV Guide
25 Sheppard Avenue W., Suite 100, Toronto, ON M2N 6S7
Phone: (416) 730-7600 Fax: (416) 733-3568
E-mail: letters@tvguide.ca
Web site: www.tvguide.ca
Contact: managing editor
Circulation: 500,000
Published weekly

Carries television listings and articles on celebrities, prime-time television shows, children's programming, sports, food, home shows, and digital television. Pay is competitive – negotiated rates paid on acceptance for articles of 500 to 800 words. "Read the magazine. Submit clips if you have them. A 1-page proposal with contacts may be requested. *TV Guide* is not a magazine for neophytes."

TV Week

4180 Lougheed Highway, 4th Floor, Burnaby, BC V6B 6A7
Phone: (604) 299-7311 Fax: (604) 299-9188
E-mail: tvweek@canadawide.com
Web site: www.canadawide.com
Contact: Brent Furdyk, editor
Circulation: 80,000
Published weekly

A television and entertainment guide. Pays 40¢/word on publication for stories of 600 to 1,100 words.

Uptown Magazine

63 Albert Street, Suite 202, Winnipeg, MB R3B 1G4
Phone: (204) 949-4370 Fax: (204) 949-4376
E-mail: john.kendle@uptownmag.com
Web site: www.uptownmag.com
Contact: John Kendle, editor
Circulation: 20,000
Published weekly

An arts, entertainment, and news weekly geared for 18- to 36-year-olds. Articles 500 to 750 words. Pay rates vary and are paid on publication. Contact editor regarding submissions.

Vancouver Magazine

2608 Granville Street, Suite 500, Vancouver, BC V6H 3V3
Phone: (604) 877-7732 Fax: (604) 877-4838
E-mail: mail@vancouvermagazine.com
Web site: www.vancouvermagazine.com
Contact: Matthew Mallon, editor
Circulation: 65,000
Published 10 times a year

The city magazine of the new Vancouver – its people, stories, and ideas – focusing on urban culture and current affairs. Articles must be Vancouver specific. Pays 60¢/word on acceptance for 300 to 3,000 words. Read the magazine before submitting. Guidelines available.

Vue Weekly
10303 – 108 Street, Edmonton, AB T5J 1L7
Phone: (780) 426-1996 Fax: (780) 426-2889
E-mail: paul@vue.ab.ca
Web site: www.vue.ab.ca
Contact: Paul Matwychuk, managing editor
Circulation: 30,000
An alternative arts and entertainment weekly with a focus on Edmonton and Alberta as well as alternative takes on politics and media. Pays on publication 8¢ to 10¢/word for articles of 600 to 2,500 words. "No fiction or poetry, please. We are especially eager to publish lively, alternative-minded media criticism with an Albertan/Canadian slant."

The Environment

Alternatives Journal: Canadian Environmental Ideas and Action
Faculty of Environmental Studies, University of Waterloo,
    Waterloo, ON N2L 3G1
Phone: (519) 888-4545 Fax: (519) 746-0292
E-mail: editor@alternativesjournal.ca
Web site: www.alternativesjournal.ca
Contact: Cheryl Lousley, executive editor
Circulation: 4,500
Published quarterly
The most widely read environmental magazine in Canada, with 30 years of journalistic experience. Articles provide a blend of practical information and analysis from across Canada and abroad. "Environment is defined in the broadest sense. Readers include environmental professionals and academics, activists, concerned citizens, and students." Feature-length articles (2,000 to 4,000

words) are peer-reviewed. Also publishes reports (750 to 1,500 words), book reviews (750 to 900 words), and humour pieces. Pay rates negotiable. Guidelines available. "Thank goodness for *Alternatives* magazine. For years I've relied on its consistently well-written, well-researched articles. Where would any environmentalist be without *Alternatives*?" – Elizabeth May, executive director of the Sierra Club of Canada.

Common Ground
3901 West Broadway, Suite 201, Vancouver, BC V6K 2G9
Phone: (604) 733-2215 Fax: (604) 733-4415
E-mail: editor@commonground.ca
Contact: Joseph Roberts, publisher/senior editor
Circulation: 70,000
Published monthly

Aims to inform, inspire, and educate readers about health, wellness, ecology, personal growth, professional development, and creativity. Pays 10¢/word on publication for articles from 800 to 2,000 words. "Send an SASE if you want materials returned. It's best to query first by e-mail. If article is already written or published, send a copy. Make your first sentence and first paragraph great or the article or query may not get read."

Green Teacher
95 Robert Street, Toronto, ON M5S 2K5
Phone: (416) 960-1244 Fax: (416) 925-3474
E-mail: info@greenteacher.com
Web site: www.greenteacher.com
Contact: Tim Grant, co-editor
Circulation: 7,200
Published quarterly

A magazine by and for educators that aims to provide ideas, inspiration, and classroom-ready materials to help all educators (including parents) promote environmental and global awareness among young people, preschool to college, in school and in the community. Articles 500 to 3,000 words. All writers are volunteers; they receive a complimentary 1-year subscription. Submissions welcome. Guidelines available on web site.

Harrowsmith Country Life
11450 Albert-Hudon Boulevard, Montreal-North, QC H1G 3J9
Phone: (514) 327-4464 Fax: (514) 327-0514
Contact: Tom Cruickshank, editor
Circulation: 165,000
Published bimonthly
   A magazine for a thoughtful, critical audience interested in all aspects of country living. Subject areas most frequently covered include rural issues, home improvement, gardening, energy and ecology, and innovative architecture. Pays a negotiated rate on acceptance for 1,000 to 1,500 words; rate varies according to complexity and writer's experience.

Nature Canada
Canadian Nature Federation, 1 Nicholas Street, Suite 606,
   Ottawa, ON K1N 7B7
Phone: (613) 562-3447 Fax: (613) 562-3371
E-mail: naturecanada@cnf.ca
Web site: www.cnf.ca
Contact: Pamela Feeny, editor
Circulation: 27,000
Published quarterly
   Mailed to members of the Canadian Nature Federation, a non-profit conservation organization. Began in 1939 as *Canadian Nature*. Aimed at people interested in learning about and protecting nature. Focuses on conservation issues related to protected federal areas, endangered species, and important bird areas. Features 650 to 2,000 words. Rates vary and are paid on publication. "E-mail queries are preferred, along with relevant samples/clips. Do not send manuscripts. Standard response time is 2 to 3 months." Check the web site for writer's guidelines, information on CNF programs, and sample columns from the magazine.

Seasons
355 Lesmill Road, Don Mills, ON M3B 2W8
Phone: (416) 444-8419 Fax: (416) 444-9866
E-mail: victoriaf@ontarionature.org
Web site: www.ontarionature.org
Contact: Victoria Foote, editor

Circulation: 15,000
Published quarterly

A nature and outdoors magazine published by the Federation of Ontario Naturalists. The editorial focus is on Ontario nature, natural history, environmental issues, and eco-tourism. Preferred length 500 to 2,500 words. Fees are negotiable, paid on acceptance. "Be familiar with the magazine before querying. We accept e-mail inquiries." Guidelines available.

The Sustainable Times

1657 Barrington Street, Unit 516, Halifax, NS B3J 2A6
Phone: (902) 423-6852 Fax: (902) 423-9736
E-mail: times@chebucto.ns.ca
Web site: www.sustainabletimes.ca
Contact: Sean Kelly, managing editor

An Internet magazine focusing on ecology, green economics, international development, and fair trade. Published by CUSO. "We believe economics should be guided by environmental protection and fairness, not just profit." Pays 40¢/word on acceptance for articles 1,000 to 2,000 words. Send initial query rather than complete article. Guidelines available.

Wildflower

P.O. Box 335, Stn. F, Toronto, ON M4Y 2L7
E-mail: editor@wildflowermag.com
Web site: www.wildflowermag.com
Contact: James Hodgins, editor
Circulation: 3,000
Published quarterly

Features popular writing for native-plant gardeners, naturalists, teachers, and botanists. Devoted to the conservation, cultivation, and study of North American native plants. Contains essays, book reviews, notices of coming events, and plant sources. Articles 1,000 to 6,000 words. Cannot pay, but will give free advertising space to contributors. Guidelines available on web site.

Feminist

Herizons
P.O. Box 128, Winnipeg, MB R3C 2G1
Phone: (204) 774-6225 Fax: (204) 786-8038
E-mail: penni@web.net
Web site: www.herizons.ca
Contact: Penni Mitchell, editor
Circulation: 5,000
Published quarterly
   A feminist periodical focusing on women's issues and the
women's movement. Articles 500 to 3,000 words. Pays 20¢/word.
Send query and sample of previous published work written from a
feminist perspective. Guidelines available on web site.

Women & Environments International Magazine
c/o I.W.S.G.S. New College, University of Toronto, 40 Willcocks
   Street, Toronto, ON M5S 1C6
Phone: (416) 978-5259 Fax: (416) 946-5561
E-mail: we.mag@utoronto.ca
Web site: www.weimag.com
Contact: Reggie Modlich, managing editor
Circulation: 2,000
Published twice a year
   A co-operative forum for discussion, review, and research on
women's built, natural, social, and political environments for femi-
nists, academics, and a broad base of grassroots groups. Articles
500 to 2,000 words. Contributors are not paid, but submission
inquiries welcome. "Clear language is essential – no academic
jargon, please. We are cross-cultural and international. All issues are
theme related. For the next 2 years, we aim to publish issues on
women, communities, health, mobility, governance, spirituality,
social change, and violence." Guidelines available.

General Interest

Alberta Views
320 – 23 Avenue S.W., Suite 208, Calgary, AB T2S 0J2
Phone: (403) 243-5334 Fax: (403) 243-8599
E-mail: contactus@albertaviews.ab.ca
Web site: www.albertaviews.ab.ca
Contacts: Jackie Flanagan, publisher/executive editor
Circulation: 20,000
Published bimonthly (9 times a year in 2005)
   Publishes insightful commentary on Alberta's politics, social issues, and culture. Articles are from 1,000 to 3,000 words. Generally pays 30¢/word on acceptance, but rates may vary. "Please send a query and writing samples. We respond to queries in 4 to 6 weeks. Features are assigned up to a year before publication." Guidelines available on web site.

The Beaver
167 Lombard Avenue, Suite 478, Winnipeg, MB R3B 0T6
Phone: (204) 988-9300 Fax: (204) 988-9309
E-mail: editors@historysociety.ca
Web site: www.thebeaver.ca
Contact: Annalee Greenberg, editor
Circulation: 48,000
Published bimonthly
   A market since 1920 for lively, well-researched, informative, expository articles on Canadian social history. "We welcome popularly written features on Canadian history, particularly those based on unpublished or new material, written from a non-traditional point of view or new interpretation of significant events or people." Interested in submissions from all parts of the country. Pays a varying rate (depending on research necessary and writer's experience) for articles of 800 to 3,500 words. "Writers should thoroughly acquaint themselves with the magazine by reading back issues." Guidelines available on web site.

Canadian Geographic

39 McArthur Avenue, Ottawa, ON KIL 8L7
Phone: (613) 745-4629 Fax: (613) 744-0974
E-mail: editorial@canadiangeographic.ca
Web site: www.canadiangeographic.ca
Contact: Rick Boychuk, editor
Circulation: 245,000
Published bimonthly

Published by the Royal Canadian Geographical Society. Describes and illuminates, with fine colour photography, all aspects of Canada: its people, places, natural resources, and wildlife. Is concerned with geography in its broadest sense, looking at the way our landscape was formed and the human impact on it, and also reporting on discoveries in the sciences, from archaeology to zoology. The magazine is widely used as a high-school and undergraduate teaching resource. Rates vary, depending on project. Fees paid on acceptance for articles of 2,000 to 3,500 words. A large paid circulation helps make it one of the more lucrative freelance opportunities. Written queries essential; unsolicited manuscripts not accepted.

Canadian Stories

P.O. Box 232, Fergus, ON N1M 2W8
Phone: (519) 787-2451 Fax: (519) 787-2451
E-mail: ejanzen@uoguelph.ca
Web site: www.canadianstories.net
Contact: Ed Janzen, publisher/editor
Circulation: 450
Published bimonthly

A collection of Canadian folk stories, old and recent, memories, memoirs, and historical articles. Readers are mostly middle aged and seniors. Preferred length of articles 200 to 1,200 words. Cannot pay but welcomes submission inquiries. Contributors are from across Canada and are mostly first-time writers. See web site for examples and guidelines.

Nuvo Magazine

460 Nanaimo Street, Suite 200, Vancouver, BC V5L 4W3
Phone: (604) 899-9380 Fax: (604) 899-1450

E-mail: editorial@nuvomagazine.com
Web site: www.nuvomagazine.com
Contact: Jim Tobler, editor
Circulation: 40,000
Published quarterly
   Canada's culture, style, and celebrity magazine with a unique
perspective on Canadian culture. Includes stories on film, music,
food and wine, sports, travel, fashion, beauty, architecture, design,
and celebrities. Articles 500 to 2,000 words. Pays on acceptance
70¢/word, although fees can be negotiated. "Please pick up a copy
of *Nuvo* and visit our web site before making your submission.
E-mail queries only; no telephone queries are accepted."
Guidelines available on web site.

Reader's Digest

1100 René Levesque Boulevard W., Montreal, QC H3B 5H5
Phone: (514) 940-0751 Fax: (514) 940-7332
E-mail: editor@readersdigest.ca
Web site: www.readersdigest.ca
Contact: editorial department
Circulation: 1,137,000
Published monthly
   This mass-interest magazine is among the freelancer's most
lucrative potential markets. Carries articles on everything from
nature, science, and politics to drama, self-improvement, and
people, prominent or otherwise. All pieces contain advice, an experience, or a philosophical message of value to the magazine's 4
million readers. No fiction or poetry. Commissions original articles
and adaptations of Canadian subjects of between 3,500 and 5,000
words, which earn $2,700. Also buys material previously published
in books, magazines, or newspapers. Buys global rights and pays on
acceptance for original articles, one-time or global rights for previously published "pickups." No unsolicited manuscripts. Send letter
of inquiry with a 2-page outline. Guidelines available on web site.

Toro

119 Spadina Avenue, Suite 502, Toronto, ON M5V 2L1
Phone: (416) 785-9446 Fax: (416) 785-9434

E-mail: info@toromagazine.ca and submissions@toromagazine.ca
Web site: www.toromagazine.ca
Contact: David Fielding, editorial assistant
Circulation: 220,000
Published 8 times a year
   A general interest magazine for men. Articles 150 to 6,000
words. Fees negotiated and paid on acceptance. "If a writer hasn't
worked with us before or is unknown to the editors, we always
suggest sending in clips along with his or her pitches." Guidelines
available on web site.

Up Here Magazine
P.O. Box 1350, Yellowknife, NT X1A 2N9
Phone: (867) 920-4343 Fax: (867) 873-2844
E-mail: liz@uphere.ca
Web site: www.uphere.ca
Contact: Liz Crompton, editor
Circulation: 30,000
Published 8 times a year
   A lively, informative magazine about travel, wildlife, arts, culture,
lifestyles, and especially the people of Canada's far northern
regions. Articles 2,200 to 3,000 words. Fees negotiable and paid on
publication. "We strongly prefer written queries that present a well-
focused story and, if not samples, then suggested leads for accompanying photography. Complete manuscripts with photos are okay,
but please be aware we cannot be responsible for unsolicited material. We're looking for solid reporting and research, and top-notch
photos. Always tell your story through the people involved."
Guidelines available.

Home & Hobby

Bloom
2137 – 33 Avenue S.W., Suite 130, Calgary, AB T2T 1Z7
Phone: (403) 243-1769 Fax: (403) 243-8456
E-mail: bloommagazine@telus.net
Contact: Carolyn Fleming, editor-in-chief

Circulation: 30,000
Published 3 times a year

Highlights gardens, gardening, and landscaping for Calgary and the area. Stories 100 to 1,000 words. Cannot pay but welcomes submission inquiries. Guidelines available.

Canadian Coin News
103 Lakeshore Road, Suite 202, St. Catharines, ON L2N 2T6
Phone: (905) 646-7744 Fax: (905) 646-0995
E-mail: bret@trajan.com
Web site: www.canadiancoinnews.com
Contact: Bret Evans, editor
Circulation: 11,000
Published biweekly

A tabloid magazine for Canadian collectors of coins and paper money. Pays a month after publication. Fees negotiable. Prefers phone or fax queries.

Canadian Gardening
340 Ferrier Street, Suite 210, Markham, ON L3R 2Z5
Phone: (905) 475-8440 Fax: (905) 475-9246
Web site: www.canadiangardening.com
Contact: Aldona Satterthwaite, editor
Circulation: 140,000
Published 8 times a year

A magazine geared toward the avid home gardener. Carries people-oriented feature articles on home gardens, garden design, and tips and techniques on gardening in the Canadian climate. Pays on acceptance $125 and up for short news items, reviews, or how-to pieces (200 to 400 words) and $350 and up for features (500 to 2,000 words). "We prefer outlines suggesting story ideas to unsolicited finished stories." Guidelines available on web site.

Canadian Home & Country
340 Ferrier Street, Suite 210, Markham, ON L3R 2Z5
Phone: (905) 475-8440 Fax: (905) 475-9246
E-mail: editorial@canadianhomeandcountry.com
Web site: www.canadianhomeandcountry.com
Contact: Suzanne Moutis, executive editor

Circulation: 100,000
Published 7 times a year

Formerly *Century Home*. A magazine for lovers of country living and country styles. Contains feature stories (800 to 1,200 words) about country houses, historic houses, artisans, entertaining, decorating, and antiques. Fees vary according to project and are paid on publication. Query first. "When pitching, queries should be accompanied by relevant scouting photos." Guidelines available.

Canadian Home Workshop

340 Ferrier Street, Suite 210, Markham, ON L3R 2Z5
Phone: (905) 475-8440 Fax: (905) 475-9560
E-mail: letters@canadianhomeworkshop.com
Web site: www.canadianhomeworkshop.com
Contact: Douglas Thomson, editor
Circulation: 108,000
Published 10 times a year

Canada's leading magazine for woodworkers and do-it-yourself home-improvement enthusiasts. Elucidates a variety of home projects, from laying floors and cleaning furnaces to renovating basements and making kitchen cabinets. Rates negotiable. Pays $300 to $800 on acceptance for features of 800 to 2,000 words. "Freelancers should have a good grounding in the subjects they query. Our step-by-step and technical articles rely on detail; generalities will not do." Guidelines available.

Canadian Homes and Cottages

2650 Meadowvale Boulevard, Unit 4, Mississauga, ON L5N 6M5
Phone: (905) 567-1440 Fax: (905) 567-1442
E-mail: editorial@homesandcottages.com
Web site: www.homesandcottages.com
Contact: Steven Chester, assistant editor
Circulation: 79,000
Published bimonthly

Canada's largest residential building magazine for consumers as well as builders, lumber retailers, and architects. Provides thought-provoking and innovative ideas and technical information to help Canadians build or renovate their homes and cottages. Articles 750 to 2,000 words. Fees vary according to complexity, but average is

$600. All articles are assigned. Pays on acceptance. "We have consumer and trade editions. We write about architecture and design, but not decorating; hard landscaping, but not gardening; cottage renovation and construction, but not cottage lifestyles." Guidelines available.

Canadian House & Home

511 King Street W., Suite 120, Toronto, ON M5V 2Z4
Phone: (416) 593-0204 Fax: (416) 591-1630
E-mail: mail@canhomepub.com
Web site: www.canadianhouseandhome.com
Contacts: Cobi Ladner, editor; Kate Quetton, managing editor
Circulation: 241,000
Published monthly

Focuses on creative home decoration and design. Inspires and teaches through pictorial essays and how-to articles featuring Canadian designers, architects, and artisans. Articles between 300 and 1,000 words. "Always include colour photos with written submissions. Stories are usually assigned based on acceptance of visuals." Pays on acceptance. Fees vary according to project.

Canadian Stamp News

103 Lakeshore Road, Suite 202, St. Catharines, ON L2N 2T6
Phone: (905) 646-7744 Fax: (905) 646-0995
E-mail: bret@trajan.com
Web site: www.canadianstampnews.ca
Contact: Bret Evans, managing editor
Circulation: 5,000
Published biweekly

A tabloid magazine serving Canadian philatelists and enthusiasts around the world who collect Canadian stamps. Pays two months after publication. Fees negotiable. Query first.

Canadian Woodworking Magazine

R.R. #3, Burford, ON N0E 1A0
Phone: (519) 449-2444 Fax: (519) 449-2445
E-mail: fulcher@canadianwoodworking.com
Web site: www.canadianwoodworking.com
Contact: Linda Fulcher, publisher

Circulation: 30,000
Published bimonthly

A special-interest publication with articles, editorials, photos, and ads for the hobbyist woodworker, beginner to advanced. Looking for articles on practical woodworking projects for the home workshop. Pays $50 to $150 on publication for articles 500 to 1,000 words.

The Craft Factor
813 Broadway Avenue, Saskatoon, SK S7N 1B5
Phone: (306) 653-3616 Fax: (306) 244-2711
E-mail: scc.editor@shaw.ca
Web site: www.saskcraftcouncil.org
Contact: Gale Hagblom Alaie, editor
Circulation: 1,500
Published twice a year

A publication pertaining to craft development in Canada, with emphasis on Saskatchewan. Highlights the work of craftspeople, provides a forum for controversial topics in the areas of craft history and theory, and generally promotes recognition of the historic and contemporary contribution of craft to Canadian culture through the appreciation of fine hand-made objects. Pays 17¢/word on publication for articles of 750 to 1,000 words.

Gardening Life
511 King Street W., Suite 120, Toronto, ON M5V 2Z4
Phone: (416) 593-0204 Fax: (416) 591-1630
E-mail: gleditorial@canhomepub.com
Web site: www.gardeninglife.ca
Contact: Danny Sinopoli, senior editor
Circulation: 98,000
Published bimonthly

Written for the avid gardener, whether novice or seasoned pro. "It is designed to inspire, to instruct, to inform, and to illuminate." Articles between 500 and 1,500 words. Pays on acceptance $1/word, although rates may vary according to project. "We do not accept unsolicited material. Always query first."

Ontario Craft

170 Bedford Road, Suite 300, Toronto, ON M5R 2K9
Phone: (416) 925-4222 Fax: (416) 925-4223
E-mail: ontariocraftcouncil@craft.on.ca
Web site: www.craft.on.ca
Contact: Sarah Mulholland, communications co-ordinator
Circulation: 2,400
Published twice a year
   Multimedia publication of the contemporary craft movement.
Profiles interesting craftspeople and reviews their work. Articles
600 to 2,000 words. Pays on publication. Fees vary. "Familiarize
yourself with *Ontario Craft* by looking through back issues. Articles
are assigned by the editor; however, submissions are welcome.
Focuses on the activities and accomplishments of the members of
the Ontario Crafts Council." Guidelines available.

Ontario Gardener

179 Carleton Street, Toronto, ON M5A 2K3
Phone: (416) 963-3934 Fax: (416) 963-5929
E-mail: shaunad@localgardener.net
Web site: www.localgardener.net
Contact: Shauna Dobbie, editor
Circulation: 20,000
Published bimonthly
   A magazine of practical information for gardeners in Ontario.
Articles 600 to 1,200 words. Pay rates vary and are paid on publi-
cation. "We look for solid but lively writing in the third person
from writers with strong, first-hand knowledge of gardening."
Guidelines available.

Photo Life

185 St. Paul Street, Quebec, QC G1K 3W2
Phone: (418) 692-2110 Fax: (418) 692-3392
E-mail: editor@photolife.com
Web site: www.photolife.com
Contacts: Anita Dammer and Darwin Wiggett, editors-in-chief
Published bimonthly
   Established 1976. Delivers serious information to photographers
from beginners to advanced in a readable way. Articles 600 to 1,200

words. Fees are negotiated. "*Photo Life* offers the opportunity for young photographers to have their work published (unpaid). We have regular contributors but welcome suggestions for future articles and submissions."

Renovation and Decor Magazine

178 Main Street, Unionville, ON L3R 2G9
Phone: (905) 479-4663 Fax: (905) 479-4482
E-mail: kwhitney@homesmag.com
Web site: www.renovationanddecor.com
Contact: Kate Whitney, managing editor
Circulation: 75,000
Published quarterly

Inspires readers with features on home renovations and decor. Also includes stories on furnishings and accessory trends, and 1-page articles on creative projects. Primary focus is on Southern Ontario. Articles 500 to 1,000 words. Pays about 25¢/word on publication, although fees vary. Guidelines available.

Style at Home

25 Sheppard Avenue W., Suite 100, Toronto, ON M2N 6S7
Phone: (416) 218-3685 Fax: (416) 218-3632
E-mail: letters@styleathome.com
Web site: www.styleathome.com
Contact: Gail Johnston Habs, editor
Circulation: 230,000
Published 10 times a year

A glossy magazine featuring Canadian home-decor stories, news, products, and trends. Rates vary with project and writer, but pays up to $1/word on acceptance for stories of 300 to 700 words. "Please read several issues of *Style at Home* before presenting queries." Guidelines available.

The Wire Artist Jeweller

32 Monteith Avenue, Thorndale, ON N0M 2P0
Phone: (519) 2461-1902 Fax: (519) 461-9007
E-mail: helen@wag.on.ca
Web site: www.wag.on.ca
Contact: Helen Goga, publisher/editor

Circulation: 9,000

Published 10 times a year

Publishes stories related to the topic of jewellery, whether or not these were made with or without the use of solder. Topics include historical information on styles of jewellery, materials used, why we wear jewellery to celebrate specific holidays, controversial subjects (such as lead in jewellery), and personal stories related to jewellery. Articles approximately 3,000 words. Sidebars and graphics are appreciated. Send all queries and submissions by e-mail. Allow 3 to 6 weeks for a response. Pays 15¢/word on publication. Guidelines available.

Lifestyle

Access Magazine

79 Portsmouth Drive, Toronto, ON M1C 5C8

Phone: (416) 335-0747 Fax: (416) 335-0748

E-mail: crossfire@accessmag.com

Web site: www.accessmag.com

Contact: Sean Plummer, editor

Circulation: 200,000

Published 6 times a year

A music/lifestyle magazine focusing on music, film, video, fashion, travel, and other lifestyle topics. Articles 120 to 1,500 words. Fees vary and are paid on publication. "We rarely take assignments on spec, but we are looking for new talent to assign features to." Phone Sean Plummer.

Alive Magazine

7436 Fraser Park Drive, Burnaby, BC V5J 5B9

Phone: (604) 435-1919 Fax: (604) 435-4888

E-mail: editorial@alive.com

Web site: www.alive.com

Contact: Terry-Lynn Stone, editor-in-chief

Circulation: 250,000

Published monthly

A national magazine for health-conscious Canadians featuring articles on whole-foods nutrition, alternative medicine, and the environment. Articles of 800 to 1,000 words by health researchers and professionals. Pays 25¢/word on publication. "Always query. Do not send unsolicited articles or manuscripts." Guidelines available.

Ascent – Yoga for an Inspired Life
837 Gilford Street, Montreal, QC H2J 1P1
Phone: (514) 499-3999 Fax: (514) 499-3904
E-mail: info@ascentmagazine.com
Web site: www.ascentmagazine.com
Contact: Juniper Glass, managing editor
Circulation: 6,500
Published quarterly

A magazine of yoga and engaged spirituality that publishes thoughtful and lively articles exploring how spiritual values are brought to life in the everyday. Each issue has a theme (e-mail managing editor for schedule of themes). Articles of 1,000 to 3,000 words. Pays 20¢/word on publication for articles and features. "We prefer to work with writers from the query stage onwards. We rarely accept unsolicited submissions." Guidelines available.

Best Wishes
65 The East Mall, Toronto, ON M8Z 5W3
Phone: (416) 537-2604 Fax: (416) 538-1794
E-mail: tracyc@parentscanada.com
Web site: www.parentscanada.com
Contact: Tracy Cooper, editor
Circulation: 100,000
Published twice a year

Given to new parents in hospitals and other medical outlets. Articles cover topics relevant to parenting a baby from birth to 6 months of age and are written by Canadian healthcare professionals. Articles 1,000 to 2,000 words. Rates vary and are paid on acceptance.

Canada's Healthy Living Guide
7436 Fraser Park Drive, Burnaby, BC V5J 5B9
Phone: (604) 435-1919 Fax: (604) 435-4888
E-mail: wendy@healthylivingguide.com
Contact: Wendy Bone, editor

Circulation: 100,000
Published monthly

Features articles on nutrition, natural health, and fitness. "Our readers are mainstream, but our information is not. We have a whole food, holistic, and true health philosophy." Articles 500 to 1,000 words. Pays 25¢/word on acceptance. Writer must have the credentials to write about a topic. Guidelines available.

The Cape Bretoner
18 Townsend Street, Sydney, NS B1P 6H1
Phone: (902) 567-6400 Fax: (902) 539-2040
E-mail: ann@cityprinters.com
Web site: www.capebretoner.com
Contact: Pat O'Neil, editor
Circulation: 8,000
Published bimonthly

Carries articles with Cape Breton themes and/or connections. Readership is almost 100% Cape Bretoners with a small percentage of non-residents who love the island. Pays approximately $100 to $150 on publication for articles 800 to 1,500 words. E-mail queries regarding guidelines.

City Parent
467 Speers Road, Oakville, ON L6K 3S4
Phone: (905) 815-0017 Fax: (905) 337-5571
E-mail: cityparent@haltonsearch.com
Web site: www.cityparent.com
Contact: Jane Muller, editor-in-chief
Circulation: 160,000
Published monthly

A magazine to inform parents of news related to children and families. Also carries arts and entertainment news. Articles 500 to 750 words. Pays about 10¢/word, depending on research and quality. Welcomes submission inquiries.

**Community Action: Canada's Community Service
    Reporter**
P.O. Box 448, Toronto, ON M3C 2T2
Phone: (416) 449-6766 Fax: (416) 444-5850

E-mail: editor@communityaction.ca
Web site: http://communityaction.ca
Contact: Leon Kumove, publisher/editor
Circulation: 12,000
Published 11 times a year
Publishes news and information on health and social services, policy, programs, publications, conferences, and funding. Articles up to 800 words, book reviews 600 words. Cannot pay but welcomes submissions.

Cottage Life
54 St. Patrick Street, Toronto, ON M5T 1V1
Phone: (416) 599-2000 Fax: (416) 599-0800
E-mail: editorial@cottagelife.com
Contact: Penny Caldwell, editor
Circulation: 70,000
Published bimonthly
An award-winning magazine directed toward those who own and spend time at cottages on Ontario's lakes. Examines and celebrates the history, personalities, and issues of cottaging. Also provides practical advice to help readers keep their cottages, docks, and boats in working order. Pays on acceptance for articles of 150 to 3,000 words. Query all ideas before submission. Guidelines available with an SASE.

The Country Connection
P.O. Box 100, Boulter, ON K0L 1G0
Phone: (613) 332-3651
E-mail: editor@pinecone.on.ca
Web site: www.pinecone.on.ca
Contact: Joanne Healy, editor
Circulation: 5,000
Published quarterly
A nature-friendly magazine for the discerning reader, with a focus on green travel, heritage, nostalgia, nature, the environment, and the arts. Articles 1,000 to 2,000 words. Submit article ideas and short fiction. Pays on publication 10¢/word for electronic submissions and 7¢/word for handwritten or typed submissions. "Visit our web site for detailed requirements for upcoming issues."

Dolce: Canada's Lifestyle Magazine

60 Winges Road, Unit 1, Woodbridge, ON L4L 6B1
Phone: (905) 264-6789 Fax: (905) 264-3787
E-mail: editor@dolcemag.com
Web site: www.dolcemag.com
Contact: Michelle Zerillo-Sosa, editor-in-chief
Circulation: 45,000
Published 10 times a year

A national lifestyle magazine featuring stories on entertainment, health, food and wine, travel, beauty, fashion, sports, and more. Articles 800 to 3,000 words. Rates vary depending on project and are paid on publication. "Please call to get a copy of our writer's guidelines."

Expecting

65 The East Mall, Toronto, ON M8Z 5W3
Phone: (416) 537-2604 Fax: (416) 538-1794
E-mail: tracyc@parentscanada.com
Web site: www.parentscanada.com
Contact: Tracy Cooper, editor
Circulation: 100,000
Published twice a year

A digest-sized parental magazine distributed to expectant parents in doctors' offices and prenatal classes. All articles must be written by Canadian healthcare professionals and deal with topics relevant to pregnancy. Articles 1,000 to 2,000 words. Pay rates vary and are paid on acceptance.

50 Plus Magazine

27 Queen Street E., Toronto, ON M5C 2M6
Phone: (416) 363-5562 Fax: (416) 363-7394
E-mail: b.baker@50plus.com
Web site: www.50plus.com
Contact: Bonnie Baker Cowan, editor
Circulation: 250,000
Published 9 times a year

The official voice of Canada's Association for the 50-Plus and a leading magazine for the over-50s. Accepts a limited number of free-lance articles each year. Pays 60¢/word on acceptance for articles of

500 to 2,000 words. "Send query and writing samples. Please don't phone." Guidelines available.

Fifty-Five Plus

3 Beaverbrook Road, Kanata, ON K2K 1L2
Phone: (613) 271-8903, ext. 6 Fax: (613) 271-8905
E-mail: editorial@sympatico.ca
Contact: Pat den Boer, editor
Circulation: 40,000
Published 8 times a year

Informs active retirees in Eastern Ontario of options and opportunities for a successful retirement. Pays $60 to $250 on publication, depending on project and length, for 800 to 2,500 words. Fees for features may be negotiated. "This is a small operation, and writers should be prepared to wait up to 6 months for a response. Photos are necessary for most stories, and submissions are accepted only on IBM disk or by e-mail." Guidelines available.

Going Natural

P.O. Box 81128, FGPO, Ancaster, ON L9G 4X1
Phone: (905) 304-4836 Fax: (905) 304-4837
E-mail: editor@fcn.ca
Web site: www.fcn.ca/gn.html
Contact: Paul Rapoport, editor
Circulation: 2,200
Published quarterly

For current and future naturists/nudists in Canada and elsewhere. "Aims for an acceptance of the entire human body, of all ages and shapes, without shame or penalty (in non-erotic contexts)." Articles 800 to 1,200 words. Cannot currently pay, but payment in future is possible. "Some types of articles may require photos. Prospective writers please contact the editor." Guidelines available.

Good Times

25 Sheppard Avenue W., Suite 100, Toronto, ON M2N 6S7
Phone: (416) 733-7600 Fax: (416) 733-7981
E-mail: goodtimes@transcontinental.ca
Web site: www.goodtimes.ca

Contact: Judy Brandow, editor-in-chief
Circulation: 150,000
Published 11 times a year

Addresses the concerns of retired Canadians and those planning retirement. Topics include financial planning, health, celebrity profiles, and leisure activities. Welcomes inquiries that note areas of expertise and suggestions along with writing samples. Articles 1,200 to 2,000 words. Buys all rights and pays 40¢/word on publication. No phone, fax, or e-mail queries.

Lethbridge Living
P.O. Box 22005, Henderson Lake P.O., Lethbridge, AB T1K 6X5
Phone: (403) 329-1008 Fax: (403) 329-0264
Web site: www.lethbridgeliving.com
Contacts: Martin Oordt, publisher/editor; Mary Oordt, publisher/managing editor
Circulation: 15,000
Published quarterly

A lifestyle magazine focusing on the concerns and interests of the people of Lethbridge and southwestern Alberta. Pays 17¢/word on publication for articles 350 to 1,200 words. "Writing samples are required. Preference is given to writers from our distribution area." Guidelines available.

Menz Magazine
2638 Allard Street, Montreal, QC H2E 2L6
Phone: (514) 769-8282 Fax: (514) 769-8189
E-mail: editor@menz.com
Web site: www.menz.com
Contact: Bill Urseth, editor-in-chief
Circulation: 15,000
Published quarterly

Established 1994. An informative lifestyle quarterly carrying adventurous features on hot travel destinations, cutting-edge technology, cars, sports, and fashion, among many other topics of interest to its intelligent, success-driven male readers aged 25 to 40. "Our emphasis is on being a participant, not a spectator." *Menz Online* enhances rather than merely duplicates the printed magazine. Pays 25¢ to 50¢/word on publication for articles from 500 to

2,000 words. Looking for articles of substance and relevance for the lives of today's men. Welcomes all ideas and submission inquiries. Guidelines available.

Natural Life
264 Queens Quay W., Suite 508, Toronto, ON M5J 1B5
Phone: (416) 260-0303
E-mail: natural@life.ca
Web site: www.naturallifemagazine.com
Contact: Wendy Priesnitz, editor
Circulation: 25,000
Published bimonthly
Provides information and inspiration about healthy, sustainable living, including articles on natural health, healthy homes, and renewable energy. Articles 1,000 to 1,500 words. Cannot pay but welcomes submission inquiries. "Please read the magazine first. Prefer queries by e-mail, not complete articles. Lots of back issues on web site." Guidelines available on web site.

New Outlook/Nouveaux Horizons
65 Front Street E., 2nd Floor, Toronto, ON M5E 1B5
Phone: (416) 360-7339 Fax: (416) 360-8846
E-mail: newoutlook@redwoodcc.com
Contact: Tracy Howard, editor
Circulation: 400,000
Published quarterly
Published in English and French for Canadian men and women aged 50 plus on behalf of Sears Canada's Mature Outlook program. Focuses on lifestyle, wellness, and travel. Articles 800 to 1,000 words. Pay varies and is paid 30 days after acceptance. "Story queries should be sent to editor by e-mail. We do not accept unsolicited manuscripts. We do not reprint articles." Guidelines available.

Okanagan Life Magazine
1753 Dolphin Avenue, Suite 10, Kelowna, BC V1Y 8A6
Phone: (250) 861-5399 Fax: (250) 868-3040
E-mail: editorial@okanaganlife.com
Web site: www.okanaganlife.com

Contact: Dona Sturmanis, associate editor
Circulation: 25,000
Published 10 times a year

A regional magazine featuring articles for affluent, active, and educated readers on homes, cuisine, fashion, and lifestyle. Pays about 15¢/word on publication for articles of 1,500 to 3,000 words. Guidelines available on web site.

The Prime Times News
63 Albert Street, Suite 202, Winnipeg, MB R3R 2H2
Phone: (204) 949-4816 Fax: (204) 949-4818
E-mail: prime.editorial@uptownmag.com
Contact: John Kendle, editor
Circulation: 10,000
Published biweekly

A tabloid-sized publication containing news, features, and games of interest to people over 50 years old. Articles 500 to 750 words. Pay rates vary and are paid on publication.

Saltscapes
4 Alderney Drive, Suite 3501, Halifax, NS B2Y 2N5
Phone: (902) 464-7258
E-mail: editor@saltscapes.com
Web site: www.saltscapes.com
Contact: Heather White, senior associate editor
Circulation: 45,000
Published 7 times a year

Focuses on the people and places of Atlantic Canada. Articles 600 to 1,500 words. Rates vary according to project and are paid on publication. Guidelines available on web site.

The Senior Times
4077 Decarie Boulevard, Montreal, QC H4A 3J8
Phone: (514) 484-5033 Fax: (514) 484-8254
E-mail: editor@theseniortimes.com
Web site: www.theseniortimes.com
Contact: Barbara Moser, managing editor/publisher
Circulation: 20,000
Published 10 times a year

An informative news source targeting the English-speaking, 50-plus community of Montreal and surrounding areas. Pays a variable fee on publication for 400 to 600 words.

Sposa
56 Temperance Street, 6th Floor, Toronto, ON M5H 3V5
Phone: (416) 364-5899 Fax: (416) 364-5996
E-mail: myspace@sposa.com
Web site: www.sposa.com
Circulation: 50,000
Published twice a year
The world's first reality-based wedding magazine, featuring witty, provocative articles about love and marriage from a global perspective. "Wit and humour much appreciated." Articles 800 to 1,000 words. Pay rates vary and are paid on acceptance. Guidelines available.

Synchronicity, the Magazine
P.O. Box 63118, 2604 Kensington Road N.W., Calgary, AB
  T2N 4S5
Phone: (403) 270-9544 Fax: (403) 270-7407
E-mail: editor@synchronicitymagazine.ca
Web site: www.synchronicitymagazine.ca
Contact: Doreen G. Nystrom, editor
Circulation: 40,000
Published bimonthly
An alternative magazine with a body-mind-spirit focus, available free on stands in Alberta and the interior of B.C. Cover features are up to 3,000 words; feature stories about 900 words; short pieces from 350 to 600 words. Pays on publication approximately 5¢/word, or $40 to $50 for 800 to 1,000 words. "We recommend that the writer obtain copies of the magazine to discover if this is their kind of writing. We encourage submission inquiries." See the web site for future themes and guidelines.

Today's Parent
1 Mount Pleasant Road, Toronto, ON M4Y 2Y5
Phone: (416) 764-1926 Fax: (416) 764-2894
E-mail: tiziana.roberts@tpg.rogers.com

Web site: www.torontofamilies.ca
Contact: Tiziana Roberts, publisher
Circulation: 80,000
Published 11 times a year
   Readers are busy, Toronto-area parents of children, newborn to
12 years old. Content must be local. Pay ranges from $150 to $400
for articles 750 to 1,200 words. Paid on acceptance. "Please send
only queries of interest to local parents. Read the publication before
submitting queries."

Today's Parent Baby & Toddler
269 Richmond Street W., Toronto, ON M5V 1X1
Phone: (416) 596-8680 Fax: (416) 596-1991
Contact: Holly Bennett, editor
Circulation: 175,000
Published twice a year
   A consumer magazine for parents with children up to the age of
3. It is distributed as a special edition of *Today's Parent* through
doctors' offices and to new subscribers of *Today's Parent* who have
babies. Supportive articles focus on health, childcare, development,
parenting, and family-life issues. Does not publish poetry or fiction.
"Because we promote ourselves as a Canadian magazine, we use
only Canadian writers." Word length and fees vary depending on
the complexity of the story, usually 500 to 2,500 words. Pays 75¢ to
$1/word on acceptance. Query in advance with samples of pub-
lished work. Guidelines available.

Today's Parent Pregnancy & Birth
269 Richmond Street W., Toronto, ON M5V 1X1
Phone: (416) 596-8680 Fax: (416) 596-1991
Contact: Holly Bennett, editor
Circulation: 200,000
Published 3 times a year
   Provides support, information, advice, and encouragement to
expectant and new parents. Articles are directed toward promoting
healthy pregnancy and an active role in the birth and early care of the
child. Encourages informed consumer choice, breastfeeding, and
gentle parenting. Pays 75¢ to $1/word on acceptance for articles from

500 and 2,500 words (less for personal stories). Rates depend on the complexity and research demands of the article. "Most editorial is provided by our regular freelancers. We are especially interested in writers with backgrounds in childbirth issues." Guidelines available.

Toronto Families
1 Mount Pleasant Road, Toronto, ON M4Y 2Y5
Phone: (416) 764-1926 Fax: (416) 764-2894
E-mail: tiziana.roberts@tpg.rogers.com
Web site: www.torontofamilies.ca
Contact: Tiziana Roberts, publisher
Circulation: 80,000
Published 11 times a year
   Readers are busy, Toronto-area parents of children, newborn to 12 years old. Content must be local. Pay ranges from $150 to $400 for articles 750 to 1,200 words. Paid on acceptance. "Please send only queries of interest to local parents. Read the publication before submitting queries."

Vitality
356 Dupont Street, Toronto, ON M5R 1V9
Phone: (416) 964-0528
Contact: Julia Woodford, editor
Circulation: 50,000
Published 10 times a year
   Toronto's wellness journal. Pays on publication 10¢/word for articles of 800 to 1,500 words. "May take up to 3 months for unsolicited manuscripts to be evaluated for publication." Send an SASE for return of unsolicited material. Guidelines available.

Weddings & Honeymoons
65 Helena Avenue, Toronto, ON M6G 2H3
Phone: (416) 653-4986 Fax: (416) 653-2291
E-mail: barwed@interlog.com
Web site: www.weddingshoneymoons.com
Contact: Joyce Barslow, editor-in-chief
Circulation: 40,000
Published quarterly

Canada's how-to bridal, travel, and lifestyle newsmagazine serving the Ontario mainstream wedding marketplace. Also includes "Honeymoons & Wedding Destinations," a regular travel section in each issue that features romantic places to get engaged, get married, or honeymoon. Articles and columns include the elements required for planning and budgeting a wedding for the bride- and groom-to-be, including fashion and accessories, beauty, ceremonies, food and cakes, wines and beverages, flowers, photography, and gifts, as well as health and wellness and newlywed information regarding homes, finance, and other real life matters. Stories range from between 50 to 500 words. Articles and photos are considered for credits. Pays a negotiated rate of $50 to $150. A free tabloid, *Weddings & Honeymoons* is distributed to major retail outlets. Include an SASE for return of material.

Westcoast Families

280 Nelson Street, Suite 224, Vancouver, BC V6B 2E2
Phone: (604) 689-1331 Fax: (604) 689-7011
E-mail: info@westcoastfamilies.com
Web site: www.westcoastfamilies.com
Contacts: Andrea Porter, publisher; Ingrid King, editor
Circulation: 50,000
Published monthly

A newspaper geared to parents of children 12 years and under. An information source and guide to fun for families in the Vancouver area. Articles 650 to 850 words. Rates vary according to project and are paid on publication. "Please do not submit humorous essays. All submissions must be relevant to Canadians; local content preferred. No phone calls, please." Guidelines available.

Western Living

2608 Granville Street, Suite 500, Vancouver, BC V6H 3V3
Phone: (604) 877-7732 Fax: (604) 877-4838
E-mail: wlmail@westernlivingmagazine.com
Web site: www.westernlivingmagazine.com
Contact: Jim Sutherland, editor
Circulation: 220,000
Published 10 times a year

A general interest and lifestyle magazine with a special emphasis on the home. The largest regional magazine in Canada. Regular features cover personalities and trends, regional and international travel, food and recipes, and homes and design, all with a western Canadian focus. All stories should have a Western Canadian focus. Articles lengths and pay rates vary; contact above for more details.

The Western Producer

P.O. Box 2500, 2310 Millar Avenue, Saskatoon, SK S7K 2C4
Phone: (306) 665-3500 Fax: (306) 934-2401
E-mail: newsroom@producer.com
Web site: www.producer.com
Contacts: Terry Fries, news editor
Circulation: 80,000
Published weekly

Publishes news and feature stories of interest to Western Canadian farmers, ranchers, and rural dwellers. Articles 500 to 800 words. Varying pay rates depending on project; paid on publication. Guidelines available.

What's Up Kids? Family Magazine

496 Metler Road, Ridgeville, ON LOS 1M0
Phone: (905) 892-7970 Fax: (905) 892-6673
E-mail: editor@whatsupkids.com
Web site: www.whatsupkids.com
Contact: Susan Pennell-Sebekos, editor
Circulation: 200,000
Published bimonthly

Focuses on issues relating to families, including discipline, diet, and health. Articles 800 to 1,800 words. Payment made on publication: $60 to $265, depending on length. E-mail story suggestions to editor. Guidelines available.

Xtra!

491 Church Street, Suite 200, Toronto, ON M4Y 2C6
Phone: (416) 925-6665 Fax: (416) 925-6503
E-mail: info@xtra.ca
Web site: www.xtra.ca

Contact: Paul Gallant, managing editor
Circulation: 42,000
Published biweekly

Toronto's gay and lesbian periodical with news, analysis, op-ed pieces, and stories on arts and entertainment. Articles 400 to 800 words. Pays about 10¢/word on publication. "No submissions on spec. Pre-assigned stories only. Queries and story pitches welcome." Guidelines available.

News, Opinions, & Issues

Adbusters Magazine
1243 West 7th Avenue, Vancouver, BC V6H 1B7
Phone: (604) 736-9401 Fax: (604) 737-6021
E-mail: info@adbusters.org
Web site: www.adbusters.org
Contact: Kalle Lasn, editor
Circulation: 120,000
Published bimonthly

Established 1989. A combative, uncompromising commentator on the politics of media control and environmental strategy. Produced by the Media Foundation. Pays 50¢/word on publication for 100 to 1,500 words, though rates vary. Contact editor first if planning a lengthy submission. Guidelines available on web site.

Alberta Sweetgrass
13245 – 146th Street, Edmonton, AB T5L 4S8
Phone: (780) 455-2700 or 1-800-661-5469 Fax: (780) 455-7639
E-mail: edsweet@ammsa.com
Web site: www.ammsa.com
Contact: Debora Steel, editor
Circulation: 7,500
Published monthly

A community newspaper highlighting Aboriginal issues, programs, people, arts, culture, and advances in Alberta. Pays $3.00 to $3.60/column inch on publication for stories of 500 to 800 words (rate depends on sources, editing, photos, etc.). Query first. Not interested in poetry or fiction. Guidelines available on web site.

Anglican Journal

80 Hayden Street, Toronto, ON M4Y 3G2
Phone: (416) 924-9192, ext. 307 Fax: (416) 921-4452
E-mail: editor@national.anglican.ca
Web site: www.anglicanjournal.com
Contact: Leanne Larmondin, editor
Circulation: 243,000
Published 10 times a year

Independently edited national publication of the Anglican Church of Canada, established in 1875. Contains news and features from across Canada and abroad. Subjects include news of all denominations and faiths, and articles on a range of social and ethical issues. Stories should be of interest to a national audience. Length 600 to maximum of 1,200 words. Pays a base rate of 23¢/published word on publication. Initial inquiry recommended. "Basic style is as for a daily newspaper. Use *CP Style Book* as a guide." Guidelines available.

The Annals of St. Anne de Beaupré

P.O. Box 1000, St. Anne de Beaupré, QC G0A 3C0
Phone: (418) 827-4538 Fax: (418) 827-4530
Contact: Father Roch Achard, editor
Circulation: 45,000
Published monthly

A general-interest religious magazine, established in 1878. Buys fiction and articles with a Catholic dimension. Pays 3¢ to 4¢/word on acceptance for "educational, inspirational, objective, and uplifting" articles up to 1,500 words. Seeks analysis rather than reporting. No poetry. Send complete manuscript, and expect a reply in 3 to 4 weeks. Unsolicited submissions are put into an "article bank" and pulled as need arises, so it can take time. "No reprints or simultaneous submissions. First North American rights only." Guidelines available.

Behind the Headlines

205 Richmond Street W., Suite 302, Toronto, ON M5V 1V3
Phone: (416) 977-9000 Fax: (416) 977-7521
E-mail: rossi@ciia.org
Web site: www.ciia.org

Contact: Michelle Rossi, program co-ordinator
Circulation: 2,000
Published quarterly

For members of the Canadian Institute of International Affairs and those with an interest in foreign policy and international affairs. Length of articles from 5,000 to 7,000 words. Cannot pay contributors but welcomes submissions. "We're a non-partisan, not-for-profit NGO. Our hallmarks are insight, criticism, perspective, dissent. Articles should address global issues from a Canadian perspective." Guidelines available.

bout de papier
47 Clarence Street, Suite 412, Ottawa, ON K1N 9K1
Phone: (613) 241-1391 Fax: (613) 241-5911
E-mail: boutdepapier@pafso.com
Web site: www.pafso.com
Contact: Debra Hulley, managing editor
Circulation: 2,500
Published quarterly

Examines all aspects of Canadian foreign policy and life in the Foreign Service. Provides a unique first-hand insight into the conduct and evolution of Canadian diplomacy. Articles are published in the language of submission. Features articles, interviews, book reviews, and commentaries from 1,000 to 2,800 words. Contributors are not paid. Welcomes submission inquiries from qualified writers.

Briarpatch
2138 McIntyre Street, Regina, SK S4P 2R7
Phone: (306) 525-2949
E-mail: briarrequest@netscape.net
Web site: www.briarpatchmagazine.com
Contact: Debra Brin, editor
Circulation: 1,500
Published 10 times a year

"*Briarpatch* is helping to build a strong activist network by covering issues and stories that expose the evils of this world and highlighting the work of people trying to make the world a better place. We provide a publishing opportunity for writers in the social

justice movement who are ignored by the mainstream media."
Carries articles of 600 to 1,200 words. Cannot pay, but submission
inquiries are welcome.

Canadian Dimension
91 Albert Street, Suite 2B, Winnipeg, MB R3B 1G5
Phone: (204) 957-1519 Fax: (204) 943-4617
E-mail: info@canadiandimension.mb.ca
Web site: www.canadiandimension.mb.ca
Contact: Kevin Matthews, office manager
Circulation: 3,000
Published bimonthly
   Established 1963. Publishes fact and analysis that bring Canada
and the world into focus. Carries alternative information on issues
concerning women, the labour movement, peace politics,
Aboriginal peoples, the environment, economics, and popular
culture. "*CD* is a magazine for people who want to change the
world. We debate issues, share ideas, recount our victories, and
evaluate our strategies for social change." Articles 600 to 2,000
words. Send written query of no more than 1 page. Can occasionally pay those whose sole income comes from writing. Guidelines
available on web site.

Canadian Lawyer
240 Edward Street, Aurora, ON L4G 3S9
Phone: (905) 841-6480 Fax: (905) 841-5078
E-mail: mfitzjames@canadalawbook.ca
Contact: Patricia Chisholm, acting editor
Circulation: 27,000
Published 11 times a year
   Sent to practising lawyers, judges, and corporate counsel, this is
the magazine Canada's legal professionals turn to for the news,
events, and issues that continually shape the profession. Pay rates
vary, depending on project. Guidelines available.

Catholic Insight
P.O. Box 625, Adelaide Stn., Toronto, ON M5C 2J8
Phone: (416) 204-9601 Fax: (416) 204-1027
E-mail: catholic@catholicinsight.com

Web site: www.catholicinsight.com
Contact: Alphonse de Valk, editor
Circulation: 3,500
Published 10 times a year

A journal of news and opinion on matters of religion, politics, society, and culture pertinent to Canada and the Catholic Church. "Most articles are pre-arranged for subject matter. Occasionally we accept an unsolicited freelance article." Length 740 to 1,400 words. Pays on publication from $150 to $350 for features, $135 for columns, and $75 for book reviews. Payment for interviews is negotiated.

Concordia University Magazine

1455 de Maisonneuve Boulevard W., FB 520, Montreal, QC
    H3G 1M8
Phone: (514) 848-2424, ext. 382   Fax: (514) 848-2826
E-mail: howard.bokser@concordia.ca
Web site: http://magazine.concordia.ca
Contact: Howard Bokser, editor
Circulation: 65,000
Published quarterly

The alumni magazine of Concordia University. It covers stories about Concordia alumni, the university, and education in Canada. Length 1,000 to 2,000 words. Fees vary and are paid on acceptance.

Education Canada

317 Adelaide Street W., Suite 300, Toronto, ON M5V 1P9
Phone: (416) 591-6300   Fax: (416) 591-5345
E-mail: glatour@cea-ace.ca
Web site: www.cea-ace.ca
Contact: Gilles Latour, production/business manager
Circulation: 4,000
Published quarterly

A theme-driven publication for Canadian educators. See web site for upcoming themes and guidelines. "Do not send articles without inquiring first." Cannot pay but welcomes inquiries.

Education Forum

60 Mobile Drive, Toronto, ON M4A 2P3
Phone: (416) 751-8300   Fax: (416) 751-3875

E-mail: grantj@osstf.on.ca
Web site: www.osstf.on.ca
Contact: J. Grant, traffic co-ordinator
Circulation: 48,000
Published 3 times a year
   A publication dealing with issues of education. Cannot pay but
welcomes submission inquiries.

Education Today
439 University Avenue, 18th Floor, Toronto, ON M5G 1Y8
Phone: (416) 340-2540 Fax: (416) 340-7571
E-mail: et@opsba.org
Web site: www.opsba.org
Contact: Catherine Watson, editor
Circulation: 3,500
Published 3 times a year
   Delivers up-to-date information and interest pieces to people
involved in or concerned about the education system. Articles 500
to 1,500 words. Rates vary with project, paid on acceptance. "Short
factual pieces on national or international education trends are
welcome." Guidelines available.

Faith Today
M.I.P. Box 3745, Markham, ON L3R 0Y4
Phone: (905) 479-5885 Fax: (905) 479-4742
E-mail: ft@efc-canada.com
Web site: www.faithtoday.ca
Contact: Gail Reid, managing editor
Circulation: 18,000
Published bimonthly
   Publishes features and news about Canadian Christians, their
thoughts, trends, issues, and events. Features 1,000 to 1,400 words.
Pays on acceptance 25¢/word for features. "We also welcome short
news items and profiles of 400 words (pays 20¢/word)." Guidelines
available on web site or upon request.

Humanist in Canada
P.O. Box 943, Duncan, BC V9L 3Y2
Phone: (250) 746-6678 Fax: (250) 746-6672

E-mail: editor@humanistincanada.com
Web site: www.humanistincanada.com
Contact: Gary Bauslaugh, editor
Circulation: 2,000
Published quarterly

Explores contemporary topics from a humanistic viewpoint, reflecting the principle that human problems can be solved rationally without relying on belief in the supernatural. For non-believers with an interest in social issues. Articles 1,000 to 2,500 words. Cannot pay (provides author copies) but welcomes submission inquiries. "A good opportunity for writers with alternative, divergent, or thought-provoking views." Guidelines available.

Inroads
280 Huron Street, New Hamburg, ON N3A 1J5
Phone: (519) 662-3390 Fax: (519) 662-3594
E-mail: inroads@canada.com
Web site: www.inroadsjournal.ca
Contact: Bob Chodos, managing editor
Circulation: 1,000
Published twice a year

Provides informed, lively commentary and analysis on issues facing Canada and the world. Readers include political scientists, policy analysts, politicians, civil servants, and interested citizens. Described by Ellen Roseman as "an energetic and eclectic read," and by Roy Romanow as "well written, balanced, and increasingly read by concerned Canadians." Articles 3,000 to 5,000 words. Cannot pay but welcomes submission inquiries. "An excellent forum for articles that are too analytical for the daily press and not academic enough for scholarly journals."

Law Times
240 Edward Street, Aurora, ON L4G 3S9
Phone: (905) 841-6481 Fax: (905) 727-0017
E-mail: lawtimes@clbmedia.ca
Web site: www.lawtimesnews.com
Contact: Gail J. Cohen, editor
Circulation: 12,000
Published weekly

Serves the Ontario legal market. Readership includes lawyers, judges, and law clerks. "If you have story ideas that would be relevant to *Law Times* readers, please feel free to send pitches to us by e-mail." Articles 800 to 1,200 words. Pay rates vary and are paid on publication.

Legion Magazine

359 Kent Street, Suite 407, Ottawa, ON K2P 0R6
Phone: (613) 235-8741 Fax: (613) 233-7159
E-mail: magazine@legion.ca
Web site: www.legionmagazine.com
Contact: Dan Black, managing editor
Circulation: 350,000
Published bimonthly
   A magazine for Canada's war veterans, RCMP members, forces personnel and their families, seniors, and the wider public. Carries news, views, and serious articles exploring Canada's military history, defence, veterans' affairs, health, and pensions. Offers humour and opinion columns, and also buys memoirs and nostalgia. Articles 600 to 2,500 words. Pays about $1,100 for 2,500 words (fee determined after final edit). "Please familiarize yourself with magazine and send an SASE with submission. Allow up to 6 months for response."

Life Learning Journal

264 Queens Quay W., Suite 508, Toronto, ON M5J 1B5
Phone: (416) 260-0303
E-mail: editor@lifelearningmagazine.com
Web site: www.lifelearningmagazine.com
Contact: Wendy Priesnitz, editor
Circulation: 25,000
Published bimonthly
   Focuses on how-to and inspirational stories about self-directed learning, unschooling, and natural parenting for a Canadian and U.S. audience. Articles 1,000 to 1,500 words. Cannot pay but welcomes submissions. Guidelines available on web site.

Living Light News

5306 – 89th Street, Suite 200, Edmonton, AB T6E 5P9
Phone: (780) 468-6397 Fax: (780) 468-6872

E-mail: shine@livinglightnews.org
Web site: www.livinglightnews.org
Contact: Jeff Caporale, editor
Circulation: 22,000
Published 7 times a year

A tabloid-sized evangelical newspaper with positive, contemporary, family-oriented appeal for Christians and spiritual seekers. Articles 450 to 800 words. Pays 10¢/word on publication for first rights, 5¢/word for reprint rights. Also pays for photos. "We are looking for writers who are evangelical Christians desiring to serve God through their writing. Our preference is on positive news that glorifies God or feature articles about well-known Christian celebrities and family-oriented subject matter." Guidelines available.

McGill News Alumni Quarterly

3640 rue de la Montagne, Montreal, QC H3G 2A8
Phone: (514) 398-3549 Fax: (514) 398-5293
E-mail: andrew.mullins@mcgill.ca
Web site: www.mcgill.ca/alumni/news
Contact: Andrew Mullins, associate editor
Circulation: 65,000 (150,000 for annual issue)
Published 3 times a year (plus annual issue)

Three issues are sent to McGill graduates and donors of the previous 2 years. Once a year, distribution is to all alumni worldwide. Also distributed to faculty and staff on campus. Features articles with a McGill connection on current affairs, entertainment, the humanities, medicine, and science, as well as profiles of graduates and students. Pays on acceptance $450 to $600, depending on complexity, for features of 1,500 to 2,000 words. Occasionally buys news stories of 250 to 500 words and 850-word personal essays for epilogue feature ($200). Publishes one article in French per issue. Prospective contributors may write for a sample copy.

Maclean's

1 Mount Pleasant Road, 11th Floor, Toronto, ON M4Y 2Y5
Phone: (416) 764-1339 Fax: (416) 764-1332
E-mail: letters@macleans.ca
Web site: www.macleans.ca

Contact: Anthony Wilson Smith, editor
Circulation: 3,100,000
Published weekly

Canada's most widely read news magazine. Examines news events, trends, and issues from a Canadian perspective. Has correspondents in 5 Canadian cities and a network of writers around the world. Staff writers and freelancers contribute to weekly sections on politics, business, entertainment, sports, leisure, education, health, science, personal finance, justice, and technology. Pays a variable but competitive fee on publication.

Monday Magazine

818 Broughton Street, Victoria, BC V8W 1E4
Phone: (250) 382-6188 Fax: (250) 381-2662
E-mail: editorial@mondaymag.com
Web site: www.mondaymag.com
Contact: Alisa Gordaneer, editor
Circulation: 40,000
Published weekly

An opinionated news and arts magazine for Victoria's progressive citizens. Articles 850 to 3,000 words. Rates vary and are paid upon publication. Seeks intelligent, inquisitive, and investigative stories with a strong Victoria focus. "Query first for most stories. We also publish personal essays (850 to 1,000 words) on a variety of topics. Send entire essay for consideration. We respond within a month, but only to submissions we're planning to publish. We prefer e-mailed submissions and queries." Guidelines available on web site.

New Socialist

P.O. Box 167, 253 College Street, Toronto, ON M5T 1R5
Phone: (416) 955-1581
E-mail: newsoc@web.net
Web site: www.newsocialist.org
Contact: editorial committee
Published bimonthly

A new left publication that aims to make changes by helping to build unions and support social movements. Publishes articles and interviews about developments in Canada and elsewhere, strategies for social change, and debates on the left by activists and writers. Welcomes letters, articles, and illustrations. Unable to pay contributors, but offers free copies of the magazine.

The NewCanadian Magazine
151 Jean Leman Boulevard, Suite 2001, Candiac, QC J5R 4V5
Phone: (450) 444-0341 Fax: (514) 221-2427
E-mail: editorial@newcanadian.com
Web site: www.newcanadian.com
Contact: Amy Luft, editorial manager
Circulation: 30,000
Published bimonthly
Focuses on Canadian culture, business, and politics. Articles 1,200 to 2,500 words. Rates vary and paid on publication.

New Internationalist
401 Richmond Street W., Suite 393, Toronto, ON M5V 3A8
Phone: (416) 588-6478 Fax: (416) 588-4285
E-mail: ni@newint.org
Web site: www.newint.org
Contact: editorial collective
Published 11 times a year
An uncompromising international periodical providing information and analysis on the major issues concerning international development. Exposes the politics of aid, militarism, and national and multinational exploitation of developing countries, and discusses racial, gender, and social politics in the developed and developing worlds. Issues are thematic. Articles 500 to 1,800 words. Pays $400 on publication for full-length articles. Guidelines available.

Off-Centre Magazine
P.O. Box 1384, Vernon, BC V1T 6N7
Phone: (250) 558-3979 Fax: (250) 558-3912
E-mail: off-centre@shaw.ca
Web site: www.off-centre.ca
Contact: Leanne Allen, publisher
Circulation: 17,000
Published monthly

An independent urban publication with witty, irreverent pieces on politics and culture. Articles 500 to 750 words. Pay varies and is paid on publication.

Our Schools Our Selves
75 Albert Street, Suite 410, Ottawa, ON K1P 5E7
Phone: (613) 563-1341 Fax: (613) 233-1458
E-mail: ccpa@policyalternatives.ca
Web site: www.policyalternatives.ca
Contact: Erika Shaker, co-editor
Circulation: 1,500
Published quarterly
A journal that provides analysis, commentary, and discussion about the education debates. Pays on acceptance for articles of 2,000 to 4,000 words. "Most articles are provided for free, or we pay for reprints." Guidelines available. "Submission information can be obtained by contacting co-editor Satu Repo at (416) 463-6978 (107 Earl Grey Road, Toronto, ON M4J 3L6)."

Our Times
P.O. Box 182, New Glasgow, NS B2H 5E2
Phone: (902) 755-6840 Fax: (902) 755-1292
E-mail: editor@ourtimes.ca
Web site: www.ourtimes.ca
Contact: Lorraine Endicott, editor
Circulation: 3,000
Published bimonthly
Published by a not-for-profit organization to promote workers' rights, unionization, and social justice. "Many articles are contributed by union activists. We pay between $100 and $400 for feature stories of 1,500 to 2,500 words from working writers." Guidelines available.

Policy Options
1470 Peel Street, Suite 200, Montreal, QC H3A 1T1
Phone: (514) 985-2461 Fax: (514) 985-2559
E-mail: policyop@irpp.org
Contact: L. Ian MacDonald, editor

Circulation: 3,000

Published 10 times a year

Published by the Institute for Research on Public Policy, a national, independent, not-for-profit think tank. Carries analyses of public policy so as to encourage wide debate on major policy issues. Articles 2,000 to 4,000 words. Contributors are unpaid, but submission inquiries by qualified writers welcome.

Presbyterian Record

50 Wynford Drive, Toronto, ON M3C 1J7

Phone: (416) 441-1111 Fax: (416) 441-2825

E-mail: pcrecord@presbyterian.ca

Web site: www.presbyterian.ca/record

Contact: David Harris, editor

Circulation: 45,000

Published 11 times a year

Primarily aimed at members of the Presbyterian Church in Canada, but carries items of interest to the Christian Church generally. Articles 750 to 1,500 words. Payment flexible and paid on publication. "Please query before submitting articles."

Queen's Alumni Review

Office of Advancement, Summerhill Building, Queen's University,
    Kingston, ON K7L 3N6

Phone: (613) 533-6000, ext. 74125 Fax: (613) 533-6828

E-mail: review@post.queensu.ca

Web site: www.alumnireview.queensu.ca

Contact: Ken Cuthbertson, editor

Circulation: 95,000

Published quarterly

Publishes news about and of interest to Queen's alumni, faculty, and friends of the university. Articles 250 to 2,500 words. Rates vary depending on project and are paid on acceptance. "We buy a limited amount of freelance material, but we are always in the market for well-written, timely articles. Would-be freelancers should study past issues before querying us." Guidelines available.

Raven's Eye: The Aboriginal Newspaper of British Columbia

13245 – 146th Street, Edmonton, AB T5L 4S8
Phone: (780) 455-2700 or 1-800-661-5469 Fax: (780) 455-7639
E-mail: bcraven@ammsa.com
Web site: www.ammsa.com
Contact: Joan Taillon, editor
Circulation: 7,000
Published monthly

Spotlights Aboriginal people and/or issues in British Columbia. Pays $3.00 to $3.60/published inch on publication for stories of 500 to 1,000 words. "We need writers/photographers located in all areas of B.C. – the farther from Vancouver the better. No poetry or fiction. Read past issues before submitting query. Focus is on Aboriginal community news." Guidelines available on web site.

Saskatchewan Sage

13245 – 146 Street, Edmonton, AB T5L 4S8
Phone: (780) 455-2700 Fax: (780) 455-7639
E-mail: edsage@ammsa.com
Web site: www.ammsa.com
Contact: Cheryl Petten, editor
Published monthly

A community newspaper featuring news, arts and entertainment, reviews, and feature articles about and by Aboriginal people of Saskatchewan. Pays $3.00 to $3.60/column inch on publication for 500 to 1,000 words. "Stories must be of provincial interest. Always query first, preferably by phone or e-mail. Guidelines available on Internet site."

Saturday Night

111 Queen Street E., Suite 450, Toronto, ON M5C 1S2
Phone: (416) 595-9944
E-mail: editor@saturdaynight.ca
Web site: www.saturdaynight.ca
Contact: Matthew Church, editor-in-chief
Circulation: 200,000
Published 10 times a year

A magazine of national scope, focus, and distribution, *Saturday Night* offers entertaining, informative, and engaging articles of interest to Canadians. Articles 1,000 to 5,000 words. Fees are negotiated and paid on acceptance.

Tandem Magazine
101 Wingold Avenue, Toronto, ON M6B 1P8
Phone: (416) 785-4300 Fax: (416) 785-4329
E-mail: tandem@corriere.com
Web site: www.tandemnews.com
Contact: Angela Baldassarre, managing editor
Circulation: 60,000
Published weekly

A news, arts, and sports magazine for 19- to 50-year-olds. Articles 500 to 1,200 words. Fees negotiated and paid on publication.

Teach Magazine
258 Wallace Avenue, Suite 206, Toronto, ON M6P 3M9
Phone: (416) 537-2103 Fax: (416) 537-3491
E-mail: info@teachmag.com
Web site: www.teachmag.com
Contact: Wili Liberman, publisher
Circulation: 22,000
Published 5 times a year

Explores pragmatic issues and ideas for educators of grades K through 12. Articles 1,500 to 2,000 words. Pay rates vary and are paid 30 to 60 days after acceptance. "Please read the publication first, then send a query letter. E-mail is fine." Guidelines available.

This Magazine
401 Richmond Street W., Suite 396, Toronto, ON M5V 3A8
Phone: (416) 979-8400 Fax: (416) 979-1143
E-mail: queries@thismagazine.ca
Web site: www.thismagazine.ca
Contact: Julie Crysler, editor
Circulation: 8,000
Published bimonthly

Canada's leading alternative magazine carrying investigative features and researched commentary on culture, politics, and the arts.

Features of 2,000 to 4,000 words earn a negotiated fee of $200 to $400 on publication. Shorter items, from 500 to 1,500 words, earn $50 to $150. "We prefer clearly focused, thoroughly researched, and sharply written investigative articles on topics the mainstream media ignore. No unsolicited poetry, fiction, or drama." Send a query letter. Guidelines available on web site.

The United Church Observer
478 Huron Street, Toronto, ON M5R 2R3
Phone: (416) 960-8500 Fax: (416) 960-8477
E-mail: general@ucobserver.org
Web site: www.ucobserver.org
Contact: Muriel Duncan, editor
Circulation: 80,000
Published 11 times a year
The national magazine of the United Church of Canada. Provides news of the church, the nation, and the world while maintaining an independent editorial policy. Prints serious articles on issues such as human rights, social justice, and Christian faith in action, and stories of personal courage – all with a Christian perspective. Also covers the religious dimensions of art, literature, and theatre. Articles 500 to 1,000 words. Fees negotiable, paid on publication. Personal stories are paid at lower rates. "Should use newsfeature treatment. Query first by fax or e-mail. Mostly staff written, but some freelance opportunities (also art and photography)." Guidelines available.

University Affairs
600 – 350 Albert Street, Ottawa, ON K1R 1B1
Phone: (613) 563-1236, ext. 228 Fax: (613) 563-9745
E-mail: pberkowi@aucc.ca
Web site: www.aucc.ca
Contact: Peggy Berkowitz, editor
Circulation: 25,000
Published 10 times a year
Canada's main source of information on university education, published by the Association of Universities and Colleges of Canada. Covers major issues and trends in higher education and other articles of interest to professors and administrators. Stories

from 300 to 2,000 words. Fees are usually 50¢/word, paid on acceptance, but can be higher for complicated features. "Please read the magazine and guidelines before submitting a story idea."

University of Toronto Magazine
21 King's College Circle, Toronto, ON M5S 3J3
Phone: (416) 946-7575 Fax: (416) 978-3958
E-mail: uoft.magazine@utoronto.ca
Web site: www.magazine.utoronto.ca
Contact: Rick Spence, editor/manager
Circulation: 260,000
Published quarterly
   Promotes the University of Toronto to its alumni, friends of the university, and the U. of T. community by publishing articles about alumni and campus news. U. of T. angle must be strong. Pays $1/word on acceptance for articles of 750 to 4,000 words.

Voices Across Boundaries
P.O. Box 54, NDG Stn., Montreal, QC H4A 3P4
Phone: (514) 223-6996 Fax: (514) 223-6997
E-mail: voices@acrossboundaries.net
Web site: www.voicesmagazine.ca
Contact: Wanda Romer Taylor, editor
Circulation: 1,200
Published quarterly
   Established 2003. Provides a venue in which people representing diverse cultures, traditions, and beliefs can share insights into contemporary issues. Directed at informing general readers. Articles 750 to 3,000 words. Pays approximately 16¢/word on publication. "*Voices* publishes theme issues, and articles are most likely to be accepted if they fit in with a theme we are covering. Check web site for upcoming themes." Guidelines available.

The Walrus Magazine
19 Duncan Street, Suite 101, Toronto, ON M5H 3H1
Phone: (416) 971-5004 Fax: (416) 971-8768
E-mail: info@walrusmagazine.com
Web site: www.walrusmagazine.com
Published 10 times a year

A general interest magazine with an international thrust. Articles 500 to 5,000 words. Pay rates vary depending on project and are paid on publication. "Please note that we do not accept unsolicited fiction or poetry submissions." Guidelines available.

Western Alumni Gazette
University of Western Ontario, Stevenson-Lawson Bldg., Room 335, London, ON N6A 5B8
Phone: (519) 661-2111, ext. 88467 Fax: (519) 661-3921
Web site: www.uwo.ca or http://communications.uwo.ca/alumni/
Contact: editor
Circulation: 130,000
Published 3 times a year
Written for Western alumni around the world. Pays on acceptance.

Windspeaker
13245 – 146 Street, Edmonton, AB T5L 4S8
Phone: (780) 455-2700 Fax: (780) 455-7639
E-mail: edwind@ammsa.com
Web site: www.ammsa.com
Contact: Debora Steel, editor
Circulation: 27,000
Published monthly
A national news magazine dealing with the issues and concerns of Aboriginal people in Canada from an Aboriginal perspective. Articles 800 to 1,000 words. Pays $3.00/published column inch on publication for single-source stories and $3.60/published column inch for multiple-source stories. "Remember the perspective; remember the audience." Guidelines available.

Special Interest

Abilities
340 College Street, Suite 650, Toronto, ON M5T 3A9
Phone: (416) 923-1885 Fax: (416) 923-9829
E-mail: able@abilities.ca
Web site: www.abilities.ca

Contact: Lisa Bendall, managing editor
Circulation: 45,000
Published quarterly

Canada's lifestyle magazine for people with disabilities. Provides inspiration, information, and opportunities to people with disabilities. Articles/stories 500 to 2,000 words. A non-profit organization that pays honoraria to writers ranging from $50 to $400 on publication. "First-hand knowledge of disability is helpful. We are interested in new ideas, resources, or strategies that will empower our readers. Avoid telling them what they already know." Guidelines available.

The Atlantic Co-operator
123 Halifax Street, Moncton, NB EIC 8N5
Phone: (506) 858-6614 Fax: (506) 858-6615
E-mail: editor@theatlanticco-operator.coop
Web site: www.theatlanticco-operator.coop
Contact: Mark Higgins, editor
Circulation: 16,000
Published 9 times a year

Established 1939. Publishes stories on local ownership and community development. Photos a plus. Articles 800 to 2,200 words. Pays 20¢/word on publication, plus an additional 2¢/word for right to post on web site. Guidelines available on web site.

Aviation Canada
72 Sunnyside Avenue, Ottawa, ON KIS ORI
Phone: (613) 730-9439 Fax: (613) 730-1321
E-mail: bob@aviationcanada.ca
Web site: www.aviationcanada.ca
Contact: Bob Baglow, publisher
Circulation: 20,000
Published quarterly

A full-colour national aviation magazine covering recreational, general, and commercial aviation. Canadian material only. Pays on publication 10¢/word for articles between 1,800 and 4,500 words. Pay rate is negotiable depending on expertise. Unsolicited material not accepted.

Canadian Classics
P.O. Box 342, O'Leary, PE COB IVO
Phone: (902) 859-3869 Fax: (902) 859-1539
E-mail: dale@lidstonepub.pe.ca
Web site: www.canadianclassicmag.com
Contact: Dale Lidstone, publisher
Circulation: 11,000
Published monthly
    A magazine specializing in antique cars. Rates vary according to project. Paid on publication.

Canadian Guider
Girl Guides of Canada, 50 Merton Street, Toronto, ON M4S 1A3
Phone: (416) 487-5281 Fax: (416) 487-5570
E-mail: CanadianGuider@girlguides.ca
Web site: www.girlguides.ca
Contact: Sharon Pruner, editor
Circulation: 36,000
Published quarterly
    A publication by the Girl Guides of Canada for anyone who works with today's youth. Includes program ideas, leadership tips, and articles on camping and the outdoors, games, and crafts. Articles from 800 to 2,000 words. Cannot pay, but welcomes submissions. Guidelines available.

Canadian Teddy Bear News
P.O. Box 457, Water Valley, AB TOM 2E0
Phone: (403) 637-2728 Fax: (403) 637-2616
E-mail: patricia@teddybearnews.com
Web site: www.teddybearnews.com
Contact: Patricia Atchison, publisher/editor
Circulation: 850
Published quarterly
    A niche market magazine for those adults interested in collecting and making teddy bears, and the Canadian teddy bear industry in general. "This magazine features approximately 95% Canadian content. Writers should be familiar with teddy bear collecting and artistry within Canada." Articles 900 to 1,500 words. Fees vary and are paid on publication. Guidelines available on web site.

Celtic Heritage Magazine

P.O. Box 805, Stn. A, Halifax, NS B3K 5H4
Phone: (902) 835-6244 Fax: (902) 835-0080
E-mail: celtic@hfx.eastlink.ca
Web site: www.celticheritage.ns.ca
Contact: Alexa Thompson, editor
Circulation: 8,000
Published bimonthly

"We welcome articles that chronicle the unique history and achievements of the various Celtic groups that have settled in Canada, especially the accounts of those individuals not generally recorded in history books." Articles from 1,000 to 1,800 words. Pays on publication $75/article and $50/review (music, books, videos). "Please submit query by e-mail or in writing. Also please be on the lookout for new story ideas of national interest." Guidelines available.

Challenging Destiny

R.R. #6, St. Marys, ON N4X 1C8
E-mail: csp@golden.net
Web site: www.challengingdestiny.com
Contact: David M. Switzer, editor/publisher
Circulation: 200
Published quarterly

Established 1997. Publishes all kinds of science fiction and fantasy short stories. Stories from 2,000 to 10,000 words. Pays 1¢/word on publication. "We're looking for interesting stories with believable characters. We like to see stories with religious or philosophical themes." Guidelines available.

Digital Journal

P.O. Box 1046, 31 Adelaide Street E., Toronto, ON M5C 2K4
Phone: (416) 410-9675
E-mail: editor@digitaljournal.com
Web site: www.digitaljournal.com
Contact: Chris Hogg, editor-in-chief
Circulation: 20,000
Published quarterly

Established on the Internet in 1998 then evolved into a printed publication. The first newsstand magazine devoted to the ongoing convergence of information technology, lifestyle, and the arts. Includes the "Essential Digital Gear" section, new product reviews, and profiles of technological visionaries and the emerging innovators in business, education, and the arts. Readers are affluent, educated urban professionals, aged 18 to 49. Articles 650 to 900 words. Pays on publication 25¢/word for articles. Guidelines available on web site.

Divorce Magazine

392 Parliament Street, Toronto, ON M5A 2Z7
Phone: (416) 368-8853 Fax: (416) 368-4978
E-mail: editors@divorcemag.com
Web site: www.DivorceMagazine.com
Contact: Diana Shepherd, editor
Circulation: 180,000
Published quarterly

A self-help magazine for people experiencing separation, divorce, and remarriage. Articles 750 to 3,000 words. Fees are negotiated based on project and paid on publication. Guidelines available.

Dogs, Dogs, Dogs!

6A – 49 The Donway W., Suite 1918, Don Mills, ON M3C 2E8
Phone: (416) 425-7534 Fax: (416) 425-5092
E-mail: info@dogsx3.com
Web site: www.dogsx3.com
Contact: Jackkie Lindsay, editor
Circulation: 13,000
Published bimonthly

Provides information for readers who considers their dog to be part of their family. Includes articles on health, training, and other activities. Articles 500 to 1,200 words. Cannot pay but welcomes submission inquiries.

Heritage

5 Blackburn Avenue, Ottawa, ON K1N 8A2
Phone: (613) 237-1066

E-mail: heritagecanada@heritagecanada.org
Web site: www.heritagecanada.org
Contact: Heather Hunter, assistant to director of communications
Circulation: 4,500
Published quarterly

The magazine for members of the Heritage Canada Foundation, a charitable, non-profit organization. Covers issues and activities in the field of preservation of heritage buildings. "Articles must address preservation issues or be about historic properties that have either been restored or are endangered." Articles 2,000 to 2,500 words. Often cannot pay, or pays on publication $500 for 2,000 to 2,500 words. Guidelines available.

Hub: Digital Living

600 – 625 Church Street, Toronto, ON M4Y 2G1
E-mail: submissions@hubcanada.com
Web site: www.hubcanada.com
Contact: Megan Johnston, editor
Circulation: 265,000
Published monthly

A publication covering new trends and technologies in computing and consumer and personal electronics. Written for a general audience and has a lifestyle focus. Articles from 250 to 1,400 words. Fees are negotiated and paid on publication. "We do not accept unsolicited material. Pitches should reflect familiarity with our magazine. We receive many pitches, so we may not reply immediately." Guidelines available.

Inside Motorcycles

P.O. Box 7100, Stn. B, Toronto, ON M5W 1X7
Phone: (416) 962-7223 Fax: (416) 962-7208
E-mail: editor@insidemotorcycles.com
Web site: www.insidemotorcycles.com
Contact: John Hopkins, editor
Circulation: 10,000
Published 10 times a year

Covers motorcycle racing and recreation with a Canadian perspective. Fees vary and are paid on publication.

The Leader Magazine
1345 Baseline Road, Suite 100, Ottawa, ON K2C 0A7
Phone: (613) 224-5131 Fax: (613) 224-3571
E-mail: leader@scouts.ca
Web site: www.scouts.ca/leader
Contact: Susan Mackie, editor
Circulation: 35,000
Published 10 times a year
  For Scouts Canada leaders. It encourages the development of youth and leaders through program-related articles on indoor and outdoor activities including camping, computers, and crafts for ages 5 to 26. Articles are 500 to 1,500 words. Does not pay, but welcomes submission inquiries. "Those who submit material should be active scouting members with program ideas to share." Guidelines available.

Muse
280 Metcalfe Street, Suite 400, Ottawa, ON K2P 1R7
Phone: (613) 567-0099
E-mail: ngauthier@museums.ca
Web site: www.museums.ca
Contact: Natasha Gauthier, editor-in-chief
Circulation: 2,500
Published bimonthly
  A source for features, news, and opinion pieces covering Canadian and international heritage institutions (museums, archives, libraries, zoos, etc.). Articles are 350 to 2,500 words. "Most articles are unpaid if they are submitted by museum professionals. However, longer features by professional, unbiased journalists may occasionally be eligible for an honorarium."

The Navigator
P.O. Box 29126, St. John's, NL A1A 5B5
Phone: (709) 754-7977 Fax: (709) 754-6225
E-mail: nav@nfld.com
Web site: www.thenavigatormagazine.com
Contact: Jim Wellman, managing editor
Circulation: 10,000
Published monthly

The voice of the commercial fishing industry in Atlantic Canada and the New England states. Articles from 750 to 1,500 words. Rates vary from 10¢ to 25¢/word, depending on project. Fees are negotiated in advance and paid on publication. "Submissions welcomed. Prospective freelancers advised to contact editor in advance for guidance."

Pets Quarterly

512 King Street E., Suite 300, Toronto, ON M5A 1M1
Phone: (416) 955-1550 Fax: (416) 955-1391
E-mail: info@capmagazine.ca
Web site: www.petsquarterly.ca
Contact: Adrienne Ramsay, office manager
Circulation: 55,000
Published quarterly

Offers timely, well-researched feature articles on subjects of interest to animal and pet lovers, including regular columns such as "Pet News," "Ask the Experts," Family Album," "Pet Press," and "Breed Profile." Readership includes veterinarians, clinics, pet retailers, groomers, and breeders. Cannot pay but welcomes submission inquiries. Guidelines available.

P.O.V. Magazine

517 College Street, Suite 325, Toronto, ON M6G 4A2
Phone: (416) 599-3844 Fax: (416) 599-0187
E-mail: info@cifc.ca
Web site: www.cifc.ca
Contact: Sandy Crawley, managing editor
Circulation: 2,000
Published quarterly

Publishes essays, reports, interviews, and news about the art and business of documentary film and video in Canada and around the world. "We target independent professionals and cinephiles with an interest in the creative and social impact of the documentary genre." Pay rates vary and are paid on publication for 700 to 2,000 words.

Stitches: The Journal of Medical Humour

240 Edward Street, Aurora, ON L4G 3S9
Phone: (905) 713-4336 Fax: (905) 727-0017

E-mail: simon@stitchesmagazine.com
Contact: Simon Hally, editor
Circulation: 39,000
Published monthly
   A magazine of humour and travel for practising physicians. Pays
40¢/word on publication for 150 to 1,500 words. "Aspiring contrib-
utors are encouraged to request a free sample copy of the magazine.
No story ideas, please; we need to see the story itself. We are eager
to hear from genuinely funny writers."

Wine Tidings
5165 Sherbrooke Street W., Suite 414, Montreal, QC H4A 1T6
Phone: (514) 481-6606 Fax: (514) 481-9699
E-mail: editor@winetidingsmag.com
Web site: www.winetidingsmag.com
Contacts: Carolyn Lavergne, circulation manager
Circulation: 20,000
Published 8 times a year
   Canada's leading national magazine dedicated to the apprecia-
tion of wine and food. Reports on the wine and spirits industry as
a whole, including vintages, trends, and profiles of well-known wine
cellars. Focuses on the Canadian wine industry as well as on travel
and recipes. Articles run from 500 to 1,500 words. Pays on publi-
cation. Knowledge of wine and spirits is a must.

World of Wheels
6200 Dixie Road, Suite 220, Mississauga, ON L5G 3M2
Phone: (905) 795-0110 Fax: (905) 795-2967
E-mail: editor@wheels.ca
Web site: www.wheels.ca
Contact: Jeremy Sinek, editor
Circulation: 50,000
Published bimonthly
   A magazine for auto enthusiasts, and for those interested in
developments in the auto industry and their impact on Canada.
Evaluates and compares the latest in cars, light pickup trucks, vans,
and sport-utility vehicles. Pays 35¢/word on publication for 1,000 to
2,000 words. Guidelines available.

Sports & Outdoors

Alberta Golf Magazine
4180 Lougheed Highway, 4th Floor, Burnaby, BC V5C 6A7
Phone: (604) 299-7311 Fax: (604) 299-9188
E-mail: bdunn@canadawide.com
Web site: www.canadawide.com
Contact: Bob Dunn, editor
Circulation: 30,000
Published quarterly
    Alberta's leading golf magazine serving the diverse interests and needs of golf enthusiasts (both serious and novice) and fans throughout the province. Pays 35¢ to 40¢/word on publication for 1,000 to 2,500 words. Pay rates vary with project. Query first; don't send completed articles on spec.

Athletics
1185 Eglinton Avenue E., Suite 302, Toronto, ON M3C 3C6
Phone: (416) 426-7215 Fax: (416) 426-7358
E-mail: ontrack@eol.ca
Web site: www.otfa.ca
Contact: John Craig, editor
Circulation: 3,500
Published 8 times a year
    Publishes in-depth stories and photographs on track and field and road running from grass roots to the Olympic level. Articles from 750 to 1,500 words. Rates vary; paid on publication.

B.C. Outdoors Hunting and Shooting
1080 Howe Street, Suite 900, Vancouver, BC V6Z 2T1
Phone: (604) 606-4644 Fax: (604) 687-1925
E-mail: bcoutdoors@oppublishing.com
Web site: www.oppublishing.com
Contact: Tracey Ellis, co-ordinating editor
Published twice a year
    "We are the source for the best hunting and shooting in B.C. We are looking for original queries from knowledgeable writers on every aspect of hunting, from heritage, wildlife management, techniques

and strategies to the very latest in shooting products and firearms issues." Carries articles from 1,800 to 2,200 words. Pays on publication. "Rates commensurate with experience and are determined by the editor." Guidelines available. "As with any publication, the best way to know what we are looking for is to read our magazine."

B.C. Outdoors Sport Fishing and Outdoor Adventure
1080 Howe Street, Suite 900, Vancouver, BC V6Z 2T1
Phone: (604) 606-4644 Fax: (604) 687-1925
E-mail: bcoutdoors@oppublishing.com
Web site: www.bcosportfishing.com
Contact: Tracey Ellis, co-ordinating editor
Circulation: 35,000
Published bimonthly
   Publishes stories about fishing in B.C. and everything that goes along with it. "We are looking for original queries from knowledgeable writers who can write factual and entertaining articles on technique, resource management, and B.C.'s world famous fishing opportunities." Carries articles from 1,800 to 2,200 words. Pays on publication. "Rates commensurate with experience and are determined by the editor." Guidelines available. "As with any publication, the best way to know what we are looking for is to read our magazine."

Below the Belt Boxing Magazine
1478 Pilgrims Way, Suite 1712, Oakville, ON L6M 3G7
Phone: (416) 336-1947
E-mail: okpasio@hotmail.com
Web site: www.belowthebelt.tv
Contact: Dameon Okpasio, publisher
Circulation: 500
Published quarterly
   A magazine aimed at fighters and those learning about boxing. Currently the only Canadian boxing publication in print. "All our writers are volunteer contributors." Welcomes submission inquiries.

Camping Canada's RV Lifestyle Magazine
1020 Brevik Place, Suite 5, Mississauga, ON L4W 4N7
Phone: (905) 624-8218 Fax: (905) 624-6764

E-mail: craig@rvlifemag.com
Web site: www.rvlife.com
Contact: Craig Ritchie, editorial director
Circulation: 51,000
Published 7 times a year

Established 1971. Geared to readers who enjoy travel and camping. Readers vary from owners of towable trailers or motorhomes to young families and entry-level campers (no tenting). Half of the articles are written by freelancers. Publishes non-fiction articles on how-to, personal experience, and travel. Buys 20 to 30 manuscripts/year of 1,800 to 2,500 words. Send photos with submission. Occasionally accepts previously published submissions, if so noted. Pay varies; received on publication. Buys first North American serial rights. Byline given. Editorial lead time 3 months. Reports in 1 month on queries, 2 months on manuscripts. Sample copy free.

Canada's Outdoor Sportsman

1080 Howe Street, Suite 900, Vancouver, BC V6Z 2T1
Phone: (604) 606-4644 Fax: (604) 687-1925
E-mail: editor@westernsportsman.com
Contact: Tracey Ellis, co-ordinating editor
Circulation: 25,000
Published bimonthly

A magazine that covers the sports of hunting and fishing, and conservation in Canada. Articles 1,800 to 2,000 words. Pays $250 on publication for articles; photos extra. Please query. Guidelines available.

Canadian Biker

735 Market Street, Victoria, BC V8T 2E2
Phone: (250) 384-0333 Fax: (250) 384-1832
E-mail: edit@canadianbiker.com
Web site: www.canadianbiker.com
Contact: John Campbell, editor
Circulation: 12,000
Published 10 times a year

A general motorcycle magazine with an emphasis on cruiser-type motorcycles and touring articles with a Canadian slant. Other subjects include custom and vintage motorcycles, personality profiles, event coverage, and new model reviews (including sport, sport-touring, and dual-sport motorcycles). "Although freelance material is actively sought, potential contributors are strongly urged to contact the editor before submitting if they wish to avoid disappointment." Preferred length 500 to 1,500 words. Pays $50 to $200 on publication. "Articles paid according to quality rather than quantity and based on topic, frequency of contributions, and originality. Preference given to work sent on disk with hard copy and a minimum of two photos (captioned)." Guidelines available.

The Canadian Fly Fisher

389 Bridge Street W., Belleville, ON K8N 4Z2
Phone: (613) 966-8017 or 1-888-805-5608 Fax: (613) 966-5002
E-mail: canflyfish@on.aibn.com
Web site: www.canflyfish.com
Contact: Chris Marshall, editor
Published quarterly

Canada's only national fly fishing magazine, with information on Canadian fly fishing destinations, techniques, fly tying, etc. Stories must have a Canadian connection. Features range from 1,800 to 2,500 words, shorter pieces from 700 to 900 words, and occasionally very short filler items are used. Sidebars are appreciated. Enclose an SASE for queries and unsolicited manuscripts that are mailed, but e-mail queries are preferred. First-time writers must include a bio of 50 to 70 words. Responds to queries in at least 4 weeks. Pays up to $300 for a feature with supporting photos and graphics, and between $100 and $200 for shorter pieces. Guidelines available on web site.

Canadian Rodeo News

2116 – 27 Avenue N.E., Suite 223, Calgary, AB T2E 7A6
Phone: (403) 250-7292 Fax: (403) 250-6926
E-mail: crn@ rodeocanada.com
Web site: www.rodeocanada.com
Contact: Jennifer James, editor
Circulation: 4,000
Published monthly

The official publication of the Canadian Professional Rodeo Association, providing articles, results, and standings. A tabloid of

news, views, and opinions from the Canadian and U.S. rodeo circuit.
Phone editor with ideas before submitting. Guidelines available.

The Canadian Sportsman
P.O. Box 129, 25 Old Plank Road, Straffordville, ON N0J 1Y0
Phone: (519) 866-5558 Fax: (519) 866-5596
E-mail: dbriggs@canadiansportsman.ca
Web site: www.canadiansportsman.ca
Contact: Dave Briggs, editor
Circulation: 5,500
Published biweekly
"The voice of harness racing since 1870." A 4-colour, high-gloss
magazine carrying features and news about harness racing in
Canada and the U.S. Features from 1,500 to 2,500 words. Rates
depend on project and are paid on publication.

Canadian Thoroughbred
225 Industrial Parkway S., P.O. Box 670, Aurora, ON L4G 4J9
Phone: (905) 727-0107 Fax: (905) 841-1530
E-mail: info@horse-canada.com
Contact: Lee Benson
Circulation: 5,000
Published bimonthly
Canada's national journal on thoroughbred racing features news
and information on horses and their owners, including pedigrees
and stable-product updates. Fees negotiable. A very specialized
market, so always inquire first.

Diver Magazine
P.O. Box 1312, Delta, BC V4M 3Y8
Phone: (604) 948-9937 Fax: (604) 948-9985
E-mail: divermag@axion.net
Web site: www.divermag.com
Contact: Peter Vassilopoulos, editor
Circulation: 7,000
Published 8 times a year
For North American sport divers. Carries regular articles on
travel destinations, snorkelling, and scuba and deep-water diving.
Also covers marine life and underwater photography. Articles 500

to 1,000 words. Pays $3/column inch after publication. Check guidelines before submitting material.

Explore: Canada's Outdoor Magazine
54 St. Patrick Street, Toronto, ON M5T 1V1
Phone: (416) 599-2000 Fax: (416) 599-0800
E-mail: explore@explore-mag.com
Web site: www.explore-mag.com
Contact: James Little, editor
Circulation: 27,000
Published bimonthly
For people who enjoy outdoor recreational activities such as backpacking, mountain biking, canoeing, kayaking, skiing, and adventure travel. Most features run from 2,000 to 5,000 words. Payment depends on quality and length, and ranges from $1,000 and up. *Explore* also has sections for shorter stories, which generally run from 250 to 1,000 words. Payment depends on quality and length, and ranges from $125 and up. "Excellent photographs are essential for almost every *Explore* story, and though we generally use the work of full-time pros, we occasionally rely on a writer to provide appropriate photo support. In these cases, we need original transparencies, not prints." Guidelines available on web site.

Family Camping Magazine
115 King Street W., Suite 220, Dundas, ON L9H 1V1
Phone: (905) 628-4309
E-mail: brobinson@andrewjohnpublishing.com
Contact: Brenda Robinson, circulation co-ordinator
Circulation: 5,000
Published 5 times a year
A publication dealing with all aspects of camping with the family. Rates vary. Pays on publication.

Gam On Yachting
250 The Esplanade, Suite 202, Toronto, ON M5A 1J2
Phone: (416) 368-1559 Fax: (416) 368-2831
E-mail: gam@passport.ca
Web site: www.gamonyachting.com
Contact: Karin Larson, publisher/editor

Circulation: 14,000
Published 8 times a year

Established 1957. A forum magazine where Canadian sailors write about their sailing experiences. "Continues to be the magazine Canadian sailors look to when purchasing new boats or to stay in touch with the sailing fraternity." Cannot pay but welcomes submission inquiries. Articles will be edited from any length.

Golf Canada

1333 Dorval Drive, Suite 1, Oakville, ON L6M 4X7
Phone: (905) 849-9700 Fax: (905) 845-7040
E-mail: golfcanada@rcga.org
Web site: www.rcga.org
Contact: John Tenpenny, editor
Circulation: 150,000
Published quarterly

The official magazine of the Royal Canadian Golf Association. Covers amateur and professional golf and golfing issues, including player profiles and related topics. Features are 750 to 3,000 words. Pays 50¢/word on acceptance. Fees are negotiated. "Interested writers are welcome to contact the editor for more information."

Horse-Canada.com Magazine

225 Industrial Parkway S., P.O. Box 670, Aurora, ON L4G 4J9
Phone: (905) 727-0107 Fax: (905) 841-1530
E-mail: info@horse-canada.com
Web site: www.horse-canada.com
Contact: Susan Jane Anstey, publisher
Circulation: 10,000
Published 5 times a year

Canada's family horse magazine for all breeds. and disciplines with emphasis on equine health and care. Includes a special pull-out section for children who love horses. Preferred length 1,000 to 2,000 words. Pays 15¢ to 20¢/word on publication. Guidelines available.

Horse Sport

225 Industrial Parkway S., P.O. Box 670, Aurora, ON L4G 4J9
Phone: (905) 727-0107 Fax: (905) 841-1530
E-mail: info@horse-canada.com

Web site: www.horse-canada.com
Contact: Susan Jane Anstey, editor
Circulation: 10,000
Published monthly

An authoritative equestrian periodical featuring articles on horse care, riding and training techniques, breeding, animal health, and the industry at large. Provides coverage of equestrian sporting events in Canada and abroad, profiles of top riders, and how-to articles. Preferred length 1,000 to 2,000 words. Pays 15¢ to 20¢/word on publication. Contact editor before submitting. Guidelines available.

Horses All
278 – 19th Street N.E., Calgary, AB T2E 8P7
Phone: (403) 248-9993 Fax: (403) 248-8839
E-mail: horsesall@northhill.net
Web site: www.horsesall.net
Contact: Jean Llewellyn, editor
Circulation: 20,000
Published monthly

An equestrian magazine for all breeds and disciplines. Readers are horse owners, riders, competitors, and breeders. Articles 800 to 1,000 words. Fees vary, but can be about $50/story paid one month after publication. "Freelance writers must be knowledgeable horse people who submit well researched articles." Prefers writers from Western Canada and the Northwestern U.S.

Impact Magazine
2007 – 2nd Street S.W., Calgary, AB T2S 1S4
Phone: (403) 228-0605 Fax: (403) 228-0627
E-mail: louise@impactmagazine.ca
Contact: Louise Hodgson-Jones, editor
Circulation: 50,000
Published bimonthly

Features health, fitness, and sports for the active and physically fit of Calgary. All content focused on Calgary and surroundings. Articles 750 to 1,500 words. Query by letter or e-mail before submitting. "Our budget is very limited. We occasionally pay a negotiated fee to freelancers."

Inside Golf
6418 Nevilane Drive, Duncan, BC V9L 5S6
Phone: (866) 764-6537 Fax: (250) 709-2141
E-mail: insidegolf@shaw.ca
Contact: Brian Outram, editor
Circulation: 25,000
Published quarterly
   Covers golf news and travel in Western Canada. Articles 500 to 1,000 words. Rates vary according to project and are paid on publication.

Inside Track Motorsport News
P.O. Box 7100, Stn. B, Toronto, ON M5W 1X7
Phone: (416) 962-7223 Fax: (416) 962-7208
E-mail: editor@insidetracknews.com
Web site: www.insidetracknews.com
Contact: Greg MacPherson, editor
Circulation: 10,000
Published 16 times a year
   Aimed at Canadian motorsport racing fans. Includes race reports, features, news, and interviews. Articles 600 to 1,200 words. Fees vary and are paid on publication. "E-mail submissions preferred. Colour photos in JPG format at 300 DPI."

Kanawa: Canada's Canoeing and Kayaking Magazine
P.O. Box 398, Merrickville, ON K0G 1N0
Phone: (613) 269-2910 Fax: (613) 269-2908
E-mail: editor@paddlingcanada.com
Web site: www.paddlingcanada.com
Contact: Judy Lord, editor
Circulation: 13,000
Published quarterly
   Canada's foremost full-colour magazine for recreational canoeing, whitewater kayaking, and sea kayaking. Articles (400 to 2,500 words) on destinations, equipment, instruction, environment, heritage, and much more. Can only pay honoraria on publication but welcomes submission inquiries. Guidelines available on web site.

Muskoka Magazine
P.O. Box 180, Bracebridge, ON P1L 1T6
Phone: (705) 646-1314 Fax: (705) 645-6424
E-mail: editor@northcountrymedia.com
Web site: www.muskokamagazine.com
Contact: Jenny Cressman, editor
Circulation: 14,000
Published 8 times a year
A publication for Muskoka residents and cottagers, or anyone with an interest in the region. Articles 1,500 to 2,000 words on the interesting individuals, activities, and history of Muskoka. Pays 10¢/word 30 days after publication. "Contact editor in advance to discuss submissions. Topics must have a Muskoka connection."

Newfoundland Sportsman
P.O. Box 13754, Stn. A, St. John's, NL A1B 4G5
Phone: (709) 754-3515 Fax: (709) 754-7490
E-mail: gfollett@newfoundlandsportsman.com
Web site: www.newfoundlandsportsman.com
Contact: Gord Follett, editor
Circulation: 15,000
Published bimonthly
Primarily focuses on hunting and fishing, but also contains articles on snowmobiling, camping, canoeing, kayaking, hiking, etc. Articles 800 to 1,500 words. Pays $100 to $300 on publication, depending on quality and if usable photos are included with article.

Ontario Golf
1074 Cooke Boulevard, Burlington, ON L7T 4A8
Phone: (905) 634-8003 Fax: (905) 634-7661
E-mail: tedbits@golfontario.ca
Web site: www.golfontario.ca
Contact: Ted McIntyre, editor
Circulation: 55,000
Published quarterly
The official publication of the Golf Association of Ontario with content of interest to all of Ontario's golf enthusiasts from features to travel, instruction to profiles, etc. Use celebrities who play golf

on covers with question-and-answer interviews inside. Negotiated fees are paid for articles 500 to 2,200 words. "We try to pay a month after submission. Stories are filed via e-mail. More than one Canadian golf writer has referred to *Ontario Golf* as the best golf magazine in Canada. Ours is a very slick publication with high standards for writing and photography." Guidelines available.

Ontario Sailor Magazine
91 Hemmingway Drive, Courtice, ON L1E 2C2
Phone: (905) 434-7409 Fax: (905) 434-1654
E-mail: sails@istar.ca
Contact: Greg McDowell
Circulation: 8,000
Published 7 times a year
   Covers the Great Lakes sailing scene in Canada and the U.S. Articles 300 to 1,500 words. Pay rates vary (start at $20/story) and are paid on publication. "Please query first. We accept freelance photos and prefer stories to be accompanied by a photo."

Outdoor Canada
340 Ferrier Street, Suite 210, Markham, ON L3R 2Z5
Phone: (905) 475-8440, ext. 158 Fax: (905) 475-9246
E-mail: walsh@outdoorcanada.ca
Web site: www.outdoorcanada.ca
Contact: Patrick Walsh, editor
Circulation: 85,000
Published 8 times a year
   Canada's only national magazine about fishing, hunting, and related conservation issues. "Our readers are passionate about this country's natural heritage, and they want to get the most out of their outdoor experiences. That's why each issue contains a solid mix of how-to articles, service pieces, entertaining features, and in-depth reporting." Articles 100 to 3,000 words. Pays on acceptance 50¢ to $1/word. Fees are established upon assignment based on complexity and length of story. "We welcome query letters from professional writers (please do not submit unsolicited manuscripts). All story ideas must be designed solely to serve the interests and needs of our readers. Contributors are therefore encouraged to first review

the magazine and familiarize themselves with its tone and specific editorial departments." Guidelines available.

Pacific Golf Magazine

4180 Lougheed Highway, 4th Floor, Burnaby, BC V5C 6A7

Phone: (604) 299-7311 Fax: (604) 299-9188

E-mail: bdunn@canadawide.com

Web site: www.canadawide.com

Contact: Bob Dunn, editor

Circulation: 30,000

Published quarterly

The West Coast's leading golf magazine serving the diverse interests and needs of golf enthusiasts (both serious and novice) and fans throughout the Pacific Northwest. Pays 35¢ to 40¢/word on publication for 1,000 to 2,500 words. Pay rates vary with project. Query first; don't send completed articles on spec.

Pacific Yachting

1080 Howe Street, Suite 900, Vancouver, BC V6Z 2T1

Phone: (604) 606-4644 Fax: (604) 687-1925

E-mail: editorial@pacificyachting.com

Web site: www.pacificyachting.com

Contact: Peter Robson, editor

Circulation: 19,000

Published monthly

Carries destination articles, cruising features, and how-to articles aimed at boaters from B.C., Western Canada, and the Northwest U.S. Stories are written from personal experience relating to powerboating and sailing on Canada's West Coast, with an emphasis on cruising, destinations, local history, and personalities. Carries racing reports, adventure, and articles 800 to 2,500 words. Fees negotiated on assignment/acceptance of article and paid on publication: 20¢ to 25¢/word or $400 to $500 for 2,500 words. Buys photos and stories together. "Writers must be familiar with our special-interest viewpoint, language, and orientation. First-hand experience of subject is essential. Know our magazine, know the B.C. coast, and know boating." Guidelines available.

The Rider
487 Book Road W., Ancaster, ON L9G 3L1
Phone: (905) 648-2035 Fax: (905) 648-6977
E-mail: therider@worldchat.com
Web site: www.therider.ca
Contact: A. W. Finn, publisher
Circulation: 6,000
Published 10 times a year
    Ontario's horse industry newspaper for English- and western-style riders. Cannot pay but welcomes submission inquiries.

Score: Canada's Golf Magazine
287 MacPherson Avenue, Toronto, ON M4V 1A4
Phone: (416) 928-2909 Fax: (416) 928-1357
E-mail: bobw@scoregolf.com
Web site: www.scoregolf.com
Contact: Bob Weeks, editor
Circulation: 200,000
Published 6 times through the golf season
    A national golf magazine with regional inserts (Ontario and Western Canada). Profiles prominent golfers and golfing personalities, and reviews courses, clubs, and equipment. Also carries articles on travel and international competitions, and instructional pieces. Pays 50¢/word on acceptance for 750 to 1,500 words, sometimes more for detailed stories. Guidelines available.

Ski Canada
117 Indian Road, Toronto, ON M6R 2V5
Phone: (416) 538-2293 Fax: (416) 538-2475
E-mail: mac@skicanadamag.com
Web site: www.skicanadamag.com
Contact: Iain MacMillan, editor
Circulation: 52,000
Published 6 times a year
    Publishes a balanced mix of entertainment and information for both the experienced and the novice-intermediate skier. "Published from early autumn through winter (with one summer issue), *SC* covers equipment, travel, instruction, competition, fashion, and

general skiing- and alpine-related news and stories. Query letters are preferred; unsolicited manuscripts rarely fit into a determined schedule. Replies will take time. Note: yearly editorial schedules are set at least six months before commencement of publishing season." Articles 400 to 2,500 words. Pays (within 30 days of publication) between $100 (news) and $500 to $800 (features), depending on length, research necessary, and writer's experience.

Ski West
1510 – 2nd Street N., Suite 200, Cranbrook, BC V1C 3L2
Phone: (250) 426-7253 Fax: (250) 426-4125
E-mail: info@kpimedia.com
Contact: Keith Powell, publisher
Circulation: 40,000
Published 3 times a year
   Primarily a destinations-type magazine looking for first-person ski travel adventure articles. Stories 500 to 800 words. Pays 15¢/word on publication.

Sno Riders West
1510 – 2nd Street N., Suite 200, Cranbrook, BC V1C 3L2
Phone: (250) 426-7253 Fax: (250) 426-4125
E-mail: info@kpimedia.com
Contact: Keith Powell, publisher
Circulation: 38,000
Published quarterly
   Primarily a destinations-type magazine looking for first-person snowmobile travel adventure articles. Stories 500 to 800 words. Pays 15¢/word on publication.

Spotlight on Skating Magazine
35 Buchanan Drive, Caledonia, ON N3W 1H1
Phone: (905) 765-5897 Fax: (905) 765-6145
E-mail: spotsk8@lara.on.ca
Web site: www.spotlightskating.com
Contact: G. Lisa Herdman, editor/president
Circulation: 15,000
Published 5 times a year

An international figure-skating magazine. Articles from 1,000 to 3,000 words. Fees negotiated and paid on publication. "Articles must be positive in nature and must be current news." Guidelines available.

WaveLength Magazine
2735 North Road, Gabriola Island, BC V0R 1X7
Phone: (250) 247-8858 Fax: (250) 247-9789
E-mail: info@WaveLengthMagazine.com
Web site: www.WaveLengthMagazine.com
Contact: Alan Wilson, editor
Circulation: 23,000
Published bimonthly

For paddlers, especially sea kayakers, and those interested in marine ecotourism and the marine environment, specifically on the West Coast. Articles from 1,000 to 1,500 words. Pays on publication $50 to $100, depending on length of article; $25 to $100 for photos. "Knowledge of kayaking (or canoeing) essential. Check our editorial calendar carefully because we are heavily feature driven. Humour and good pictures are an asset." Guidelines available.

Western Sportsman
1080 Howe Street, 9th Floor, Vancouver, BC V6Z 2T1
Phone: (604) 606-4644 Fax: (604) 687-1925
E-mail: editor@westernsportsman.com
Web site: www.oppublishing.com
Contact: Tracey Ellis, co-ordinating editor
Circulation: 25,000
Published bimonthly

Publishes articles on recreational fishing, hunting, and conservation from west of the Rockies to Manitoba. Stories 1,600 to 2,000 words. Pays on publication. Please query. Guidelines available.

Travel & Tourism

Airlines
3600A – 12th Street N.E., Calgary, AB T2E 6N1
Phone: (403) 215-0030 Fax: (403) 230-2088

Web site: www.airlinesmagazine.com
Contact: Colleen Seto, editor
Circulation: 400,000
Published monthly

Airlines is WestJet's in-flight magazine. Interested in stories in the following broad categories: travel, adventure, business, art and culture, and Canada. Prefers articles 350 to 1,500 words. Rates vary, depending on project, and are paid on publication. Guidelines available on web site.

DreamScapes Travel and Lifestyle Magazine
642 Simcoe Street, S.S. 1, Niagara-on-the-Lake, ON LOS 1J0
Phone: (905) 468-4021 Fax: (905) 468-2382
E-mail: editor@dreamscapes.ca
Web site: www.dreamscapes.ca
Contact: Donna Vieira, editor
Circulation: 110,000
Published 8 times a year

Distributed to subscribers of the *Globe and Mail* across Canada. See web site for publishing and editorial schedule. Articles from 500 to 1,200 words. Pays 30¢/word on publication; this fee covers both the printed magazine format and the online version. "Photos must accompany all editorials. We do not pay for them, although we do give a photo credit." Guidelines available.

enRoute
4200 Saint-Laurent Boulevard, Suite 707, Montreal, QC H2W 2R2
Phone: (514) 844-2001 Fax: (514) 844-6001
E-mail: info@enroutemag.net
Web site: www.enroutemag.net
Contact: Julie Roy, editorial assistant
Circulation: 170,000
Published monthly

Air Canada's inflight magazine. A general lifestyle publication featuring trends, travel, entertainment, social stories, fashion, and food. Aimed at a high-end market. Articles 200 to 2,000 words. Pay rates vary. Paid on acceptance. Inquire first with ideas. Always enclose tearsheets. Guidelines available.

Journeywoman: The Premier Travel Resource for Women
50 Prince Arthur Avenue, Toronto, ON M5R 1B5
Phone: (416) 929-7654
E-mail: editor@journeywoman.com
Web site: www.journeywoman.com
Contact: Evelyn Hannon, publisher/editor
Circulation: 365,000

An online international travel resource that publishes stories and tips focusing on the specific needs and interests of women travellers. Stories up to 900 words, with two additional sidebars and a 2- to 3-line bio. Pays a $35 honorarium for articles. Each published article is eligible for the Annual Journeywoman Travel Writing Contest, with two top prizes of $100 each. "We welcome requests for guidelines and submissions (by e-mail only), especially from women who are starting out as writers and looking for an avenue in which to publish their travel stories."

Saskatchewan Naturally Magazine
P.O. Box 520, Norquay, SK S0A 2V0
Phone: (306) 594-2455 Fax: (306) 594-2119
E-mail: editor@sasknaturally.com
Web site: www.sasknaturally.com
Contact: Lionel Hughes, publisher/editor
Circulation: 11,000
Published quarterly

A regional publication with international readership featuring high-quality photography for travel-oriented, Saskatchewan-loving people mostly in their mid-50s. Articles 1,500 to 2,500 words. Pays on publication 25¢/word. Guidelines available.

The Student Traveller
45 Charles Street E., Suite 100, Toronto, ON M4Y 1S2
Phone: (416) 966-2887 Fax: (416) 966-4043
E-mail: stutrav@travelcuts.com
Web site: www.travelcuts.com
Contact: Sherry Brown, managing editor
Circulation: 130,000
Published twice a year

A travel magazine geared toward student and budget travellers aged 18 to 35. Pays 10¢/word on publication for articles 500 to 1,200 words and 25¢/photo published. Welcomes submission inquiries. Guidelines available.

Westworld Alberta / Westworld B.C. / Westworld Saskatchewan / Going Places Magazine

4180 Lougheed Highway, 4th Floor, Burnaby, BC V5C 6A7
Phone: (604) 299-7311 Fax: (604) 299-9188
E-mail: editorial@canadawide.com
Web site: www.canadawide.com
Contact: Anne Rose, editor
Circulations: 600,000
Published quarterly

Publishes travel and outdoor living magazine in Alberta, B.C., Saskatchewan, and Manitoba (*Going Places Magazine*). Pays 50¢ to $1/word for articles of 500 to 2,000 words. Kill fees are 50%. "Please mail or e-mail for submission guidelines before sending queries with an SASE."

Where Calgary

125 – 9 Avenue S.E., Suite 250, Calgary, AB T2G 0P6
Phone: (403) 299-1888 Fax: (403) 299-1899
E-mail: info_calgary@where.ca
Web site: www.where.ca/calgary
Contact: Melanie Jones, editor
Circulation: 50,000
Published bimonthly

News of events and attractions for visitors. Covers local dining, shopping, fine art, and Calgary and Alberta attractions. Cover stories highlight things to do and see. Pays about 50¢/word on acceptance. Word count and rates vary with project. "Query first with résumé and clips. Please don't send spec manuscripts, fiction, or poetry."

Where Edmonton

9343 – 50th Street, 4 Parkwood Office Centre, Edmonton, AB
  T6B 2L5

Phone: (780) 465-3362 Fax: (780) 448-0424
E-mail: askus@whereedmonton.com
Web site: www.whereedmonton.com
Contact: Tracy Cooper-Posey, editor
Circulation: 40,000
Published bimonthly

Features dining, shopping, and entertainment news and information for visitors to Edmonton. Articles range from 800 to 1,200 words, although the longer length is rare. Length is determined by the editorial calendar and the importance of the subject. "Study the magazine! You have to know the city of Edmonton well, and understand the format and readership of the magazine. This magazine is freely distributed, so back and current issues are not expensive to acquire and study. Articles must be timely and should point toward something the visitor to Edmonton can see or do while she is in the city." New freelance writers are paid 18¢/word on publication; rates will rise as more stories are completed. Sometimes pre-article fees are negotiated. "We pay extra for photographs, from a basic $10/published photo or higher, depending on quality." Guidelines available.

Where Halifax

1300 Hollis Street, Halifax, NS B3J 1T6
Phone: (902) 420-9943 Fax: (902) 429-9058
E-mail: publishers@metroguide.ca
Contact: Trevor J. Adams, editor
Circulation: 25,000
Published 10 times a year

What to do and where to go in the Halifax area. Shopping, sightseeing, events – anything of interest to visitors. Welcomes written inquiries with story ideas. Articles/pieces 500 to 800 words. Fees average $150 for 800 words, paid on publication.

Where Vancouver

2208 Spruce Street, Vancouver, BC V6H 2P3
Phone: (604) 736-5586 Fax: (604) 736-3465
Contact: Louise Phillips, co-editor
Circulation: 50,000
Published monthly

A visitors' guide incorporating entertainment listings, *Where Vancouver* aims to provide an intelligent magazine and city guide for the upscale traveller. Monthly events sections are popular features. Articles 800 to 1,000 words. Pay rates vary depending on project and are paid on acceptance. "Our need for freelance submissions is minimal." Writers should first contact editor, since all projects are assigned.

Whistler This Week
4370 Lorimer Road, Suite 238, Whistler, BC V0N 1B4
Phone: (604) 935-3113 Fax: (604) 935-3114
E-mail: editor@whistlerthisweek.com
Web site: www.whistlerthisweek.com
Contact: Steven Hill, editor
Circulation: 10,000
Published weekly

Caters to the destination-visitor market with a focus on nightlife, entertainment, and recreation. "Our goal is to inform visitors about what they can do 'this week' in Whistler. We don't really review events after the fact." Articles 500 to 1,000 words. Pays on publication about 10¢/word. Guidelines available.

Women's

Chatelaine
1 Mount Pleasant Road, 8th Floor, Toronto, ON M4Y 2Y5
Phone: (416) 764-2421 Fax: (416) 764-2431
E-mail: editors@chatelaine.com
Web site: www.chatelaine.com
Contact: Trish Snyder, assistant managing editor
Circulation: 700,000
Published monthly

A high-quality glossy magazine addressing the needs, interests, and preferences of Canadian women. Covers current issues, personalities, lifestyles, health, relationships, travel, and politics. Features of 1,000 to 2,500 words earn $1,250 and up; one-page columns start at $350. "For all serious articles, deep, accurate, and thorough research and rich details are required. Features on beauty, food, fashion, and home decorating are supplied by staff writers and editors only." Buys first North American serial rights in English and French (to cover possible use in French-language edition). Pays on acceptance. Query first with brief outline, but does not accept e-mail queries. Guidelines available on web site (type *guidelines* in search category).

City Woman Business
6025 Flewellyn Road, Suite 125, Ottawa, ON K2S 1B6
Phone: (613) 831-0980 Fax: (613) 831-0838
E-mail: info@denboer.ca
Web site: www.execwoman.com
Contact: Patricia den Boer, publisher
Circulation: 40,000
Published quarterly in 2004, monthly by 2005

A new print and online publication designed to provide women in leadership positions in the private, public, and not-for-profit sectors with information and advice, and a forum to share ideas on how to lead organizations while maintaining balance in their own lives. Articles of 800 to 1,000 words describe how women in some of the world's best known and emerging organizations are changing the face of business and society. Fees negotiated and paid on publication. Guidelines available.

The Compleat Mother
P.O. Box 38033, Calgary, AB T3K 5G9
Phone: (403) 255-0246
E-mail: thecompleatmother@shaw.ca
Web site: www.compleatmother.com/canada
Contact: Angela van Son, publisher/editor
Circulation: 10,000
Published quarterly

The magazine of pregnancy, birth, and breastfeeding, focusing on mothers from all walks of life. "We publish articles ranging from birth stories to experiences relating to weaning and everything in between." Cannot pay, but welcomes submission inquiries. "Articles considered if they are passionate, gutsy, hysterical, or brilliant. We also love to receive photos, drawings, cartoons, etc., to print alongside articles." Guidelines available.

Elle Canada
25 Sheppard Avenue W., Suite 100, Toronto, ON M2N 6S7
Phone: (416) 227-8210 Fax: (416) 733-7981
E-mail: editors@ellecanada.com
Circulation: 100,000
Published monthly
   Features stories on women's beauty, fashion, and lifestyle. Articles 300 to 1,200 words. Pays $1/word on acceptance.

good girl
837 Gilford Street, Montreal, QC H2J 1P1
Phone: (514) 935-7659
E-mail: submissions@goodgirl.ca
Web site: www.goodgirl.ca
Contact: Nikko Snyder, publisher
Published quarterly
   Aimed at women from 18 to 35, *good girl* is dedicated to publishing ideas that challenge, critique, and break the rules of the status quo. Showcases young writers in a forum for progressive, challenging, and engaging ideas. Submissions should be e-mailed, they must not exceed 2,000 words, and should include an author bio of 50 words or less. Reviews of books, movies, music, and zines are also welcome. Unable to pay but accepted writers will receive a complimentary subscription. Guidelines available on web site.

Homemaker's Magazine
25 Sheppard Avenue W., Suite 100, North York, ON M2N 6S7
Phone: (416) 733-7600 Fax: (416) 733-3398
E-mail: letters@homemakers.com
Web site: www.homemakers.com
Contact: Kathryn Dorrell, associate editor
Circulation: 1.3 million
Published 10 times a year
   A national magazine of current affairs and service articles directed toward women aged 25 to 54. Feature articles, which average about 2,000 words, deal with issues of particular concern to women, their families, and communities. Also published in French as *Madame au Foyer*. Pays up to $1/word on acceptance for features, less for personal essays and pieces requiring less research. "We

prefer queries in writing – 1 or 2 pages that outline the proposed article and the direction the writer intends to take. Finished articles on spec are also welcome. We have a special need for dramatic first-person stories ('Challenges')." Guidelines available.

Snap
Box 130, 2137 – 33 Avenue S.W., Calgary, AB T2T 1Z7
Phone: (403) 243-1769
E-mail: featureseditor@snapmagazine.com
Web site: www.snapmagazine.com
Contact: Carolyn Fleming, editor-in-chief
Circulation: 30,000
Published quarterly
   Speaks to professional women about cutting-edge technology, design, business, events, and people. Articles 200 to 3,000 words. Rates vary depending on project. Paid on publication. "Please send well-focused queries." Guidelines available.

Women's Post
365 Bloor Street E., Suite 1706, Toronto, ON M4W 3L4
Phone: (416) 964-5850 Fax: (416) 964-6142
E-mail: editor@womenspost.ca
Web site: www.womenspost.ca
Contact: Sarah Thomson, publisher
Circulation: 75,000
Published monthly
   A magazine targeting professional women between the ages of 25 and 55. Articles should be intimate first-person narratives from 700 to 900 words. Pays approximately $75/story on publication. Guidelines available.

Youth & Children's

Chickadee
49 Front Street E., 2nd Floor, Toronto, ON M5E 1B3
Phone: (416) 340-2700 Fax: (416) 340-9769
E-mail: chickadee@owlkids.com
Web site: www.owlkids.com

Contact: Mary Vincent, assistant editor
Circulation: 95,000
Published 10 times a year

Through this magazine, kids from 6 to 9 discover a world of people, places, and animals. Bright and lively text and visuals make this a great publication for beginner readers. No unsolicited manuscripts. Pays $350 on acceptance for stories between 600 and 650 words. "Please read the magazine in order to get a feel for the tone. Also, we work several months in advance, and each story is linked to a theme." Guidelines available.

Chirp

49 Front Street E., 2nd Floor, Toronto, ON M5E 1B3
Phone: (416) 340-2700 Fax: (416) 340-9769
Web site: www.owlkids.com
Contact: Angela Keenlyside, editor
Circulation: 70,000
Published 10 times a year

The "see and do" magazine for children aged 2 to 6. Publishes puzzles, games, rhymes, stories, and songs to entertain and teach preschoolers about animals, nature, letters, numbers, and more. No unsolicited manuscripts. Prefers complete articles of 300 to 450 words (fees range between $100 and $350). Short poems (25 to 40 words) are paid $50. Query first.

Fashion18

59 Front Street E., Toronto, ON M5E 1B3
Phone: (416) 364-3334 Fax: (416) 594-3374
E-mail: letters@fashion18.com
Web site: www.fashion18.com
Contact: Karine Ewart, deputy editor
Circulation: 62,000
Published quarterly

A fashion magazine for teenagers. Pay rates vary and are paid on acceptance. Guidelines available.

Faze Magazine

4936 Yonge Street, Suite 2400, Toronto, ON M2N 6S3
Phone: (416) 222-3060 Fax: (416) 222-2097

E-mail: editor@fazeteen.com
Web site: www.fazeteen.com
Contact: Lorraine Zander, editor-in-chief
Circulation: 375,000
Published quarterly
Offers Canadian teenagers a look at real life issues, entertainment, global issues, health, personal style, careers, and technology. Strives to be both entertaining and empowering. Rates vary depending on project and are paid on publication. Guidelines available.

Fuel Magazine
401 Richmond Street W., Suite 245, Toronto, ON M5V 1X3
Phone: (416) 595-1313 Fax: (416) 595-1312
E-mail: kaaren@youthculture.com
Web site: www.fuelpowered.com
Contact: Kaaren Whitney, president
Circulation: 100,000
Published 7 times a year
Targeted to males aged 12 to 17. Articles 350 to 1,000 words. Pay rates vary and are paid on publication.

OWL
49 Front Street E., 2nd Floor, Toronto, ON M5E 1B3
Phone: (416) 340-2700 Fax: (416) 340-9769
E-mail: owl@owlkids.com
Web site: www.owlkids.com
Contact: Marybeth Leatherdale, editor
Circulation: 75,000
Published 10 times a year
A general interest magazine for 9- to 13-year-olds. Entertains and informs on the topics and issues that concern them. Topics include everything from sports to the environment, and pop culture to peer relationships. Pays $500 and up on publication for 600 to 800 words. Prefers submission inquiries; no unsolicited manuscripts. Strongly recommends writers check back issues (available in libraries) for a sense of *OWL*'s approach.

Verve Magazine
401 Richmond Street W., Suite 245, Toronto, ON M5V 1X3
Phone: (416) 595-1313, ext. 259   Fax: (416) 595-1312
E-mail: editor@youthculture.com
Web site: www.vervegirl.com
Contact: Jaishree Drepaul, editor
Circulation: 180,000
Published 7 times a year
   Geared toward teenaged girls across Canada. "Our mission is to inform readers about what's going on in the world and to provide the latest information on what's hot and what's not." Articles 750 to 1,500 words. Pay rates vary and are paid on publication.

What Magazine
93 Lombard Avenue, Suite 108, Winnipeg, MB R3B 3B1
Phone: (204) 985-8160   Fax: (204) 957-5638
E-mail: what@whatmagazine.ca
Web site: www.whatmagnet.ca
Contact: Barbara Chabai, editor-in-chief
Published bimonthly
   A pop-culture, entertainment, and teen-lifestyle publication distributed through high schools across Canada. Articles 350 to 1,200 words. Pay rates vary depending on project, and payment made on publication. Guidelines available.

Youthink Magazine
1275 West 6th Avenue, Suite 206, Vancouver, BC V6H 1A6
Phone: (604) 732-6397   Fax: (604) 732-6390
E-mail: submit@youthink.ca
Web site: www.youthink.ca
Contact: Lotte Ewald, editor
Circulation: 80,000
Published 10 times a year
   Connects high-school students across Vancouver's Lower Mainland and publishes writing by local high-school students only. Articles 50 to 300 words. Cannot pay but welcomes inquiries.

2

LITERARY & SCHOLARLY PUBLICATIONS

It's ironic that literary and scholarly journals, which are among the most prestigious outlets for a writer's work, can least afford to pay their contributors. Many journals rely on funding from arts councils, or from academic or professional sources, and still run at a loss. They have relatively small subscription lists, perhaps two or three unpaid or part-time staff, and attract little or no advertising support. They can rarely afford to pay their contributors much, and in many cases, modest funding and low revenues preclude payment altogether, or limit it to small honoraria or free copies.

Writers would be unwise to look to this sector of publishing as a significant source of income. Qualified writers would be just as unwise to neglect it because of this. Publishing your work in a distinguished literary or scholarly journal can add immeasurably to your reputation, and may well open up other publishing opportunities. This chapter lists many of Canada's most notable journals and literary magazines. Use the information presented in each entry to help you choose the most appropriate publications to approach.

Contributors to scholarly journals are frequently graduate students, salaried academics, or professionals, who draw on current areas of research. For graduate students, journal publication is often an essential element of their professional development. The successful applicant for a university teaching position, for instance, will usually have a substantial publishing history.

Before you make your submission, familiarize yourself thoroughly with the journal to which you hope to contribute. Editors take a dim view of submissions from writers who are obviously unfamiliar with their publication. Study several recent issues, or better still, subscribe. Learn what you can of the editors' approaches and points of view and the kind of work they favour. Determine who their readers are. If they have a web site, be sure to visit it.

Always request writers' guidelines, and follow these closely to ensure you meet the editors' needs. Remember to include an SASE whenever you expect a response. Refereed journals will require several copies of your submission. Scholarly articles will need to be accompanied by full documentation. Fiction, poetry, reviews, and criticism must be carefully targeted and professionally presented. The extra care and attention will pay dividends.

Acadiensis: Journal of the History of the Atlantic Region
University of New Brunswick, P.O. Box 4400, Fredericton, NB
  E3B 5A3
Phone: (506) 453-4978 Fax: (506) 453-5068
E-mail: acadnsis@unb.ca
Web site: www.lib.unb.ca/texts/acadiensis
Contact: Bill Parenteau, editor
Circulation: 850
Published twice a year
  Includes original academic research, review articles, documents, notes, and a running bibliography compiled by librarians in the four Atlantic provinces. "Canada's most ambitious scholarly journal" – Michael Bliss, *Journal of Canadian Studies*. Articles published in English and in French. Cannot pay but welcomes submission inquiries. Guidelines available.

Alberta History
95 Holmwood Avenue N.W., Calgary, AB T2K 2G7
Phone: (403) 289-8149 Fax: (403) 289-8144
E-mail: potaina@aol.com
Contact: Hugh Dempsey, editor
Circulation: 1,200
Published quarterly

Publishes articles on Alberta history from 3,000 to 5,000 words to a mostly province-wide audience. Cannot pay, but welcomes submission inquiries. Guidelines available.

The Antigonish Review

St. Francis Xavier University, P.O. Box 5000, Antigonish, NS
   B2G 2W5
Phone: (902) 867-3962   Fax: (902) 867-5563
E-mail: tar@stfx.ca
Web site: www.antigonishreview.com
Contacts: B. Allan Quigley, co-editor; Jeanette Lynes, co-editor
Circulation: 1,000
Published quarterly

A creative literary review featuring poetry, fiction, reviews, and critical articles using original graphics to enliven the format. Directed at a general audience. Preferred length 1,500 to 5,000 words. Payment negotiated with editor, paid upon publication. Rights remain with author. Guidelines available at web site.

Arc

P.O. Box 7219, Ottawa, ON K1L 8E4
E-mail: arc.poetry@cyberus.ca
Web site: www.cyberus.ca/~arc.poetry
Contact: Anita Lahey, managing editor
Circulation: 1,000
Published twice a year

Publishes poetry from Canada and abroad, as well as reviews, interviews, and articles on poetry and poetry related subjects. No fiction or drama. Poetry submissions must be typed and include 5 to 8 unpublished poems. Reviews, interviews, and other prose, including how poems work, must be queried first. Pays $30/published page on publication. Guidelines and other information available on web site.

BC Studies: The British Columbian Quarterly

University of British Columbia, 1866 Main Mall, Buchanan E162,
   Vancouver, BC V6T 1Z1
Phone: (604) 822-3727   Fax: (604) 822-0606
E-mail: write-us@bcstudies.com

Web site: www.bcstudies.com
Contact: Carlyn Craig, managing editor
Circulation: 650

Established in 1968, an interdisciplinary academic journal on the economic, political, and cultural life of B.C., past and present. Aims to present original scholarship in an accessible form to a wide readership. Articles 7,000 to 8,000 words. Cannot pay for submissions and retains all rights to articles published. Guidelines available.

Brick, A Literary Journal
P.O. Box 537, Stn. Q, Toronto, ON M4T 2M5
E-mail: info@brickmag.com
Web site: www.brickmag.com
Contact: Vivien Leong, managing editor
Circulation: 2,400
Published twice a year

Publishes literary non-fiction about books, writers, and literary pursuits. Pays $100 to $500 on publication for articles 250 to 7,500 words. Fees based on type of article and are paid on publication. "We do not read fiction or poetry. E-mail submissions to the magazine are welcome. Please read the magazine to get an idea of what kind of work we publish." Guidelines available on web site.

Canadian Children's Literature
Department of English, 4th Floor, MacKinnon Building,
    University of Guelph, Guelph, ON N1G 2W1
Phone: (519) 824-4120, ext. 53189 Fax: (519) 837-1315
E-mail: ccl@uoguelph.ca
Web site: www.uoguelph.ca/ccl
Contact: Benjamin Lefebvre, administrator
Circulation: 800
Published quarterly

Presents in-depth criticism and reviews of Canadian literature for children and young adults. Directed toward teachers, librarians, academics, and parents. Scholarly articles (2,000 to 8,000 words), interviews, profiles, and reviews are supplemented by illustrations and photographs. Now also covers film and electronic media. Cannot pay but welcomes submissions. Guidelines available.

Canadian Ethnic Studies

Department of History, University of Calgary, 2500 University
   Drive N.W., Calgary, AB T2N 1N4
Phone: (403) 220-7257 Fax: (403) 210-8764
E-mail: ces@ucalgary.ca
Web site: www.ss.ucalgary.ca/ces
Contact: Jo-Ann Cleaver, managing editor
Circulation: 800
Published 3 times a year

An interdisciplinary journal devoted to the study of ethnicity, immigration, inter-group relations, and the history and cultural life of ethnic groups in Canada. Also carries book reviews, opinions, memoirs, creative writing, and poetry, and has an ethnic voice section. All material should address Canadian ethnicity. Must be a member of the association to be published. "We accept short poetry, book review queries, and ethnic memoirs. Querying first is always helpful; we do not return unused manuscripts." Contributors are not paid. Guidelines available. See web site for more information.

The Canadian Historical Review

UTP Journals, 5201 Dufferin Street, North York, ON M3H 5T8
Phone: (416) 667-7994 Fax: (416) 667-7881
E-mail: chr@utpress.utoronto.ca
Contacts: Arthur J. Ray and Wendy Mitchinson, co-editors
Circulation: 1,800
Published quarterly

Publishes original research articles in all areas of Canadian history as well as research notes and book reviews. For academics and graduate students of Canadian history. Preferred length 5,000 to 10,000 words. Cannot pay but welcomes submission inquiries.

Canadian Journal of Film Studies

Editorial Office, Department of Art History and Communication
   Studies, McGill University, 853 Sherbrooke Street W.,
   Montreal, QC H3A 2T6
Phone: (514) 398-4935 Fax: (514) 398-7247
E-mail: william.wees@mcgill.ca
Web site: www.film.queensu.ca/fsac/cjfs.html
Contacts: William C. Wees, editor; Blaine Allan, managing editor

Circulation: 600
Published twice a year
   Distributed to members of the Film Association of Canada, to
Canadian and international libraries, and to individual subscribers.
Length of articles up to 5,000 words. Rates vary according to project.

Canadian Journal of History

Department of History, 9 Campus Drive, University of
   Saskatchewan, Saskatoon, SK S7N 5A5
Phone: (306) 966-5794 Fax: (306) 966-5852
E-mail: cjh@duke.usask.ca
Web site: www.usask.ca/history/cjh
Contact: Christopher Kent, editor
Published 3 times a year
   Publishes general history in all periods and all fields other than
Canadian. Articles to be based on original research with primary
sources. Usually assessed by readers before publication. Detailed
style guide on web site.

Canadian Journal on Aging

McMaster Centre for Gerontological Studies, McMaster
   University, 1280 Main Street W., KTH 226, Hamilton, ON
   L8S 4M4
Phone: (905) 525-9140, ext. 22517 Fax: (905) 525-4198
E-mail: crosent@mcmaster.ca
Web site: www.cjarcv.ca
Contact: Carolyn Rosenthal, editor-in-chief
Circulation: 1,200
Published quarterly
   A refereed publication of the Canadian Association on Geron-
tology. It publishes manuscripts concerned with biology, health sci-
ences, social sciences, and psychology. Contributors are not paid.
Articles 4,500 to 6,000 words. Guidelines available.

Canadian Literature

University of British Columbia, 1866 Main Mall, Buchanan E158,
   Vancouver, BC V6T 1Z1
Phone: (604) 822-2780 Fax: (604) 822-5504
E-mail: canlit@ubc.ca

Web site: www.cdnlit.ubc.ca
Contact: Laurie Ricou, editor
Circulation: 1,200
Published quarterly

Devoted to studying many aspects of Canadian literature and offering a literary critique of Canadian writers. For academics, researchers, libraries, schools, and universities. Contributors are not paid. Maximum length of articles 6,500 words, including notes and works cited. Must be double-spaced and submitted in triplicate with author's name removed. A few poems by Canadian writers accepted for each issue. Guidelines available.

Canadian Modern Language Review

UTP Journals, 5201 Dufferin Street, Toronto, ON M3H 5T8
Phone: (416) 667-7994 Fax: (416) 667-7881
E-mail: cmlr@utpress.utoronto.ca
Web site: www.utpjournals.com/cmlr
Contacts: Sharon Lapkin and Larry Vandergrift, co-editors
Circulation: 1,000
Published quarterly

Publishes applied, linguistic, second-language theory, and pedagogical articles, book reviews, current advertisements, and other material of interest to high-school and university language teachers and academics. A balance of theory and practice. All articles are voluntarily submitted rather than assigned, and are refereed. Length to 6,500 words. Contributors are not paid, but submissions are welcome. Consult "Guide to Authors" in each issue and write to editors for further information.

Canadian Poetry: Studies, Documents, Reviews

University of Western Ontario, Department of English, London,
    ON N6A 3K7
Phone: (519) 661-3403 Fax: (519) 661-3776
E-mail: canadianpoetry@uwo.ca
Web site: www.canadianpoetry.ca
Contact: D. M. R. Bentley, editor
Circulation: 400
Published twice a year

A scholarly and critical refereed journal devoted to the study of poetry from all periods and regions of Canada. Prints articles, reviews, and documents – 500 to 5,000 words – directed toward university and college students and teachers. *No original poetry.* Cannot pay but welcomes submissions. Follow *MLA Handbook* for style. Guidelines available.

Canadian Public Administration/Administration publique du Canada

1075 Bay Street, Suite 401, Toronto, ON M5S 2B1
Phone: (416) 924-8787 Fax: (416) 924-4992
E-mail: ntl@ipaciapc.ca
Web site: www.ipaciapc.ca
Contact: Allan Tupper, editor
Circulation: 3,500
Published quarterly

A refereed journal, written by public administrators and academics, that examines structures, processes, and outcomes of public policy and public management related to executive, legislative, judicial, and quasi-judicial functions in municipal, provincial, and federal spheres of government. "We are a high-quality, well-established journal that is distinctive in terms of its objectives and contents." Articles from 10 to 30 pages. Contributors are unpaid. Guidelines available on web site.

Canadian Social Work

383 Parkdale Avenue, Suite 402, Ottawa, ON K1Y 4R4
Phone: (613) 729-6668 Fax: (613) 729-9608
E-mail: casw@casw-acts.ca
Web site: www.casw-acts.ca
Contact: Paul Lagevin
Circulation: 15,500
Published 3 times a year

Publication of the Canadian Association of Social Workers. A bilingual forum for social-work professionals through which social workers and others share their knowledge, skills, research, and information with each other and with the general public. Peer reviewed. Articles from 2,500 to 5,000 words and shorter articles

250 to 1,000. Cannot pay but welcomes submission inquiries. First preference given to CASW members. Guidelines available.

Canadian Woman Studies

212 Founders College, York University, 4700 Keele Street, North
   York, ON M3J 1P3
Phone: (416) 736-5356 Fax: (416) 736-5765
E-mail: cwscf@yorku.ca
Contact: Luciana Ricciutelli, managing editor
Circulation: 5,000
Published quarterly

A bilingual, thematic journal featuring current scholarly writing and research on a wide variety of feminist topics. Welcomes creative writing, poetry, experiential articles, and essays of 750 to 3,000 words, as well as book reviews. Contributors are unpaid but receive a complimentary copy of the issue containing their work. Guidelines available.

The Capilano Review

2055 Purcell Way, North Vancouver, BC V7J 3H5
E-mail: tcr@capcollege.bc.ca
Web site: www.capcollege.bc.ca/dept/tcr
Contact: Carol Hamshaw, managing editor
Circulation: 900
Published 3 times a year

Established 1972. A showcase of innovative literary and visual art. Pays $50/page, to a maximum of $200, on publication. Carries stories up to 8,000 words. Guidelines available with an SASE or on web site. Read the magazine before submitting; sample copies $9.

Challenger international

Phone: (250) 991-5567
E-mail: lukivdan@hotmail.com
Web site: http://challengerinternational.20m.com/index.html
Contact: Dan Lukiv, editor
Circulation: 60
Published once a year

This low-budget, high school–based literary journal publishes poetry and fiction by children through to seasoned authors.

Distributed to Quesnel District high school students. Encourages young writers, especially teenagers, to submit poetry. Experimental work welcome if it makes sense. "We like poetry with vivid images and clear themes." Stories to 1,000 words. No profanity or pornography. Submissions by e-mail only. Include author details. Contributors paid in copies.

Contemporary Verse 2: The Canadian Journal of Poetry and Critical Writing

100 Arthur Street, Suite 207, Winnipeg, MB R3B 1H3
Phone: (204) 949-1365 Fax: (204) 942-5754
E-mail: cv2@mb.sympatico.ca
Web site: www.contemporaryverse2.ca
Contact: Clarise Foster, managing editor
Circulation: 700
Published quarterly

Established 1975 by Dorothy Livesay, *CV2* is Canada's oldest and best read poetry quarterly. Publishes critical writing (including interviews, articles, essays, and regular features on poetry) and original verse. Brings together established and emerging writers in a discussion of poetry that will appeal to a wide variety of readers, both the seasoned reader and the student of poetry. Each issue features interviews with experienced poets about their work, including popular trends, work habits, form, styles, and the importance of poetry. Poets recently published in *CV2* include George Elliott Clarke, P. K. Page, Gregory Schofield, Lorna Crozier, Marvin Francis, Catherine Hunter, Michael Crummey, Stephanie Bolster, and Carol Shields.

Preferred length of submission is 4 to 6 poems. For critical writing, please query first. Submission guidelines available upon request and on web site. Pays $20/poem; $40 for reviews. Fees for other writing are available by e-mail consultation only. "Please send a short bio and an SASE with your submission." Guidelines available.

The Dalhousie Review

6209 University Avenue, Dalhousie University, Halifax, NS
    B3H 1X1
Phone: (902) 494-2541 Fax: (902) 494-3561

E-mail: Dalhousie.Review@Dal.ca
Web site: www.dal.ca/~dalrev/
Contact: Ronald Huebert, editor
Circulation: 500
Published 3 times a year

Welcomes submissions of poetry, short fiction, and articles up to 5,000 words in such fields as history, literature, political science, sociology, and philosophy. Prefers poetry of fewer than 40 lines. Contributors to this distinguished quarterly, first published in 1921, are given 10 off-prints and 2 complimentary copies of the issue. "Please enclose an SASE for return of your manuscript." See web site for guidelines and excerpts from past issues.

Dandelion

Department of English, University of Calgary, 2500 University
    Drive N.W., Calgary, AB T2N 2B3
Phone: (403) 220-4679 Fax: (403) 289-1123
Web site: www.english.ucalgary.ca/dandelion/
Contact: Jill Hartman, editor
Circulation: 500
Published twice a year

Publishes experimental prose and poetry, including visual and concrete poetry. "We look for innovative form and content. We do not currently pay for submissions but provide published authors/artists with 2 copies of the issue." Guidelines available.

The Danforth Review

P.O. Box 72056, 1562 Danforth Avenue, Toronto, ON M4J 5C1
E-mail: danforthreview@canada.com
Web site: www.danforthreview.com
Contact: Michael Bryson, editor
Circulation: 2,000 hits/month

A web-based literary magazine that focuses on the Canadian small-press scene. "We publish fiction and poetry, plus book reviews, interviews, and feature articles on Canadian book issues." Stories from 1,000 to 5,000 words. Pay rates vary and are paid upon publication.

Descant

P.O. Box 314, Stn. P, Toronto, ON M5S 2S8

Phone: (416) 593-2557 Fax: (416) 593-9362

E-mail: descant@web.net

Web site: www.descant.on.ca

Contact: Mary Newberry, managing editor

Circulation: 1,200

Published quarterly

A literary journal publishing short fiction, poetry, essays, drama, interviews, photography, and art. Pays an honorarium of $100 to all contributors on publication. "Each manuscript submission receives a critical reading and must be approved by three members of our editorial board before acceptance. This process can take 3 to 9 months. Only unpublished material will be considered, and we request first publication rights." Guidelines available.

The Devil's Artisan (DA)

c/o The Porcupine's Quill, 68 Main Street, Erin, ON N0B 1T0

Phone: (519) 833-9158 Fax: (519) 833-9845

E-mail: pql@sentex.net

Web site: www.sentex.net/~pql

Contact: Elke Inkster, general manager

Circulation: 500

Published twice a year

The devil's artisan was a medieval term for a practitioner of the art and mystery of printing. "In publishing this journal, our desire is to maintain that early sense of curiosity about the craft of printing and bookmaking. We also present information on bibliographic and historic matters, and on communicative, sociological, and technical subjects related to printing. Each issue contains a hand-printed keepsake." Pays $100 per article upon publication.

Environments: A Journal of Interdisciplinary Studies

University of Waterloo, Heritage Resources Centre, Waterloo, ON
   N2L 3G1

Phone: (519) 888-4567, ext. 2072 Fax: (519) 746-2031

E-mail: environments@civics.ca

Web site: www.fes.uwaterloo.ca/research/environments/

Contact: Gordon Nelson, editor-in-chief
Circulation: 500
Published 3 times a year

A refereed journal for scholars and practitioners. Promotes greater understanding of environmental, economic, and social change through articles (2,000 to 5,000 words) that assess the implications of change and provide information for improved decision-making. Oriented to academics, students, professionals, and concerned citizens. For more information, check inside front cover. Cannot pay but welcomes submission inquiries. Guidelines available.

Event: The Douglas College Review
Douglas College, P.O. Box 2503, New Westminster, BC V3L 5B2
Phone: (604) 527-5293   Fax: (604) 527-5095
E-mail: event@douglas.bc.ca
Web site: http://event.douglas.bc.ca
Contact: Carolyn Robertson, assistant editor
Circulation: 1,000
Published 3 times a year

Features poetry, fiction, creative non-fiction, and reviews of Canadian books. Stories and non-fiction up to 5,000 words or up to 8 poems per submission. Pays $22/page on publication. Include a brief cover letter and an SASE with Canadian postage or an International Reply Coupon. Guidelines available on web site.

existere quarterly
121 Vanier College, 4700 Keele Street, York University, Toronto,
   ON M3J 1P3
E-mail: existere@yorku.ca
Web site: www.yorku.ca/existere
Contact: Richard Laporte, editor

The literary and arts quarterly of York University. Submissions must be accompanied by a brief letter of introduction. Pieces of all genres and forms are welcome, including short plays, reviews, critical essays, etc. Prose submissions of no longer than 3,500 words; a maximum of 2 pieces of short fiction; 5 postcard stories; and/or 6 graphics will be considered from one submitter at one time. Mail queries must be accompanied by an SASE. Unable to pay. Guidelines available on web site.

The Fiddlehead

Campus House, 11 Garland Court, University of New Brunswick,
  P.O. Box 4400, Fredericton, NB E3B 5A3
Phone: (506) 453-3501 Fax: (506) 453-5069
E-mail: fiddlehd@unb.ca
Web site: www.lib.unb.ca/texts/fiddlehead
Contact: Sabine Campbell, managing editor
Circulation: 1,000
Published quarterly

A highly respected literary journal, established in 1945, publishing
poetry, short fiction, and some book reviews. Focuses on freshness
and vitality. While retaining an interest in writers of Atlantic Canada,
it is open to outstanding work from all over the English-speaking
world. Stories from 50 to 3,000 words, poetry up to 10 poems. Pays
$20/published page on publication. "Find yourself an issue and read
it to get an idea of what we're about. Do not fax or e-mail submissions, and include an SASE for replies." Guidelines available.

filling Station

P.O. Box 22135, Bankers Hall, Calgary, AB T2P 4J5
Phone: (403) 294-7492
E-mail: editor@fillingstation.ca
Web site: www.fillingstation.ca
Contact: Natalie Simpson, managing editor
Circulation: 700
Published 3 times a year

Publishes poetry, fiction, one-act plays, and essays. Preferred
length for prose 1,000 to 2,500 words. Submission deadlines
March 15, July 15, and November 15. Pays with a 1-year subscription for accepted submissions. Guidelines available on web site.

Geist Magazine

1014 Homer Street, Suite 103, Vancouver, BC V6B 2W9
Phone: (604) 681-9161 Fax: (604) 669-8250
E-mail: geist@geist.com
Web site: www.geist.com
Contact: Barbara Zatyko, managing editor
Circulation: 8,000
Published quarterly

"Each issue of *Geist* is a meditation on the imaginary country we inhabit. Often that imaginary country has something to do with some part of Canada." Preferred length for creative non-fiction 200 to 1,000 words, for essays and short stories 2,000 to 5,000 words. Rates vary depending on project and are paid on publication. "We only accept submissions by snail mail. Please see our web site for guidelines and read the magazine."

Grain

P.O. Box 67, Saskatoon, SK S7K 3KI
Phone: (306) 244-2828   Fax: (306) 244-0255
E-mail: grain.mag@sasktel.net
Web site: www.grainmagazine.ca
Contact: Kent Bruyneel, editor
Circulation: 1,600
Published quarterly

A literary journal of national and international scope published by the Saskatchewan Writers Guild since 1973. Prints previously unpublished work by emerging and established writers that is fresh, startling, and imaginative. The work represents a range of mainstream poetry, prose, and occasionally creative non-fiction from writers in Canada and the world. Pays $40/page, up to $175, on publication, plus 2 complimentary copies of the issue. Read back issues before submitting. Guidelines available.

International Journal

205 Richmond Street, Suite 302, Toronto, ON M5V 1V3
Phone: (416) 977-9000 or 1-800-668-2442   Fax: (416) 977-7521
Web site: www.ciia.org
Contact: Adrienne Guthrie, managing editor
Published quarterly

Established 1946. Recognized as Canada's preeminent scholarly publication on international relations. Writers are a mixture of scholars, practitioners, and policy-makers, Canadian and non-Canadian. Each issue has a specific theme. Length must not exceed 7,000 words. Articles assessed by 2 reviewers. Cannot pay contributors but welcomes submissions. Guidelines available on web site.

Journal of the Association for Research on Mothering
York University, 4700 Keele Street, 726 Atkinson, Toronto, ON
    M3J 1P3
Phone: (416) 736-2100, ext. 60366
E-mail: arm@yorku.ca
Web site: www.yorku.ca/crm
Contact: Cheryl Dobinson, managing editor
Circulation: 2,500
Published twice a year
    Written for scholars, researchers, artists, activists, and feminist mothers. Maximum length of articles 3,750 words. Cannot pay but welcomes submission inquiries. Guidelines available.

Journal of Bahá'í Studies
34 Copernicus Street, Ottawa, ON K1N 7K4
Phone: (613) 233-1903 Fax: (613) 233-3644
E-mail: abs-na@bahai-studies.ca
Contact: Wendy Heller, managing editor
Circulation: 2,100
Published twice a year
    Founded in 1975. The journal of the Association for Bahá'í Studies aims to promote courses of study on the Bahá'í faith, to foster relationships with various leaders of thought and persons of capacity, to publish scholarly materials examining the Bahá'í faith, especially on the application to the concerns and needs of humanity, and to demonstrate the value of this scholarly approach in reinforcing the endeavours of the Bahá'í community to reach the diverse strata of society. Cannot pay but welcomes submissions.

Journal of Canadian Studies/Revue d'études canadiennes
1600 West Bank Drive, Trent University, Peterborough, ON
    K9J 7B8
Phone: (705) 748-1279 Fax: (705) 748-1110
Contact: Kerry Cannon, managing editor
Circulation: 1,200
Published quarterly
    A journal that focuses on all areas related to Canada and things Canadian in the humanities and social sciences (in French and English). Articles 5,000 to 9,000 words. Cannot pay.

Labour/Le travail

Memorial University, Faculty of Arts Publications, FM2005, St.
  John's, NL AIC 5S7
Phone: (709) 737-2144 Fax: (709) 737-4342
E-mail: cclh@mun.ca
Web site: www.mun.ca/cclh
Contact: Irene Whitfield, managing editor
Circulation: 900
Published twice a year

A bilingual, interdisciplinary historical journal concerned with
work, workers, and the labour movement. Includes articles of 5,000
to 10,000 words, book notes, archival notes, and an annual bibliography of Canadian labour studies. Cannot pay but welcomes submission inquiries. Guidelines available.

lichen literary Journal

701 Rossland Road E., Suite 234, Whitby, ON LIN 9K3
E-mail: info@lichenjournal.ca
Web site: www.lichenjournal.ca
Contact: editorial board
Circulation: 400
Published twice a year

Publishes fiction, poetry, plays, essays, reviews, and black-and-
white art and photography by local, Canadian, and international
writers and artists. Presents a unique mix of city and country, of
innovation and tradition. Stories 250 to 3,000 words. Contributors
receive a copy of the issue and a 1-year subscription. "Send us
something more than unfocused anger, gratuitous sex, or chatty
confession. If you can write beyond your own skin with a memo-
rable voice, play freely with elements of the craft, and take risks, you
have our attention." Guidelines available.

The Literary Review of Canada

581 Markham Street, Toronto, ON M6G 2L7
Phone: (416) 531-1383 Fax: (416) 531-1612
E-mail: review@lrcreview.com
Web site: www.reviewcanada.ca
Contact: Bronwyn Drainie, editor-in-chief

Circulation: 5,000

Published 10 times a year

A tabloid in the style of *The New York Review of Books*, carrying substantive book reviews of Canadian non-fiction and fiction, although it also publishes poetry, occasional essays, and excerpts. Provides a forum for intellectual curiosity, critical thinking, and the vigorous examination of ideas. Intriguing, incisively written, and informative, it attracts a highly educated readership. Reviews are 2,000 to 3,500 words. Prefers e-mailed proposals and outlines over those faxed or mailed, but they are also acceptable. Payment negotiable.

The Malahat Review

University of Victoria, P.O. Box 1700, Stn. CSC, Victoria, BC
    V8W 2Y2

Phone: (250) 721-8524 Fax: (250) 472-5051

E-mail: malahat@uvic.ca

Web site: www.malahatreview.ca

Contact: John Barton, editor

Circulation: 1,000

Published quarterly

A distinguished, award-winning literary journal publishing Canada's best poets and short-story writers. Pays $30/estimated published page on acceptance. Use e-mail address for queries only. For poetry, submit 6 to 10 pages of poems; for fiction, send 1 complete story. Write for guidelines.

Mosaic, A Journal for the Interdisciplinary Study of Literature

208 Tier Building, University of Manitoba, Winnipeg, MB
    R3T 2N2

Phone: (204) 474-9763 Fax: (204) 474-7584

E-mail: mosaic_journal@umanitoba.ca

Web site: www.umanitoba.ca/publications/mosaic

Contact: Jackie Pantel, manager

Circulation: 900

Published quarterly

Explores the interaction between literary study and research in other disciplines. The journal features well-established scholars, as well as emerging researchers, all of whom contribute lively discussions about literature and literary issues from all periods and genres. Invites provocative, interdisciplinary submissions (6,500 to 7,500 words) that identify and engage key issues in a variety of areas, including memory, the archive, reconsidering the documentary, post-colonial literatures, the idea of community, travel writing, the interrelations of literature and film, cryptographic imagination, architecture and text, the poetics of space, and the literary signature. Contributors are unpaid. Submission inquiries welcome. Guidelines available.

The New Quarterly
c/o St. Jerome's University, 200 University Avenue W., Waterloo, ON N2L 3G3
Phone: (519) 884-8111, ext. 290 Fax: (519) 884-5759
E-mail: newquart@watarts.uwaterloo.ca
Web site: www.newquarterly.uwaterloo.ca
Contact: Kim Jernigan, editor
Circulation: 900
   Publishes short and long fiction, poetry, and essays on writing, with a focus on "new directions in Canadian writing." Prose can be anything from postcard fiction to novellas. "Reading us is the best way to get our measure. We don't have preconceived ideas about what we're looking for other than it must be by Canadian authors. We want something that is fresh, something that will repay a second reading, something in which the language soars." Pays $150 for fiction, $100 for essays, $30 for postcard fiction, and $25/poem, on publication. Tries to publish at least 1 or 2 new writers in each issue. "We are a volunteer-run magazine so writers must anticipate long waits on manuscripts – 3 to 6 months is typical." Guidelines available.

NFG Magazine
P.O. Box 43112, Sheppard Centre, Toronto, ON M2N 6N1
Fax: (416) 226-0994
E-mail: mrspeabody@nfg.ca
Web site: www.nfg.ca
Contact: Mrs. Peabody
Circulation: 5,000
Published 3 times a year

An international literary magazine that offers fiction with an attitude. "Selected for quality, and never limited by conformity to mere genre, our content runs the gamut from poetry to short stories, comics to art. If it titillates the mind, twists the subconscious, or delivers an unexpected slap, you'll find it pinned between our covers." Preferred length for stories 1,001 to 7,500 words. Rates vary (see web site), but usually pays on acceptance 5¢/word (minimum $15) for articles up to 1,000 words and 3¢/word (minimum $50) for longer stories. Pays $35 for poetry, $30 to $175 for comics, and $40 to $200 for art. "Our staff covers the globe. We're fully automated online from point of submission to production. Artists submitting to us are kept up-to-date on the status of their work and may log on at any time to read comments by the editors." Guidelines available on web site.

Ontario History
34 Parkview Avenue, Willowdale, ON M2N 3Y2
Phone: (416) 226-9011 Fax: (416) 226-2740
E-mail: rbfleming@lindsay.igs.net
Web site: www.ontariohistoricalsociety.ca
Contact: R. B. Fleming, editor
Circulation: 1,200
Published twice a year
Specializes in the history of Ontario in any period: Native to newcomer to new millennium. Articles are scholarly yet accessible to all intelligent readers. Articles 5,000 to 6,000 words. Cannot pay but welcomes submission inquiries. Do not submit before contacting the editor for guidelines.

Optimum: The Journal of Public Sector Management
180 Elgin Street, 8th Floor, Ottawa, ON K2P 2K3
Phone: (613) 688-0763 Fax: (613) 688-0767
E-mail: info@optimumonline.ca
Web site: www.optimumonline.ca
Contact: McEvoy Galbreath, publisher
Circulation: 7,500
Published quarterly
Newly released on the Internet only. Includes articles of interest to senior federal government executives on public sector

management. Articles from 2,000 to 4,000 words. Cannot pay but welcomes submission inquiries. Guidelines available.

Other Voices
P.O. Box 52059, 8210 – 109 Street, Edmonton, AB T6E 1N3
Phone: (780) 424-5059
E-mail: info@othervoices.ca
Web site: www.othervoices.ab.ca
Contact: Rachel Sentes, president
Circulation: 500
Published twice a year
  A small literary journal seeking fiction, poetry, creative non-fiction, reviews, photographs, and artwork. Payment of 1-year subscription for stories up to 2,500 words. "Please check web site for contests and current payment rates. Please query on reviews. We welcome established and new writers." Guidelines available.

Pacific Affairs
1855 West Mall, Suite 164, University of British Columbia,
  Vancouver, BC V6T 1Z2
Phone: (604) 822-6508, ext. 4534 Fax: (604) 822-9452
E-mail: enquiry@pacificaffairs.ubc.ca
Web site: www.pacificaffairs.ubc.ca
Contact: Timothy Cheek, editor
Circulation: 2,400
Published quarterly
  A source of scholarly insight into the current social, cultural, political, and economic issues of Asia and the Pacific region, directed toward universities, institutions, governments, embassies, consulates, and increasingly, the business sector. Articles and review articles are contributed by authors from around the world. Reviews about 50 books each issue. Length must not exceed 8,000 words. Contributors are not paid. Submission inquiries welcome. Guidelines available.

Pagitica in Toronto
P.O. Box 591, Stn. P, Toronto, ON M5S 2T1
Phone: (416) 966-3459
E-mail: editor@pagitica.com

Web site: www.pagitica.com
Contact: Andrew Leith Macrae, managing and fiction editor
Circulation: 1,000
Published quarterly

Mingles literature with the other arts, emerging talents with established writers, and Canadian voices with international. "Our design and typography are held to a high standard, reflecting our belief that quality of presentation enhances the quality of the content. Exploring fiction, poetry, essays, criticism, and the total range of art forms, *Pagitica* is Canada's voice for new literature." Accepts submissions up to 10,000 words, sometimes longer. Cannot pay at this time, except with copies. Guidelines available on web site. *Pagitica* also operates a monthly reading series.

paperplates
19 Kenwood Avenue, Toronto, ON M6C 2R8
Phone: (416) 651-2551 Fax: (416) 651-2910
E-mail: info@paperplates.org
Web site: www.paperplates.org
Contact: Bernard Kelly, publisher/editor
Circulation: 2,000
Published 3 times a year

An online publication that publishes poetry, fiction, plays, travel pieces, essays, interviews, and memoirs. Length 2,500 to 7,500 words. Cannot pay but welcomes submission inquiries. Guidelines available.

Pottersfield Portfolio
9879 Kempt Head Road, Ross Ferry, NS B1X 1N3
Web site: www.magomania.com
Contact: Douglas A. Brown, managing editor
Circulation: 1,500
Published twice a year

"Innovative and bold writing appears in *Pottersfield Portfolio* first. Offers readers, institutions, writers, and photographers an entry point to an enviable selection of the best Canadian writing and photography." Publishes short stories, non-fiction, and photography from Canadians and Canadian expatriates (non-Canadian writers by invitation only). Stories up to 4,000 words. Pays

$10/page on publication to a maximum of $50. "Writers submitting material must follow submission guidelines, available upon request. No fax or e-mail submissions or inquiries."

Prairie Fire
100 Arthur Street, Suite 423, Winnipeg, MB R3B 1H3
Phone: (204) 943-9066 Fax: (204) 942-1555
E-mail: prfire@mts.net
Web site: www.prairiefire.mb.ca
Contact: Andris Taskans, managing editor
Circulation: 1,500
Published quarterly

Publishes poetry, fiction, creative non-fiction, interviews, reviews, and occasionally literary criticism. Submissions may be from 200 to 5,000 words. Pays on publication: for fiction/poetry, $50 for first page, $45 for each additional page (max. $500); for essays/articles/editorials, $45 for first page, $40 for each additional page (max. $250); for interviews/profiles, $25 for first page, $30 for each additional page (max. $200); and for reviews, 5¢/word. Guidelines and full payment schedule available. All submissions must be accompanied by an SASE.

Prairie Forum
Canadian Plains Research Center, University of Regina, Regina,
    SK S4S 0A2
Phone: (306) 585-4758 Fax: (306) 585-4699
E-mail: brian.mlazgar@uregina.ca
Web site: www.cprc.uregina.ca
Contact: Patrick Douaud, editor
Circulation: 300
Published twice a year

An interdisciplinary scholarly journal that publishes interdisciplinary scholarly research on the Canadian plains region. Market largely comprises university professors. Articles 3,500 to 10,000 words. Welcomes inquiries. No fees are paid. Guidelines available.

Prairie Journal
P.O. Box 61203, Brentwood P.O., Calgary, AB T2L 2K6
E-mail: prairiejournal@yahoo.com

Web site: www.geocities.com/prairiejournal
Contact: A. Burke, editor
Circulation: 600
Published twice a year

A literary journal featuring new and established Canadian writers of reviews, interviews, and creative and critical writing. Any payment depends on grant. Query with samples before submitting reviews. No e-mail submissions accepted. "We acquire first North American rights only." Guidelines available on web site. "We also publish online (poems only). We welcome freelance submissions."

PRISM international

Creative Writing Program, University of British Columbia, 1866
    Main Mall, Buch E462, Vancouver, BC V6T 1Z1
Phone: (604) 822-2514 Fax: (604) 822-3616
E-mail: prism@interchange.ubc.ca
Web site: www.prism.arts.ubc.ca
Contact: editors
Circulation: 1,250
Published quarterly

Features innovative new fiction, poetry, drama, literary non-fiction, and translation from Canada and around the world. The oldest literary journal in Western Canada. Welcomes submissions of 250 to 5,000 words from established and unknown writers. Pays $40/published page for poetry, $20/published page for prose, on publication. No multiple submissions. "We are looking for innovative, striking work in all areas. Show us originality of thought and close attention to language. No genre fiction, please." Guidelines available.

Public

York University, 4700 Keele Street, 279 Winters College, Toronto,
    ON M3J 1P3
Phone: (416) 736-2100, ext. 70106 Fax: (416) 650-8034
Web site: www.yorku.ca/public
Contact: Public Access collective
Circulation: 1,000
Published twice a year

An interdisciplinary journal combining scholarly and critical writing in cultural studies, focusing on the visual arts, performance, and literature. Dedicated to providing a forum in which artists, critics, and theorists exchange ideas on topics previously segregated by ideological boundaries of discipline. Has limited funds to pay for contributions. Guidelines available.

Queen Street Quarterly

P.O. Box 311, Stn. P, 704 Spadina Avenue, Toronto, ON M5S 2S8
Phone: (416) 760-0831
E-mail: theqsq@hotmail.com
Contact: Suzanne Zelazo, publisher/editor
Circulation: 800

A literary journal that provides a forum for experimental and traditional poetry, fiction, and intermedia. Publishes stories from 800 to 2,500 words. Pays, on publication, $20 for stories, $7 for poems. Welcomes submission inquiries. "Where possible, submissions should be accompanied by a PC-readable disk." Guidelines available.

Queen's Quarterly

Queen's University, 144 Barrie Street, Kingston, ON K7L 3N6
Phone: (613) 533-2667 Fax: (613) 533-6822
E-mail: qquarter@post.queensu.ca
Web site: http://info.queensu.ca/quarterly
Contact: Boris Castel, editor
Circulation: 3,000

A distinctive and multidisciplinary university-based review with a Canadian focus and an international outlook. First published in 1893. Features scholarly articles (2,000 to 3,000 words) of general interest on politics, history, science, the humanities, and arts and letters, plus regular music and science columns, original poetry, fiction, and extensive book reviews. Fees, which are paid on publication, are negotiated. Guidelines available.

Resources for Feminist Research

OISE/UT, 252 Bloor Street W., Toronto, ON M5S 1V6
Phone: (416) 923-6641 Fax: (416) 926-4725
E-mail: rfrdrf@oise.utoronto.ca
Web site: www.oise.utoronto.ca/rfr
Contact: Philinda Masters, editor

Circulation: 2,000
Published quarterly

A journal of feminist scholarship containing research articles, abstracts, book reviews, and bibliographies. "*RFR* is an academic journal, so we accept research articles within a feminist perspective." Preferred length 7,000 to 10,000 words. Cannot pay but welcomes submissions. Guidelines are outlined on inside back cover of journal.

Rhubarb

100 Arthur Street, Suite 606, Winnipeg, MB R3B 1B3
Phone: (204) 956-0500
E-mail: rhubarb@mts.net
Circulation: 1,000
Published twice a year

Publishes new art and writing by people of Mennonite heritage for a general reading public. Stories 500 to 2,500 words. Pays $25 to $100 on publication.

RicePaper

P.O. Box 74174, Hillcrest RPO, Vancouver, BC V5V 5C8
Phone: (604) 879-5962 Fax: (604) 879-5962
E-mail: hanako@interchange.ubc.ca
Web site: www.ricepaperonline.com
Contact: Hanako Masutani
Circulation: 2,000
Published quarterly

Focuses on Asian-Canadian art and culture. Publishes reviews, previews, interviews, profiles, essays, short fiction, poetry, visual artwork, scripts, and features on visual arts, music, dance, poetry, theatre, and culture. Short features are 750 to 1,200 words, long features from 1,500 to 3,000 words, fiction no longer than 3,500 words (no minimum), poetry no longer than 3,000 words (no minimum), and reviews from 500 to 1,000 words. Pays in copies and a 1-year subscription. Welcomes submission inquiries.

Room of One's Own

P.O. Box 46160, Stn. D, Vancouver, BC V6J 5G5
E-mail: contactus@roommagazine.com

Web site: www.roommagazine.com
Contact: editorial collective
Circulation: 1,100
Published quarterly

Established 1975. Solicits fine writing and editing from women authors in Canada and other countries, both well-known and unknown. Features original poetry, fiction, reviews, artwork, and occasionally, creative non-fiction. Length 2,000 to 5,000 words. Pays $35 honorarium plus 2 copies of issue on publication. Guidelines are available, but reading recent back issues will provide the best guidance.

Scrivener Creative Review

853 Sherbrooke Street W., Montreal, QC H3A 2T6
Phone: (514) 398-6588
E-mail: scrivenermag@hotmail.com
Web site: www.scrivenercreativereview.org
Contact: Anca Szilágyi, co-ordinating editor
Circulation: 300
Published annually

Publishes poetry, fiction, and photography from new and established talent in Canada and abroad. Stories 200 to 9,000 words. Cannot pay but welcomes submissions. Guidelines available on web site.

Studies in Canadian Literature/Études en littérature canadien

University of New Brunswick, English Department, P.O. Box 4400, Fredericton, NB E3B 5A3
Phone: (506) 453-3501 Fax: (506) 453-5069
E-mail: scl@unb.ca
Web site: www.lib.unb.ca/Texts/Scl
Contacts: John C. Ball and Jennifer Andrews, editors
Circulation: 450
Published twice a year

A bilingual, refereed journal of Canadian literary criticism. Carries essays and author interviews of 6,000 to 8,000 words. Contributors receive a complimentary 1-year subscription. Guidelines in journal. Use *MLA Handbook* for style. "Papers are vetted by 2 members of an advisory board, so 2 copies are required. Author's name should be on a separate sheet."

sub-TERRAIN Magazine
P.O. Box 3008, MPO, Vancouver, BC V6B 3X5
Phone: (604) 876-8710   Fax: (604) 879-2667
E-mail: subter@portal.ca
Web site: www.anvilpress.com/subterrain
Contact: Brian Kaufman, editor-in-chief
Circulation: 4,000
Published 3 times a year

Publishes first-time and established writers from across North America. Interested in progressive writing – fiction, commentary, and poetry. Preferred length 1,000 to 4,000 words. Pays on publication $25/page for prose, $20/poem. Read the magazine before submitting (sample copy $5). Guidelines available on web site.

Taddle Creek
P.O. Box 611, Stn. P, Toronto, ON M5S 2Y4
E-mail: editor@taddlecreekmag.com
Web site: www.taddlecreekmag.com
Contact: Conan Tobias, editor-in-chief
Circulation: 1,000
Published twice a year

Publishes urban fiction and poetry by Toronto authors. Only submissions of fiction and poetry are accepted. Authors must currently be residing in Toronto. Fees are negotiated. Guidelines available on web site. "Authors should not submit before reading guidelines."

Teacher Librarian: The Journal for School Library Professionals
101 – 1001 West Broadway, Suite 343, Vancouver, BC V6H 4E4
Phone: (604) 925-0266   Fax: (604) 925-0566
E-mail: admin@teacherlibrarian.com
Web site: www.teacherlibrarian.com
Contact: Ken Haycock, editor
Circulation: 10,000
Published 5 times a year

Publishes articles on teacher librarianship. Pays a small honorarium on publication for articles. Guidelines available on web site.

TickleAce
P.O. Box 5353, St. John's, NL A1C 5W3
Phone: (709) 754-6610 Fax: (709) 754-5579
E-mail: tickleace@nfld.com
Web site: www.magomania.com
Contact: Bruce Porter, editor
Circulation: 1,100
Published twice a year

Publishes poetry, fiction, book reviews, visual art, and literary interviews with a focus on (but not restricted to) Newfoundland and Labrador. Stories run from 500 to 6,000 words. Pays on publication an average of $35/page to a maximum of $350, depending on availability of funds. Guidelines available.

Urban History Review
Becker Associates, P.O. Box 507, Stn. Q, Toronto, ON M4T 2M5
Phone: (416) 483-7282 Fax: (416) 489-1713
E-mail: jbecker@interlog.com
Contact: John Becker, managing editor
Circulation: 500
Published twice a year

A bilingual interdisciplinary and refereed journal presenting lively articles covering such topics as architecture, heritage, urbanization, housing, and planning, all in a generously illustrated format. Regular features include in-depth articles, research notes, two annual bibliographies covering Canadian and international publications, comprehensive book reviews, and notes and comments on conferences, urban policy, and publications. Contributors are unpaid.

West Coast Line
2027 East Annex, 8888 University Drive, Simon Fraser
   University, Burnaby, BC V5A 1S6
Phone: (604) 291-4287 Fax: (604) 291-4622
E-mail: wcl@sfu.ca
Web site: www.sfu.ca/west-coast-line

Contact: Karen Earl, managing editor
Circulation: 800
Published 3 times a year

Publishes work by contemporary writers and artists who are experimenting with or expanding the boundaries of conventional forms and contexts. Interested in work that is engaged with problems of representation, race, culture, gender, sexuality, technology, media, urban/rural spaces, nature, and language. "We advise those considering submitting work to first familiarize themselves with the journal and with the work of our recent contributors by purchasing a recent issue ($12). Recently we have published poetry by Bruce Andrews, Charles Bernstein, Wayde Compton, Dan Farrell, and Fred Wah; prose essays by Di Brandt, Margot Leigh Butler, Peter Culley, Paul Kelley, Scott McFarlane, Larissa Lai, Roy Miki, and Janice Williamson; visual art by David Garneau, Laiwan, Ashok Mathur, Chick Rice, and Jan Wade. Recent special issues have included "Writing Rupture: Iranian Emigration Literature," guest edited by Peyman Vahabzadeh, and "Woodsquat," a compilation of writings and documents on the Woodward's squat in Vancouver. Fiction up to 7,000 words; poetry up to 400 lines. Pays $10/page after publication. Query first. Guidelines available.

3

TRADE, BUSINESS, FARM,&
PROFESSIONAL PUBLICATIONS

Trade publications are a potentially lucrative sector of the writer's market that is often overlooked. Although most pay no more than $500 for a full-length article, and usually less, the writing may require considerably fewer sources than are needed for consumer magazine features. An article can often be completed in a day or two, sometimes after research and interviews conducted solely by telephone. In terms of hours spent, therefore, the pay is generally relatively good. What's more, trade editors are often keen to find competent new writers.

The secret to making money from these publications is to work frequently for as many as possible, always bearing in mind that they may want a degree of technical detail that will inform readers already well acquainted with the specific fields they serve. If you have an area of specialist knowledge, you have a significant advantage. If not, you would do well to familiarize yourself with at least one trade or business area and the publications that serve it. Most trade periodicals, however, deliberately avoid becoming too technical, and aim to appeal to a wider readership. It bears repeating that before submitting, you must familiarize yourself with the magazine thoroughly by reading back issues.

Magazines in each of the following categories carry pieces about new products and developments, unusual marketing and promotion ideas, innovative management techniques, and prominent people and events specific to the industry, trade, or profession they serve. The regional business journals are highly recommended for freelance writers with business knowledge, since they often pay top dollar for timely and well-informed contributions. Those writers who have found markets through the main business section in Chapter 1 may profitably pursue this specialty further in the business listing below.

In many cases, staff writers produce the bulk of the feature writing and call on outside experts to provide specific material. But editors will often utilize freelancers when there is an editorial shortfall. Some cultivate long-term relationships with regular freelancers, who produce much of their copy. Often one editor is involved in several magazines, so making yourself and your work known to him or her can lead to further commissions, especially if you show yourself to be reliable and adaptable.

This chapter offers a broadly representative selection of trade publications across a wide range of industrial and professional areas, including many well-established, dependable employment sources, and provides a solid resource for the freelance writer looking to break into a new market. However, this is perhaps the most fluid sector in publishing: periodicals come and go, and reappear under a new masthead; editors move from job to job relatively often in response to industry and structural changes. Chapter 11, Resources, lists some of the larger publishers of trade magazines in Canada, who can be contacted for a list of their publications.

For a monthly updated reference source, consult Rogers's *CARD* directory or refer to *Matthews Media Directory*, published four times a year, at your library. Check *CARD*, too, or the annual supplement *Publication Profiles* for upcoming editorial themes, media profiles, circulation figures, and other useful information.

Advertising, Marketing, & Sales

Adnews Insight Magazine
80 Parklawn Road, Suite 212, Toronto, ON M8Y 3H8
Phone: (416) 252-9400 Fax: (416) 252-8002
E-mail: info@adnews.com

Contact: Derek Winkler, editor
Published quarterly

Blitz Magazine
1489 Marine Drive, West Vancouver, BC V7T 1B8
Phone: (604) 921-8735 or 1-866-632-5489 Fax: (604) 921-8738
E-mail: blitzmag@smartt.com
Contact: Louise Aird, publisher/editor-in-chief
Published bimonthly

Canadian Retailer
1255 Bay Street, Suite 800, Toronto, ON M5R 2A9
Phone: (416) 922-6678 or 1-888-373-8245 Fax: (416) 922-8011
E-mail: general@dvtail.com
Contact: Pamela Addo, editor-in-chief
Published bimonthly

Direct Marketing News
137 Main Street N., Suite 302, Markham, ON L3P 1Y2
Phone: (905) 201-6600 Fax: (416) 201-6601
Contact: Ron Glen, editor
Published monthly

Government Purchasing Guide
15 Wertheim Court, Suite 710, Richmond Hill, ON L4B 3H7
Phone: (905) 771-7333 Fax: (905) 771-7336
Contact: Blair Adams, editorial director
Published bimonthly

Marketing
1 Mount Pleasant Road, 7th Floor, Toronto, ON M4Y 2Y5
Phone: (416) 764-1570
Contact: Stan Sutter, editorial director
E-mail: paul.ferriss@marketingmag.rogers.com
Web site: www.marketingmag.ca
Published 42 times a year

Marketnews
701 Evans Avenue, Suite 102, Toronto, ON M9C 1A3

Phone: (416) 667-9945 Fax: (416) 667-0609
E-mail: mail@marketnews.ca
Contact: Robert Franner, editor
Published monthly

Pool & Spa Marketing
270 Esna Park Drive, Unit 12, Markham, ON L3R 1H3
Phone: (905) 513-0090 Fax: (905) 513-1377
Contact: David Barnsley, editor
Published 7 times a year

Sales Promotion
3228 South Service Road, Suite 209, Burlington, ON L7N 3H6
Phone: (905) 634-2100 Fax: (905) 634-2238
E-mail: nmallett@clbmedia.ca
Web site: www.sp-mag.com
Contact: Nathan Mallett, editor
Published bimonthly

Strategy
366 Adelaide Street W., Suite 500, Toronto, ON M5V 1R9
Phone: (416) 408-2300 Fax: (416) 408-0870
Contact: Susan Linton, publisher
Published 25 times a year

Architecture, Building, Engineering, & Heavy Construction

Aggregates & Roadbuilding Magazine
4999 St. Catherine Street W., Suite 215, Montreal, QC H3Z 1T3
Phone: (514) 487-9868 Fax: (514) 487-9276
E-mail: rocktoroad@sympatico.ca
Contact: Robert L. Consedine, publisher/editor
Published 8 times a year

Alberta Construction Magazine
1333 – 8 Street S.W., Suite 800, Calgary, AB T2R 1M6
Phone: (403) 265-3700 or 1-888-563-2946 Fax: (403) 265-3706

Contact: Darrell Stonehouse, editor
Published bimonthly

Atlantic Construction Journal
11 Thornhill Drive, Halifax, NS B3B 1R9
Phone: (902) 468-8027 Fax: (902) 468-2425
E-mail: nsbj@hfxnews.southam.ca
Contact: Lori McKay, editor
Published quarterly

Award Magazine
4180 Lougheed Highway, 4th Floor, Burnaby, BC V5C 6A7
Phone: (604) 299-7311 Fax: (604) 299-9188
Contact: Les Wiseman, editor
Published bimonthly

Building & Construction Trades Today
29 Bernard Avenue, Toronto, ON M5R 1R3
Phone: (416) 690-2860 Fax: (416) 944-80133
E-mail: jleckie@ca.inter.net
Contact: John Leckie, assembly editor
Published 8 times a year

Building Magazine
360 Dupont Street, Toronto, ON M5R 1V9
Phone: (416) 966-9944 Fax: (416) 966-9946
E-mail: info@building.ca
Contact: Albert Warson, editor
Published bimonthly

Canadian Architect
1450 Don Mills Road, Toronto, ON M3B 2X7
Phone: (416) 442-5600 Fax: (416) 442-2214
Contact: Ian Chodikoff, editor
Published monthly

The Canadian Civil Engineer
4920 de Maisonneuve Boulevard W., Suite 201, Montreal, QC
    H3Z 1N1

Phone: (514) 933-2634 Fax: (514) 933-3504
E-mail: info@csce.ca
Contact: Michel Langelier, executive director
Published bimonthly

Canadian Consulting Engineer

1450 Don Mills Road, Toronto, ON M3B 2X7
Phone: (416) 442-2266 Fax: (416) 442-2214
E-mail: bparsons@ccemag.com
Contact: Bronwen Parsons, editor
Published 7 times a year

Canadian Roofing Contractor

92 Church Street, Suite 107, Ajax, ON L1S 6B4
Phone: (905) 427-0080 Fax: (905) 427-0087
Contact: Tanja Nowotny, editor
Published quarterly

Construction Alberta News

17704 – 103rd Avenue, Suite 104, Edmonton, AB T5S 1J9
Phone: (780) 424-1146 Fax: (780) 425-5886
E-mail: canews@telus.net
Contact: Grant Bush, editor
Published twice a week

Construction Canada

15 Wertheim Court, Suite 710, Richmond Hill, ON L4B 3H7
Phone: (905) 771-7333 or 1-800-409-8688 Fax: (905) 771-7336
Contact: Blair Adams, editorial director
Published twice a week

Contractors Rental

2323 Boundary Road, Suite 201, Vancouver, BC V5M 4V8
Phone: (604) 291-9900 Fax: (604) 291-1906
Contact: Keith Barker, editor
Published bimonthly

Daily Commercial News
500 Hood Avenue, 4th Floor, Markham, ON L3R 9Z3
Phone: 1-800-465-6475 Fax: (905) 752-5450
E-mail: dcnsub@cmdg.com
Contact: Andrew Cook, publisher

Design Engineering
1 Mount Pleasant Road, 7th Floor, Toronto, ON M4Y 2Y5
Phone: (416) 764-1555 Fax: (416) 764-1686
Contact: Renee Wilson, editor
Published 8 times a year

Engineering Dimensions
25 Sheppard Avenue W., Suite 1000, Toronto, ON M2N 6S9
Phone: (416) 224-1100 Fax: (416) 224-8168
Contact: Joan Bailey, editor
Published bimonthly

Equipment Journal
5160 Explorer Drive, Unit 6, Mississauga, ON L4W 4T7
Phone: (905) 629-7500 or 1-800-667-8541 Fax: (905) 629-7988
E-mail: office@equipmentjournal.com
Contact: Michael Anderson, editor
Published 17 times a year

Geomatica
1390 Prince of Wales Drive, Suite 400, Ottawa, ON K2C 3N6
Phone: (613) 224-9851 Fax: (613) 224-9577
E-mail: editgeo@magma.com
Contact: Mike Pinch, editor
Published quarterly

Heavy Construction News On-Site
1 Mount Pleasant Road, 7th Floor, Toronto, ON M4Y 2Y5
Phone: (416) 764-1494 Fax: (416) 764-1733
E-mail: jim.barnes@on-sitemag.rogers.com
Contact: Jim Barnes, editor
Published 8 times a year

Home Builder Magazine
4819 St. Charles Boulevard, Montreal, QC H9H 3C7
Phone: (514) 620-2200 Fax: (514) 620-6300
Contact: Frank O'Brien, editor
Published bimonthly

Home Improvement Retailing
245 Fairview Mall Drive, Suite 501, Toronto, ON M2J 4T1
Phone: (416) 494-1066 Fax: (416) 494-2536
E-mail: jhornyak@powershift.ca
Contact: Joe Hornyak, executive editor
Published bimonthly

Innovation
4010 Regent Street, Suite 200, Burnaby, BC V5C 6N2
Phone: (604) 929-6733 Fax: (604) 929-6753
E-mail: apeginfo@apeg.bc.ca
Contact: Wayne Gibson, editor
Published 10 times a year

Journal of Commerce
4285 Canada Way, Burnaby, BC V5G 1H2
Phone: (604) 433-8164 Fax: (604) 433-9549
Published twice a week

Ontario Home Builder
1074 Cooke Boulevard, Burlington, ON L7T 4A8
Phone: (905) 634-8003 Fax: (905) 634-7661
E-mail: steve@homesontario.com
Contact: Steve McNeil, editor
Published 5 times a year

The Pegg
10060 Jasper Avenue N.W., 1500 Scotia One, Edmonton, AB
    T5J 4A2
Phone: (780) 426-3990 Fax: (780) 425-1722
Contact: George Lee, manager, editorial services
Published 10 times a year

Perspectives
512 King Street E., Suite 300, Toronto, ON M5A 1M1
Phone: (416) 955-1550 Fax: (416) 955-1391
E-mail: info@capmagazines.ca
Contact: Gordon Grice, editor
Published quarterly

Toronto Construction News
500 Hood Avenue, 4th Floor, Markham, ON L3R 9Z3
Phone: 1-800-465-6475 Fax: (905) 752-5450
Contact: Andrew Cook, publisher
Published quarterly

Wood
26 Raymond Boulevard, Gatineau, QC I8Y 1R4
Phone: (613) 235-4469 Fax: (613) 235-4613
Contact: Don Griffith, editor
Published quarterly

Yardstick
2020 Portage Avenue, Unit 3C, Winnipeg, MB R3J 0K4
Phone: (204) 985-9780 Fax: (204) 985-9795
Contact: Terry Ross, editor
Published bimonthly

Automotive (see also Transportation & Cargo)

Aftermarket Canada
6200 Dixie Road, Suite 220, Mississauga, ON L5T 2E1
Phone: (905) 795-0110 Fax: (905) 795-2967
Contact: Jack Kazmierski, editor
Published bimonthly

AP & T
130 Belfield Road, Toronto, ON M9W 1G1
Phone: (416) 614-0955 Fax: (416) 614-2781
E-mail: info@apt-mag.ca

Contact: Allan Janssen, editor
Published bimonthly

Bodyshop
1450 Don Mills Road, Toronto, ON M3B 2X7
Phone: (416) 442-5600 Fax: (416) 442-2213
Contact: Lowell Conn, editor
Published 7 times a year

Canadian Auto World
6200 Dixie Road, Suite 220, Mississauga, ON L5T 2E1
Phone: (905) 795-0110 Fax: (905) 795-2967
Contact: Michael Goetz, editor
Published monthly

Canadian Automotive Fleet
95 Barber Greene Road, Suite 207, Toronto, ON M3C 3E9
Phone: (416) 383-0302 Fax: (416) 383-0313
Contact: Kevin Sheehy, managing editor
Published bimonthly

Car & Truck Digest
95 Barber Greene Road, Suite 207, Toronto, ON M3C 3E9
Phone: (416) 383-0302 Fax: (416) 383-0313
E-mail: digest@fleetbusiness.com
Contact: Kevin Sheehy, managing editor
Published quarterly

Collision Repaire Magazine
86 John Street, Markham, ON L3T 1Y2
Phone: (905) 889-3544 Fax: (905) 252-4680
E-mail: collisionrepair@rogers.com
Contact: Darryl Simmons, publisher
Published bimonthly

Jobber News
1450 Don Mills Road, Toronto, ON M3B 2X7
Phone: (416) 442-5600 Fax: (416) 442-2213

E-mail: aross@jobbernews.com
Contact: Andrew Ross, publisher/editor
Published monthly

Motor Fleet Management
77 Nipissing Crescent, 2nd Floor, Brampton, ON L6S 4Z8
Phone: (905) 451-4199 Fax: (905) 451-2938
E-mail: motorfleet@rogers.com
Contact: Dan Radulescu, publisher/editorial director
Published bimonthly

Octane
1333 – 8th Street S.W., Suite 800, Calgary, AB T2R 1M6
Phone: (403) 265-3700 or 1-888-563-2946 Fax: (403) 265-3706
Contact: Gordon Jaremko, editor
Published bimonthly

SSGM (Service Station & Garage Management)
1450 Don Mills Road, Toronto, ON M3B 2X7
Phone: (416) 442-5600 Fax: (416) 442-2213
Contact: Jim Anderton, editor
Published monthly

Taxi News
38 Fairmount Crescent, Toronto, ON M4L 2H4
Phone: (416) 466-2328 Fax: (416) 466-4220
E-mail: taxinews@the.wire.com
Contact: William McQuat, editor
Published monthly

Aviation & Aerospace

Airforce
P.O. Box 2460, Stn. D, Ottawa, ON K1P 5W6
Phone: (613) 992-5184 Fax: (613) 995-2196
E-mail: vjohnson@airforce.ca
Contact: Vic Johnson, editor
Published quarterly

Airports Americas
2323 Boundary Road, Suite 203, Vancouver, BC V5M 4V8
Phone: (604) 298-3005 Fax: (604) 298-3966
Contact: Rick Steadman, editor
Published quarterly

Aviator
3318 Oak Street, Suite 19, Victoria, BC V8X 1R1
Phone: (250) 658-6575 or 1-800-656-7598 Fax: (250) 658-6576
E-mail: pilotpress@shaw.ca
Contact: Garth Eichel, editor
Published 9 times a year

Helicopters
6200 Dixie Road, Suite 220, Mississauga, ON L5T 2E1
Phone: (905) 795-0110 Fax: (905) 795-2967
E-mail: info@helicoptersmagazine.com
Contact: David Carr, editor
Published quarterly

ICAO Journal
999 University Street, Montreal, QC H3C 5H7
Phone: (514) 954-8222 Fax: (514) 954-6376
E-mail: emacburnie@icao.int
Contact: Eric MacBurnie, editor
Published 9 times a year

Wings
6200 Dixie Road, Suite 220, Mississauga, ON L5T 2E1
Phone: (905) 795-0110 Fax: (905) 795-2967
E-mail: info@wingsmagazine.com
Contact: David Carr, senior editor
Published bimonthly

Business, Commerce, Banking, Law, Insurance, & Pensions

Alberta Venture
10350 – 124 Street, Suite 201, Edmonton, AB T5N 3V9
Phone: (780) 990-0839 Fax: (780) 425-4921
E-mail: admin@albertaventure.com
Contact: Ruth Kelly, publisher/editor-in-chief
Published 10 times a year

BC Business Service
1122 Mainland Street, Suite 310, Vancouver, BC V6B 5L1
Contact: John Merrick, publisher
Published quarterly

Benefits and Pensions Monitor
245 Fairview Mall Drive, Suite 501, Toronto, ON M2J 4T1
Phone: (416) 494-1066 Fax: (416) 494-2536
E-mail: jmclaine@powershift.ca
Web site: www.bpmmagazine.com
Contact: John L. McLaine, publisher/editorial director
Published bimonthly

Benefits Canada
1 Mount Pleasant Road, 12th Floor, Toronto, ON M4Y 2Y5
Phone: (416) 764-3813
Contact: Jim MacDonald, editor
Published monthly

BIZ
1074 Cooke Boulevard, Burlington, ON L7T 4A8
Phone: (905) 634-8003 Fax: (905) 634-7661
Contact: Jannene McNeil, editor
Published quarterly

The Bottom Line
75 Clegg Road, Markham, ON L6G 1A1
Phone: (905) 415-5804 or 1-800-668-6481 Fax: (905) 479-3758

Contact: Patrick McManus, editor
Published 19 times a year

Business Careers Canada
512 King Street E., Suite 300, Toronto, ON M5A 1M1
Phone: (416) 955-1550 Fax: (416) 955-1391
E-mail: mandrews@capmagazines.ca
Contact: Marni Andrews, editor
Published twice a year

The Business Executive
466 Speers Road, Suite 220, Oakville, ON L6K 3W9
Phone: (905) 845-8300 Fax: (905) 845-9086
Contact: Wendy Peters, associate publisher/editor
Published monthly

Business in Calgary
P.O. Box 2400, Stn. M, Calgary, AB T2P 0W8
Phone: (403) 569-4700 Fax: (403) 569-4799
E-mail: infor@businessincalgary.com
Contact: Richard Bronstein, editor
Published monthly

Business in Vancouver
1155 West Pender Street, Suite 500, Vancouver, BC V6E 2P4
Phone: (604) 688-2398 Fax: (604) 688-1963
Contact: Ian Noble, editor
Published weekly

Business Trends
1283 Confederation Street, Sarnia, ON N7S 5P1
Phone: (519) 336-1100 Fax: (519) 336-1833
E-mail: businesstrends@cogeco.net
Contact: Gayle Nichol, editor
Published monthly

BusinessWoman Canada
P.O. Box 31010, Barrie, ON L4N 0B3
Phone: (877) 251-7226 Fax: (704) 722-7268

E-mail: admin@smallbusinesscanada.ca
Contact: Hayden Bradshaw, production manager
Published quarterly

CA Magazine
277 Wellington Street W., Toronto, ON M5V 3H2
Phone: (416) 977-3222 Fax: (416) 977-8585
Contact: Louis D'Souza, associate publisher
Published 10 times a year

Canadian German Trade
480 University Avenue, Suite 1410, Toronto, ON M5G 1V2
Phone: (416) 598-3355 Fax: (416) 598-1840
E-mail: info.toronto@germanchamber.ca
Contact: Lutz Renner, editor
Published bimonthly

Canadian Insurance
111 Peter Street, Suite 500, Toronto, ON M5V 2H1
Phone: (416) 599-0772 Fax: (416) 599-0867
Contact: Barbara Aarsteinsen, editor
Published monthly

Canadian Investment Review
1 Mount Pleasant Road, 12th Floor, Toronto, ON M4Y 2Y5
Phone: (416) 764-3816 Fax: (416) 764-3934
Web site: www.investmentreview.com
Contact: Jim MacDonald, editor
Published quarterly

The Canadian Manager
2175 Sheppard Avenue E., Suite 310, Toronto, ON M2J 1W8
Phone: (416) 493-0155 Fax: (416) 491-1670
E-mail: office@cim.ca
Contact: Ruth Max, editor
Published quarterly

Canadian Underwriter
1450 Don Mills Road, Don Mills, ON M3B 2X7
Phone: (416) 442-2133 Fax: (416) 442-2213
E-mail: sean@canadianunderwriter.com
Contact: Sean Van Zyl, managing editor
Published monthly

Central Nova Business News
228 Main Street, Bible Hill, NS B2N 1H0
Phone: (902) 895-7948 Fax: (902) 893-1427
Contact: Shannon Berry, editor-in-chief
Published monthly

CGA Magazine
1188 West Georgia Street, Suite 800, Vancouver, BC V6E 4A2
Phone: (604) 669-3555 Fax: (604) 689-5845
E-mail: public@cga-canada.org
Contact: Peggy Homan, editor
Published bimonthly

China's Wired!
202 Torrens Avenue, Toronto, ON M4J 2P5
Phone: (416) 423-4857 Fax: (416) 423-6058
E-mail: stonecut@ultratech.net
Contact: Bob Tytus, managing editor
Published monthly

Commerce and Industry
1839 Inkster Boulevard, Winnipeg, MB R2X 1R3
Phone: (204) 954-2085 Fax: (204) 954-2057
Contact: Kelly Gray, editor
Published bimonthly

Commerce News
10123 – 99th Street, Suite 600, Edmonton, AB T5J 3G9
Phone: (780) 426-4620 Fax: (780) 424-7946
Contact: Terry Smith, editor
Published 11 times a year

Durham Business Times

138 Commercial Avenue, Ajax, ON L1S 2H5
Phone: (905) 426-4676 Fax: (905) 426-6598
Contact: Joanne Burghardt, editor-in-chief
Published monthly

Edge

25 Sheppard Avenue W., Suite 100, Toronto, ON M2N 6S7
Phone: (416) 227-8312 or 1-800-387-5012 Fax: (416) 227-6324
Contact: Joe Tersigni, publisher
Published monthly

Franchise Canada

530 Century Street, Suite 225, Winnipeg, MB R3H 0Y4
Phone: (204) 957-0265 or 1-888-573-1136 Fax: (204) 957-0217
E-mail: info@august.ca
Contact: Jackie Johnson, editor
Published bimonthly

Human Resources Professional

100 Sutherland Avenue, Winnipeg, MB R3L 1H9
Phone: 1-800-665-2456 Fax: 1-800-709-5551
Contact: Frank Robinson, publisher
Published bimonthly

Huronia Business Times

400 Bayfield Street, Suite 242, Barrie, ON L4M 5A1
Phone: (705) 734-1728 Fax: (705) 734-9600
E-mail: hbt@simcoe.com
Contact: Martin Melbourne, editor
Published monthly

In Business Windsor

1775 Sprucewood, La Salle, ON N9J 1X7
Phone: (519) 250-2825 Fax: (519) 250-2881
E-mail: inbiz@mnsl.net
Contact: Gary Baxter, general manager
Published monthly

Investment Executive
25 Sheppard Avenue W., Suite 100, Toronto, ON M2N 6S7
Phone: (416) 733-7600 Fax: (416) 218-3624
Contact: Tessa Wilmott, editor
Published 16 times a year

Investor's Digest of Canada
133 Richmond Street W., Suite 700, Toronto, ON M5H 3M8
Phone: (416) 869-1177 Fax: (416) 869-0616
Contact: Michael Popovitch, editor
Published 24 times a year

Kootenay Business Magazine
1510 – 2nd Street N., Suite 200, Cranbrook, BC V1C 3L2
Phone: (250) 426-7253 or 1-800-663-8555 Fax: (250) 426-4125
E-mail: info@kpimedia.com
Web site: www.koocanusapublications.com
Contact: Brian Coombs, editor
Published bimonthly

The Lawyers Weekly
75 Clegg Road, Markham, ON L6G 1A1
Phone: (905) 415-5804 or 1-800-668-6481 Fax: (905) 479-3758
Contact: Thomas Claridge, managing editor
Published 48 times a year

Management for Strategic Business Ideas
1 Robert Speck Parkway, Suite 1400, Mississauga, ON L4Z 3M3
Phone: (905) 949-3130 or 1-800-263-7622 Fax: (905) 949-0888
Contact: Robert Colman, editor-in-chief
Published 9 times a year

Manitoba Business
294 Portage Avenue, Suite 508, Winnipeg, MB R3C 0B9
Phone: (204) 943-2931 Fax: (204) 943-2942
Contact: Ritchie Gage, editor
Published 10 times a year

Mississauga Business Times
3145 Wolfedale Road, Mississauga, ON L5C 3A9
Phone: (905) 273-8222 Fax: (905) 273-8118
E-mail: webmaster@mississauga.net
Contact: Rick Drennan, managing editor
Published monthly

Montreal Business Magazine
204 St. Sacrement, Suite 201, Montreal, QC H2Y 1W8
Phone: (514) 286-8038 Fax: (514) 287-7346
E-mail: info@mbm-minc.com
Contact: Michael Carin, editor
Published bimonthly

National
1 Mount Pleasant Road, 12th Floor, Toronto, ON M4Y 2Y5
Phone: (416) 764-3910 Fax: (416) 764-3933
Contact: Jordan Furlong, editor
Published 8 times a year

Northern Ontario Business
158 Elgin Street, Sudbury, ON P3E 3N5
Phone: (705) 673-5667 Fax: (705) 673-4652
E-mail: info@nob.on.ca
Contact: Sari Huhtala, managing editor
Published monthly

Northwest Business Magazine
3907 – 3A Street N.E., Bay 114, Calgary, AB T2E 6S7
Phone: (403) 250-1128 Fax: (403) 250-1194
Contact: Kathryn Engel, editor
Published bimonthly

Okanagan Business Journal
591 Bernard Avenue, Suite 104, Kelowna, BC V1V 6N9
Phone: (250) 763-8509 Fax: (250) 763-8529
E-mail: publisher@businessjournal.ca
Contact: Devon Brooks, managing editor
Published 9 times a year

Ottawa Business Journal
1400 St-Laurent, Suite 200, Ottawa, ON K1K 4H4
Phone: (613) 744-4800 Fax: (613) 744-0866
Contact: Anne Howland, editor
Published 51 times a year

Silicon Valley North
99 Atlantic Avenue, Suite 309, Toronto, ON M6K 3J8
Phone: (416) 368-1886 Fax: (416) 368-1889
E-mail: jcarson@siliconvalleynorth.com
Contact: John Carson, editor
Published monthly

Small Business Canada Magazine
P.O. Box 31010, Barrie, ON L4N 0B3
Phone: 1-877-251-7226 Fax: (705) 722-7268
E-mail: admin@smallbusinesscanada.ca
Contact: Hayden Bradshaw, production manager
Published bimonthly

Sounding Board
999 Canada Place, Suite 400, Vancouver, BC V6C 3E1
Phone: (604) 681-2111 Fax: (604) 681-0437
Contact: Tracy Campbell, editor
Published 10 times a year

Today's Corporate Investor
77 Nipissing Crescent, 2nd Floor, Brampton, ON L6S 4Z8
Phone: (905) 451-4199 Fax: (905) 451-2938
Contact: Anne Pamehl, managing editor
Published bimonthly

Toronto Business Magazine
11966 Woodbine Avenue, Gormley, ON L0H 1G0
Phone: (905) 887-5048 Fax: (905) 887-0764
Contact: Kate Fleming, editor
Published bimonthly

Toronto Business Times
100 Tempo Avenue, Toronto, ON M2H 3S5
Phone: (416) 493-4400 Fax: (416) 493-4703
Contact: Deborah Bodine, editor-in-chief
Published monthly

Computers & Data Processing

CIO Canada
55 Town Centre Court, Suite 302, Toronto, ON M1P 4X4
Phone: (416) 290-0240 Fax: (416) 290-0238
E-mail: cio_canada@itworldcanada.com
Contact: Blair McQuillan, assistant editor
Published monthly

Communications & Networking
25 Sheppard Avenue W., Suite 100, Toronto, ON M2N 6S7
Phone: (416) 733-7600 or 1-800-387-5012 Fax: (416) 227-8324
Contact: Joe Tersigni, publisher
Published monthly

Computer Dealer News
25 Sheppard Avenue W., Suite 100, Toronto, ON M2N 6S7
Phone: (416) 733-7600 or 1-800-387-5012 Fax: (416) 227-8324
Contact: Joe Tersigni, publisher
Published 18 times a year

Computerworld
55 Town Centre Court, Suite 302, Toronto, ON M1P 4X4
Phone: (416) 290-0240 Fax: (416) 290-0238
E-mail: computerworld_canada@itworldcanada.com
Contact: Michael MacMillan, editor
Published 25 times a year

Computing Canada
25 Sheppard Avenue W., Suite 100, Toronto, ON M2N 6S7
Phone: (416) 733-7600 or 1-800-387-5012 Fax: (416) 227-8324

Contact: Joe Tersigni, publisher
Published twice a month

IT Focus
55 Town Centre Court, Suite 302, Toronto, ON M1P 4X4
Phone: (416) 290-0240 Fax: (416) 290-0238
E-mail: smaclean@itworldcanada.com
Contact: Susan Maclean, editor
Published monthly

NetworkWorld Canada
55 Town Centre Court, Suite 302, Toronto, ON M1P 4X4
Phone: (416) 290-0240 Fax: (416) 290-0238
Contact: Greg Enright, editor
Published 24 times a year

Technology in Government
25 Sheppard Avenue W., Suite 100, Toronto, ON M2N 6S7
Phone: (416) 733-7600 Fax: (416) 227-8324
Contact: Joe Tersigni, publisher
Published 11 times a year

Education & School Management

Canadian Vocational Journal
P.O. Box 3435, Stn. D, Ottawa, ON K1P 6L4
Phone: (613) 838-6012 Fax: (613) 838-6012
Published 3 times a year

Educational Digest
11966 Woodbine Avenue, Gormley, ON L0H 1G0
Phone: (905) 887-5048 Fax: (905) 887-0764
Contact: Janet Gardiner, publisher
Published quarterly

Professionally Speaking
121 Bloor Street E., 6th Floor, Toronto, ON M4W 3M5

Phone: (416) 961-8800 Fax: (416) 961-8822
Contact: Philip Carter, editor
Published quarterly

Quebec Home & School News
3285 Cavendish Boulevard, Suite 560, Montreal, QC H4B 2L9
Phone: (514) 481-5619 Fax: (514) 481-5610
Published quarterly

University Manager
2020 Portage Avenue, Suite 3C, Winnipeg, MB R3J 0K4
Phone: (204) 985-9780 Fax: (204) 985-9795
E-mail: kelman@videon.wave.ca
Contact: Craig Kelman, editor
Published quarterly

Electronics & Electrical

Cabling Systems
1450 Don Mills Road, Don Mills, ON M3B 2X7
Phone: (416) 442-2124 Fax: (416) 442-2200
Contact: Paul Barker, editor
Published 8 times a year

Canadian Electronics
240 Edward Street, Aurora, ON L4G 3S9
Phone: (905) 727-0077 Fax: (905) 727-0017
Contact: Tim Gouldson, editor
Published 7 times a year

Electrical Business
240 Edward Street, Aurora, ON L4G 3S9
Phone: (905) 727-0077 Fax: (905) 727-0017
E-mail: jcoombes@clbmedia.ca
Contact: Jennifer Coombes, managing editor
Published monthly

Electrical Line
3105 Benbow Road, West Vancouver, BC V7V 3E1
Phone: (604) 922-5516 Fax: (604) 922-5312
E-mail: kenb@electricalline.com
Contact: Ken Buhr, editor
Published bimonthly

Electricity Today
15 Harwood Avenue S., Suite 205, Ajax, ON L1S 2B9
Phone: (905) 686-1040 Fax: (905) 686-1078
E-mail: hq@electricityforum.com
Contact: Kelly Jones Johnston, editor
Published 10 times a year

EP & T (Electronic Products and Technology)
1200 Aerowood Drive, Unit 27, Mississauga, ON L4W 2S7
Phone: (905) 624-8100 Fax: (905) 624-1760
E-mail: eptech@ept.ca
Contact: Steven Law, editor
Published 8 times a year

Energy, Mining, Forestry, Lumber, Pulp & Paper, & Fisheries

Atlantic Fisherman
130 Wright Avenue, Halifax, NS B3B 1R6
Phone: (902) 422-4990 Fax: (902) 422-4728
Contact: Shirley McLaughlin, editor
Published monthly

Canadian Forest Industries
90 Morgan Road, Unit 14, Baie d'Urfe, QC H9X 3A8
Phone: (514) 457-2211 Fax: (514) 457-2558
Contact: Scott Jamieson, editor
Published 8 times a year

Canadian Miner
285 Lynn Avenue, North Vancouver, BC V7J 2C3

Phone: (604) 980-0794 Fax: (604) 980-7123
Contact: Michael J. McGrath, editor
Published quarterly

Canadian Mining Journal
1450 Don Mills Road, Toronto, ON M3B 2X7
Phone: (416) 442-5600 Fax: (416) 442-2181
Contact: Ray Perks, publisher
Published 9 times a year

Canadian Wood Products
90 Morgan Road, Unit 14, Baie d'Urfe, QC H9X 3A8
Phone: (514) 457-2211 Fax: (514) 457-2558
Contact: Scott Jamieson, editor
Published bimonthly

Energy Manager
135 Spy Court, Markham, ON L3R 5H6
Phone: (905) 477-3222 Fax: (905) 477-4320
Contact: Peter West, managing editor
Published bimonthly

Energy Processing/Canada
900 – 6th Avenue S.W., Suite 500, Calgary, AB T2P 3K2
Phone: (403) 263-6881 or 1-800-526-4177 Fax: (403) 263-6886
E-mail: nstar@northernstar.ab.ca
Contact: Alister Thomas, managing editor
Published bimonthly

The Fisherman
326 – 12th Street, 1st Floor, New Westminster, BC V3M 4H6
Phone: (604) 519-3638 Fax: (604) 224-6944
E-mail: fisherman@ufawu.org
Contact: Sean Griffin, editor
Published quarterly

The Forestry Chronicle
151 Slater Street, Suite 606, Ottawa, ON K1P 5H3
Phone: (613) 234-2242 Fax: (613) 234-6181

Contact: B. Haddon, editor
Published bimonthly

Forum
1188 West Georgia Street, Suite 1030, Vancouver, BC V6E 4A2
Phone: (604) 687-8027 Fax: (604) 4687-3264
E-mail: forum@rpf-bc.org
Contact: Sandra Sauer, editor
Published bimonthly

Hiballer Forest Magazine
P.O. Box 16052, Lynn Valley PO, North Vancouver, BC V7J 2P0
Phone: (604) 984-2002 Fax: (604) 984-2820
Contact: Paul Young, publisher/managing editor
Published bimonthly

Logging & Sawmilling Journal
P.O. Box 86670, North Vancouver, BC V7L 4L2
Phone: (604) 990-9970 or 1-866-405-6462 Fax: (604) 990-9971
Contact: Paul MacDonald, editor
Published 10 times a year

Mill Product News
2323 Boundary Road, Suite 203, Vancouver, BC V5M 4V8
Phone: (604) 298-3005 Fax: (604) 298-3966
E-mail: hbaum@baumpub.com
Contact: Heri R. Baum, publisher
Published bimonthly

Mining Review
4180 Lougheed Highway, 4th Floor, Burnaby, BC V5C 6A7
Phone: (604) 299-7311 Fax: (604) 299-9188
Contact: Peter Legge, publisher
Published quarterly

Northern Aquaculture
5001 Forbidden Plateau Road, Courtenay, BC V9J 1R3
Phone: (250) 478-3973 or 1-800-661-0368 Fax: (250) 338-2466
E-mail: naquasuib@mars.ark.com

Contact: Peter Chettleburgh, editor
Published monthly

The Northern Miner
1450 Don Mills Road, Toronto, ON M3B 2X7
Phone: (416) 442-5600 Fax: (416) 442-2181
Contact: Doug Donnelly, publisher
Published weekly

Oilweek
9915 – 56 Avenue N.W., Edmonton, AB T6E 5L7
Phone: (780) 944-9333 Fax: (780) 944-9500
Contact: Gordon Jaremko, editor
Published monthly

Propane/Canada
900 – 6th Avenue S.W., Suite 500, Calgary, AB T2P 3K2
Phone: (403) 263-6881 or 1-800-526-4177 Fax: (403) 263-6886
E-mail: nstar@northernstar.ab.ca
Contact: Alister Thomas, managing editor
Published bimonthly

Pulp & Paper Canada
1 Holiday Street, East Tower, Suite 705, Montreal, QC H9R 5N3
Phone: (514) 630-5955 or 1-800-363-1327 Fax: (514) 630-5980
Contact: Anya Orzechowska, managing editor
Published monthly

The Roughneck
900 – 6th Avenue S.W., Suite 500, Calgary, AB T2P 3K2
Phone: (403) 263-6881 Fax: (403) 263-6886
E-mail: nstar@northernstar.ab.ca
Contact: Scott Jeffrey, publisher
Published monthly

The Sou'Wester
P.O. Box 128, Yarmouth, NS B5A 4B1
Phone: (902) 742-7111 Fax: (902) 742-2311

Contact: Alain Meuse, editor
Published 24 times a year

Trucklogger Magazine
4180 Lougheed Highway, 4th Floor, Burnaby, BC V5C 6A7
Phone: (604) 684-4291 Fax: (604) 684-7134
Contact: Sandra Bishop, editor
Published quarterly

Environmental Science & Management

Canadian Environmental Protection
2323 Boundary Road, Suite 201, Vancouver, BC V5M 4V8
Phone: (604) 291-9900 Fax: (604) 291-1906
Contact: Morena Zanotto, editor
Published 8 times a year

Environmental Science & Engineering
220 Industrial Parkway S., Unit 30, Aurora, ON L4G 3V6
Phone: (905) 727-4666 Fax: (905) 841-7271
Contact: Tom Davey, publisher/editor
Published bimonthly

HazMat Management
1450 Don Mills Road, Don Mills, ON M3B 2X7
Phone: (416) 442-5600 Fax: (416) 442-2026
Contact: Connie Vitello, editor
Published bimonthly

Recycling Product News
2323 Boundary Road, Suite 201, Vancouver, BC V5M 4V8
Phone: (604) 291-9900 Fax: (604) 291-1906
Contact: Keith Barker, editor
Published 9 times a year

Solid Waste & Recycling
1450 Don Mills Road, Toronto, ON M3B 2X7

Phone: (416) 442-5600 Fax: (416) 442-2204
Contact: Guy Crittenden, editor-in-chief
Published bimonthly

Water & Pollution Control
11966 Woodbine Avenue, Gormley, ON L0H 1G0
Phone: (905) 887-5048 Fax: (905) 887-0764
Contact: Amy Margaret, editor
Published quarterly

Farming

Alberta's Farm Gateway
P.O. Box 3326, Leduc, AB T9E 6M1
Phone: (780) 986-1787 or 1-866-986-1787 Fax: (780) 980-5303
E-mail: farmgateway@msapublishing.com
Contact: Cait Wills, editor
Published 11 times a year

Better Farming
58 Teal Drive, Guelph, ON N1C 1G4
Phone: (519) 763-4044 Fax: (519) 763-4482
E-mail: rirwin@betterfarming.com
Web site: www.betterfarming.com
Contact: Robert Irwin, senior staff editor
Published 10 times a year

Canadian Hereford Digest
5160 Skyline Way N.E., Calgary, AB T2E 6V1
Phone: (403) 274-1734 Fax: (403) 275-4999
Contact: Kurt Gilmore, publisher/editor
Published 7 times a year

Canadian Jersey Breeder
350 Speedvale Avenue W., Unit 9, Guelph, ON N1H 7M7
Phone: (519) 821-9150 Fax: (519) 821-2723
E-mail: breeder@jerseycanada.com

Contact: Betty Clements, editor
Published 10 times a year

Canadian Poultry
222 Argyle Avenue, Delhi, ON N4B 2Y2
Phone: (519) 582-2513 Fax: (519) 582-3412
E-mail: mwhite@canadianpoultrymag.com
Web site: www.canadianpoultrymag.com
Contact: Marilyn White, editor
Published monthly

Canola Guide
P.O. Box 6600, Winnipeg, MB R3C 3K7
Phone: (204) 944-5569
Contact: Jay Whetter, editor
Published bimonthly

Cattlemen
P.O. Box 6600, Winnipeg, MB R3C 3K7
Phone: (204) 944-5760
Contact: G. Winslow, editor
Published 13 times a year

Country Guide
P.O. Box 6600, Winnipeg, MB R3C 3K7
Phone: (204) 944-5569 Fax: (204) 942-8463
Contact: Dave Wreford, editor
Published 9 times a year

Country Life in B.C.
10317 – 158A Street, Surrey, BC V4N 2M5
Phone: (604) 951-4444 Fax: (604) 951-4445
E-mail: countrylife@telus.net
Contact: Peter Wilding, publisher/editor
Published monthly

Dairy Contact
P.O. Box 549, 4914 – 50th Street, Onoway, AB T0E 1V0

Phone: (780) 967-2929 Fax: (780) 967-2930
E-mail: dccontact@icrossroads.com
Contact: Allen F. Parr, publisher/editor
Published monthly

Dairy Update
P.O. Box 6600, Winnipeg, MB R3C 3K7
Phone: (204) 944-5569
Contact: G. Winslow, editor
Published 9 times a year

Farm Business Journal
1147 Gainsborough Road, London, ON N6H 5L5
Phone: 1-800-567-3276
Contact: Isobel Carew, office manager
Published bimonthly

Farm Focus
P.O. Box 128, Yarmouth, NS B5A 4B1
Contact: Mark Richardson, publisher
Published 24 times a year

Farm Market
930 Richmond Street, Chatham, ON N7M 5J5
Phone: (519) 351-7331 Fax: (519) 351-2452
E-mail: farmmarketnews@bowesnet.com
Contact: Peter Epp, editor
Published 25 times a year

Fruit & Vegetable Magazine
222 Argyle Avenue, Delhi, ON N4B 2Y2
Phone: (519) 582-2513 Fax: (519) 582-4040
E-mail: mland@annexweb.com
Contact: Margaret Land, editor
Published 8 times a year

Germination
897 Corydon Avenue, Suite 203, Winnipeg, MB R3M 0W7
Phone: (204) 453-1965 Fax: (204) 475-5247

E-mail: issues@issuesink.com
Contact: Robynne Anderson, editor
Published 5 times a year

Grainews
P.O. Box 6600, Winnipeg, MB R3C 3K7
Phone: (204) 944-5569
Contact: Andy Sirski, editor
Published 18 times a year

The Grower
355 Elmira Road N., Unit 105, Guelph, ON N1K 1S5
Phone: (519) 763-6160 Fax: (519) 763-6604
E-mail: editor@thegrower.org
Contact: Jamie Reaume, editor
Published monthly

Holstein Journal
9120 Leslie Street, Unit 105, Richmond Hill, ON L4B 3J9
Phone: (905) 886-4222 Fax: (905) 886-0037
E-mail: peter@holsteinjournal.com
Contact: Bonnie Cooper, editor
Published monthly

Manitoba Co-Operator
P.O. Box 6600, Winnipeg, MB R3C 3K7
Phone: (204) 944-5569
Contact: Andy Sirski, editor
Published weekly

Niagara Farmers' Monthly
P.O. Box 52, Smithville, ON L0R 2A0
Phone: (905) 957-3751 Fax: (905) 957-0088
E-mail: editor@niagarafarmers.com
Contact: Steve Ecker, publisher/editor
Published 11 times a year

Ontario Corn Producer
90 Woodlawn Road W., Guelph, ON N1H 1B2

Phone: (519) 837-1660 Fax: (519) 837-1674
Published 9 times a year

Ontario Dairy Farmer
P.O. Box 7400, London, ON N5Y 4X3
Phone: (519) 473-0010 Fax: (519) 473-2256
Contact: Paul Mahon, editor-in-chief
Published 8 times a year

Ontario Farmer
P.O. Box 7400, London, ON N5Y 4X3
Phone: (519) 473-0010 Fax: (519) 473-2256
Contact: Paul Mahon, editor-in-chief
Published weekly

Ontario Milk Producer
6780 Campobello Road, Mississauga, ON L5N 2L8
Phone: (905) 821-8970 Fax: (905) 821-3160
E-mail: questions@milk.org
Contact: Bill Dimmick, editor
Published monthly

Quebec Farmers' Advocate
P.O. Box 80, Ste. Anne de Bellevue, QC H9X 3L4
Phone: (514) 398-7844 Fax: (514) 398-7972
Contact: Susanne J. Brown, managing editor
Published 11 times a year

Rural Roots
30 – 10th Street E., Prince Albert, SK S6V 0Y5
Fax: (306) 922-4237
Contact: Ruth Griffiths, editor
Published weekly

Saskatchewan Farm Life
2206A Avenue C North, Saskatoon, SK S7L 6C3
Phone: 1-888-924-6397
Published biweekly

Top Crop Manager
145 Thames Road W., Exeter, ON N0M 1S3
Phone: (519) 235-2400 Fax: (519) 235-0798
Contact: Peter Darbishire, managing editor
Published monthly

Voice of the Farmer
P.O. Box 490, Dresden, ON N0P 1M0
Phone: (519) 683-4485 Fax: (519) 683-4355
Contact: Janice Myers, editor
Published biweekly

Western Dairy Farmer Magazine
4504 – 61 Avenue, Leduc, AB T9E 3Z1
Phone: (780) 986-2271 Fax: (780) 986-6397
E-mail: leducrep@ccinet.ab.ca
Contact: Diana MacLeod, editorial
Published bimonthly

Food, Drink, Hostelry, & Hotel & Restaurant Supplies

Atlantic Restaurant News
2065 Dundas Street E., Suite 201, Mississauga, ON L4X 2W1
Phone: (905) 206-0150 or 1-800-201-8596 Fax: (905) 206-9972
Contact: Mike Cormack, managing editor
Published bimonthly

Bakers Journal
222 Argyle Avenue, Delhi, ON N4B 2Y2
Phone: (519) 582-2513 Fax: (519) 582-4040
E-mail: editor@bakersjournal.com
Web site: www.bakers.retailfoodservice.com
Contact: Jane Ayer, editor
Published 10 times a year

Bar & Beverage Business Magazine
1839 Inkster Boulevard, Winnipeg, MB R2X 1R3
Phone: (204) 954-2085 Fax: (204) 954-2057

E-mail: mp@mercury.mb.ca
Contact: Kelly Gray, editor
Published bimonthly

Canada's Foodservice News
295 The West Mall, Suite 215, Toronto, ON M9C 4Z4
Phone: (416) 695-9229 or 1-888-736-6661 Fax: 1-800-598-9906
E-mail: info@cfsn.ca
Contact: Ellie Chesnutt, editor
Published 9 times a year

Canadian Grocer
1 Mount Pleasant Road, 7th Floor, Toronto, ON M4Y 2Y5
Phone: (416) 764-1679 Fax: (416) 764-1523
Contact: Jerry Tutunjian, editor
Published 10 times a year

Canadian Pizza Magazine
222 Argyle Avenue, Delhi, ON N4B 2Y2
Phone: (519) 582-2513 Fax: (519) 582-4040
E-mail: dmaccarthy@annexweb.com
Contact: Drew McCarthy, editor
Published 8 times a year

Food in Canada
1 Mount Pleasant Road, 7th Floor, Toronto, ON M4Y 2Y5
Phone: (416) 764-1502 Fax: (416) 764-1755
E-mail: sandra.eagle@food.rogers.com
Web site: www.foodincanada.com
Contact: Sandra Eagle, editor
Published 9 times a year

Foodservice and Hospitality
23 Lesmill Road, Suite 101, Toronto, ON M3B 3P6
Phone: (416) 447-0888 Fax: (416) 447-5333
E-mail: rcaira@foodservice.ca
Contact: Rosanna Caira, publisher/editor
Published monthly

Grocer Today
4180 Lougheed Highway, 4th Floor, Burnaby, BC V5C 6A7
Phone: (604) 299-7311 Fax: (604) 299-9188
Contact: Les Wiseman, editor
Published 8 times a year

Hotelier
23 Lesmill Road, Suite 101, Don Mills, ON M3B 3P6
Phone: (416) 447-0888 Fax: (416) 447-5333
E-mail: rcaira@foodservice.ca
Contact: Rosanna Caira, publisher/editor
Published 8 times a year

Ontario Restaurant News
2065 Dundas Street E., Suite 201, Mississauga, ON L4X 2W1
Phone: (905) 206-0150 or 1-800-201-8596 Fax: (905) 206-9972
Contact: Mike Deibert, editor
Published monthly

The Supermarket Journal
P.O. Box 96510, Maple, ON L6A 1W5
Phone: (905) 760-9228 Fax: (905) 761-9961
E-mail: supermkt@idirect.com
Contact: Mel Fruitman, editor
Published bimonthly

Western Grocer
1839 Inkster Boulevard, Winnipeg, MB R2X 1R3
Phone: (204) 954-2085 Fax: (204) 954-2057
Contact: Kelly Gray, editor
Published bimonthly

Your Convenience Manager
508 Lawrence Avenue W., Suite 201, Toronto, ON M6A 1A1
Phone: (416) 504-0504 Fax: (416) 256-3002
E-mail: sinfo@fulcrum.ca
Contact: Jane Widerman, editor
Published bimonthly

Health, Dentistry, Medicine, Pharmacy, & Nursing

The Alberta Doctors' Digest
12230 – 106th Avenue N.W., Edmonton, AB T5N 3Z1
Phone: (780) 482-2626 Fax: (780) 482-5445
E-mail: amamail@albertadoctors.org
Contact: G. L. Higgins, editor
Published bimonthly

British Columbia Medical Journal
1665 West Broadway, Suite 115, Vancouver, BC V6J 5A4
Phone: (604) 736-5551 Fax: (604) 733-7317
E-mail: journal@bcma.bc.ca
Contact: Jamy Draper, managing editor
Published 10 times a year

Canadian Family Physician
2630 Skymark Avenue, Mississauga, ON L4W 5A4
Phone: (905) 629-0900 Fax: (905) 629-0893
Contact: Anthony Reid, scientific editor
Published monthly

Canadian Healthcare Manager
1 Mount Pleasant Road, 12th Floor, Toronto, ON M4Y 2Y5
Phone: (416) 764-3867 Fax: (416) 764-3937
Contact: Don Bish, editor
Published 7 times a year

Canadian Healthcare Technology
1118 Centre Street, Suite 207, Markham, ON L4J 7R9
Phone: (905) 709-2330 Fax: (905) 709-2258
E-mail: info@canhealth.com
Contact: Jerry Zeidenberg, publisher
Published 8 times a year

Canadian Journal of Clinical Pharmacology
2902 South Sheridan Way, Oakville, ON L6J 7L6
Phone: (905) 829-4770 Fax: (905) 829-4799

E-mail: pulsus@pulsus.com
Contact: Neil H. Shear, editor-in-chief
Published quarterly

Canadian Journal of Continuing Medical Education
955 St. Jean Boulevard, Suite 306, Montreal, QC H9R 5K3
Phone: (514) 695-7623 Fax: (514) 695-8554
E-mail: www.clinicien@sta.ca
Contact: Paul F. Brand, executive editor
Published monthly

The Canadian Journal of Hospital Pharmacy
1145 Hunt Club Road, Suite 350, Ottawa, ON K1V 0Y3
Phone: (613) 736-9733 Fax: (613) 736-5660
Contact: Scott Walker, editor
Published 7 times a year

Canadian Journal of Public Health
1565 Carling Avenue, Suite 400, Ottawa, ON K1Z 8R1
Phone: (613) 725-3769 Fax: (613) 725-9826
Contact: Gerald H. Dafoe, managing editor
Published bimonthly

Canadian Medical Association Journal
1867 Alta Vista Drive, Ottawa, ON K1G 3Y6
Phone: 1-800-663-7336, ext. 2111 Fax: (613) 565-7488
Web site: www.cmaj.ca
Contact: John Hoey, editor
Published biweekly

Canadian Nurse
50 Driveway, Ottawa, ON K2P 1E2
Phone: (613) 237-2133 Fax: (613) 237-3520
E-mail: cnj@cna-aiic.ca
Published 10 times a year

Canadian Pharmaceutical Journal (CPJ)
1785 Alta Vista Drive, Ottawa, ON K1G 3Y6
Phone: (613) 523-7877 or 1-800-917-9489 Fax: (613) 523-0445

Contact: Chris Thatcher, managing editor
Published 10 times a year

The Care Connection
5025 Orbitor Drive, Building 4, Suite 200, Mississauga, ON
    L4W 4Y5
Phone: (905) 602-4664 Fax: (905) 602-4666
Contact: Joanne Young Evans, editor
Published quarterly

Dental Practice Management
1450 Don Mills Road, Toronto, ON M3B 2X7
Phone: (416) 442-5600 Fax: (416) 442-2214
Contact: Catherine Wilson, managing editor
Published quarterly

Doctor's Review
400 McGill Street, 3rd Floor, Montreal, QC H2Y 2G1
Phone: (514) 397-8833 Fax: (514) 397-0228
E-mail: drreview@parkpub.com
Contact: Annarosa Sabbadini, editor
Published monthly

Geriatrics Today
3100 Bayview Avenue, Unit 4, Toronto, ON M2N 5L3
Phone: (416) 224-5055 Fax: (416) 224-5455
E-mail: medicine@bellnet.ca
Contact: William Dalziel, editor
Published quarterly

Healthbeat
9768 – 170 Street, Suite 319, Edmonton, AB T5T 5L4
Phone: (780) 413-9342 or 1-800-727-0782 Fax: (780) 413-9328
E-mail: info@mccronehealthbeat.com
Published monthly

Healthcare Management Forum
9 – 5th Avenue, Chateauguay, QC J6K 3L5

Phone: (450) 691-9515 Fax: (450) 699-8869
Contact: Patricia Brown, managing editor
Published quarterly

Hospital News
15 Apex Road, Toronto, ON M6A 2V6
Phone: (416) 781-5516 Fax: (416) 781-5499
E-mail: hospitalnews@rogers.com
Contact: Julie Abelsohn, editor
Published monthly

Journal of the Canadian Dental Association
1815 Alta Vista Drive, Ottawa, ON K1G 3Y6
Phone: (613) 523-1770 Fax: (613) 523-7736
Contact: John O'Keefe, editor-in-chief
Published 11 times a year

Long Term Care
345 Renfrew Drive, Suite 102–202, Markham, ON L3R 9S9
Phone: (905) 470-8995 Fax: (905) 470-9595
Published quarterly

The Medical Post
1 Mount Pleasant Road, 12th Floor, Toronto, ON M4Y 2Y5
Phone: (416) 764-3902 Fax: (416) 764-1207
Contact: Nancy Kent, associate publisher
Published 46 times a year

Nursing BC
2855 Arbutus Street, Vancouver, BC V6J 3Y8
Phone: (604) 736-7331 Fax: (604) 738-2272
Contact: Bruce Wells, editor
Published 5 times a year

Ontario Dentist
4 New Street, Toronto, ON M5R 1P6
Phone: (416) 922-3900 Fax: (416) 922-9005
E-mail: comm@oda.on.ca

Contact: Mark Levine, publisher
Published 10 times a year

Ontario Medical Review
525 University Avenue, Suite 300, Toronto, ON M5G 2K7
Phone: (416) 599-2580 Fax: (416) 599-9309
E-mail: public_affairs@oma.org
Contact: Jeff Henry, editor
Published 11 times a year

Oral Health
1450 Don Mills Road, Toronto, ON M3B 2X7
Phone: (416) 442-5600 Fax: (416) 442-2214
Contact: Catherine Wilson, managing editor
Published monthly

Parkhurst Exchange
400 McGill Street, 3rd Floor, Montreal, QC H2Y 2G1
Phone: (514) 397-8833 Fax: (514) 397-0228
E-mail: parkex@parkpub.com
Contact: Milena Katz, managing editor
Published monthly

Patient Care
1 Mount Pleasant Road, 12th Floor, Toronto, ON M4Y 2Y5
Phone: (416) 764-3912
Contact: Golda Goldman, editor
Published monthly

Pharmacy Practice
1 Mount Pleasant Road, 12th Floor, Toronto, ON M4Y 2Y5
Phone: (416) 764-3926
Contact: Ruth Hanley, editor
Published monthly

Industrial

Accident Prevention
207 Queens Quay W., Suite 550, Toronto, ON M5J 2Y3
Phone: (705) 444-5402 or 1-800-669-4939 Fax: (416) 506-8880
E-mail: apmag@iapa.ca
Contact: Scott Williams, editor
Published bimonthly

Advanced Manufacturing
3228 South Service Road, Suite 209, Burlington, ON L7N 3H8
Phone: (905) 634-2100 Fax: (905) 634-2238
E-mail: tphillips@clbmedia.ca
Contact: Todd Phillips, editor
Published bimonthly

Canadian Chemical News
130 Slater Street, Suite 550, Ottawa, ON K1P 6E2
Phone: (613) 232-6252 Fax: (613) 232-5862
Web site: www.accn.ca
Published 10 times a year

Canadian Industrial Equipment News
1450 Don Mills Road, Toronto, ON M3B 2X7
Phone: (416) 442-3396 Fax: (416) 442-2214
Contact: Olga Markovich, associate publisher/editor
Published monthly

Canadian Machinery and Metalworking
1 Mount Pleasant Road, 12th Floor, Toronto, ON M4Y 2Y5
Phone: (416) 764-1508 Fax: (416) 764-1735
Contact: Kim Laudrum, editor
Published 7 times a year

Canadian Occupational Safety
135 Spy Court, Markham, ON L3R 5H6
Phone: (905) 477-3222 Fax: (905) 477-4320
E-mail: mgault@clbmedia.ca

Contact: Michelle Gault, editor
Published bimonthly

Canadian Packaging

1 Mount Pleasant Road, 12th Floor, Toronto, ON M4Y 2Y5
Phone: (416) 764-1505
Contact: George Guidoni, editor
Published 11 times a year

Canadian Plastics

1450 Don Mills Road, Toronto, ON M3B 2X7
Phone: (416) 422-2290 Fax: (416) 442-2213
Contact: Michael LeGault, editor
Published 12 times a year

Canadian Process Equipment & Control News

343 Eglinton Avenue E., Toronto, ON M4P 1L7
Phone: (416) 481-6483 Fax: (416) 481-6436
E-mail: cpe@cpecn.com
Contact: Laura Gardash, editor
Published bimonthly

Canadian Textile Journal

3000 Boulle, St-Hyacinthe, QC J2S 1H9
Phone: (450) 778-1870 Fax: (450) 778-3901
E-mail: rleclerc@ctt.ca
Contact: Roger Leclerc, editor-in-chief
Published bimonthly

Hardware Merchandising

1 Mount Pleasant Road, 7th Floor, Toronto, ON M4Y 2Y5
Phone: (416) 764-1662 Fax: (416) 764-1484
Contact: Robert Gerlsbeck, editor
Published 8 times a year

Heating–Plumbing–Air Conditioning

1 Mount Pleasant Road, 7th Floor, Toronto, ON M4Y 2Y5
Phone: (416) 764-1549 Fax: (416) 764-1746

Contact: Kerry Turner, editor
Published 7 times a year

Industrial Process Products & Technology
1011 Upper Middle Road E., Suite 1235, Oakville, ON L6H 5Z9
Phone: (905) 642-1215 Fax: (905) 642-1229
Contact: Glen Scholey, editor
Published bimonthly

Laboratory Product News
1450 Don Mills Road, Toronto, ON M3B 2X7
Phone: (416) 442-2052 Fax: (416) 442-2213
E-mail: lburt@labcanada.com
Contact: Leslie Burt, publisher/editor
Published 7 times a year

Machinery & Equipment MRO
1450 Don Mills Road, Toronto, ON M3B 2X7
Phone: (416) 442-2089 Fax: (416) 442-2214
Contact: William Roebuck, editor
Published bimonthly

Metalworking Production & Purchasing
240 Edward Street, Aurora, ON L4G 3S9
Phone: (905) 727-0077 Fax: (905) 727-0017
Contact: Jerry Cook, editor
Published bimonthly

OH & S Canada
1450 Don Mills Road, Toronto, ON M3B 2X7
Phone: (416) 442-2997 Fax: (416) 442-2200
E-mail: astelmakowich@ohscanada.com
Web site: www.ohscanada.com
Contact: Angela Stelmakowich, editor
Published 8 times a year

Plant, Canada's Industry Newspaper
1 Mount Pleasant Road, 7th Floor, Toronto, ON M4Y 2Y5

Phone: (416) 764-1546 Fax: (416) 764-1742
Contact: Joe Terrett, editor
Published 14 times a year

Plant Engineering & Maintenance
3228 South Service Road, Suite 209, Burlington, ON L7N 3H6
Phone: (905) 634-2100 Fax: (905) 634-2238
E-mail: rrobertson@clbmedia.ca
Contact: Rob Robertson, editor
Published 7 times a year

Landscaping & Horticulture

Canadian Florist
222 Argyle Avenue, Delhi, ON N4B 2Y2
Phone: (519) 582-2510 Fax: (519) 582-4040
E-mail: khall@annexweb.com
Contact: Karen Hall, editor
Published 8 times a year

Greenhouse Canada
222 Argyle Avenue, Delhi, ON N4B 2Y2
Phone: (519) 582-2513 Fax: (519) 582-4040
Contact: Dave Harrison, editor
Published monthly

GreenMaster
15 Wertheim Court, Suite 710, Richmond Hill, ON L4B 3H7
Phone: (905) 771-7333 or 1-800-409-8688 Fax: (905) 771-7336
Contact: Blair Adams, editorial director
Published bimonthly

Hortwest
5830 – 176A Street, Suite 101, Surrey, BC V3S 4H5
Phone: (604) 574-7772 Fax: (604) 574-7773
E-mail: kdejong@telus.net
Contact: Karen DeJong, managing editor
Published 10 times a year

Landscape Trades
7856 Fifth Line S., R.R. #4, Milton, ON L9T 2X8
Phone: (905) 875-1805 Fax: (905) 875-0183
E-mail: lo@hort-trades.com
Contact: Linda Erskine, editor
Published 9 times a year

Landscaping & Groundskeeping Journal
2323 Boundary Road, Suite 201, Vancouver, BC V5M 4V8
Phone: (604) 291-9900 Fax: (604) 291-1906
Contact: Lawrence Buser, editorial director
Published bimonthly

Prairie Landscape Magazine
P.O. Box 85127, APPO, Calgary, AB T2A 7R7
Phone: (403) 273-6917 Fax: (403) 207-6797
E-mail: prairielandscape@shaw.ca
Contact: Jennett Jackson, publisher
Published bimonthly

Turf & Recreation
275 James Street, Delhi, ON N4B 2B2
Phone: (519) 582-8873 Fax: (519) 582-8877
Contact: Mike Jiggens, editor
Published 7 times a year

Media, Music, & Communications

Broadcast Dialogue
414 St. Germain Avenue, Toronto, ON M5M 1W7
Phone: (416) 782-6482 Fax: (416) 782-9993
E-mail: broadcastdialogue@rogers.com
Contact: Howard Christensen, publisher
Published 10 times a year

Broadcaster
1450 Don Mills Road, Don Mills, ON M3B 2X7
Phone: (416) 510-6865 Fax: (416) 442-2213

Contact: Greg O'Brien, editor
Published 8 times a year

Cablecaster
1450 Don Mills Road, Toronto, ON M3B 2X7
Phone: (416) 510-6865 Fax: (416) 442-2213
Contact: Greg O'Brien, editor
Published 8 times a year

Canadian Music Trade
23 Hannover Drive, Unit 7, St. Catharines, ON L2W 1A3
Phone: (905) 641-3471 Fax: (905) 641-1648
E-mail: mail@nor.com
Contact: Jeff MacKay, editor
Published bimonthly

News Canada
111 Peter Street, Suite 810, Toronto, ON M5V 2H1
Phone: (416) 599-9900 Fax: (416) 599-9700
Contact: Ruth Douglas, publisher
Published monthly

Playback
366 Adelaide Street W., Suite 500, Toronto, ON M5V 1R9
Phone: (416) 408-2300 Fax: (416) 408-0870
E-mail: cmacdonald@brunico.com
Contact: Claire MacDonald, publisher
Published 25 times a year

Premiere Video Magazine
102 Atlantic Avenue, Suite 100, Toronto, ON M6K 1X9
Phone: (416) 539-8800 Fax: (416) 539-8511
Contact: Salah Bachir, editor
Published monthly

Press Review
P.O. Box 368, Stn. A, Toronto, ON M5W 1C2
Phone: (416) 368-0512 Fax: (416) 366-0104

Contact: Irene Papakonstantinou, managing editor
Published quarterly

Professional Sound

23 Hannover Drive, Unit 7, St. Catharines, ON L2W 1A3
Phone: (905) 641-3471 Fax: (905) 641-1648
E-mail: mail@nor.com
Web site: www.nor.com/upload
Contact: Jeff MacKay, editor
Published bimonthly

WholeNote

720 Bathurst Street, Suite 503, Toronto, ON M5S 2R4
Phone: (416) 323-2232 Fax: (416) 603-4791
E-mail: info@thewholenote.com
Contact: David Perlman, editorial
Published 10 times a year

Miscellaneous Trade & Professional

Blue Line Magazine

12A – 4981 Highway 7E, Suite 254, Markham, ON L3R 1N1
Phone: (905) 640-3048 Fax: (905) 640-7547
E-mail: blueline@blueline.ca
Contact: Morley S. Lymburner, publisher/editor
Published 10 times a year

Canadian Apparel

124 O'Connor Street, Suite 504, Ottawa, ON K1P 5M9
Phone: (613) 231-3220 or 1-800-661-1187 Fax: (613) 231-2305
E-mail: editor@apparel.ca
Contact: Marsha Ross, managing editor
Published bimonthly

Canadian Defence Review

132 Adrian Crescent, Markham, ON L3P 7B3
Phone: (905) 472-2801 Fax: (905) 472-3091

E-mail: editor@canadiandefencereview.com
Contact: Peter A. Kitchen, editor-in-chief
Published bimonthly

Canadian Facility Management & Design
4195 Dundas Street W., Suite 338, Toronto, ON M8X 1Y4
Phone: (416) 236-5856 Fax: (416) 236-5219
E-mail: cfm@sympatico.ca
Contact: Tom Kelly, editor
Published 7 times a year

The Canadian Firefighter and EMS Quarterly
222 Argyle Avenue, Delhi, ON N4B 2Y2
Phone: (519) 582-2513 Fax: (519) 582-4040
E-mail: cfirefight@annexweb.com
Contact: Jim Haley, editor
Published quarterly

Canadian Footwear Journal
750 Marcel Laurin, Suite 220, Montreal, QC H4M 2M4
Phone: (514) 744-5858 Fax: (514) 744-6377
E-mail: group@shoetrades.com
Contact: Barbara McLeish, editor
Published 7 times a year

The Canadian Funeral Director Magazine
21 Lennon Court, Whitby, ON L1P 1P4
Phone: (905) 430-2288 Fax: (905) 430-3004
E-mail: info@thefuneralmagazine.com
Contact: Scott Hillier, publisher/editor
Published monthly

Canadian Funeral News
101 – 6th Avenue S.W., Suite 1025, Calgary, AB T2P 3P4
Phone: (403) 264-3270 Fax: (403) 264-3276
Contact: Julie Peterson, editor
Published monthly

Canadian Hairdresser Magazine
11 Spadina Road, Toronto, ON M5R 2S9
Phone: (416) 923-1111 Fax: (416) 968-1031
E-mail: joan@canhair.com
Contact: Joan Harrison, managing editor
Published 10 times a year

Canadian Home Economics Journal
151 Slater Street, Suite 307, Ottawa, ON K1P 5H3
Phone: (613) 238-8817 Fax: (613) 238-8972
E-mail: general@chea-acef.ca
Contact: Glenda Everett, editor
Published twice a year

Canadian Home Style Magazine
146 Cavendish Court, Oakville, ON L6J 5S2
Phone: (905) 338-0799 Fax: (905) 338-5657
E-mail: homestylemag@home.com
Contact: Laurie O'Halloran, publisher/editorial director
Published bimonthly

Canadian HR Reporter
1 Corporate Plaza, 2075 Kennedy Road, Toronto, ON M1T 3V4
Phone: (416) 298-5141 Fax: (416) 298-5031
E-mail: john.hobel@thomson.com
Contact: John Hobel, managing editor
Published 22 times a year

Canadian Interiors
360 Dupont Street, Toronto, ON M5R 1V9
Phone: (416) 966-9944 Fax: (416) 966-9946
E-mail: info@canadianinteriors.com
Contact: Kelly Rude, editorial director
Published bimonthly

Canadian Jeweller
555 Richmond Street W., Suite 701, Toronto, ON M5V 3B1
Phone: (416) 203-6737 Fax: (416) 203-1057

E-mail: style@style.ca
Contact: Carol Besler, editor
Published 7 times a year

Canadian Property Management
5255 Yonge Street, Suite 1000, Toronto, ON M2N 6P4
Phone: (416) 512-8186 Fax: (416) 512-8344
E-mail: infor@mediaedge.ca
Contact: Robert Colman, editor
Published 8 times a year

Canadian Rental Service
145 Thames Road W., Exeter, ON N0M 1S3
Phone: (519) 235-2400 Fax: (519) 235-0798
E-mail: ais@aiscommunications.net
Contact: Peter Darbishire, managing editor
Published 9 times a year

Canadian Retailer
1255 Bay Street, Suite 800, Toronto, ON M5R 2A9
Phone: (416) 922-6678 or 1-888-373-8245 Fax: (416) 922-8011
E-mail: general@dvtail.com
Contact: Pamela Addo, editor-in-chief
Published bimonthly

Canadian Security
240 Edward Street, Aurora, ON L4G 3S9
Phone: (905) 727-0077 Fax: (905) 727-0017
Contact: Stacey Hunt, editor
Published 9 times a year

Canadian Textile Journal
3000 Boulle, St-Hyacinthe, QC J2S 1H9
Phone: (450) 778-1870 Fax: (450) 778-3901
E-mail: rleclerc@ctt.ca
Contact: Roger Leclerc, editor-in-chief
Published bimonthly

The Canadian Veterinary Journal
339 Booth Street, Ottawa, ON K1R 7K1
Phone: (613) 236-1162 Fax: (613) 236-9681
Contact: Doug Hare, editor
Published monthly

CM Condominium Manager
2121 Argentina Road, Suite 404, Mississauga, ON L5N 2X4
Phone: (905) 826-6890 Fax: (905) 826-4873
Contact: Susan Howard, executive editor
Published quarterly

Coatings
1 Mount Pleasant Road, 7th Floor, Toronto, ON M4Y 2Y5
Phone: (416) 764-1540 Fax: (416) 764-1740
E-mail: lisa.wichmann@coatings.rogers.com
Contact: Lisa Wichmann, managing editor
Published 7 times a year

Cosmetics
1 Mount Pleasant Road, 7th Floor, Toronto, ON M4Y 2Y5
Phone: (416) 764-1680
Contact: Ron Wood, editor
Published bimonthly

Eyecare Visionary
21 Hay Avenue, Toronto, ON M8Z 1G2
Phone: (416) 966-8826 Fax: (416) 966-5152
E-mail: dgolab@pathcom.com
Contact: Ian Corks, editor
Published quarterly

Fire Fighting in Canada
222 Argyle Avenue, Delhi, ON N4B 2Y2
Phone: (519) 582-2513 Fax: (519) 582-4040
E-mail: firefight@annexweb.com
Contact: Jim Haley, editor
Published 8 times a year

Gifts and Tablewares
1450 Don Mills Road, Toronto, ON M3B 2X7
Phone: (416) 442-2151 Fax: (416) 442-2213
E-mail: lsmith@gifts-and-tablewares.com
Web site: www.gifts-and-tablewares.com
Contact: Lori Smith, editor
Published 7 times a year

Glass Canada
145 Thames Road W., Exeter, ON N0M 1S3
Phone: (519) 235-2400 Fax: (519) 235-0798
E-mail: ais@aiscommunications.net
Contact: Peter Darbishire, managing editor
Published bimonthly

The Hill Times
69 Sparks Street, Ottawa, ON K1P 5A5
Phone: (613) 232-5952 Fax: (613) 232-9055
Contact: Kate Malloy, managing editor
Published weekly

Lighting Magazine
135 Spy Court, Markham, ON L3R 5H6
Phone: (905) 477-3222 Fax: (905) 477-4320
Published bimonthly

Luggage, Leathergoods & Accessories
96 Karma Road, Markham, ON L3R 4Y3
Phone: (905) 944-0265
E-mail: info@llanda.com
Contact: Vida Jurisic, editor
Published quarterly

Municipal World
42860 Sparta Line, Union, ON N0L 2L0
Phone: (519) 633-0031 Fax: (519) 633-1001
E-mail: mwadmin@municipalworld.com
Contact: Susan Gardner, executive editor
Published monthly

Optical Prism
250 The East Mall, Suite 1113, Toronto, ON M9B 6L3
Phone: (416) 699-4874 or 1-877-677-7476 Fax: (416) 233-1746
Contact: Craig Saunders, editor
Published 10 times a year

REM Canada's Magazine for Real Estate Professionals
115 Thorncliffe Park Drive, Toronto, ON M4H 1M1
Phone: (416) 425-3504 Fax: (416) 425-0040
Contact: Jim Adair, editor
Published monthly

Salon Magazine
555 Richmond Street W., Suite 701, Toronto, ON M5V 3B1
Phone: (416) 203-6737 or 1-800-720-6665 Fax: (416) 203-1057
E-mail: salon@beautynet.com
Contact: Jill Maynard, editor
Published 8 times a year

Spa Management
P.O. Box 365, Place d'Armes, Montreal, QC H2Y 3H1
Phone: (514) 274-0004 Fax: (514) 274-5004
Contact: Guy Jonkman, executive director
Published 10 times a year

Style
555 Richmond Street W., Suite 701, Toronto, ON M5V 3B1
Phone: (416) 203-6737 or 1-800-720-6665 Fax: (416) 203-1057
E-mail: style@style.ca
Contact: Jill Maynard, editor
Published monthly

Tour of Duty
180 Yorkland Boulevard, Toronto, ON M2J 1R5
Phone: (416) 491-4301 Fax: (416) 491-7421
E-mail: editor@tpassn.com
Contact: Elizabeth Alexander, editor
Published monthly

Toys & Games
61 Alness Road, Suite 224, Toronto, ON M3J 2H2
Phone: (416) 663-9229 Fax: (416) 663-2353
E-mail: toymag@idirect.com
Contact: Lynn Winston, editor
Published bimonthly

Woodworking
240 Edward Street, Aurora, ON L4G 3S9
Phone: (905) 727-0077 Fax: (905) 727-0017
Contact: Kerry Knudsen, editor
Published 7 times a year

Workplace News
240 Edward Street, Aurora, ON L4G 3S9
Phone: (905) 841-6481 Fax: (905) 841-5078
E-mail: lawtimes@clbmedia.ca
Contact: Gail Cohen, editor
Published monthly

Printing & Photography

Canadian Printer
1 Mount Pleasant Road, 7th Floor, Toronto, ON M4Y 2Y5
Phone: (416) 764-1530 Fax: (416) 764-1738
Contact: Doug Picklyk, editor
Published 8 times a year

Graphic Monthly
1606 Sedlescomb Drive, Unit 8, Mississauga, ON L4X 1M6
Phone: (905) 625-7070 Fax: (905) 625-4856
E-mail: ftamburri@graphicmonthly.ca
Contact: Filomena Tamburri, editor
Published bimonthly

Photonews & Electronic Imaging
101 Thorncliffe Park Drive, Toronto, ON M4H 1M2

Phone: (416) 421-7944 Fax: (416) 421-0966
E-mail: reception@bcsgroup.com
Contact: Gunter Ott, editor
Published twice a year

PrintAction
4580 Dufferin Street, Suite 404, Toronto, ON M3H 5Y2
Phone: (416) 665-7333 Fax: (416) 655-7226
Contact: John Robinson, editor
Published monthly

Second Impressions
35 Mill Drive, St. Albert, AB T8N 1J5
Phone: (780) 458-9889 Fax: (780) 458-9839
E-mail: secimp@telusplanet.net
Contact: Loretta Puckrin, publisher
Published bimonthly

Transportation & Cargo

Atlantic Transportation Journal
11 Thornhill Drive, Halifax, NS B3B 1R9
Phone: (902) 468-8027 Fax: (902) 468-2425
E-mail: atj@hfxnews.southam.ca
Contact: Lori McKay, managing editor
Published quarterly

Canadian Transportation & Logistics
1450 Don Mills Road, Toronto, ON M3B 2X7
Phone: (416) 442-2922 Fax: (416) 442-2214
E-mail: lsmyrlis@businessinformationgroup.ca
Contact: Lou Smyrlis, editor
Published 11 times a year

Harbour & Shipping
1865 Marine Drive, Suite 200, West Vancouver, BC V7V 1J7
Phone: (604) 922-6717 Fax: (604) 922-1739

E-mail: harbour&shipping@telus.net
Contact: Kirstin Hodge, editor
Published monthly

HighwayStar
130 Belfield Road, Toronto, ON M9W IGI
Phone: (416) 614-5825 Fax: (416) 614-8861
Contact: Rolf Lockwood, editor
Published monthly

Logistics Magazine
916 Ste-Adele, Suite 115, Sainte-Adele, QC J8B 2N2
Phone: (450) 229-7777 Fax: (450) 229-3233
E-mail: info@vlogistics-mag.com
Contact: Michel Trudeau, editor
Published bimonthly

Motor Truck
1450 Don Mills Road, Toronto, ON M3B 2X7
Phone: (416) 442-2922 Fax: (416) 442-2092
E-mail: lsmyrlis@businessinformationgroup.ca
Contact: Lou Smyrlis, editor
Published bimonthly

Over the Road
18 Park Glen Drive, Ottawa, ON K2G 3G9
Phone: (613) 224-9947 or 1-800-416-8712 Fax: (613) 224-8825
E-mail: otr@otr.on.ca
Contact: Peter Charboneau, publisher
Published monthly

Today's Trucking
130 Belfield Road, Toronto, ON M9W IGI
Phone: (416) 614-5826 Fax: (416) 614-8861
Contact: Stephen Petit, editor
Published 10 times a year

Truck News
1450 Don Mills Road, Toronto, ON M3B 2X7

Phone: (416) 442-2922 Fax: (416) 442-2213
E-mail: lsmyrlis@businessinformationgroup.ca
Contact: Lou Smyrlis, editor
Published monthly

Travel

Canadian Traveller
1260 Hornby Street, Suite 104, Vancouver, BC V6Z 1W2
Phone: (604) 669-9990 Fax: (604) 669-9993
E-mail: info@canadiantraveller.net
Contact: Rex Armstead, publisher/editor-in-chief
Published monthly

GSA: The Travel Magazine for Western Canada
1104 Hornby Street, Suite 200, Vancouver, BC V6Z 1V8
Phone: (604) 689-2909 Fax: (604) 689-2989
E-mail: editor@gsapublishing.com
Contact: Lynda Cumming, editor
Published 24 times a year

Meetings & Incentive Travel
1 Mount Pleasant Road, 7th Floor, Toronto, ON M4Y 2Y5
Phone: (416) 764-1640 Fax: (416) 764-1419
Contact: Janet White-Bardwell, editor
Published bimonthly

The Road Explorer
920 Yonge Street, 6th Floor, Toronto, ON M4W 3C7
Contact: Frank Robinson, publisher
Published 3 times a year

Special Events & Travel
77 Nipissing Crescent, 2nd Floor, Brampton, ON L6S 4Z8
Phone: (905) 451-4199 Fax: (905) 451-2938
E-mail: specialevents@rogers.com
Contact: Nancy Larin, editor
Published bimonthly

Travel Courier
310 Dupont Street, Toronto, ON M5R 1V9
Phone: (416) 968-7252 Fax: (416) 968-2377
E-mail: tc@baxter.net
Contact: Edith Baxter, editor-in-chief
Published weekly

Travel Press
310 Dupont Street, Toronto, ON M5R 1V9
Phone: (416) 968-7252 Fax: (416) 968-2377
E-mail: ctp@baxter.net
Contact: Edith Baxter, editor
Published weekly

Travelweek Bulletin
282 Richmond Street E., Suite 100, Toronto, ON M5A 1P4
Phone: 1-800-727-1429
Contact: Patrick Dineen, editor
Published weekly

4

DAILY NEWSPAPERS

There are almost a hundred English-language daily newspapers in Canada, making this a significant potential market for both experienced and less-seasoned freelance writers. Remember that many successful writing careers began in the pages of a local daily or small community newspaper.

Many of the larger city dailies pay as much as or more than the average consumer magazine for well-written, well-researched articles on important or intriguing subjects. And they settle faster: most pay at the end of the month, some even on acceptance.

Two keys to writing for newspapers are the accuracy of the story and delivering it on time. Because news loses its value as quickly as it changes, it is usually gathered hurriedly, on large and small papers, by staff reporters. Therefore, it is to your advantage to concentrate on background stories about ongoing issues or to write profiles of prominent, interesting, or unusual local citizens or institutions.

Editors look for feature articles with body and strength, as well as originality and freshness. Timing is important. Keep a calendar of dates for seasonal stories – Halloween, Thanksgiving, Christmas, Chinese New Year, Canada Day, and so on – and read behind the news for feature ideas.

The travel section of a paper typically buys the most freelance work, followed by the food section, but other categories where freelancers often contribute include hobbies, lifestyles, personal finance, business, and strong human-interest pieces, which are among the most popular in any newspaper. Most editors like to build up a resource of articles that do not have to be used immediately.

Your best preparation in tackling the newspaper market is to carefully read several issues of a specific paper. Note its editorial approach, style, story lengths, use of photographs, and the difference in content, construction, and tone between its news stories and feature articles. If you have never studied journalism, you might want to refer to *News Reporting and Writing*, by Melvin Mencher, a professor at Columbia University's School of Journalism (see Chapter ii, Resources).

You will, of course, need more experience to sell to large well-staffed metropolitan dailies such as the *Toronto Star* or the *Winnipeg Free Press*. But even here, the outside contributor has a chance, provided he or she has some specialized knowledge, can handle human-interest material deftly, and can write full-bodied issue stories with conviction and authority.

When approaching a newspaper, the freelancer should not use the same procedures as for magazines. Speed is a primary factor here. If you are planning to write about a breaking news event, it is permissible to telephone the editor for his or her okay. Even for less time-sensitive articles, a query letter would take too long. Instead, send the completed piece to the editor along with an SASE and a cover letter. In the letter convince the editor that he or she should buy your article, include a short outline of your experience (with tearsheets of your published work and copies of any of your letters that that paper may have published), and note the availability of photographs.

To stretch the earning potential of your newspaper article, it is acceptable to sell it to more than one paper at a time, as long as the publications serve completely different regions and one of the papers is not a national.

Don't forget to also target the magazine-style weekly supplements put out by most newspapers. Here general-interest stories usually prevail, and opportunities exist for the freelance writer. Your first approach to the editor of a supplement should either be via a query letter or else by sending in the completed article.

If you are just beginning your writing career and need to gain confidence and assemble a file of tearsheets, consider weekly community newspapers as a good starting point. With small staffs, low budgets, and no wire services to rely on, their editors are often happy to accept outside contributions, particularly feature articles that cover the local scene. And since payment is modest, there is little competition from more experienced writers. Phone the editors directly, since they have neither the time nor the resources to respond to written queries.

In addition to writing for your city paper, look for opportunities to act as a correspondent, or stringer, for one published elsewhere. The full listing of English-language Canadian daily newspapers that follows will prove useful. For suburban weeklies, check the *CARD* directory. Canadian newspapers are also listed in *Matthews Media Directory* and annual publications such as the *Canadian Almanac & Directory* and *Scott's Canadian Sourcebook* (see Chapter 11, Resources).

Alberta

The Calgary Herald
215 – 16th Street S.E., P.O. Box 2400, Stn. M, Calgary, AB
  T2P 0W8
Phone: (403) 235-7100 Fax: (403) 235-7379
E-mail: news@theherald.canwest.ca
Web site: www.canada.com/calgary

The Calgary Sun
2615 – 12th Street N.E., Calgary, AB T2E 7W9
Phone: (403) 250-4122 Fax: (403) 250-4180
E-mail: callet@calgarysun.com
Web site: www.calgarysun.com

Edmonton Journal
10006 – 101st Street, Edmonton, AB T5J 0S1
Phone: (780) 429-5100 Fax: (780) 429-5500
E-mail: city@thejournal.southam.ca
Web site: www.canada.com/edmonton/edmontonjournal

The Edmonton Sun

4990 – 92nd Avenue, Suite 250, Edmonton, AB T6B 3A1
Phone: (780) 468-0100 Fax: (780) 468-0139
E-mail: edm-citydesk@edm.sunpub.com
Web site: www.fyiedmonton.com

Fort McMurray Today

8550 Franklin Avenue, Bag 4008, Fort McMurray, AB T9H 3G1
Phone: (780) 743-8186 Fax: (780) 715-3820
E-mail: today@bowesnet.com
Web site: www.fortmcmurraytoday.com

Grande Prairie Daily Herald-Tribune

10604 – 100th Street, Bag 3000, Grande Prairie, AB T8V 6V4
Phone: (780) 532-1110 Fax: (780) 532-2120
E-mail: dht@bowesnet.com
Web site: www.dailyheraldtribune.com

The Lethbridge Herald

504 – 7th Street S., P.O. Box 670, Lethbridge, AB T1J 3Z7
Phone: (403) 328-4411 Fax: (403) 329-9355
E-mail: dmackinnon@lethbridgeherald.com
Web site: www.mysouthernalberta.com/leth

Medicine Hat News

3257 Dunmore Road S.E., P.O. Box 10, Medicine Hat, AB
  T1A 7E6
Phone: (403) 527-1101 Fax: (403) 527-1244
E-mail: mail@medicinehatnews.com
Web site: www.medicinehatnews.com

Red Deer Advocate

2950 Bremner Avenue, Bag 5200, Red Deer, AB T4N 5G3
Phone: (403) 343-2400 Fax: (403) 341-6560
E-mail: editorial@reddeeradvocate.com
Web site: www.reddeeradvocate.com

British Columbia

Alaska Highway News
9916 – 98th Street, Fort St. John, BC V1J 3T8
Phone: (250) 785-5631 Fax: (250) 785-3522
E-mail: ahnews@awink.com
Web site: www.canada.com/fortstjohn

Alberni Valley Times
4918 Napier Street, P.O. Box 400, Port Alberni, BC V9Y 7N1
Phone: (250) 723-8171 Fax: (250) 723-0586
E-mail: avtimes@shaw.ca

Daily Bulletin
335 Spokane Street, Kimberley, BC V1A 1Y9
Phone: (250) 427-5333 Fax: (250) 427-5336
E-mail: bulletin@cyberlink.bc.ca
Web site: www.dailytownsman.com/bulletin

Daily Courier
550 Doyle Avenue, Kelowna, BC V1Y 7V1
Phone: (250) 762-4445 Fax: (250) 762-3866
E-mail: john.harding@ok.bc.ca
Web site: www.kelownadailycourier.ca

The Daily News
393 Seymour Street, Kamloops, BC V2C 6P6
Phone: (250) 371-6149 Fax: (250) 374-3884
E-mail: kamloopsnews@telus.net
Web site: www.kamloopsdailynews.ca

The Daily News
801 – 2nd Avenue W., Prince Rupert, BC V8J 1H6
Phone: (250) 624-6781 Fax: (250) 624-2851
E-mail: prdnews@citytel.net

Daily Townsman
822 Cranbrook Street N., Cranbrook, BC V1C 3R9

Phone: (250) 426-5201   Fax: (250) 426-5003
E-mail: editorial@dailytownsman.com
Web site: www.dailytownsman.com

Nanaimo Daily News
2575 McCullough Road, Suite B-1, Nanaimo, BC V9S 5W5
Phone: (250) 729-4200   Fax: (250) 729-4288
E-mail: dnews@island.net
Web site: www.canada.com/nanaimo

Nelson Daily News
266 Baker Street, Nelson, BC V1L 4H3
Phone: (250) 352-3552   Fax: (250) 352-2418
E-mail: news@nelsondailynews.com
Web site: www.nelsondailynews.com

Peace River Block News
901 – 100th Avenue, Dawson Creek, BC V1G 1W2
Phone: (250) 782-4888   Fax: (250) 782-6770
E-mail: prbnews@pris.bc.ca
Web site: www.sterlingnews.com/peace

Penticton Herald
186 Nanaimo Avenue W., Suite 101, Penticton, BC V2A 1N4
Phone: (250) 492-4002   Fax: (250) 492-2403
E-mail: andre.martin@ok.bc.ca
Web site: www.pentictonherald.ca

Prince George Citizen
150 Brunswick Street, P.O. Box 5700, Prince George, BC V2L 5K9
Phone: (250) 562-2441   Fax: (250) 562-7453
E-mail: news@princegeorgecitizen.com
Web site: www.princegeorgecitizen.com

The Province
200 Granville Street, Suite 1, Vancouver, BC V6C 3N3
Phone: (604) 605-2222   Fax: (604) 605-2720
E-mail: tabtips@png.canwest.com
Web site: www.canada.com/vancouver

Times Colonist
2621 Douglas Street, P.O. Box 300, Victoria, BC V8T 4M2
Phone: (250) 380-5211 Fax: (250) 380-5353
E-mail: edit@times-colonist.com
Web site: www.canada.com/victoria/timescolonist

Trail Daily Times
1163 Cedar Avenue, Trail, BC V1R 4B8
Phone: (250) 364-1242 Fax: (250) 368-8550
E-mail: editor@trailtimes.ca
Web site: www.canada.com/trail

The Vancouver Sun
200 Granville Street, Suite 1, Vancouver, BC V6C 3N3
Phone: (604) 605-2000 Fax: (604) 605-2720
E-mail: sunfile@png.canwest.com
Web site: www.canada.com/vancouver

Manitoba

The Brandon Sun
501 Rosser Avenue, Brandon, MB R7A 0K4
Phone: (204) 727-2451 Fax: (204) 727-0385
E-mail: opinion@brandonsun.com
Web site: www.brandonsun.com

The Daily Graphic
1941 Saskatchewan Avenue W., P.O. Box 130, Portage La Prairie,
   MB R1N 3B4
Phone: (204) 857-3427 Fax: (204) 239-1270
E-mail: news.dailygraphic@shawcable.com
Web site: www.bowesnet.com/dailygraphic

The Reminder
10 North Avenue, Flin Flon, MB R8A 0T2
Phone: (204) 687-3454 Fax: (204) 687-4473
E-mail: reminder@mb.sympatico.ca

Winnipeg Free Press
1355 Mountain Avenue, Winnipeg, MB R2X 3B6
Phone: (204) 697-7000 Fax: (204) 697-7412
E-mail: margo.goodhand@freepress.mb.ca
Web site: www.winnipegfreepress.com

The Winnipeg Sun
1700 Church Avenue, Winnipeg, MB R2X 3A2
Phone: (204) 694-2022 Fax: (204) 697-0759
E-mail: citydesk@wpgsun.com
Web site: www.fyiwinnipeg.com/winsun.html

New Brunswick

The Daily Gleaner
P.O. Box 3370, Fredericton, NB E3B 2T8
Phone: (506) 452-6671 Fax: (506) 452-7405
E-mail: dgnews@nbnet.nb.ca
Web site: www.canadaeast.com

The Saint John Telegraph-Journal
P.O. Box 2350, Saint John, NB E2L 3V8
Phone: (506) 632-8888 Fax: (506) 633-6758
E-mail: newsroom@nbpub.com
Web site: www.canadaeast.com

The Times & Transcript
P.O. Box 1001, Moncton, NB E1C 8P3
Phone: (506) 859-4900 Fax: (506) 859-4904
E-mail: news@timestranscript.com
Web site: www.canadaeast.com

Newfoundland & Labrador

The Telegram
1 Columbus Drive, P.O. Box 5970, St. John's, NL A1C 5X7
Phone: (709) 364-6300 Fax: (709) 364-9333

E-mail: telegram@thetelegram.com
Web site: www.thetelegram.com

The Western Star
106 West Street, P.O. Box 460, Corner Brook, NL A2H 6E7
Phone: (709) 634-4348 Fax: (709) 637-4675
E-mail: newsroom@thewesternstar.com
Web site: www.canada.com/cornerbrook

Nova Scotia

Cape Breton Post
255 George Street, P.O. Box 1500, Sydney, NS B1P 6K6
Phone: (902) 564-5451 Fax: (902) 562-7077
E-mail: news@cbpost.com
Web site: www.capebretonpost.com

Daily News
10 Lawrence Street, Amherst, NS B4H 3Z2
Phone: (902) 667-5102 Fax: (902) 667-0419
E-mail: editdept@cumberlandpublishing.com
Web site: www.cumberlandpublishing.com

The Daily News
P.O. Box 8330, Stn. A, Halifax, NS B3K 5M1
Phone: (902) 468-1222 Fax: (902) 468-2645
E-mail: citydesk@hfxnews.ca
Web site: www.canada.com/halifax/dailynews

The Evening News
352 East River Road, P.O. Box 159, New Glasgow, NS B2H 5E2
Phone: (902) 752-3000 Fax: (902) 752-1945
E-mail: news@newglasgownews.com
Web site: www.newglasgownews.com

The Mail-Star/Chronicle-Herald/Sunday Herald
1650 Argyle Street, P.O. Box 610, Halifax, NS B3J 2T2
Phone: (902) 426-1187 Fax: (902) 426-1158

E-mail: newsroom@herald.ns.ca
Web site: www.halifaxherald.com

Truro Daily News
6 Louise Street, Truro, NS B4H 3Z2
Phone: (902) 893-9405 Fax: (902) 893-0518
E-mail: news@trurodaily.com
Web site: www.canada.com/truro

Ontario

The Beacon Herald
16 Packham Road, P.O. Box 430, Stratford, ON N5A 6T6
Phone: (519) 271-2220 Fax: (519) 271-1026
E-mail: beaconherald@bowesnet.com
Web site: www.stratfordbeaconherald.com

The Burlington News
44 Frid Street, P.O. Box 300, Hamilton, ON L8N 3G3
Phone: (905) 526-3333 Fax: (905) 526-4657
E-mail: letters@thespec.com
Web site: www.hamiltonspectator.com

Chatham Daily News
45 – 4th Street, P.O. Box 2007, Chatham, ON N7M 5M6
Phone: (519) 354-2000 Fax: (519) 354-9489
E-mail: news@chathamdailynews.ca
Web site: www.chathamdailynews.ca

Chronicle-Journal
75 South Cumberland Street, Thunder Bay, ON P7B 1A3
Phone: (807) 343-6215 Fax: (807) 343-9409
Web site: www.chroniclejournal.com

The Daily Bulletin
116 First Street E., P.O. Box 339, Fort Frances, ON P9A 3M7
Phone: (807) 274-5373 Fax: (807) 274-7286

E-mail: news@fortfrancesonline.com
Web site: www.fftimes.com

The Daily Miner and News

33 Main Street S., P.O. Box 1620, Kenora, ON P9N 3X7
Phone: (807) 468-5555 Fax: (807) 468-4318
E-mail: minerandnews@norcomcable.ca
Web site: www.kenoradailyminerandnews.com

The Daily Observer

186 Alexander Street, Pembroke, ON K8A 4L9
Phone: (613) 732-3373 Fax: (613) 732-2226
E-mail: editor@thedailyobserver.ca
Web site: www.thedailyobserver.ca

The Daily Press

187 Cedar Street S., Timmins, ON P4N 7G1
Phone: (705) 268-5050 Fax: (705) 268-7373
E-mail: tdpnews@vianet.ca
Web site: www.timminspress.com

Daily Star

99 King Street W., P.O. Box 400, Cobourg, ON K9A 4L1
Phone: (905) 372-0131 Fax: (905) 372-4966
E-mail: editorial@northumberlandtoday.com
Web site: www.northumberlandtoday.com

The Examiner

16 Bayfield Street N., Barrie, ON L4M 4Z9
Phone: (705) 726-6537 Fax: (705) 726-5414
E-mail: news@thebarrieexaminer.com
Web site: www.thebarrieexaminer.com

The Examiner

730 The Kingsway, P.O. Box 3890, Peterborough, ON K9J 8L4
Phone: (705) 745-4641 Fax: (705) 743-4581
E-mail: news1@ptbo.igs.net
Web site: www.thepeterboroughexaminer.com

The Expositor
53 Dalhousie Street, P.O. Box 965, Brantford, ON N3T 5S8
Phone: (519) 756-2020   Fax: (519) 756-9470
E-mail: expnews@brt.southam.ca
Web site: www.brantfordexpositor.ca

The Globe and Mail
444 Front Street W., Toronto, ON M5V 2S9
Phone: (416) 585-5000   Fax: (416) 585-5085
E-mail: newsroom@globeandmail.com
Web site: www.globeandmail.com

The Guelph Mercury
14 Macdonell Street, Suite 8, P.O. Box 3604, Guelph, ON N1H 6P7
Phone: (519) 822-4310   Fax: (519) 767-1681
E-mail: editor@guelphmercury.com
Web site: www.guelphmercury.com

The Intelligencer
45 Bridge Street E., P.O. Box 5600, Belleville, ON K8N 5C7
Phone: (613) 962-9171   Fax: (613) 962-9652
E-mail: newsroom@intelligencer.ca
Web site: www.intelligencer.ca

Kingston Whig-Standard
6 Cataraqui Street, P.O. Box 2300, Kingston, ON K7L 4Z7
Phone: (613) 544-5000   Fax: (613) 530-4118
E-mail: kinwhig@thewhig.com
Web site: www.thewhig.com

Lindsay Daily Post
15 William Street N., Lindsay, ON K9V 3Z8
Phone: (705) 324-2113   Fax: (705) 324-0174
E-mail: lineditorial@thepost.ca
Web site: www.thepost.ca

The London Free Press
369 York Street, P.O. Box 2280, London, ON N6A 4G1
Phone: (519) 667-5451   Fax: (519) 667-4528

E-mail: newsdesk.lfpress.com
Web site: www.fyilondon.com/londonfreepress

National Post
1450 Don Mills Road, Suite 300, Don Mills, ON M3B 3R5
Phone: (416) 383-2300 Fax: (416) 442-2209
E-mail: queries@nationalpost.com
Web site: www.nationalpost.com

The Niagara Falls Review
4801 Valley Way, P.O. Box 270, Niagara Falls, ON L2E 6T6
Phone: (905) 358-5711 Fax: (905) 374-0461
E-mail: reporter@nfreview.com
Web site: www.niagarafallsreview.ca

Northern Daily News
8 Duncan Avenue, P.O. Box 1030, Kirkland Lake, ON P2N 3L4
Phone: (705) 567-5321 Fax: (705) 567-6162
E-mail: news@northernnews.ca
Web site: www.northernnews.ca

The Nugget
259 Worthington Street W., P.O. Box 570, North Bay, ON P1B 3B5
Phone: (705) 472-3200 Fax: (705) 472-1438
E-mail: news@nugget.ca
Web site: www.nugget.ca

Observer
140 South Front Street, P.O. Box 3009, Sarnia, ON N7T 7M8
Phone: (519) 344-2112 Fax: (519) 344-8301
E-mail: editorial.observer-sarnia.com
Web site: www.observer-sarnia.com

The Ottawa Citizen
1101 Baxter Road, P.O. Box 5020, Ottawa, ON K2C 3M4
Phone: (613) 829-9100 Fax: (613) 726-1198
E-mail: letters@thecitizen.southam.ca
Web site: www.canada.com/ottawa/ottawacitizen

The Ottawa Sun
380 Hunt Club Road, P.O. Box 9729, Stn. T, Ottawa, ON K1G 5H7
Phone: (613) 739-7000 Fax: (613) 739-8041
E-mail: ottawa.citydesk@ott.sunpub.com
Web site: www.fyiottawa.com

The Packet & Times
31 Colborne Street E., P.O. Box 220, Orillia, ON L3V 1T4
Phone: (705) 325-1355 Fax: (705) 325-4033
E-mail: news@orilliapacket.com
Web site: www.orilliapacket.com

Port Hope Evening Guide
73 Mill Street S., P.O. Box 296, Port Hope, ON L1A 2S8
Phone: (905) 885-2471 Fax: (905) 885-7442
E-mail: phenews@northumberlandtoday.com
Web site: www.northumberlandtoday.com

The Record
225 Fairway Road S., P.O. Box 938, Kitchener, ON N2G 4E5
Phone: (519) 894-2231 Fax: (519) 894-3912
E-mail: newsroom@therecord.com
Web site: www.therecord.com

The Recorder & Times
1600 California Avenue, Brockville, ON K6V 5T8
Phone: (613) 342-4441 Fax: (613) 342-4456
E-mail: editor@recorder.ca
Web site: www.recorder.ca

St. Thomas Times-Journal
16 Hincks Street, St. Thomas, ON N5R 5Z2
Phone: (519) 631-2790 Fax: (519) 631-5653
E-mail: news@stthomastimesjournal.com
Web site: www.stthomastimesjournal.com

Sault Star
145 Old Garden River Road, P.O. Box 460, Sault Ste. Marie, ON
   P6A 5M5

Phone: (705) 759-3030 Fax: (705) 942-8690
E-mail: ssmstar@saultstar.com
Web site: www.saultstar.com

Simcoe Reformer
105 Donly Drive S., P.O. Box 370, Simcoe, ON N3Y 4L2
Phone: (519) 426-5710 Fax: (519) 426-9255
E-mail: refedit@annexweb.com
Web site: www.annexweb.com/reformernet

The Spectator
44 Frid Street, P.O. Box 300, Hamilton, ON L8N 3G3
Phone: (905) 526-3333 Fax: (905) 526-0147
E-mail: letters@thespec.com
Web site: www.hamiltonspectator.com

The Standard
17 Queen Street, St. Catharines, ON L2R 5G5
Phone: (905) 684-7251 Fax: (905) 684-6032
E-mail: standard@scs.southam.ca
Web site: www.stcatharinesstandard.ca

Standard-Freeholder
44 Pitt Street, Cornwall, ON K6J 3P3
Phone: (613) 933-3160 Fax: (613) 933-3664
E-mail: maned@standard-freeholder.com
Web site: www.standard-freeholder.com

The Sudbury Star
33 MacKenzie Street, Sudbury, ON P3C 4Y1
Phone: (705) 674-5271 Fax: (705) 674-0624
E-mail: editorial@thesudburystar.com
Web site: www.thesudburystar.com

The Sun Times
290 – 9th Street E., P.O. Box 200, Owen Sound, ON N4K 5P2
Phone: (519) 376-2250 Fax: (519) 376-7190
E-mail: news@owensoundsuntimes.com
Web site: www.owensoundsuntimes.com

Toronto Metro
1 Concorde Gate, Suite 300, Toronto, ON M3C 3N6
Phone: (416) 486-4900 Fax: (416) 489-2068
E-mail: newsdesk@metronews.ca
Web site: www.metropoint.com

The Toronto Star
1 Yonge Street, Toronto, ON M5E 1E6
Phone: (416) 367-2000 Fax: (416) 869-4328
E-mail: editorial@thestar.ca
Web site: www.thestar.com

The Toronto Sun
333 King Street E., Toronto, ON M5A 3X5
Phone: (416) 947-2222 Fax: (416) 947-1664
E-mail: tor_news@tor.sunpub.com
Web site: www.torontosun.com

Toronto 24 Hours (weekdays)
333 King Street E., Toronto, ON M5A 3X5
Phone: (416) 350-6400 Fax: (416) 350-6524
E-mail: 24news@tor.sunpub.com

The Tribune
228 East Main Street, P.O. Box 278, Welland, ON L3B 5P5
Phone: (905) 732-2411 Fax: (905) 732-4883
E-mail: tribune@iaw.on.ca
Web site: www.wellandtribune.ca

The Windsor Star
167 Ferry Street, Windsor, ON N9A 4M5
Phone: (519) 255-5711 Fax: (519) 255-5515
E-mail: letters@thestar.canwest.com
Web site: www.canada.com/windsor

Woodstock Sentinel-Review
16 Brock Street, P.O. Box 1000, Woodstock, ON N4S 8A5
Phone: (519) 537-2341 Fax: (519) 537-8542

E-mail: sentinel@annexweb.com
Web site: www.annexweb.com/sentinel

Prince Edward Island

The Guardian
165 Prince Street, P.O. Box 760, Charlottetown, PE C1A 7L8
Phone: (902) 629-6000 Fax: (902) 566-3808
E-mail: newsroom@theguardian.pe.ca
Web site: www.theguardian.pe.ca

Journal-Pioneer
4 Queen Street, P.O. Box 2480, Summerside, PE C1N 4K5
Phone: (902) 436-2125 Fax: (902) 436-3027
E-mail: info@journalpioneer.com
Web site: www.journalpioneer.com

Quebec

The Gazette
250 St. Antoine Street W., Montreal, QC H2Y 3R7
Phone: (514) 987-2222 Fax: (514) 987-2399
E-mail: letters@thegazette.canwest.com
Web site: www.montrealgazette.com

The Record
1195 Galt Street E., Sherbrooke, QC J1G 1Y7
Phone: (819) 569-6345 Fax: (819) 569-3945
E-mail: newsroom@sherbrookerecord.com
Web site: www.sherbrookerecord.com

Saskatchewan

The Daily Herald
30 – 10th Street E., P.O. Box 550, Prince Albert, SK S6V 0Y5
Phone: (306) 764-4276 Fax: (306) 763-3331

E-mail: editorial@paherald.sk.ca
Web site: www.paherald.sk.ca

The Leader-Post
1964 Park Street, P.O. Box 2020, Regina, SK S4P 3G4
Phone: (306) 565-8211 Fax: (306) 565-8812
E-mail: editorial@leaderpost.com
Web site: www.canada.com/regina/leaderpost

The StarPhoenix
204 – 5th Avenue N., Saskatoon, SK S7K 2P1
Phone: (306) 652-9200 Fax: (306) 664-0433
E-mail: spnews@thesp.com
Web site: www.canada.com/saskatoon/starphoenix

Times-Herald
44 Fairford Street W., P.O. Box 3000, Moose Jaw, SK S6H 1V1
Phone: (306) 692-6441 Fax: (306) 692-2101
E-mail: editorial@mjtimes.sk.ca
Web site: www.mjtimes.sk.ca

Yukon

The Whitehorse Star
2149 – 2nd Avenue, Whitehorse, YT Y1A 1C5
Phone: (867) 667-2013 Fax: (867) 668-7130
E-mail: star@whitehorsestar.com
Web site: www.whitehorsestar.com

5

BOOK PUBLISHERS

The first-time author should be under no illusions about the difficulties of breaking into book publishing – still less, of making a living from the often-slender proceeds, unless you are phenomenally talented or hit on that rare winning formula. Nonetheless, every year brings a new success story – another brilliant unknown author who takes the publishing world by storm. Every writer must be a realist, and an optimist.

Small presses are more likely to take an interest in an unpublished writer, and are generally more receptive to unsolicited manuscripts. They also may be more accessible, offer more personal attention to their authors, and be more willing to take a risk. Nino Ricci's prize-winning first novel, *Lives of the Saints*, was published by Cormorant Books, having been rejected by a raft of the larger players. But he had no difficulty placing his eagerly awaited second novel with McClelland & Stewart. Small presses almost always work with unagented writers. On the down side, small publishers offer small advances or none at all, their print runs tend to be low, and their distribution systems and marketing expertise cannot match those of the big houses.

Before you make any approaches to publishers, do some research. Use the following list to whittle down a selection of houses whose programs seem most compatible with your own work, then check out some of their books. Another approach is to browse through a bookstore compiling a list of publishers who are releasing books similar to yours. You can write to their publicity departments, including a large SASE, to request current catalogues, and visit their web sites to learn more about their publishing programs. Familiarity with the focus of several houses can help you develop an attractive proposal, as well as target the most appropriate potential publishers.

It is important to note the difference in selling fiction and non-fiction manuscripts to book publishers. Typically a manuscript of fiction must be fully finished before you approach an editor. For non-fiction, you must have done considerable research on your topic, but usually you are required to produce only a synopsis of your story, a chapter outline, and two or three sample chapters. Remember that whether your manuscript is fiction or non-fiction, it is imperative that it begin with a strong, attention-grabbing start. If you don't capture an editor's interest in the first few minutes, he or she is likely to set aside your work and move on to the next manuscript in the pile.

The Query Letter

If you are aiming to sell your manuscript directly to a book publisher without the benefit of a literary agent, your first approach should be through a query letter. This initial correspondence is extremely important. A poorly composed letter can nix your chances of getting published before an editor has even looked at your manuscript. A compelling query letter may get your manuscript onto someone's desk for a first read.

Your letter should be typed in a plain, readable font on unadorned, business-like stationery. Include your name, address, telephone and fax numbers, and your e-mail address. Refer to the editor (or other contact person) by name, and address him or her as Mr. or Ms.

In a letter of no more than two pages, plus enclosures, you must convince a publishing house to at least consider investing considerable money and effort in your manuscript. Spend time to craft it in your best writing style and seize the editor's attention with a gripping intro. Remember, an editor doesn't yet have your manuscript to read; his or her judgement will be based largely upon the strength of your query.

Tell the editor the working title of your book and describe what it is about; if it is fiction, outline the characters and provide a short plot synopsis. Next, mention any special qualifications you have to write this manuscript. These might include a background in the subject covered or special access to research sources. Indicate your publishing history, who published your previous books, how many copies were sold, and if any foreign rights were bought.

Tell the editor what competing books on a similar subject are in the marketplace, and confidently assert why yours will do equally well or be more successful. Also describe what makes your manuscript different from all the others; after all, publishers want something original. Inform the editor about any research you have done to determine the markets for your book and ideas you may have for promotion.

For non-fiction queries, include a one-page synopsis of your manuscript if it could not be adequately described in your letter. Also enclose a table of contents with a brief description of what each chapter is about and an indication of the research you will undertake in writing this book. You may send one or two sample chapters or wait for a request by the editor. For a fiction query, send along a one-page synopsis and three sample chapters (including the first chapter).

If you haven't received a reply after two months, you may wish to send the editor a note attached to a copy of your original query letter. But if after three months you still haven't heard, move on to another publisher. Due to long delays, which are typical in book publishing, it is permissible to send out multiple queries.

Sending the Manuscript

If you have received a positive reply from a query letter, or if you have targeted a publisher that will accept full manuscripts without an initial query, there is a certain protocol to follow when submitting your work.

Manuscripts should be prepared as indicated in the Introduction; that is, on 8-by-11-inch bond paper, typed on a computer in a readable font and double-spaced. Of course, you should never send the only copy of your work. Manuscripts should not be stapled, but fastened with elastic bands and held between two sheets of cardboard, front and back, or better still, placed in a box.

A covering letter should accompany your work. If this is an unsolicited manuscript, include a letter similar to the query letter (above), one that sells both you and your book to the prospective publisher. When an editor has asked to see your manuscript in response to a query, enclose a covering letter reminding him or her of your previous correspondence.

It may take three months or longer for a publisher to reply to your submission, so it is advisable to include a self-addressed stamped postcard so they can acknowledge its receipt. Be sure to also send a postage-paid envelope large enough for your manuscript so an editor can return your work if it is not accepted, otherwise you may not receive it back.

While it is perfectly permissible to send out multiple submissions, there is a general protocol that you should follow. Indicate in your covering letter that you have sent the manuscript to other publishers; you do not need to specify which publishers these are. Also state a deadline for their decision – three months is standard – before which time you must not sign a contract from one publisher without allowing the others to make counter-offers.

Contracts

Receiving a contract from a book publisher is a dream come true. While your tendency may be to sign anything that will bring your manuscript into book form, it is a very important legal document, and you must proceed with caution.

First of all, you need to seek the advice of a professional who will explain the rights, obligations, and rewards being offered by such a document. You must understand the rights you are selling and agree that the compensation is fair, or negotiate to try to improve it. You should never sign away the copyright to your work.

Royalty rates vary, but average around 10 per cent for hardcover books and in the 8-per-cent range for paperbacks. Sometimes a sliding scale is offered whereby you receive a higher rate if your book sells more than a certain number of copies. For regular sales of your book (which doesn't include book-club sales or discount sales), you should receive the royalty as a percentage of the list price of the book, not the publisher's net.

An advance is a payment against the royalties your publisher expects the book will earn. It is typically paid in either two or three installments: when the contract is signed, when the manuscript is accepted, and sometimes when the book is published. While some small presses are unable to offer their authors advances, in the industry overall advances are rising, due to the increasing aggressiveness of Canadian publishers and agents, as well as international recognition of Canadian fiction. It is rare for a first-time novelist to receive over $15,000 as an advance; for business books, an average advance would range from $5,000 to $10,000.

As print-on-demand systems and e-books gain in popularity, new contractual issues arise. When a book is out of print for a certain period of time, the rights revert to the author. But now in the United States, those rights may not revert if the book exists in electronic form. In addition, if a book appears in an electronic medium, the writer has to ensure that he or she will receive adequate compensation.

For advice on publishing contracts, contact a lawyer who specializes in the publishing field, an experienced literary agent, or the Writers' Union of Canada.

Before outlining what we cover in the rest of this chapter, perhaps it's worth clarifying what we don't. Educational publishers are not listed unless they have a significant trade-publishing arm. Today more than ever, educational publishers are commissioning their books in close collaboration with schools and colleges to meet specific curricular needs. These texts are nearly always written by specialists in the field. Very few educational publishers consider unsolicited manuscripts or proposals, and fewer still are likely to look favourably upon them unless their author has a proven track record in the area. Neither, with a few exceptions, have we included publishers that specialize in poetry. For a comprehensive listing, consult *Poetry Markets for Canadians* (7th edition), published by the League of Canadian Poets, or *Poet's Market*, an annual publication by Writer's Digest Books.

The following list of publishers comprises English-language publishing houses only. It includes the major companies, as well as most of the mid-range and many of the smaller trade publishers currently operating in Canada. Some have large general-interest lists; others are more specialized, either in their subject areas or in their regional concerns.

Aardvark Enterprises

204 Millbank Drive S.W., Calgary, AB T2Y 2H9
Phone: (403) 256-4639
Contact: J. Alvin Speers, publisher/editor

Established 1962; active publishing began 1978. Produces at least 4 books per year (83 titles in catalogue, which is free on request). Publishes several how-to books helpful to writers. No unsolicited manuscripts. Accepts written inquiries. Author guidelines available on request. "As in any field of endeavour, there are 3 kinds of writers: those who make things happen, those who watch things happen, and some who wonder what happened."

Notable 2003 title: *Second 1,000 Poems*, J. Alvin Speers.

Abbeyfield Publishers

1 Benvenuto Place, Suite 103, Toronto, ON M3V 2L1
Phone: (416) 925-6458 Fax: (416) 925-4165
E-mail: abbeyfld@istar.ca
Web site: www.abbeyfieldpublishers.com
Contact: Bill Belfontaine, publisher

Publishes non-fiction, biographies, memoirs, books about the holocaust, corporate books, books on social issues, and custom books. No fiction, children's books, or art books. Produces 5 new titles a year. No unsolicited manuscripts. Inquire by telephone first. Author guidelines available.

Notable 2003 title: *Gabriel's Dragon*, Fr. Anthony Gabriel.

ABC Publishing

Anglican Book Centre, 80 Hayden Street, Toronto, ON M4Y 3G2
Phone: (416) 924-9192 Fax: (416) 968-7983
E-mail: abcpublishing@national.anglican.ca
Web site: www.abcpublishing.com
Contact: Robert Maclennan, publishing manager

Publishes books by Canadian authors on practical spirituality for everyday living and on church liturgy, ministry, mission, and education. Produced 15 new titles in 2003. No unsolicited manuscripts. Accepts inquiries. Author guidelines available.

Notable 2003 title: *Oceans of Grief and Healing Waters*, Marian Jean Haggerty.

Acorn Press

P.O. Box 22024, Charlottetown, PE C1A 1Y1
Phone: (902) 892-8151 or (902) 566-0956 Fax: (902) 566-0756
E-mail: brinklow@upei.ca
Web site: www.acornpresscanada.com
Contact: Laurie Brinklow, publisher

Publishes books about Prince Edward Island by Prince Edward Islanders. Releases about 4 new titles a year. Accepts unsolicited manuscripts about P.E.I. only, but send inquiry first. Guidelines available.

Notable 2003 title: *The Betrayer*, Michael Hennessey.

Thomas Allen Publishers

145 Front Street E., Suite 209, Toronto, ON M5A 1E3
Phone: (416) 361-0233 Fax: (416) 203-2773
E-mail: tap@tallen.com
Web site: www.thomas-allen.com
Contact: Patrick Crean, publisher

Publishes literary fiction and non-fiction. Non-fiction categories include history, memoirs, travel, nature, religion, and popular culture. No cookbooks, genre fiction, DIY, or financial books. Produces 15 new titles annually. Accepts unsolicited manuscripts, but send an inquiry first. "Do not send your entire manuscript if we haven't asked for it. Materials returned only with SASE with adequate postage. Familiarize yourself with our list before submitting your proposal." Author guidelines available.

Notable 2003 title: *Sitting Practice*, Caroline Anderson.

Annick Press

15 Patricia Avenue, Willowdale, ON M2M 1H9
Phone: (416) 221-4802 Fax: (416) 221-8400
E-mail: annick@annickpress.com
Web site: www.annickpress.com
Contact: Sandra Booth, assistant editor

Established 1975. Publishes children's literature, including picture books, teen and middle-reader fiction, and non-fiction. "We seek out works that crackle with originality and become a passage-way to new ideas. Our list is designed to excite, entertain, and promote self-awareness." Releases 28 new titles annually. Accepts unsolicited manuscripts, but first send an outline. "Please see our web site for full submission details."

Notable 2003 title: *Made You Look: How Advertising Works and Why You Should Know*, Sheri Graydon.

Anvil Press

P.O. Box 3008, MPO, Vancouver, BC V6B 3X5
Phone: (604) 876-8710 Fax: (604) 879-2667
E-mail: subter@portal.ca
Web site: www.anvilpress.com
Contact: Brian Kaufman, publisher

An independent literary press interested in work from new and established writers. Publishes contemporary work in all genres. Releases 8 to 10 books a year. Accepts unsolicited manuscripts. Send synopsis with sample chapter or two. Expect a wait of 4 to 6 months for reply. Send a #10 SASE for reply without manuscript. "Get our guidelines online, look at our books and catalogue to get a sense of the press, and submit if you feel your work is in line with our program."

Apple Press Publishing

810 Landresse Court, Newmarket, ON L3X 1M6
Phone: (905) 853-7979 Fax: (905) 853-1175
E-mail: info@applepressbooks.com
Contact: Deborah Sherman, editor

Publishes social studies workbooks/activity books for students across Canada, grades 1 to 8, and map skills books for the educa-tional market. "We do not publish poetry or other kinds of children's books." Releases 2 to 4 new titles annually. Accepts unsolicited man-uscripts, but first send an outline. Author guidelines available.

Notable 2003 title: *Map Book 4*, George Quinn.

Arbeiter Ring Publishing

121 Osborne Street, Suite 201E, Winnipeg, MB R3L 1Y4

Phone: (204) 942-7058 Fax: (204) 944-9198
E-mail: info@arbeiterring.com
Web site: www.arteiterring.com
Contact: Carolynn Smallwood, administration

Publishes a combination of serious cultural work and non-fiction titles with an emphasis on progressive political analysis of social and cultural issues. Releases 3 or 4 titles a year. Accepts unsolicited manuscripts, but send an inquiry first. "Consult our web site to determine if your manuscript accords with our house publishing agenda."

Notable 2003 title: *"As Many Liars": The Story of the 1995 Manitoba Vote-Splitting Scandal*, Doug Smith.

Arsenal Pulp Press
1014 Homer Street, Suite 103, Vancouver, BC V6B 2W9
Phone: (604) 687-4233 Fax: (604) 687-4283
E-mail: contact@arsenalpulp.com
Web site: www.arsenalpulp.com
Contact: Brian Lam, publisher

Established 1971. Independent publisher specializing in literary fiction, pop culture, multicultural literature, gay and lesbian literature, cookbooks, guidebooks, and visual arts. Releases 14 to 18 titles a year. Accepts unsolicited manuscripts, but send an inquiry or sample chapters first. Will not respond without an SASE. Does not accept submissions by fax or e-mail. Guidelines available on web site.

Notable 2003 title: *I, Shithead: A Life in Punk*, Joey Keithley.

Art Gallery of Greater Victoria
1040 Moss Street, Victoria, BC V8V 4P1
Phone: (250) 384-4171 Fax: (250) 361-3995
E-mail: aggv@aggv.bc.ca
Web site: www.aggv.bc.ca
Contacts: Barry Hill, curator, Asian art; Lisa Baldissera, curator,
    contemporary art

Publications are produced in conjunction with gallery exhibitions to illustrate and describe the thesis of the exhibition. Released 4 titles in 2003. Does not accept unsolicited manuscripts.

Notable 2003 title: *Ceramics of Asia*, Barry Hill.

Banff Centre Press

P.O. Box 1020, 107 Tunnel Mountain Drive, Banff, AB TIL 1H5
Phone: (403) 762-7532 Fax: (403) 762-6699
E-mail: press@banffcentre.ca
Web site: www.banffcentre.ca/press
Contact: Jennifer Nault, managing editor

The Banff Centre Press specializes in publications on contemporary art, culture, and literature. It seeks to explore, disseminate, and garner support for the arts. Releases 4 to 6 new titles annually. Does not accept unsolicited manuscripts; send an inquiry first. Guidelines available.

Notable 2003 title: *Mary of Canada: The Virgin Mary in Canadian Culture, Spirituality, History, and Geography*, Joan Skogan.

The Battered Silicon Dispatch Box

P.O. Box 204, Shelburne, ON L0N 1S0
Fax: (519) 925-3482
E-mail: gav@bmts.com
Contact: George A. Vanderburgh, publisher

A small press specializing in detective fiction from the golden age. "A Sherlockian publisher of first and last resort." Does not accept unsolicited manuscripts; send an inquiry first.

Beach Holme Publishing

409 Granville Street, Suite 1010, Vancouver, BC V6C 1T2
Phone: (604) 733-4868 Fax: (604) 733-4860
E-mail: bhp@beachholme.bc.ca
Web site: www.beachholme.bc.ca
Contact: Michael Carroll, publisher

Formerly Press Porcépic, established 1971. Exclusively a literary fiction, non-fiction, and poetry house. Historical and contemporary young adult fiction with teacher's guides as well as black-and-white illustrated juvenile fiction under the Sandcastle imprint; literary fiction and poetry under the Porcépic imprint; and creative non-fiction under the Prospect Books imprint. Publishes 10 to 14 titles a year. Accepts unsolicited manuscripts, but first send an inquiry with the first three chapters. Send manuscript with an SASE and correct postage. No multiple submissions.

Response time up to 6 months. Canadian citizens only. Guidelines available on web site.

Notable 2003 title: *Kameleon Man*, Kim Barry Brunhuber.

Between the Lines
720 Bathurst Street, Suite 404, Toronto, ON M5S 2R4
Phone: (416) 535-9914 Fax: (416) 535-1484
E-mail: btlbooks@web.ca
Web site: www.btlbooks.com
Contact: Paul Eprile, editorial co-ordinator
Established 1977. Publishes critical, accessible non-fiction, primarily on Canadian history, economics, culture, and social issues. Produced 10 new titles in 2003. Accepts unsolicited manuscripts, but prefers to receive an inquiry first with an outline.

Notable 2003 titles: *Booze: A Distilled History*, Craig Heron; *User Error: Resisting Computer Culture*, Ellen Rose.

Big Splash Books
5549 Merkel Place, Halifax, NS B3K 2H7
Phone: (902) 454-0134 Fax: (902) 654-2353
E-mail: quoddy@ns.sympatico.ca or info@bigsplashbooks.com
Web site: www.bigsplashbooks.com
Contact: Karin Cope, managing editor
A new national press with a mandate to publish fiction of a national and international scope, can-do books of environmental interest (a series called Building on Kyoto), and books that explore the relationship between health and the creative arts. Will publish 4 or 5 new titles in 2004. Accepts unsolicited manuscripts, but prefers to receive an inquiry first with return postage. Author guidelines available.

Notable 2003 titles: *The Killing Ear*, Marike Finlay-de Monchy.

Black Moss Press
2450 Byng Road, Windsor, ON N8W 3E8
Fax: (519) 253-7809
Web site: www.blackmosspress.com
Contact: Marty Gervais, editor
Seeking new poetry, fiction, and non-fiction. Publishes two

theme anthologies each year. "Looking for new and innovative writing with an edge." Produced 11 new titles in 2003. Accepts unsolicited manuscripts, but send an inquiry first.

Notable 2003 title: *Wrapped within Again: Selected Poems by Robert Hilles*.

Borealis Press
8 Mohawk Crescent, Nepean, ON K2H 7G6
Phone: (613) 829-0150 Fax: (613) 829-7783
E-mail: drt@borealispress.com
Web site: www.borealispress.com

Established 1972. A general publisher, but specializes in Canadiana, including the Tecumseh Press subsidiary reserved for Canadian material. "We do not consider multiple submissions or unsolicited full manuscripts. Query first, including synopsis and a sample chapter or equivalent, together with return postage or international postal coupons and adequate-sized envelope." Guidelines available on web site.

Notable 2003 title: *Stories from Stones: Cairns of Ontario*, Marion Heath.

The Boston Mills Press
132 Main Street, Erin, ON N0B 1T0
Phone: (519) 833-2407 Fax: (519) 833-2195
E-mail: books@bostonmillspress.com
Web site: www.bostonmillspress.com
Contact: John Denison, publisher

Established 1974. Specializes in historical works. Publishes local or regional history, guidebooks, and large-format pictorials. Releases 25 new titles a year. "We are interested in book ideas on the following topics: Ontario; outdoors, especially hiking and canoeing; Ontario's cottage country; transportation; and local histories." Accepts unsolicited manuscripts, but first send an inquiry with outline and sample chapter. Send an SASE for catalogue.

Notable 2003 title: *Canadian Pacific*, Greg McDonnell.

Robin Brass Studio
10 Blantyre Avenue, Toronto, ON M1N 2R4
Phone: (416) 698-5848 Fax: (416) 698-2120

E-mail: rbrass@sympatico.ca
Web site: www.rbstudiobooks.com
Contact: Robin Brass, publisher
Publishes books on Canadian history and other non-fiction. Military history is a major topic, but they are not limited to that area. Releases about 4 to 5 new titles a year. Does not accept unsolicited manuscripts. Send an inquiry, outline, and sample chapters. Guidelines available on web site.
Notable 2003 title: *A Very Brilliant Affair: The Battle of Queenston Heights*, Robert Malcomson.

Breakwater Books
P.O. Box 2188, 100 Water Street, St. John's, NL A1C 6E6
Phone: (709) 722-6680 Fax: (709) 753-0708
E-mail: info@breakwater.nf.net
Web site: www.breakwater.nf.net
Contact: Clyde Rose, president
Publishes fiction, non-fiction, and educational titles, especially those related to the culture and history of Newfoundland and Labrador. Releases about 15 new titles a year. Does not accept unsolicited manuscripts. Send an inquiry with outline and sample chapters.
Notable 2003 title: *Undertow*, Thomas Rendall Curran.

Brick Books
431 Boler Road, P.O. Box 20081, London, ON N6K 4G6
Phone: (519) 657-8579
E-mail: brick.books@sympatico.ca
Web site: www.brickbooks.ca
Contact: Kitty Lewis, general manager
Established 1975. Publishes Canadian poetry by Canadian authors only. Reads manuscripts January 1 through April 30 every year. Releases 6 to 7 new titles annually. Accepts unsolicited manuscripts, but first send an inquiry. Guidelines available.
Notable 2003 title: *Concrete and Wild Carrot*, Margaret Avison.

Broadview Press
P.O. Box 1243, Peterborough, ON K9J 7H5
Phone: (705) 743-8990 Fax: (705) 743-8353

E-mail: customerservice@broadviewpress.com
Web site: www.broadviewpress.com
Contact: Michael Harrison, vice president
Established 1985. Specializes in the arts and social sciences, incorporating a variety of viewpoints: liberal, conservative, libertarian, feminist, and Marxist. Subject areas include anthropology, politics, history, philosophy, sociology, English literature, and medieval studies. Most titles are relevant for undergraduate course use. About 60 new titles a year. Very rarely accepts unsolicited manuscripts. Send an inquiry with an outline. Guidelines available on web site.

Notable 2003 title: *The Broadview Anthology of Drama: Plays from the Western Theatre*, edited by Jennifer Wise and Craig S. Walker.

Broken Jaw Press
P.O. Box 596, Stn. A, Fredericton, NB E3B 5A6
Phone: (506) 454-5127 Fax: (506) 454-5127
E-mail: jblades@brokenjaw.com
Web site: www.brokenjaw.com
Contact: Joe Blades, publisher
An independent literary arts publisher with Canadian-authored poetry, fiction, drama, and creative non-fiction as the focus. Publishes works in translation (especially from Spanish) with poetry often in bilingual editions. Released 9 new titles in 2003. Does not accept unsolicited manuscripts, except from those who enter the Annual Poets' Corner Award contest for book-length poetry. Guidelines available at www.brokenjaw.com/submissions.htm.

Notable 2003 title: *Groundswell: The Best of Above-Ground Press, 1993–2003*, edited by Rob McLennan.

Caitlin Press
P.O. Box 2387, Prince George, BC V2N 2S6
Phone: (250) 964-4953 Fax: (604) 648-9992
E-mail: caitlin_press@telus.net
Web site: www.caitlin_press.com
Contact: Cynthia Wilson, managing editor
Established 1977. A regional publisher specializing in trade books by B.C. Interior authors. Some literary titles by B.C. authors. Publishes 5 titles each year. "We are interested primarily in Canada's North, and more particularly northern British Columbia."

Accepts unsolicited manuscripts that meet these criteria. Send outline and sample chapters. Guidelines available on web site. "Please follow those guidelines."

Notable 2003 titles: *A Northern Woman*, Jacqueline Baldwin; *A Jewel in the Wilderness*, Suzanne Leblanc.

Canadian Circumpolar Institute (CCI) Press
University of Alberta, 8625 – 112 Street, Suite 308, Campus
  Tower, Edmonton, AB T6E OHI
Phone: (780) 492-4512 Fax: (780) 492-1153
E-mail: ccinst@ualberta.ca
Web site: www.ualberta.ca/~ccinst
Contact: Elaine L. Maloney, assistant director CCI/managing
  editor CCI Press

Publishes peer-reviewed scholarly works, educational volumes, and trade titles on northern polar and circumpolar subjects. Thematic series include Studies in Whaling, Northern Hunter-Gatherer Research, Solstice (Community Voices), and the Circumpolar Research Series. Publishes 4 to 5 titles a year. Accepts unsolicited manuscripts, but first send an inquiry, outline, and sample chapters. Guidelines available.

Notable 2003 title: *People of the Robin*, James MacDonald.

Canadian Museum of Civilization
100 Laurier Street, P.O. Box 3100, Stn. B, Gatineau, QC J8X 4H2
Phone: (819) 776-8394 Fax: (819) 776-8393
E-mail: pam.coulas@civilization.ca
Web site: www.civilization.ca
Contact: Pam Coulas, promotional co-ordinator

Publishes research and disseminates information on the disciplines of Canadian history, ethnography, archaeology, and folk culture. Publishes 15 titles a year. Does not accept unsolicited manuscripts.

Notable 2003 title: *Adventures in the New World: The Saga of the Coureurs des Bois*, Georges-Hébert Germain.

Canadian Scholar's Press
180 Bloor Street W., Suite 801, Toronto, ON M5S 2V6
Phone: (416) 929-2774 Fax: (416) 929-1926

E-mail: aprince@cspi.org
Web site: www.cspi.org
Contact: Althea Prince, managing editor

A publisher of scholarly books and textbooks. No unsolicited manuscripts; send an inquiry, an outline, and sample chapters. "All academic and scholarly book submissions are welcome." Guidelines available on web site.

Notable 2003 title: *Teaching for Equity and Diversity*, Patrick Solomon and Cynthia Lavine-Rasky.

CHA Press

17 York Street, Ottawa, ON K1N 9J6
Phone: (613) 241-8005, ext. 264 Fax: (613) 241-5055
E-mail: chapresss@cha.ca
Web site: www.cha.ca/publishing
Contact: Eleanor Sawyer, director, publishing

CHA Press, the publisher for the Canadian Healthcare Association, is a direct-mail, specialty publisher whose mission is to support Canadian authors writing about issues concerning the delivery of healthcare across the system. "Our target audience are the senior/middle managers of health facilities/agencies in Canada's health delivery system, including its governors." Publishes 4 titles a year. Send an inquiry with an outline and sample chapters. Guidelines available.

Notable 2003 title: *Strengthening the Quality of Cancer Services in Ontario*, edited by Terrence Sullivan et al.

Captus Press

1600 Steeles Avenue W., Units 14 & 15, Concord, ON L4K 4M2
Phone: (416) 736-5537 Fax: (416) 736-5793
E-mail: info@captus.com
Web site: www.captus.com
Contact: Pauline Lai, manager

As well as textbooks and professional books, Captus Press publishes non-fiction trade books. Accepts unsolicited manuscripts. Guidelines available. "We assist authors in development of their books, with emphasis on those designed to enhance post-secondary education and furnish information to practising professionals. To determine the feasibility of your project, submit an author/

editor questionnaire at www.captus.com/information/manuscript-contents.htm. We will contact you with our initial assessment and offer publishing suggestions. We may also wish to review sample chapters as soon as they are available, which would assist us to confirm the acceptance of your project for publication."

Chestnut Publishing Group
4005 Bayview Avenue, Suite 610, Toronto, ON M2M 3Z9
Phone: (416) 224-5824 Fax: (416) 486-4752
E-mail: hgoldhar@sympatico.ca or sharkstark@sympatico.ca
Web site: www.chestnutpublishing.com
Contacts: Harry Goldhar, vice-president, editorial; Stanley
    Starkman, president
Publishes children's literature, general trade titles, education books for school and college, books for reluctant readers, and books on English as a second language. Produced 8 new titles in 2003. Accepts unsolicited manuscripts; send an outline and sample chapters first.
Notable 2003 title: *Die Wealthy and Broke*, Gopala Alampur.

Coach House Books
401 Huron Street (rear – on bpNichol Lane), Toronto, ON
    M5S 2G5
Phone: (416) 979-2217 Fax: (416) 977-1158
E-mail: mail@chbooks.com
Web site: www.chbooks.com
Contacts: Alana Wilcox, senior editor; Jason McBride, managing
    editor
Publishes innovative poetry, fiction, and drama by Canadian writers. Releases approximately 15 new titles annually. Does not accept unsolicited manuscripts. Send an inquiry. Guidelines available.
Notable 2003 title: *All My Friends Are Superheroes*, Andrew Kaufman.

Colombo & Company
42 Dell Park Avenue, Toronto, ON M6B 2T6
Phone: (416) 782-6853 Fax: (416) 782-0285
E-mail: jrc@ca.inter.net

Web site: www.colombo.ca
Contact: John Robert Colombo
  Publishes about 6 new titles annually; 82 in print. Does not accept unsolicited manuscripts. "Demonstrate that you have read at least 5 of our publications before sending an inquiry."

Cordillera Books

8415 Granville Street, P.O. Box 46, Vancouver, BC V6P 4Z9
Phone: (604) 261-1695 Fax: (604) 266-4469
E-mail: richbook@ca.inter.net
Contact: S. C. Heal, president
  Specializes in maritime history, shipping, tug and barge transportation, and fishing industry books. Does not accept unsolicited manuscripts; send an inquiry first. "We have a full publishing program for 2004–2005. Not considering any fresh works at this time."
  Notable 2003 titles: Books in The West Coast Maritime Series, S. C. Heal.

Cormorant Books

215 Spadina Avenue, Studio 230, Toronto, ON M5T 2C7
Phone: (416) 929-4957 Fax: (416) 929-3596
E-mail: cormorantbooksinc@bellnet.ca
Web site: www.cormorantbooks.com
Contact: J. M. Côté, publisher
  Publishes literary fiction and non-fiction that represents the diversity of Canadian society. Released 11 new titles in 2003. Accepts unsolicited manuscripts; send an inquiry first. "We receive 1,000 submissions a year, the vast majority of which are wrong for our list. Please visit the web site and become familiar with our list before submitting." Guidelines available.
  Notable 2003 title: *Still Life with June*, Darren Greer.

Coteau Books

2206 Dewdney Avenue, Suite 401, Regina, SK S4R 1H3
Phone: (306) 777-0170 Fax: (306) 522-5152
E-mail: coteau@coteaubooks.com
Web site: www.coteaubooks.com
Contact: Nik L. Burton, managing editor

Established 1975. Publishes fiction, poetry, juvenile fiction, books on women's issues, and quality and popular non-fiction. Published 18 new titles in 2003. "Coteau publishes only Canadian authors, in all categories. We do not accept simultaneous/multiple submissions. Check our recent titles on our web site." Accepts unsolicited manuscripts; send an inquiry with sample chapters. Guidelines available.

Notable 2003 title: *A Song for Nettie Johnson*, Gloria Sawai.

Crabtree Publishing Co.

612 Welland Avenue, St. Catharines, ON L2M 5V6
Phone: (905) 682-5221 Fax: (905) 682-7166
E-mail: editor@crabtreebooks.com
Web site: www.crabtreebooks.com
Contact: Heather Fitzpatrick, production co-ordinator

Established 1978. Publishes children's illustrated non-fiction series written at a specific reading level to meet educational demands for the children's library market. Main subjects are social studies and science. Releases 50 to 100 new titles a year. "We do not accept unsolicited manuscripts and discourage fiction, as it is not our market."

Notable 2003 title: *Famous Native North Americans*, Bobbie Kalman.

Creative Book Publishing

P.O. Box 8660, St. John's, NL A1B 3T7
Phone: (709) 722-8500 Fax: (709) 579-7745
E-mail: books@rb.nf.ca
Web site: www.nfbooks.com
Contact: Dawn Roche, publisher/general manager

Established 1983. Publishes under 3 imprints, each having a distinctive focus. Titles released under its Creative Publishers imprint include primarily histories, biographies, pictorials, cookbooks, books of humour, and travel/guide books. Under its Killick Press imprint, the company publishes poetry, fiction, drama, creative non-fiction, belles lettres, essays, feminist literature, and fine art reproduction. The Tuckamore Books imprint is devoted to children's books and young-adult literature. Publishes 10 to 14 books a year. Send a cover letter describing the genre of the manuscript and the intended audience, an author résumé, a manuscript summary, the full manuscript, and an SASE.

Creative Bound International
P.O. Box 424, Carp, ON K0A 1L0
Phone: (613) 831-3641 or 1-800-287-8610 Fax: (613) 831-3643
Web site: www.creativebound.com
Contacts: Gail Baird, president; Lindsay Pike, director

Publishes resources for personal growth and enhanced performance in business. "We help experts get their messages out." Releases 6 to 8 new titles annually. Send an outline and sample chapters.

Notable 2003 title: *Six Legs Jazz Club: A Journey to Uncovering Your Best Life*, Dick Cappon and John Christensen.

Creekstone Press
7456 Driftwood Road, Smithers, BC V0J 2N7
Phone: (250) 847-3663 Fax: (250) 847-3663
E-mail: creekstone@bulkley.net
Web site: www.creekstonepress.com
Contact: Lynn Shervill, president

Provides a vehicle for creative writers and artists in northern British Columbia. "Diversity of expression, accuracy, originality, craftsmanship, and regional relevance govern selection. Creekstone Press applies exacting design and production standards, which complement and enhance selected works." Publishes 1 new title a year. No unsolicited manuscripts. Send an inquiry. Guidelines available.

Cumulus Press
P.O. Box 5205, Stn. B, Montreal, QC H3B 4B5
Phone: (514) 522-5404
E-mail: cumulus@cumuluspress.com
Web sites: www.cumuluspress.com
Contact: David Widgington, publisher

Established 1998. "Cumulus Press takes the stairs instead of the escalator. Gravity is an ally. Poetry, fiction, social justice, the Tendril Anthology Series, and the open road fill the space between the cracks. All of our titles are well crafted, one by one." Publishes 2 books a year. Does not accept unsolicited manuscripts. Send an outline first. "Seeking submissions by talented and emerging writers under the age of 25 for Tendril Anthology Series, Book 3, Biography." Guidelines available on web site.

Notable 2003 title: *Rising to a Tension: New Short Fiction by Thirteen Writers Under 25*, edited by Neale McDevitt and Tom Abray.

DC Books
P.O. Box 662, 950 Decane, Ville St. Laurent, QC H4L 4V9
Phone: (514) 843-8130 Fax: (514) 939-0569
E-mail: dcbooks@videotron.ca
Contact: Steve Luxton, editor-in-chief
A literary publisher specializing in fiction, poetry, and drama. Published 5 books in 2003. Accepts unsolicited manuscripts but prefers inquiries.

Notable 2003 title: *Career Suicide: Canadian Literary Humour*, edited by Jon Paul Fiorentino.

DESPUB (David E. Scott Publishing)
2340B Clifton Street, Allanburg, ON L0S 1A0
Phone: (905) 680-7884 or 1-866-471-4123 Fax: (905) 680-7884
E-mail: despub@niagara.com
Contact: David E. Scott, editor-in-chief
Established 2001. Publishes fun Canadian books that are in good taste. Averages 4 new titles a year. Send an outline, a sample chapter, your ideas on sales and marketing potential, and an SASE. All proposals will be considered promptly and carefully. "Please do not send poetry or anything autobiographical unless the experiences described are genuinely unique and will amuse and entertain the reader. Ask yourself, 'Who would want to spend money to read this story?'"

Notable 2003 title: *Northern Ontario: There's More to Northern Ontario Than Just Rocks, Trees and Lakes*, Geoffrey Corfield.

Detselig Enterprises
1220 Kensington Road N.W., Unit 210, Calgary, AB T2N 3P5
Phone: (403) 283-0900 Fax: (403) 283-6947

E-mail: temeron@telusplanet.net
Web site: www.temerondetselig.com
Contact: T. E. Giles, president

Established 1975. Publishes academic (education, social science, and the humanities) and general trade books. Averages 14 new books each year. Accepts unsolicited manuscripts, but first send inquiry letter with outline and sample chapters.

Notable 2003 title: *Awed, Amused and Alarmed*, Faye Holt.

Doubleday Canada
1 Toronto Street, Suite 300, Toronto, ON M5C 2V6
Phone: (416) 364-4449 Fax: (416) 957-1587
Web site: www.randomhouse.ca
Contact: acquisitions editor

Publishes quality trade fiction and non-fiction by leading and award-winning authors. Published 59 new titles in 2003. Does not accept unsolicited manuscripts. An inquiry should be accompanied by an outline and sample chapters.

Notable 2003 title: *The In-Between World of Vikram Lall*, M. G. Vassanji.

Douglas & McIntyre Publishing Group
2323 Quebec Street, Suite 201, Vancouver, BC V5T 4S7
Phone: (604) 254-7191 Fax: (604) 254-9099
E-mail: dm@douglas-mcintyre.com
Web site: www.douglas-mcintyre.com
Contact: editorial department

Established 1964. Publishes general trade books in 3 publishing units: Douglas & McIntyre, Greystone Books, and Groundwood Books (see separate listing). Douglas & McIntyre specializes in Canadian art and culture, particularly militaria, maritime history, and northwest coast and Inuit literary fiction. Greystone Books specializes in natural history, ecology and the environment, popular science, health, and travel and outdoor guidebooks. Produces 60 new titles annually. Toronto office handles only children's books and adult fiction. Submit an outline with 2 or 3 sample chapters.

Notable 2003 titles: *Village of the Small Houses*, Ferguson (Douglas & McIntyre), and *Temptress: From the Original Bad Girls to Women on Top*, Billinghurst (Greystone).

DreamCatcher Publishing

105 Prince William Street, Saint John, NB E2L 2B2
Phone: (506) 632-4008 Fax: (506) 632-4009
E-mail: dcpub@fundy.net
Web site: www.dreamcatcher.nb.ca
Contact: Elizabeth Margaris, publisher

Publishes good mainstream fiction, with first consideration to Atlantic Canadian writers. "Especially interested in 'green' theme fiction, 'hope' non-fiction (autobiographies), and quality stories for children." Produces 6 to 9 new titles annually. No unsolicited manuscripts. Send an inquiry. "Make your query letter businesslike. We think it is a myth that queries have to be 'creative.' Clever tactics irk us."

Notable 2003 title: *Something Lovely*, Alan Weatherley.

The Dundurn Group

8 Market Street, Suite 200, Toronto, ON M5E 1M6
Phone: (416) 214-5544 Fax: (416) 214-5556
E-mail: info@dundurn.com
Web site: www.dundurn.com
Contact: Kirk Howard, publisher

Established 1973. Publishes Canadian history (notably of Ontario), biography, art, and literary criticism. Encompasses Dundurn (serious non-fiction), Hounslow (popular non-fiction), Simon & Pierre (literary), the Castle Street Mysteries, and Boardwalk (young adult) imprints. Averages 50 new titles annually. Accepts unsolicited manuscripts, but first send outline and sample chapters, and identify your prospective market. Allow 4 to 12 weeks for reply.

Notable 2003 title: *60 Years Behind the Wheel*, Bill Sherk.

Duval House Publishing

18228 – 102 Avenue, Edmonton, AB T5S 1S7
Phone: (780) 488-1390 or 1-800-267-6187 Fax: (780) 482-7213
E-mail: duvalhouse@duvalhouse.com
Web site: www.duvalhouse.com
Contact: Glenn Rollans, publisher

A Canadian producer of learning materials for students in kindergarten to grade 12. Publishes social studies, science, and language learning resources in English, French, Cree, Blackfoot, and other languages. Does not accept unsolicited manuscripts; initiates most projects in-house.

ECW Press
2120 Queen Street E., Suite 200, Toronto, ON M4E 1E2
Phone: (416) 694-3348 Fax: (416) 698-9906
E-mail: info@ecwpress.com
Web site: www.ecwpress.com
Contact: Tracey Millen, managing editor
Established 1974. Traditionally a publisher of reference books and literary criticism on Canadian writers and their works, ECW has now been transformed into a vigorous literary and trade house focusing on poetry, fiction, biography, sports books, and non-fiction. Releases about 45 titles annually. Does not accept unsolicited manuscripts. Send a query first. Guidelines available. "Authors should include an SASE if they wish their material returned."
Notable 2003 title: *Wrestlecrap*, Randy Baer.

EDGE Science Fiction & Fantasy Publishing
P.O. Box 1714, Calgary, AB T2P 2L7
Phone: (403) 254-0160 Fax: (403) 254-0456
Web site: www.edgewebsite.com
Contact: Kimberly Gammon, editorial manager
"We are dedicated to producing thought-provoking, intelligent and well-written novel-length science fiction and fantasy works between 75,000 and 100,000 words in length." Publishes 6 to 8 new titles annually. Accepts unsolicited manuscripts, but first send outline, sample chapters, and an SASE. Web site has complete submission information. No electronic submissions.
Notable 2003 title: *Dreams of the Sea*, Elisabeth Vonarburg.

Ekstasis Editions
P.O. Box 8474, Main Postal Outlet, Victoria, BC V8W 3S1
Phone: (250) 361-9941 Fax: (250) 385-3378
E-mail: ekstasis@islandnet.com
Web site: www.ekstasiseditions.com
Contact: Richard Olafson, publisher

A literary press dedicated to publishing poetry, fiction, belle lettres, and translation. Averages 15 new titles annually. Accepts unsolicited manuscripts, but send sample chapters first. "Always send an SASE for a reply or return of materials." Guidelines available.

Notable 2003 title: *Passages*, Émile Ollivier.

Empty Mirrors Press

6252 Jubilee Road, Halifax, NS B3H 2G5

Phone: (902) 425-3725

E-mail: aaosl@chebucto.ns.ca

Web site: www.chebucto.ns.ca/~aaosl/empty_mirrors.html

Contact: Christopher Majka, publisher

Publishes selected works of interest to the publisher. Releases 1 new title a year. Does not accept unsolicited manuscripts. "We seek out manuscripts of interest to us."

Fernwood Publishing

8422 St. Margaret's Bay Road, Site 2A, Box 5, Black Point, NS
    BOJ 1B0

Phone: (902) 857-1388   Fax: (902) 857-1328

E-mail: info@fernwoodbooks.ca

Web site: www.fernwoodbooks.ca

Contact: Errol Sharpe, publisher

Publishes critical non-fiction that provides insight and challenges existing norms, focusing on the social sciences and humanities. Released 19 new titles in 2003. Does not accept unsolicited manuscripts; send an inquiry and outline. Guidelines available.

Notable 2003 title: *Accounting for Genocide*, Dean Neu and Richard Terrian.

Fifth House Publishers

1800 – 4th Street S.W., Suite 1511, Calgary, AB T2S 2S5

Phone: (403) 571-5232   Fax: (403) 571-5235

E-mail: charlene@hillsboro.ca

Web site: www.fitzhenry.ca

Contact: Charlene Dobmeier, publisher

Established 1982. Publishes general trade non-fiction, specializing in Western Canadiana, emphasizing history, biography, gardening, nature, and First Nations titles. Releases approximately 16 books a year. Accepts unsolicited manuscripts, but send an inquiry with an outline and sample chapters first. "No phone calls, please."

Notable 2003 title: *All Hell Can't Stop Us: The On-to-Ottawa Trek and Regina Riot*, Bill Waiser.

Firefly Books
66 Leek Crescent, Richmond Hill, ON L4B 1H1
Phone: (416) 499-8412 Fax: (416) 499-8313
E-mail: service@fireflybooks.com
Web site: www.fireflybooks.com

Publishes practical how-to and illustrated books, with a special interest in gardening, cooking, astronomy, natural history, and sports for the Canadian and U.S. markets. No unsolicited manuscripts.

Formac Publishing Company
5502 Atlantic Street, Halifax, NS B3H 1G4
Phone: (902) 421-7022 Fax: (902) 425-0166
E-mail: eeve@formac.ca
Web site: www.formac.ca
Contact: Elizabeth Eve, senior editor

Publishes trade guides for Canadian destinations, children's books (series), and a wide range of illustrated and text-only books for the regional market. Releases 15 new titles a year. Accepts unsolicited manuscripts, but send an outline first. "For children's books, note that we publish in only 2 genres: series and regional interest. E-mail petitions are welcome." Guidelines available on web site.

Notable 2003 title: *Heritage Houses of Nova Scotia*, Sheila Stevenson and Stephen Archibald.

Garamond Press
63 Mahogany Court, Aurora, ON L4G 6M8
Phone: (905) 841-1460 Fax: (905) 841-3031
E-mail: garamond@web.ca
Web site: www.garamond.ca
Contact: Peter Saunders, publisher

Established 1981. Publishes academic monographs and university texts offering a critical perspective. Subject areas include women's studies, cultural and labour studies, education, the Third World, and ethnicity. Releases about 6 new titles a year. No unsolicited manuscripts. Written inquiries only. Specific submission guidelines available on web site.

Notable 2003 title: *Hidden Knowledge: Organized Labour in the Information Age*, Livingstone and Sawchuk.

Gaspereau Press

1 Church Avenue, Kentville, NS B4N 2M7
Phone: (902) 678-6002 Fax: (902) 678-7845
E-mail: info@gaspereau.com
Web site: www.gaspereau.com
Contact: Kate Kennedy, associate editor

Publishes literary and creative non-fiction titles in quality first-edition paperbacks and limited hardcover books aimed at the Canadian and U.S. markets. Releases 9 new titles a year. Accepts unsolicited manuscripts and sample chapters. Guidelines available. "Please include a cover letter with all submissions. Samples and full manuscripts accepted. Please include a detailed synopsis of the work in full. No e-mail submissions."

General Store Publishing House

499 O'Brien Road, P.O. Box 415, Renfrew, ON K7V 4A6
Phone: (613) 432-7697 or 1-800-465-6072 Fax: (613) 432-7184
E-mail: publisher@gsph.com
Web site: www.gsph.com
Contact: Tim Gordon, publisher

Established 1980. Publishes history, military, cookbooks, regional titles pertaining to the Ottawa Valley, and sports books. Releases 20 to 25 titles a year. Accepts unsolicited manuscripts, but phone first. Guidelines available.

Notable 2003 title: *An Ovarian Cancer Companion*, Diane Sims.

Goose Lane Editions

469 King Street, Fredericton, NB E3B 1E5
Phone: (506) 450-4251 Fax: (506) 459-4991
Web site: www.gooselane.com
Contacts: Laurel Boone, editorial director; Ross Leckie, poetry
    editor

Established 1954. Publishes Canadian adult literary fiction, non-fiction, and poetry. Produces about 18 paper books each year and

10 audio books. Considers unsolicited manuscripts. "Query first for poetry, story collections, and non-fiction. Send outline or synopsis and a 30- to 50-page sample for novels. No electronic queries or submissions, please." Guidelines available with an SASE.

Notable 2003 title: *Elle*, Douglas Glover.

Granville Island Publishing

1656 Duranleau, Suite 212, Vancouver, BC V6H 3S4
Phone: (604) 688-0320 or 1-877-688-0320 Fax: (604) 688-0132
E-mail: info@granvilleislandpublishing.com
Web site: www.granvilleislandpublishing.com
Contact: Jo Blackmore, publisher

Publishes books that are financed by the author. The publisher provides publicity and marketing, and distributes the books in Canada and the U.S. "Authors should be prepared to promote their work after they commit to this way of publishing. We are now publishing more health and medical books." Released 9 books in 2003. Does not accept unsolicited manuscripts; send a query first. Guidelines available.

Notable 2003 title: *Faces of Courage: Young Heroes of World War II*, Sally Rogow.

Great Plains Publications

70 Arthur Street, Suite 420, Winnipeg, MB R3B 1G7
Phone: (204) 475-6799 Fax: (204) 475-0138
E-mail: info@greatplains.mb.ca
Web site: www.greatplains.mb.ca
Contact: Gregg Shilliday, publisher

An independent regional publisher specializing in prairie history and fiction. Publishes 8 to 10 titles a year. Accepts unsolicited manuscripts; send an outline and sample chapters first. Guidelines available.

Notable 2003 title: *Nowhere to Run: The Killing of Constable Dennis Strongquill*, Mike McIntyre.

Groundwood Books

720 Bathurst Street, Suite 500, Toronto, ON M5S 2R4
Phone: (416) 537-2501 Fax: (416) 537-4647

E-mail: genmail@groundwooddm.com
Web site: www.groundwoodbooks.com
Contact: Nan Froman, managing editor

Publishes high quality Canadian picture books, both fiction and non-fiction, plus a new line of Spanish-language titles, Libras Tigrillo, aimed at the U.S. Latino market and the export market in Mexico and Central America. Released 29 new titles in 2003. Accepts unsolicited manuscripts; send a synopsis and sample chapters first. No e-mail submissions. Guidelines available on web site.

Notable 2003 title: *Inanna: From the Myths of Ancient Sumer*, Kim Echlin (illustrations by Linda Wolfsgruber).

Guernica Editions
P.O. Box 117, Stn. P, Toronto, ON M5S 2S6
Phone: (416) 658-9888 Fax: (416) 657-8885
E-mail: guernicaeditions@cs.com
Web site: www.guernicaeditions.com
Contact: Antonio D'Alfonso, editor

Established 1978. Specializes in fiction, non-fiction, plays, poetry, and translations that address the Italian/North American experience. Also translates Québécois authors. Publishes about 23 new titles a year. No unsolicited manuscripts. Inquiries welcome. "A publisher is not just an outlet. It is the home for minds with similar ideas on what literature is about."

Notable 2003 title: *A Demon in My View*, Len Gasparin.

Hancock House Publishers Ltd.
19313 Zero Avenue, Surrey, BC V3S 9R9
Phone: (604) 538-1114 Fax: (604) 538-2262
E-mail: promo@hancockhouse.com
Web site: www.hancockhouse.com
Contact: Melanie Clark, promotional manager

Established 1970. Specializes in Pacific Northwest history and biography, Native culture, nature guides, and natural history. A second division focuses on international nature and conservation books. Publishes about 20 titles a year. Accepts unsolicited manuscripts. "Send printed copies of complete manuscripts, including photos and illustrations." Guidelines available on web site.

Harbour Publishing

P.O. Box 219, Madeira Park, BC V0N 2H0
Phone: (604) 883-2730 Fax: (604) 883-9451
E-mail: info@harbourpublishing.com
Web site: www.harbourpublishing.com
Contact: Shyla Seller, assistant to the publisher

Primarily focuses on regional non-fiction titles, but publishes in all genres, mainly on topics concerning the West Coast of B.C. Publishes about 20 titles a year. Accepts unsolicited manuscripts, but first send an inquiry with an outline and sample chapters. "Please contact the publisher for a catalogue or browse our book list at www.harbourpublishing.com for examples of the kinds of books we publish." Guidelines available.

Notable 2003 title: *Raincoast Chronicles 19*, edited by Howard White.

Harlequin Enterprises

225 Duncan Mill Road, Don Mills, ON M3B 3K9
Phone: (416) 445-5860 Fax: (416) 445-8655
Web site: www.eharlequin.com (also www.mirabooks.com;
   www.reddressink.com; www.luna-books.com;
   www.steeplehill.com)
Contact: Isabel Swift, vice-president, editorial

Established 1949. Each year they publish more than 1,100 new titles in all formats (mass-market, trade, and hardcover), including series romance (Harlequin and Silhouette imprints), single-title women's fiction (MIRA Books, Red Dress Ink, and IIQN imprints), inspirational fiction (Steeple Hill imprint), fantasy (Luna imprint), and mystery and action adventure (Gold Eagle and Worldwide Library imprints). Accepts query letters. Tip sheets available. Check web site for updated information, especially the Learn to Write channel. New authors are contracted only on full manuscript.

HarperCollins Publishers

2 Bloor Street E., 20th Floor, Toronto, ON M4W 1A8
Phone: (416) 975-9334 Fax: (416) 975-5223
Web site: www.harpercanada.com
Contact: editorial department

Publishes a wide range of fiction, non-fiction, business, young-adult, and children's books. Produces over 50 new titles each year. No unsolicited manuscripts or proposals.

The Frederick Harris Music Co.

5865 McLaughlin Road, Unit 1, Mississauga, ON L5R 1B8
Phone: (905) 501-1595, ext. 230 Fax: (905) 501-0929
E-mail: fhmc@frederickharrismusic.com
Web site: www.frederickharrismusic.com
Contact: Trish Sauerbrei, editor-in-chief
Established 1904. A not-for-profit publisher of music education materials, particularly curriculum material for the Royal Conservatory of Music. Released about 50 new titles in 2003. Send sample chapters. Guidelines available.
Notable 2003 title: *Celebrate Piano! A Comprehensive Piano Method*, C. Albergo, J. M. Kolar, M. Mrozinski.

Heritage House Publishing Co. Ltd.

3555 Outrigger Road, Suite 301, Nanoose Bay, BC V9P 9K1
Phone: (250) 468-5328 Fax: (250) 468-5318
E-mail: publisher@heritagehouse.ca
Web site: www.heritagehouse.ca
Contact: Rodger Touchie, publisher
The Heritage publishing program emphasizes Canadian non-fiction with a focus on subjects of regional interest in British Columbia and Alberta. Releases about 20 titles annually. Accepts unsolicited manuscripts, but send an outline first. Guidelines available on web site. "Check our web site for full review of what we publish. With outline include letter about why you think your book would sell and who would buy it."
Notable 2003 title: *Fortress of the Grizzlies: The Khutzeymateen Grizzly Bear Sanctuary*, Dan Wakeman and Wendy Shymanski.

Highway Book Shop

R.R. #1, Cobalt, ON P0J 1C0
Phone: (705) 679-8375 Fax: (705) 679-8511
E-mail: bookshop@nt.net
Web site: www.abebooks.com/home/highwaybooks
Contact: Lois Pollard, assistant manager

Publishes mostly histories of northeastern Ontario. Averages 5 titles a year. Accepts unsolicited manuscripts, but send sample chapters first. No colour photographs; black-and-white photos or drawings only. Guidelines available.

Notable 2003 title: *New Liskeard: The Pioneer Years*, Bruce W. Taylor.

House of Anansi Press
110 Spadina Avenue, Toronto, ON M5V 2K4
Phone: (416) 363-4343 Fax: (416) 363-1017
E-mail: info@anansi.ca
Web site: www.anansi.ca
Contact: editorial department

Publishes literary fiction, non-fiction, and poetry. Releases 15 to 20 new titles a year. Accepts unsolicited manuscripts, but first send an outline and sample chapters. "We regret that we are unable to respond to queries regarding our submission guidelines. For complete guidelines, please visit our web site."

Notable 2003 title: *UN*, Dennis Lee.

Hushion House Publishing
36 Northline Road, Toronto, ON M4B 3E2
Phone: (416) 285-6100 Fax: (416) 285-1777
Web site: www.hushion.com
Contact: Bill Hushion, president

"We do not publish; we act as a distributor for self-published books." Represents over 400 self-published titles. "If you are considering self-publishing, please contact us at least six months prior to publication."

Hyperion Press Limited
300 Wales Avenue, Winnipeg, MB R2M 2S9
Phone: (204) 256-9204 Fax: (204) 255-7845
E-mail: tamos@mts.net
Contact: Dr. Marvis Tutiah, president

Established 1978. Specializes in craft and how-to books for all ages, and children's picture books for under-12s. Averages 8 to 10 new titles a year. Accepts unsolicited manuscripts.

Insomniac Press
192 Spadina Avenue, Suite 403, Toronto, ON M5T 2C2
Phone: (416) 504-6270 Fax: (416) 504-9313
E-mail: mike@insomniacpress.com
Web site: www.insomniacpress.com
Contact: Mike O'Connor, publisher
  Established 1992. Publishes fiction, non-fiction in a wide variety of areas, and poetry. "Please visit our web site for an idea of the books we have published recently." Releases about 20 new titles annually. Accepts unsolicited manuscripts, but first send sample chapters by mail only. Guidelines available on web site.
  Notable 2003 title: *The Lover's Tongue*, Mark Morton.

ISER Books, Faculty of Arts Publications (Institute of
  Social and Economic Research)
Memorial University of Newfoundland, St. John's, NL A1C 5S7
Phone: (709) 737-7474 Fax: (709) 737-7560
E-mail: iser-books@mun.ca
Web site: www.mun.ca/iser
Contact: Al Potter, manager
Publishes research relevant to Newfoundland and Labrador, and the North Atlantic Rim, especially research pertaining to social and economic development in Newfoundland and Labrador. Specializes in anthropology, sociology, folklore, women's studies, geography, history, and economics. Periodic collections on Native peoples and the nation-state, social-science advocacy, and the fishing crisis. Publishes 3 or 4 titles each year. Does not accept unsolicited manuscripts. Send an inquiry with an outline. Guidelines available.
  Notable 2003 title: *A Way of Life That Does Not Exist: Canada and the Extinguishment of the Innuit*, Colin Samson.

Island Scholastic Press
Phone: (250) 991-5567
E-mail: lukivdan@hotmail.com
Contact: Dan Lukiv, editor
  Established 1997. Showcases authors published in the *Challenger international* literary journal. Released 3 titles in 2003.

Accepts unsolicited manuscripts, but send a sample chapter first.
Submissions by e-mail only.

Notable 2003 title: *Summer Soliloquy*, Dolores Guglielmo.

Island Studies Press

Institute of Island Studies, University of Prince Edward Island,
Charlottetown, PE C1A 4P3
Phone: (902) 566-0956 Fax: (902) 566-0756
E-mail: brinklow@upei.ca
Web site: www.islandstudies.com
Contact: Laurie Brinklow, publishing co-ordinator

Releases about 2 new titles a year. Accepts unsolicited manuscripts about P.E.I. and other islands, mostly with a scholarly focus, but send inquiry first. Guidelines available.

Notable 2003 title: *Letters from the Manse*, Joan Archibald Colborne.

Jesperson Publishing

100 Water Street, 3rd Floor, P.O. Box 2188, St. John's, NL A1C 6E6
Phone: (709) 757-2216 Fax: (709) 753-0708
E-mail: info@jespersonpublishing.nf.net
Web site: www.jespersonpublishing.nf.net
Contact: Rebecca Rose, vice president

Publishes fiction and non-fiction, especially that which is related to the culture of Newfoundland and Labrador and to Canada. Releases 5 or 6 new titles a year. Accepts unsolicited manuscripts. Guidelines available.

Notable 2003 title: *Peril on the Sea: The Trinity Bay Disaster of 1892*, Eldon Drodge.

Kegedonce Press

Cape Croker First Nation, R.R. #5, Wiarton, ON N0H 2T0
Phone: (519) 371-1434 Fax: (519) 371-5011
E-mail: info@kegedonce.com
Web site: www.kegedonce.com
Contact: R. K. Abram, publishing co-ordinator

Committed to the development, promotion, and publication of the work of indigenous writers. Released 2 titles in 2003. Accepts unsolicited manuscripts, but first send an inquiry and sample chapters. "Prior publishing credits (magazines, etc.) are required for serious consideration. Aboriginal/indigenous authors only." Guidelines available on web site.

Notable 2003 title: *Without Reservation: Indigenous Erotica*, edited by Katiri Akiwenzie-Damon.

Key Porter Books
70 The Esplanade, Toronto, ON M5E 1R2
Phone: (416) 862-7777 Fax: (416) 862-2304
E-mail: info@keyporter.com
Web site: www.keyporter.com
Contact: editorial department
Established 1980. Specializes in high-profile non-fiction books on politics, history, biography, celebrities, cooking, natural history, and the environment. Also publishes literary fiction, short-story collections, and children's fiction and non-fiction. "We do not publish poetry, novellas, speculative fiction, or mysteries." Publishes approximately 75 new titles a year. No unsolicited manuscripts. Accepts outlines and sample chapters. See web site for guidelines.

Notable 2003 title: *The Player: The Life and Times of Dalton Camp*, Geoffrey Stevens.

Kids Can Press
29 Birch Avenue, Toronto, ON M4V 1E2
Phone: (416) 925-5437 Fax: (416) 960-5437
E-mail: info@kidscan.com
Web site: www.kidscanpress.com
Contact: Valerie Hussey, publisher
Established 1973. Publishes quality books for children of all ages, including picture books, poetry, non-fiction, fiction, crafts, and activity books. Averages 70 new titles each year. Accepts unsolicited manuscripts. Send outline and sample chapters of longer fiction. "Please familiarize yourself with our list before sending a manuscript. Request a catalogue if you're having trouble getting a good sense of the entire publishing program." Guidelines available on web site.

Notable 2003 title: *Suki's Kimono*, Chieri Uegake (illustrations by Stéphanie Jorisch).

Alfred A. Knopf Canada

1 Toronto Street, Suite 300, Toronto, ON M5C 2V6
Phone: (416) 364-4449 Fax: (416) 364-6863
Web site: www.randomhouse.ca
Contact: Angelika Glover, editorial assistant

"Knopf Canada publishes exceptional literary fiction and non-fiction from Canada and around the world." Releases approximately 30 new titles a year. Does not accept unsolicited manuscripts.

Notable 2003 title: *The Way the Crow Flies*, Ann-Marie MacDonald.

Lone Pine Publishing

10145 – 81st Avenue, Edmonton, AB T6E 1W9
Phone: (780) 433-9333 Fax: (780) 433-9646
E-mail: info@lonepinepublishing.com
Web site: www.lonepinepublishing.com

Established 1980. Specializes in natural history, outdoor recreation, regional gardening, and popular history. Most books have a regional focus. Has offices in Edmonton and Washington State. Publishes about 35 new titles each year. Accepts unsolicited manuscripts, but first send an inquiry by mail (after familiarizing yourself with Lone Pine's current titles). Guidelines available.

James Lorimer & Company

35 Britain Street, Toronto, ON M5A 1R7
Phone: (416) 362-4762 Fax: (416) 362-3939
E-mail: production@lorimer.ca
Web site: www.lorimer.ca
Contact: Chad Fraser, production editor

Seeking manuscripts on the following Canadian topics: biography, history, cookbooks (with a Canadian or regional focus), education, public issues, and travel. Published 22 new titles in 2003. Does not accept unsolicited manuscripts. Send an inquiry with sample chapters. Guidelines available.

Notable 2003 title: *Paul Martin: CEO for Canada?* Murray Dobbin.

Lost Moose – The Yukon Publishers

58 Kluane Crescent, Whitehorse, YT Y1A 3G7

Phone: (867) 668-5076
E-mail: lmoose@yknet.ca
Publishes books from the North about the North. Has a new literary imprint. Publishes 2 or 3 new titles annually. Accepts unsolicited manuscripts, but send an inquiry first. Guidelines available.

Lynx Images
P.O. Box 5961, Stn. A, Toronto, ON M5W 1P4
Phone: (416) 925-8422 Fax: (416) 925-8352
E-mail: sales@lynximages.com
Web site: www.lynximages.com
Contact: Russell Floren, publisher
Publishes books on Canadian history and Great Lakes travel. Averages 4 new titles a year. Accepts unsolicited manuscripts. Send an inquiry first. Guidelines available.
Notable 2004 title: *Vanished in the Mist*.

McArthur & Company Publishing
322 King Street W., Suite 402, Toronto, ON M5V 1J2
Phone: (416) 408-4007, ext. 21 Fax: (416) 408-4081
E-mail: info@mcarthur-co.com
Web site: www.mcarthur-co.com
Contact: Ann Ledden, vice president, sales
Publishes quality Canadian and international fiction, and nonfiction for adults and children. Produced 49 new titles in 2003. Does not accept unsolicited manuscripts. Send an inquiry first. "Please see our web site for further information on our company."
Notable 2003 title: *An Adoration*, Nancy Huston.

McClelland & Stewart Ltd.
481 University Avenue, Suite 900, Toronto, ON M5G 2E9
Phone: (416) 598-1114 Fax: (416) 598-7764
Web site: www.mcclelland.com
Contact: editorial department
Established 1906. Publishes a wide selection of fiction and nonfiction books on biography, history, natural history, politics, art, religion, and sports. Also publishes poetry and reference books. Releases about 80 titles a year. "We are 'The Canadian Publishers' and take our role to publish the best in Canadian fiction, non-fiction,

and poetry very seriously. With a stable of authors ranging from Margaret Atwood through to Roy MacGregor on to Leonard Cohen and then to Alice Munro and Rohinton Mistry, this house is not an easy point of entry for the beginning author." No unsolicited manuscripts; send an inquiry for fiction, an outline for non-fiction. See web site for guidelines.

Notable 2003 title: *Oryx and Crake*, Margaret Atwood.

McGill-Queen's University Press

Montreal office: McGill University, 3430 McTavish Street,
    Montreal, QC H3A 1X9
Phone: (514) 398-3750 Fax: (514) 398-4333
E-mail: mqup@mqup.mcgill.ca
Web site: www.mcgill.ca/mqup
Contact: Philip Cercone, editor-in-chief
Kingston office: Queen's University, Kingston, ON K7L 3N6
Phone: (613) 533-2155 Fax: (613) 533-6822
E-mail: mqup@post.queensu.ca
Contact: D. H. Akenson, senior editor

Established 1969. A non-profit joint venture of McGill and Queen's Universities. Its mission is to serve the Canadian and international scholarly communities as a vehicle for the publication of scholarly works of the highest quality. Publishes scholarly books on northern studies and history, political science, Canadian literature, anthropology, architecture, philosophy, and religion. Does not publish works of fiction. Averages 130 new titles a year, a third of which are destined for the trade market. Submit a proposal before sending manuscript. Guidelines available on web site.

Notable 2003 title: *The American Empire and the Fourth World*, Tony Hall.

Maple Tree Press

51 Front Street E., Suite 200, Toronto, ON M5E 1B3
Phone: (416) 304-0702 Fax: (416) 304-0525
E-mail: info@mapletreepress.com
Web site: www.mapletreepress.com
Contact: submissions editor

Publishes high-quality, innovative information books, activity books, and picture books with an emphasis on science, nature, animals, and children's activities such as crafts. Averages 8 to 10 new titles a year. Accepts unsolicited manuscripts, but first send query and outline for longer non-fiction works, the full manuscript for picture books. "Before submitting, spend some time familiarizing yourself with Maple Tree Press books in the library or on our web site. An SASE is required for any response. Maple Tree Press does not accept electronic submissions and does not publish novels." Guidelines available.

Notable 2003 title: *Canadian Dinosaurs*, Elin Kelsey.

Micromedia ProQuest
20 Victoria Street, Toronto, ON M5C 2N8
Phone: (416) 362-5211 Fax: (416) 362-6161
E-mail: sabram@micromedia.ca
Web site: www.micromedia.ca
Contact: Stephen Abram, vice-president

Electronic-database publisher specializing in Canadian serials, government documents, and corporate information for libraries, information centres, and research departments. Products available on CD-ROM, WWW, print, and microform. Frequently offers employment to indexers and abstracters. Releases 6 new titles annually. No unsolicited manuscripts. First send an inquiry.

Moose Enterprise Book and Theatre Play Publishing
684 Walls Road, Sault Ste. Marie, ON P6A 5K6
Phone: (705) 779-3331 Fax: (705) 779-3331
E-mail: mooseenterprises@on.aibn.com
Contact: Richard Mousseau, editor

"We assist the new and up-and-coming writer, those needing help developing their work. We accept submissions from unpublished and published authors." Released 5 titles in 2003. Accepts unsolicited manuscripts, but first send a query. "We accept only works of moral content." Guidelines available.

Notable 2003 title: *Realm of the Golden Feather*, Cory Ginter.

Morgaine House
P.O. Box 1027, Pointe Claire, QC H9S 4H9
E-mail: kamouraska3@sympatico.ca
Contact: Mary Gurekas, editor

Established 1994. A small literary press interested in well-crafted manuscripts of poetry and short fiction. Publishes 2 to 5 new titles annually. No unsolicited manuscripts. Queries only.

Notable 2003 title: *Between Cup and Lip*, Jean Mallinson.

Mosaic Press

1252 Speers Road, Units 1 & 2, Oakville, ON L6L 5N9
Phone: (905) 825-2130 Fax: (905) 825-2130
E-mail: mosaicpress@on.aibn.com
Web site: www.mosaic-press.com
Contact: Keith Daniel, managing director

Focuses on literature, including fiction, short fiction, and poetry; the arts, including theatre, art, architecture, and music; social studies; and international studies. Publishes 20 new titles annually. Accepts unsolicited manuscripts; send sample chapters first.

Notable 2003 title: *A Garden of Anchors: New and Selected Poems*, Joy Kagawa.

Napoleon Publishing/Rendez Vous Press

178 Willowdale Avenue, Suite 201, Toronto, ON M2N 4Y8
Phone: (416) 730-9052 Fax: (416) 730-8096
E-mail: editorial@transmedia95.com
Web site: www.napoleonpublishing.com
Contact: Allister Thompson, editor

Publishers of children's fiction, picture books, and educational resources. Adult imprint focuses primarily on Canadian crime fiction. Released 10 new titles in 2003. "We will not be accepting unsolicited submissions in 2004. We will resume in 2005." Send queries. Guidelines available.

Notable 2003 title: *The Deep End Gang*, Peggy Dymond Leavey.

Natural Heritage Books

P.O. Box 95, Stn. O, Toronto, ON M4A 2M8
Phone: (416) 694-7907 Fax: (416) 690-0819
E-mail: info@naturalheritagebooks.com
Web site: www.naturalheritagebooks.com
Contact: Jane Gibson, editor

Primarily a non-fiction press specializing in history, heritage, out-of-doors, natural history, and the environment. Committed to quality Canadian non-fiction. Averages 14 titles a year, including 1 or 2 works of poetry. No unsolicited manuscripts. First send inquiry with outline and sample chapters including idea of intended audience. Guidelines available.

Notable 2003 title: *Family Secrets: Crossing the Colour Line*, Catherine Slaney.

New Society Publishers

P.O. Box 189, Gabriola Island, BC V0R 1X0
Phone: (250) 247-9737 Fax: (250) 247-7471
E-mail: info@newsociety.com
Web site: www.newsociety.com
Contact: Chris Plant, editor

NSP's mission is to publish books that contribute in fundamental ways to building an ecologically sustainable and just society, and to do so in a manner that models this vision with the least possible impact on the Earth. Dedicated to social change through non-violent action. Releases approximately 20 to 25 new titles a year. Send inquiry first. Guidelines available. "All of NSP's new titles are printed on acid-free paper that is 100% old-growth-forest free, processed chlorine free. Each book contains an eco audit."

Notable 2003 title: *Diary of a Compost Hotline Operator*, Spring Gillard.

New Star Books

3477 Commercial Drive, Suite 107, Vancouver, BC V5N 4E8
Phone: (604) 738-9429 Fax: (604) 738-9332
E-mail: info@newstarbooks.com
Web site: www.newstarbooks.com
Contact: Melva McLean, managing editor

Publishes progressive books on social issues, politics, British Columbia, and the West, along with literary novels and short fiction. Released 10 new titles in 2003. Does not accept unsolicited manuscripts of poetry. Send an inquiry with sample chapters for non-fiction and the complete manuscript for fiction. Guidelines available. "No fax, e-mail, or disk submissions, and no telephone inquiries, please."

Notable 2003 title: *Field Day: Getting Society Out of School*, Matt Hern.

New World Publishing

P.O. Box 36075, Halifax, NS B3J 3S9
Phone: (902) 576-2055 Fax: (902) 576-2095
E-mail: editor@newworldpublishing.com
Web site: www.newworldpublishing.com
Contact: Francis Mitchell, managing editor

Publishes books and music that make a difference in people's lives, including alternative-health and children's books, and include important messages relating to self-esteem, improvement in health, etc. All non-fiction, except children's books, but there must be an uplifting message built in. "Please do not submit fiction." Releases 2 to 3 new books a year. Does not accept unsolicited manuscripts. Send an inquiry and an outline. Guidelines available on web site.

Notable 2003 title: *Free to Fly: A Journey Toward Wellness*, Judet Rajhathy.

NeWest Publishing

8540 – 109th Street, Suite 201, Edmonton, AB T6G 1E6
Phone: (780) 432-9427 Fax: (780) 433-3179
E-mail: info@newestpress.com
Web site: www.newestpress.com
Contact: Ruth Linka, general manager

A literary publisher that focuses on Western Canadian authors of fiction, poetry, drama, literary criticism, and regional non-fiction. Releases approximately 15 new books a year. Accepts unsolicited manuscripts. "Manuscripts are reviewed by an editorial board, and it can take up to 6 months to receive a response." Guidelines available on web site.

Notable 2003 title: *Playing Dead*, Ruby Wiebe.

Nimbus Publishing

3731 Mackintosh Street, P.O. Box 9166, Halifax, NS B3K 5M8
Phone: (902) 455-5956 Fax: (902) 455-5440
E-mail: smcintyre@nimbus.ns.ca
Web site: www.nimbus.ns.ca
Contact: Sandra McIntyre, managing editor

Established 1978. The largest trade publisher in Atlantic Canada. Publishes and distributes books on all aspects of Atlantic Canada. Non-fiction topics include natural history, political and social issues, and history. Also publishes guidebooks, cookbooks, and books of photography, children's literature, and fiction. Does not publish poetry or genre fiction. Releases about 25 new titles each year. Accepts unsolicited manuscripts, but first send outline and sample chapters. "Writers are encouraged to submit proposals that fit within our publishing mandate." Guidelines available.

Notable 2003 title: *Inspired Halifax: The Art of Dusan Kadlec*, Dusan Kadlec with text by Cynthia Mahoney.

Northstone Publishing

9025 Jim Bailey Road, Kelowna, BC V4V 1R2
Phone: (250) 766-2778 Fax: (250) 766-2736
E-mail: info@woodlake.com
Web site: www.joinhands.com
Contact: Michael Schwartentuber, editor

"Our products are truth seeking and life affirming, and reflect our mission to promote positive social and spiritual values." Publishes about 10 titles a year. Accepts unsolicited manuscripts, but first send a query. Guidelines available.

Notable 2003 title: *Gen X: Y Faith*, Ross Lockhart.

Novalis

Saint Paul University, 223 Main Street, Ottawa, ON K1S 1C4
Phone: (613) 236-1393, ext. 2200 Fax: (613) 751-4020
E-mail: kburns@ustpaul.ca
Web site: www.novalis.ca
Contact: Kevin Burns, commissioning editor

Established 1936. Publishes resources that help people explore the dynamics of their faith, to pray, and to foster their spiritual growth. Founded by a Roman Catholic yet dedicated to ecumenical and interfaith dialogue and understanding. Releases about 30 new books each year in English and a similar number in French. Also publishes a number of periodicals, including *Living with Christ, Celebrate!* and *Words of Life*. Accepts unsolicited manuscripts, but first send an inquiry with sample chapters and author résumé. Guidelines available.

"Developing a book is a long, slow creative process. Approach us early with your idea. Since we publish both periodicals and books, we let our periodicals address short-term and topical subjects. By comparison, we like to choose books that will have a longer than usual shelf life. We look for subject matter and literary approaches that will not fade with yesterday's headlines. We are interested in reaching people who are searching for meaning, while at the same time we support those with a clear faith commitment."

Notable 2003 title: *The Human Right to Peace*, Douglas Roche.

Oberon Press
350 Sparks Street, Suite 400, Ottawa, ON K1R 7S8
Phone: (613) 238-3275 Fax: (613) 238-3275
Web site: www3.sympatico.ca/oberon
Contact: Nicholas Macklem, general manager

Established 1966. Publishes Canadian literary fiction, poetry, and non-fiction (biographies, memoirs, literary criticism, and essays). No genre fiction. Averages 12 new books a year. Accepts unsolicited manuscripts, but first send outline and sample chapters. Multiple submissions not considered. Guidelines available.

Notable 2003 title: *03: Best Canadian Stories*, edited by Douglas Glover.

Oolichan Books
P.O. Box 10, Lantzville, BC V0R 2H0
Phone: (250) 390-4839 Fax: (250) 390-4839
E-mail: oolichan@island.net
Web site: www.oolichan.com
Contact: Ron Smith, publisher

Established 1974. Publishes literary fiction, poetry, and literary non-fiction. Releases 7 new titles a year. Considers unsolicited submissions, but send initial letter of inquiry and sample. Guidelines available on web site. "We accept multiple submissions. Please do not send children's or young-adult manuscripts, or fantasy, horror, science-fiction, romance, thriller, gothic, or mass-market fiction."

Notable 2003 title: *Time's Reach*, Rachel Wyatt.

Orca Book Publishers
P.O. Box 5626, Stn. B, Victoria, BC V8R 6S4
Phone: (250) 380-1229 Fax: (250) 380-1892
E-mail: orca@orcabook.com
Web site: www.orcabook.com

Contacts: Bob Tyrrell or Andrew Wooldridge for teen fiction;
   Andrew Wooldridge for juvenile fiction and Soundings;
   Maggie de Vries for early readers and picture books
   Established 1984. Publishes award-winning books for young readers by Canadian authors, including picture books, first readers, and juvenile and teen fiction. Only occasionally publishes non-fiction. Releases approximately 40 new titles a year. Unsolicited manuscripts accepted for picture books (send an SASE); for novels, send query, outline, and sample chapters (send an SASE). Guidelines available on web site. No submissions via e-mail.
   Notable 2003 title: *Under a Prairie Sky*, Anne Laurel Carter.

Oxford University Press
70 Wynford Drive, Don Mills, ON M3C 1J9
Phone: (416) 441-2941 Fax: (416) 444-0427
Web site: www.oup.com/ca
Contact: Leslie Anne Connell, director, trade and reference division
   Established in Canada 1904. The Canadian trade publishing program is small and focuses mainly on history and reference. It includes only books intended for a general audience, and everything on this list either has a Canadian subject or examines a topic from a distinctly Canadian point of view. No novels, short stories by 1 author, how-to or self-help books, cookbooks, coffee-table books, books of poetry, or books for children or young adults. Accepts unsolicited manuscripts, but first send a query with a brief synopsis. Guidelines available on web site.

Pedlar Press
P.O. Box 26, Stn. P, Toronto, ON M5S 2S6
Phone: (416) 534-2011 Fax: (416) 535-9677
E-mail: feralgrl@interlog.com
Web site: www.pedlarpress.com
Contact: Beth Follett, publisher/editor
   Publishes Canadian fiction, poetry, and art books. Sees its role as an innovator. Releases 5 new titles each year. Accepts unsolicited manuscripts, but first send an inquiry, outline, and sample chapters. Guidelines available.
   Notable 2003 title: A *Novel by Ken Sparling*.

Pemmican Publications Inc.
150 Henry Avenue, Winnipeg, MB R3B 0J7
Phone: (204) 589-6346 Fax: (204) 589-2063
E-mail: pemmicanpublications@hotmail.com
Web site: www.pemmican.mb.ca
Contact: Audreen Hourie, managing editor
  Established 1980 by the Manitoba Métis Federation as a creative and vocational venue for the Métis people of Manitoba. "A cultural and educational publishing house, the only established Métis book publisher in Canada. Pemmican is renowned for colour children's books. We also publish poetry, novels, and non-fiction." Releases 4 to 5 new titles each year. Accepts unsolicited manuscripts, but first send sample chapters. Guidelines available.

Penguin Group (Canada)
10 Alcorn Avenue, Suite 300, Toronto, ON M4V 3B2
Phone: (416) 925-2249 Fax: (416) 925-0068
Web site: www.penguin.ca
Contact: Helen Reeves, editorial assistant
  Established in Canada in 1974. Mainstream publisher that features fiction, fantasy fiction, non-fiction, and young-adult titles for 8- to 12-year-olds. Notable authors include Michael Ignatieff, John Ralston Saul, Stuart McLean, Mark Kingwell, Guy Gavriel Kay, Nega Mezlekia, and Joan Clark. Released 75 new titles in 2003. No unsolicited manuscripts.
  Notable 2003 title: *Vinyl Cafe Diaries*, Stuart McLean.

Penumbra Press
1225 Potter Drive, Manotick, ON K4M 1C9
Phone: (613) 692-5590 Fax: (613) 692-5589
E-mail: john@penumbrapress.com
Web site: www.penumbrapress.com
Contact: John Flood, president
  Publishes northern, eastern Ontario, and Native literature and art, Scandinavian literature in translation, archives of Canadian art, children's books, and poetry books. Releases about 10 new titles a year. Accepts unsolicited manuscripts, but first send an inquiry with outline and sample chapters.

Playwrights Canada Press
215 Spadina Avenue, Suite 230, Toronto, ON M5T 2C7
Phone: (416) 703-0013 Fax: (416) 408-3402
Web site: www.playwrightscanada.com
Contact: Angela Rebeiro, publisher
   Established 1972. Publishes drama only, and only those plays
that have had professional theatre production. Published 20 plays
in 2003. Accepts unsolicited manuscripts. Guidelines available.
   Notable 2003 title: *Einstein's Gift*, Vern Thiessen.

Polar Bear Press
35 Prince Andrew Place, Toronto, ON M3C 2H2
Phone: (416) 449-4000 Fax: (416) 449-9924
Contact: Michelle Hayles
   Publishes books on Ontario history and humour, non-fiction
only. Releases 4 new titles annually. Does not accept unsolicited
manuscripts. Send an outline and sample chapters. "Please send an
SASE for return of any unsolicited material."

The Porcupine's Quill
68 Main Street, Erin, ON N0B 1T0
Phone: (519) 833-9158 Fax: (519) 833-9845
E-mail: pql@sentex.net
Web site: www.sentex.net/~pql
Contact: John Metcalf, senior fiction editor
   Established 1974. Specializes in Canadian literary fiction.
Published 12 new titles in 2003. Does not accept unsolicited
manuscripts.
   Notable 2003 title: *Always Now*, Margaret Avison.

Portage & Main Press
318 McDermot Avenue, Suite 100, Winnipeg, MB R3A 0A2
Phone: (204) 987-3500 Fax: (204) 947-0080
E-mail: books@portageandmainpress.com
Web site: www.portageandmainpress.com
Contact: Catherine Gerbasi, director
   Publishes books by education professionals for teachers of grades
K to 6 in all subjects. Publishes about 20 new titles a year. Does not
accept unsolicited manuscripts. Send a query. Guidelines available.

Notable 2003 title: *The Guide to Textiles for Interiors* (3rd edition), Dianne Jackman, Mary Dixon, and Jill Conora.

Pottersfield Press

83 Leslie Road, East Lawrencetown, NS B2Z 1P8
Web site: www.pottersfieldpress.com
Contact: Lesley Choyce, editor
Established 1979. Publishes general non-fiction, novels, and books of interest to Atlantic Canada. Particularly interested in biography proposals. Averages 6 new titles a year. Accepts proposals and/or full manuscripts. No phone calls, please.

Productive Publications

P.O. Box 7200, Stn. A, Toronto, ON M5W 1X8
Phone: (416) 483-0634 Fax: (416) 322-7434
Web site: www.productivepublications.ca
Contact: Iain Williamson, publisher
Publishes softcover books on small business, entrepreneurship, business management, computers, and the Internet. Publishes about 16 new titles a year. Accepts unsolicited manuscripts, but send an inquiry first. Guidelines available. "We are looking for books of 100 to 200 pages that are well written by people who know their subject well."
Notable 2003 title: *Entrepreneurship and Starting a Business*.

Ptarmigan Press

1372 16th Avenue, Campbell River, BC V9W 2E1
Phone: (250) 286-0878 Fax: (250) 286-9749
E-mail: info@kaskgraphics.com
Web site: www.ptarmiganpress.com; www.kaskgraphics.com
Contact: Ann Kask, manager
Specializes in non-fiction, local history, and cookbooks. Published 4 new books in 2003. Accepts unsolicited manuscripts, but first send an inquiry.
Notable 2003 title: *Rivers of Return*, Van Egan.

Raincoast Books

9050 Shaughnessy Street, Vancouver, BC V6P 6E5
Phone: (604) 323-7100 Fax: (604) 323-2600

E-mail: info@raincoast.com
Web site: www.raincoast.com
Contacts: editorial department
   Publishes regional, national, and international titles on the environment/nature, sports, travel, and cooking, as well as children's, YA, and adult fiction, poetry, and picture books. Publishes about 30 new titles a year. Does not accept unsolicited manuscripts or queries by e-mail. Send query letter by mail, allowing 8 to 16 weeks for a reply. Guidelines available on web site.

Random House Canada
1 Toronto Street, Suite 300, Toronto, ON M5C 2V6
Phone: (416) 364-4449 Fax: (416) 364-6863
Web site: www.randomhouse.ca
Contact: Paul Robertson, editorial assistant
   A general trade publisher of quality fiction and non-fiction, primarily general interest, literary, and culinary titles. No unsolicited manuscripts. Send an inquiry with an outline and sample chapters. No e-mail submissions.
   Notable 2003 title: *Shake Hands with the Devil*, Romeo Dallaire.

Red Deer Press
2500 University Drive N.W., MLT-813, Calgary, AB T2N 1N4
Phone: (403) 220-4334 Fax: (403) 210-8191
E-mail: rdp@ucalgary.ca
Web site: www.reddeerpress.com
Contacts: Dennis Johnson, managing editor; Peter Carver, children's editor
   Established 1975. Publishes literary fiction and non-fiction for adults and children, illustrated children's books, young-adult and teen fiction, poetry, and drama. Produced 15 books in 2001. Accepts unsolicited manuscripts. Send an inquiry with sample chapters first. Canadian authors only. "Children's list is usually booked 2 to 3 years in advance. Reports in 4 to 6 months." Guidelines available on web site.
   Notable 2003 title: *Amber Waiting*, Nan Gregory.

Rocky Mountain Books
4 Spruce Centre S.W., Calgary, AB T3C 3B3

Phone: (403) 249-9490 Fax: (403) 249-2968
E-mail: tonyd@rmbooks.com
Web site: www.rmbooks.com
Contact: Tony Daffern, publisher

Established 1976. Specializes in outdoor recreational guides to the Canadian Rockies and Western Canada, and books on mountain culture, mountaineering, mountain people, and local history in mountain areas. Averages 6 new titles a year. Does not accept unsolicited manuscripts. Send an query letter and outline after visiting the web site to review the booklist and consult the author guidelines.

Notable 2003 title: *The Yam: 50 Years of Climbing on Yamnuska*, Chic Scott, Dave Dornian, and Ben Gadd.

Ronsdale Press
3350 West 21st Avenue, Vancouver, BC V6S 1G7
Phone: (604) 738-4688 Fax: (604) 731-4548
E-mail: ronhatch@pinc.com
Web site: www.ronsdalepress.com
Contact: Ronald B. Hatch, director

Established in 1988. A literary press specializing in fiction, poetry, biography, regional literature, and books of ideas. Also children's literature, but not picture books. Interested in quality and experimental literature. Released 10 new titles in 2003. Accepts unsolicited manuscripts. "We expect our authors to read widely in contemporary and past literature. Poets must have some publishing credits. With children's literature, we are interested in Canadian historical fiction. No picture books, please." Guidelines available on web site.

Notable 2003 title: *Strongman: The Doug Hepburn Story*, Tom Thurston.

Roseway Publishing Co. Ltd.
R.R. #1, Lockeport, NS B0T 1L0
Phone: (902) 656-2223 Fax: (902) 656-2223
E-mail: kathleen.tudor@ns.sympatico.ca
Web site: www.rosewaypublishing.com
Contact: Kathleen Tudor, CEO

Publishes Nova Scotian authors and is particularly interested in high-quality poetry, fiction, plays, issue-related non-fiction, and children's literature. Releases 1 or 2 titles annually. Accepts unsolicited manuscripts, but first send an inquiry. "Authors should become familiar with publisher's list before submitting material." Guidelines available.

Notable 2003 title: *Among the Saints*, Donna E. Smyth.

Royal BC Museum

Publishing, 675 Belleville Street, Victoria, BC V8W 9W2
Phone: (250) 387-2478 Fax: (250) 952-6825
E-mail: gtruscott@royalbcmuseum.bc.ca
Web site: www.royalbcmuseum.bc.ca
Contact: Gerry Truscott, publisher

Established 1891. Publishes scholarly and popular non-fiction concerning the human and natural histories of British Columbia, and the museum's activities. All manuscripts must be sponsored by an RBCM curator or department. Produces about 4 new titles a year. No unsolicited manuscripts. Send an inquiry. Guidelines available.

Notable 2003 title: *Songhees Pictorial*, Grant Keddie.

Rubicon Publishing

595 Argus Road, Oakville, ON L6J 3J4
Phone: (905) 849-8777 Fax: (905) 849-7579
E-mail: contact@rubiconpublishing.com
Web site: www.rubiconpublishing.com
Contact: Reg Neill, general manager

Publishes educational and trade titles. Releases about 20 books a year. Accepts unsolicited manuscripts, but first send an outline and sample chapters.

Notable 2003 title: *Northern Lights: Outstanding Canadian Women*, J. Green, L. Palazzi, and M. Senecal.

Saxon House Canada

P.O. Box 6947, Stn. A, Toronto, ON M5W 1X6
Phone: (416) 488-7171 Fax: (416) 488-2989
Contact: W. H. Wallace, general manager

Seeking works of history, philosophy, and fiction with literary integrity, historical accuracy, and fresh narrative skills. No longer publishes poetry. Averages 4 titles a year. Send an inquiry and outline.

Notable 2003 title: *The Journey to Canada*, David Mills.

Scholastic Canada Ltd.

175 Hillmount Road, Markham, ON L4C 1Z7
Phone: (905) 887-7323 Fax: (905) 887-3643
Web site: www.scholastic.ca
Contact: editor

Publishes books for children and young people up to age 14 with a focus on Canadian authors and illustrators. Produces about 75 new English trade books a year. No unsolicited manuscripts. Send an inquiry. For guidelines, see www.scholastic.ca/guideline.html.

Notable 2003 title: *Pippin the Christmas Pig*, Jean Little and Werner Zimmermann.

Second Story Press

720 Bathurst Street, Suite 301, Toronto, ON M5S 2R4
Phone: (416) 537-7850 Fax: (416) 537-0588
E-mail: info@secondstorypress.ca
Web site: www.secondstorypress.ca
Contact: Margie Wolfe, publisher

A women's press specializing in quality fiction and non-fiction (women's health and contemporary social issues are of particular interest), children's picture books, and juvenile novels. Released 10 titles in 2003. Accepts unsolicited manuscripts, but first send outline and sample chapters. Guidelines available.

Notable 2003 title: *Night Spies*, Kathy Kacer.

Self-Counsel Press

1481 Charlotte Road, North Vancouver, BC V7J 1H1
Phone: (604) 986-3366 Fax: (604) 986-3947
E-mail: editor@self-counsel.com
Web site: www.self-counsel.com
Contact: Richard Day, acquisitions editor

Established 1971. Publishes non-fiction in 3 categories: legal series for lay readers, business series for small-business operators, and how to start and run a specific type of business. Also publishes how-to books on topics such as buying a house and understanding accounting. Produces at least 24 new titles each year. Accepts unsolicited manuscripts, but first send an outline, sample chapter, a résumé of your credentials, and the reasons this book is needed. "We seek fact-rich books written by experts in their field. Most manuscripts accepted are 70,000 to 80,000 words. We publish for the Canadian and U.S. markets." Guidelines available on web site.

J. Gordon Shillingford Publishing
P.O. Box 86, RPO, Winnipeg, MB R3M 3S3
Phone: (204) 779-6967 Fax: (204) 779-6970
E-mail: jgshill@allstream.net
Contact: Gordon Shillingford, president

Publishes Canadian drama, poetry, and non-fiction (social history, biography, native issues, and politics). Produces about 12 new titles a year. No unsolicited manuscripts. Send an inquiry. "We do not publish fiction or children's books."

Notable 2003 title: *In Muddy Water: Conversations with 11 Poets*.

Shoreline
23 Ste-Anne, Ste-Anne-de-Bellevue, QC H9X 1L1
Phone: (514) 457-5733 Fax: (514) 457-5733
E-mail: shoreline@sympatico.ca
Web site: www.shorelinepress.ca
Contact: Judy Isherwood, editor

Focuses on biographies and memoirs, some local history, and some poetry. Released 7 new titles in 2003. No unsolicited manuscripts. "We are a very small press and booked through 2005."

Notable 2003 title: *Sheila's Take*, Sheila Kindellan-Sheehan.

Signature Editions
P.O. Box 206, RPO Corydon, Winnipeg, MB R3M 3S7
Phone: (204) 779-7803 Fax: (204) 779-6970
E-mail: signature@allstream.net
Web site: www.signature-editions.com
Contact: Karen Haughian, publisher

Publishes literary works by Canadians in the genres of fiction, non-fiction, poetry, and drama. Accepts unsolicited manuscripts by mail only with a covering letter, a synopsis, and a C.V. specifying previous published works. Include an SASE for a reply. Guidelines available on web site.

Notable 2003 title: *Last Days of Montreal*, John Brooke.

Smart Cookie Publishing

2017 West 15th Avenue, Suite 4, Vancouver, BC V6J 2L4
E-mail: smartcookiebooks@yahoo.ca
Web site: www.webspotter.com/smartcookie
Contact: Chris Rothstein, editor

A micro press that publishes zines, chapbooks, and books with a smart and funny perspective on underground and alternative culture. "Our interest is in shorter runs, unusual book forms, and in risky, unusual, and experimental styles and ideas. No mainstream writing." Releases 2 new titles a year. Accepts unsolicited manuscripts, but first send a sample (30 pages maximum). Guidelines available.

Notable 2003 title: *Number One Fan: How Pop Culture Changed My Life*.

Sound and Vision Publishing

359 Riverdale Avenue, Toronto, ON M4J 1A4
Phone: (416) 465-2828 Fax: (416) 465-0755
E-mail: sales@soundandvision.com
Web site: www.soundandvision.com
Contact: Geoff Savage, publisher

A specialist press featuring books on musical humour. Also publishes Quotable Books, a series of titles containing quotations from famous musical, literary, and historical figures. "Writers should check out our web site to see the kind of books we publish." Releases an average of 3 new titles a year. Does not accept unsolicited manuscripts. Send queries with outlines and sample chapters.

Notable 2003 title: *The Music Lover's Quotation Book*, David W. Barber.

Talonbooks

P.O. Box 2076, Vancouver, BC V6B 3S3
Phone: (604) 444-4889 Fax: (604) 444-4119

E-mail: talon@pinc.com
Web site: www.talonbooks.com
Contact: Karl Siegler, publisher

Established 1967. Specializes in drama, serious fiction, poetry, women's literature, social issues, and ethnography. Publishes about 20 new titles annually. No unsolicited poetry manuscripts. For the rest, first send an inquiry. "We consider for publication only playscripts that have been professionally produced. We do not publish historical, romance, adventure, or sci-fi fiction, or children's literature." Guidelines available.

Notable 2003 title: *Birth of a Bookworm*, Michel Tremblay.

Theytus Books
Lot 45, Green Mountain Road, R.R. #2, Site 50 Comp. 8,
    Penticton, BC V2A 6J7
Phone: (250) 493-7181 Fax: (250) 493-5302
E-mail: theytusbooks@vip.net
Web site: www.theytusbooks.ca
Contacts: Anita Large, publishing manager; Leanne Flett Kruger,
    production and distribution manager

An Aboriginal-owned and -run publishing house that publishes Aboriginal authors. Theytus is an Salishan word that means "preserving for the sake of handing down." "We strive to produce appropriate reading material and information about Aboriginal peoples through the promotion of Aboriginal authors." Publishes about 8 new titles a year. Accepts unsolicited manuscripts. Guidelines available.

Notable 2003 title: *The Little Duck*, Beth Cuthand.

Thistledown Press
633 Main Street, Saskatoon, SK S7H 0J8
Phone: (306) 244-1722 Fax: (306) 244-1762
E-mail: tdpress@thistledown.sk.ca
Web site: www.thistledown.sk.ca
Contact: Jackie Forrie, publications co-ordinator

Established 1975. Aims to publish Canadian literature of the highest quality, representing the wealth of the nation's culture and heritage. Specializes in Canadian fiction, poetry, and young-adult fiction. Publishes about 14 new titles a year. The New Leaf Editions series is devoted to books of 64 pages by previously unpublished writers from Saskatchewan. Does not accept unsolicited manuscripts. Query first. Guidelines available on web site.

Notable 2003 title: *Coyote*, Brian Brett.

timeless (Canada)
P.O. Box 9, Kootenay Bay, BC VOB IXO
Phone: (250) 227-9224 Fax: (250) 227-9494
E-mail: contact@timeless.org
Web site: www.timeless.org
Contact: Andrew Wedman, co-ordinator

Publishes the works of Swami Sivananda Radha and others who teach yoga in her tradition. Publishes 1 new title a year. Does not accept unsolicited manuscripts.

Notable 2003 title: *Radha: Diary of a Woman's Search*, Swami Sivananda Radha.

Touchwood Editions
356 Simcoe Street, Suite 6, Victoria, BC V8V ILI
Phone: (250) 360-0829 Fax: (250) 385-0829
E-mail: touchwoodeditions@shaw.ca
Web site: www.touchwoodeditions.com
Contact: Vivian Sinclair, managing editor

Publishes mostly non-fiction, with a focus on creative non-fiction and some historical fiction, history, biography, and nautical subjects, all relevant to B.C. or Western Canada. Released 17 titles in 2003. Accepts unsolicited manuscripts, but first send an inquiry with an outline and sample chapters. Guidelines available.

Notable 2003 title: *Painter, Paddler: The Art and Adventures of Stewart Marshall*, Andrew Scott.

Tundra Books
481 University Avenue, Suite 900, Toronto, ON M5G 2E9
Phone: (416) 598-4786 Fax: (416) 598-0247
Web site: www.tundrabooks.com
Contact: Tamara Sztainbok, editor

Established 1967. Specializes in literary children's books, including picture books with outstanding art, chapter books, and young-adult novels. Averages 36 new titles a year. Does not accept unsolicited manuscripts.

Turnstone Press
100 Arthur Street, Suite 607, Winnipeg, MB R3B 1H3
Phone: (204) 947-1555 Fax: (204) 942-1555
E-mail: info@turnstonepress.com
Web site: www.turnstonepress.com
Contact: Todd Besant, managing editor

Established 1976. A literary press publishing fiction, poetry, non-fiction, and literary criticism. Through its imprint Ravenstone, it publishes non-formula genre fiction. Releases 12 new titles a year. Accepts unsolicited manuscripts. Send sample chapters first. Guidelines available on web site.

Notable 2003 title: *Kilter: 55 Fictions*, John Gould.

UBC Press
2029 West Mall, Vancouver, BC V6T 1Z2
Phone: (604) 822-5959 Fax: (604) 822-6083
E-mail: info@ubcpress.ca
Web site: www.ubcpress.ca
Contact: Jean Wilson, associate director, editorial

Established 1971. Publishes non-fiction for scholarly, educational, and general audiences in the humanities, social sciences, and natural sciences. Subject areas include history, political science, Native studies, natural resources, Asian studies, and law and society. Releases 50 new titles each year. No unsolicited manuscripts. Send an inquiry with outline and sample chapters. Guidelines available.

Notable 2003 title: *Unnatural Law: Rethinking Canadian Environmental Law and Policy*, David R. Boyd.

Ulysses Travel Guides
4176 St. Denis, Montreal, QC H2W 2M5
Phone: (514) 843-9882 Fax: (514) 843-9448
E-mail: info@ulysses.ca
Web site: www.ulyssesguides.ca
Contact: Daniel Desjardins, president

Publishes travel guides and outdoor activity guides for Canadians. Released 6 new titles in 2003. Accepts unsolicited manuscripts, but first send an outline and sample chapters.

Notable 2003 title: *The Trans-Canada Trail in Quebec*, Yves Seguin.

United Church Publishing House

3250 Bloor Street W., Suite 300, Toronto, ON M8X 2Y4
Phone: (416) 231-5931 Fax: (416) 231-3103
Web site: www.united-church.ca
Contact: Rebekah Chevalier, senior editor

Established in 1829 as Ryerson Press. Aims to meet the spiritual needs of both its church members and others. Committed to publishing books that help people engage in Christian ministry, attracting readers, regardless of denomination or faith, to consider the spiritual aspects of their lives. Not accepting unsolicited manuscripts.

Notable 2003 title: *Faithful Moments*, compiled by Jackie Harper.

University of Alberta Press

Ring House 2, University of Alberta, Edmonton, AB T6G 2E1
Phone: (780) 492-3662 Fax: (780) 492-0719
E-mail: u.a.p@ualberta.ca
Web site: www.uap.ualberta.ca
Contact: Linda D. Cameron, director

Established 1969. The UAP publishing program includes important scholarly works and fine books for broad audiences. "Our list is strong in western and northern Canadian topics, including history, Native studies, health sciences, natural history, and the environment. Recent additions include biography, travel writing, business, and international relations." Publishes about 22 new titles a year. No unsolicited manuscripts. Inquiries accepted. Guidelines available on web site.

Notable 2003 title: *The Canadian Dictionary of ASL*, edited by Carole Sue Bailey and Kathy Dolby.

University of Calgary Press

2500 University Drive N.W., Calgary, AB T2N 1N4
Phone: (403) 220-7578 Fax: (403) 282-0085

E-mail: whildebr@ucalgary.ca
Web site: www.uofcpress.com
Contact: Sharon Boyle, marketing manager

Established 1981. Publishes academic and trade books and journals that engage academic, industry/business, government, and public communities. "We focus on works that give voice to the heartland of the continent (the Canadian Northwest, the American West, including the mountain region and the Great Plains); are innovative, experimental, and offer alternative perspectives on established canons and subjects; and resonate with international themes, bringing diverse voices and views to the forefront." Releases 15 to 20 new titles annually. Accepts unsolicited manuscripts, but first send an inquiry with an outline and sample chapters. Guidelines available.

Notable 2003 title: *Madwoman in the Academy: 43 Women Boldly Take on the Ivory Tower*, edited by D. Keahey and D. J. Schnitzer.

University College of Cape Breton Press

P.O. Box 5300, Sydney, NS B1P 6L2
Phone: (902) 563-1955 Fax: (902) 563-1177
E-mail: uccb_press@uccb.ca
Web site: www.uccbpress.ca
Contact: Mike Hunter, editor-in-chief

Serves as a link between the University College of Cape Breton and its broader communities, publishing literature of significance to Cape Breton Island that enhances knowledge about the island, its history, and cultural preservation. A leading publisher of works related to community development (CED), which are read by scholars and activists around the world. Released 4 new titles in 2003. Accepts unsolicited manuscripts, but first send an inquiry and outline. Guidelines available.

Notable 2003 title: *The Loom of Change: Weaving a New Economy*, Patterson and Biag.

University of Manitoba Press

301 St. John's College, Winnipeg, MB R3T 2M5
Phone: (204) 474-9495 Fax: (204) 474-7566
Web site: www.umanitoba.ca/uofmpress
Contact: David Carr, director

Established 1967. Publishes non-fiction for trade and academic markets in Western Canadian history and Native studies. Averages 5 new titles each year. No unsolicited manuscripts. Send an inquiry with an outline and sample chapters first. Guidelines available. "Please confine inquiries to manuscripts that pertain to the fields in which we publish."

Notable 2003 title: *Alien Heart: The Life and Work of Margaret Laurence*, Lyall Powers.

University of Ottawa Press
542 King Edward Avenue, Ottawa, ON KIN 6N5
Phone: (613) 562-5246 Fax: (613) 562-5247
E-mail: press@uottawa.ca
Web site: www.uopress.uottawa.ca
Contact: Ruth Bradley St-Cyr, editor-in-chief

Reflecting the major interests of its parent institute, the UOP publishes scholarly works, textbooks, and general interest books. Areas of interest include Canadian studies, Canadian literature, history, governance, criminology, women's studies, religion, and translation. "We do not publish fiction, poetry, plays, memoirs, or works that claim to 'explain everything.'" Releases about 20 new titles annually. Accepts unsolicited manuscripts, but first send an inquiry. Guidelines available.

Notable 2003 title: *Windows and Words: A Look at Canadian Children's Literature in English*, edited by Aïda Hudson and Susan-Ann Cooper.

University of Toronto Press
10 St. Mary Street, Suite 700, Toronto, ON M4Y 2W8
Phone: (416) 978-2239 Fax: (416) 978-4738
E-mail: publishing@utpress.utoronto.ca
Web site: www.library.utoronto.ca/www/utpress/publish/
  publish.htm

Established 1901. A large university press publishing scholarly and general works, and many academic journals. Editorial program includes classical, medieval, Renaissance, and Victorian studies, modern languages, English and Canadian literature, literary theory and criticism, women's studies, social sciences, Native studies, philosophy, law, religion, music, education, modern history, geography, and political science. Accepts unsolicited manuscripts, but first send inquiry with outline and sample chapter. Use *Chicago* or *MLA* for style, though internal consistency is the most important.

Notable 2003 title: *Forever Young: The 'Teen-Aging' of Modern Culture*, Marcel Danesi.

Vanwell Publishing

1 Northrup Crescent, P.O. Box 2131, St. Catharines, ON L2R 7S2
Phone: (905) 937-3100 Fax: (905) 937-1760
E-mail: editor@vanwell.com
Contact: Angela Dobler, editor

Established 1983. Canada's leading publisher of quality military, naval, and aviation books. Releases about 9 new titles a year. Reviews unsolicited manuscripts, but first send an outline or sample chapters. Guidelines available.

Notable 2003 title: *No Higher Purpose: The Official History of the Royal Canadian Navy in the Second World War, 1939–1945* (volume 2, part 1), Douglas, Sarty, and Whitby.

Véhicule Press

P.O. Box 125, Place du Parc, Montreal, QC H2X 4A3
Phone: (514) 844-6073 Fax: (514) 844-7543
E-mail: vp@vehiculepress.com
Web site: www.vehiculepress.com
Contact: Vicki Marcok, general manager

Established 1973. Publishes fiction, non-fiction, and poetry within the context of social history. "In 2003, our 30th anniversary, a new fiction series, Esplanade Books, was inaugurated. Editor Andrew Steinmetz will be looking at novels only in 2004." Released 13 titles in 2003. Accepts unsolicited manuscripts, but first send covering letter, sample chapters, and return postage if you want manuscript returned. Guidelines available.

Notable 2003 title: *A House by the Sea*, Sikeena Karmali.

Whitecap Books

351 Lynn Avenue, North Vancouver, BC V7J 2C4
Phone: (604) 980-9852 Fax: (604) 980-8197
E-mail: whitecap@whitecap.ca

Web site: www.whitecap.ca
Contact: Michael Burch, president
Established 1977. Publishes books on cookery, gardening, and travel, as well as children's fiction and non-fiction. Focused on themes of nature, wildlife, and natural history with national and/or international potential. Releases about 40 books a year. Accepts unsolicited manuscripts. "Please research our list before submitting." Guidelines available.

Notable 2003 title: *British Columbia Wine Country*, John Schreiner and Kevin Miller.

Wilfrid Laurier University Press
75 University Avenue W., Waterloo, ON N2L 3C5
Phone: (519) 884-0710, ext. 6124 Fax: (519) 725-1399
E-mail: press@wlu.ca
Web site: www.press.wlu.ca or www.wlupress.wlu.ca
Contact: Jacqueline Larson, acquisitions editor
Established 1974. Publishes scholarly books (and academic journals) in the humanities and social sciences, and literary non-fiction. Subject areas include film, literature, literary criticism, literature in translation, cultural studies, native studies, religious studies, Canadian studies, life writing, philosophy, history, and women's studies. Produces 20 to 30 new books a year. Accepts unsolicited manuscripts, but first send c.v., outline, and sample chapter. Guidelines available on web site.

Wolsak and Wynn Publishers
192 Spadina Avenue, Suite 315, Toronto, ON M5T 2C2
Phone: (416) 603-3085 Fax: (416) 603-9935
E-mail: wolsakwynn@rogers.com
Web site: www.poets.ca/wolsakwynn
Contact: Maria Jacobs, publisher/editor
Publishes poetry exclusively. "We do so because we believe in poetry's power to crystallise and express the diverse life of the country and in the importance of widening the audience for poetry in Canada and keeping it vital. The authors we publish display widely divergent styles and approaches to writing. We favour no one style over any other; we publish to no agenda beyond that of presenting the best in Canadian poetry from fresh new voices to

assured, familiar ones." Accepts submissions during the first quarter of the year. Guidelines available.

Notable 2003 title: *(sub rosa)*, Stan Rogal (illustrations by Jacquie Jacobs).

Women's Press
180 Bloor Street W., Suite 801, Toronto, ON M5S 2V6
Phone: (416) 929-2774 Fax: (416) 929-1926
E-mail: aprince@cspi.org
Web site: www.womenspress.ca
Contact: Althea Prince, managing editor

A publisher of feminist writing. No unsolicited manuscripts for fiction; send a letter of inquiry. For academic books, send an inquiry, outline, and sample chapters. Guidelines available on web site.

Notable 2003 title: *Afraid of the Day*, Nancy Graham.

XYZ Publishing
Editorial office: P.O. Box 250, Lantzville, BC V0R 2H0
Phone: (250) 390-2352 Fax: (250) 390-2329
E-mail: xyzed@shaw.ca
Web site: www.xyzedit.qc.ca
Contact: Rhonda Bailey, editorial director

The English-language imprint of XYZ éditeur, a distinguished Montreal literary press. Publishes approximately 8 titles per year in the Quest Library, a series of biographies of great Canadians. Also publishes fiction. Does not accept unsolicited manuscripts. Send an inquiry first. "In consultation with the editorial board, the editorial director commissions titles for the Quest Library, but we are interested in considering novels for our fiction list. Please send an inquiry with an SASE." Guidelines available on web site.

Notable 2003 title: *Nellie McClung: Voice for the Voiceless*, Margaret MacPherson.

6

LITERARY AGENTS

Acquiring a literary agent can sometimes be more challenging than finding a publisher. So why bother? Why pay a percentage of your hard-earned royalties to someone who didn't share those long hours writing at your computer, agonizing over every word, tormented with insecurity and overwork?

If you focus your writing on periodicals, you probably will not require an agent, but if your aspiration is to have a book published, an agent is someone you should seriously consider. As has been the case in the United States for many years, Canadian book publishers are increasingly reluctant to deal with unagented manuscripts, or if they do accept them, they are often not given the same serious scrutiny as work that comes from an agent. Publishers respect the professionalism of agents and realize that if they consider a manuscript to be worth their while, it must be a saleable commodity.

Good agents have extensive contacts in the publishing industry, affording them valuable insight as to which publishers and editors to approach with your project. They are experienced in negotiating the most favourable contracts for their clients, obtaining the best royalty rate and highest advance, and typically do business with the larger publishers, those who have the most money to spend. Agents will attempt to retain as many rights to their clients' work as possible, then pursue the sale of subsidiary rights, which may include foreign and film rights. They will follow up on contracts to ensure that all obligations are fulfilled, examining royalty statements and collecting all monies due. An agent's expertise is in the business side of publishing, an area in which most writers have neither the time nor inclination to become proficient.

In addition, agents can provide writers with professional career guidance and be an invaluable sounding-board for ideas, since they are acutely familiar with the marketplace. They will critique your work so changes can be made before a publisher has the opportunity to turn it down.

Finding an agent to represent you can be a difficult task, especially if you are an unpublished author. Typically, agencies work overtime to represent the clients they already have and are often reluctant to invest their time and money in an unproven entity. That is why some of them charge a reading fee. A referral from an interested publisher or from one of their clients could help pique some interest, but getting your foot in an agent's door is not an easy process.

Although this chapter lists most of the active literary agencies in Canada, you will notice that many of them will not accept unsolicited manuscripts. In such cases, a query letter will be your first entry into an agent's office. Resist the urge to send out a mass mailing to every agent in the country. First, examine their subject interests and specialties, as indicated below, noting only the agencies that represent the type of work you are writing, then target those. Contacting agencies who do not handle your area of interest is a waste of everyone's time.

A query letter to an agent should contain a brief outline of the work you want him or her to sell and a description of your writing experience. If you have previously had a book in print, a prospective agent will want to know who published it and how many copies and which foreign rights were sold. In other words, a busy agency must be convinced that your work has earning power. If you have no publishing history, your query letter needs to persuade an agent that your project will appeal to a lucrative market. Enclose an SASE for his or her reply.

Before agreeing to be represented by an agency, you should check its track record and ask for a client list. You may wish to obtain specialized legal advice before signing a contract with them or, alternatively, contact the Writers' Union of Canada or your regional branch of the Canadian Authors Association to assist you with any questions you may have.

Agents in Canada usually charge 15 per cent of the value of all rights sold, which may increase to 20 per cent for foreign sales. Some agencies also tack on fees for reading, evaluation, and editorial services, as well as charging the author for such office costs as photocopying, postage, couriers, and long-distance telephone and fax expenses. Be certain that all such obligations are disclosed and agreed to before you become that agency's client, and insist on an accounting of fees and expenses, as well as an upper limit to such charges.

Acacia House Publishing Services Ltd.

51 Acacia Road, Toronto, ON M4S 2K6
Phone: (416) 484-8356 Fax: (416) 484-8356
E-mail: fhanna.acacia@rogers.com
Contacts: Frances Hanna and Bill Hanna

Subject interests: Fiction with international potential. No horror, occult, science fiction, or adult fantasy. For non-fiction, no self-help, fitness, true crime, or business books. Special non-fiction interest in history and military subjects.

Comments: Accepts unsolicited queries only, with writing sample (up to 50 double-spaced pages). Reads unpublished writers. Does not charge evaluation, editorial, or other handling fees. All queries and submissions must be accompanied by an SASE.

Author Author Literary Agency Ltd.

P.O. Box 56534, Lougheed Town Centre, Burnaby, BC V3J 7W2
Phone: (604) 415-0056
E-mail: joan@authorauthorliteraryagency.com
Web site: www.authorauthorliteraryagency.com
Contact: Joan Rickard

Subject interests: Book-length adult/juvenile fiction and non-fiction. No poetry, screenplays, or magazine-length stories/articles.

Comments: Welcomes unpublished writers. No evaluation fees for authors with a book already published in the same genre as current endeavours (excluding electronic, print-on-demand, and self-published books). Otherwise, there is a refundable entry evaluation fee of $75 U.S. per proposal (certified cheques or bank money orders; international bank money order if outside Canada). Submit hard copy only (no faxed or disk submissions). Reports in about 8 weeks from receipt of submission.

"Study thoroughly your chosen genre to learn writing techniques and what publishers are buying. Ensure manuscripts are properly formatted: double-spaced with 1-inch borders. Provide an SASE, International Reply Coupon, certified cheque, or adequate funds for response to inquiries and/or return of manuscripts. For writers' guidance, we offer a 22-page booklet, 'Crash Course for Proposals to Book and Magazine Publishers: Business Letters, Basic Punctuation/Information Guidelines and Manuscript Formatting' for $8.95 U.S., including S/H."

Authors Marketing Services Ltd.
P.O. Box 84668, 2336 Bloor Street W., Toronto, ON M6S 4Z7
Phone: (416) 763-8797 Fax: (416) 763-1504
E-mail: authorslhoffman@cs.com
Contact: Larry Hoffman
Subject interests: Adult fiction and non-fiction.
Comments: Accepts unsolicited queries, but no unsolicited manuscripts. Unpublished writers are charged evaluation/handling fees.

Christopher Banks & Associates Inc.
6 Adelaide Street E., Suite 610, Toronto, ON M5C 1H6
Phone: (416) 214-1155 Fax: (416) 214-1150
E-mail: info@chrisbanks.com
Contact: Patricia Ney
Subject interests: Dramatic works only (stage, screen, radio).
Comments: Roster is full, but unsolicited queries (not manuscripts) are considered. Unpublished writers are read by professional recommendation. No fees are charged.

Johanna M. Bates Literary Consultants Inc.
171 Somme Avenue S.W., Calgary, AB T2T 5J8
Phone: (403) 282-7370
E-mail: query@telusplanet.net
Web site: www.batesliterary.com
Contact: Johanna M. Bates

Subject interests: Literary fiction, children's books, and thriller/suspense novels.

Comments: Accepts queries from unpublished writers. No unsolicited manuscripts. An evaluation fee is charged.

Rick Broadhead & Associates Literary Agency

47 St. Clair Avenue W., Suite 501, Toronto, ON M4V 3A5

Phone: (416) 929-0516   Fax: (416) 927-8732

E-mail: rickb@rbaliterary.com

Web site: www.rbaliterary.com

Contact: Rick Broadhead

Subject interests: Seeking new titles in a variety of non-fiction categories including health and medicine, politics, business, sports, science, history, humour, food/wine, self-help, pop culture, parenting, gift books, memoirs, travel, music/entertainment, true crime, television tie-ins, narrative non-fiction, investigative journalism, and quirky/offbeat reference. Occasionally accepts novels.

Comments: Has made sales in Canada, the U.S., the U.K., Australia, and New Zealand to major publishers such as Random House, Chronicle Books, Wiley, and Jossey Bass. Especially interested in books that have a unique "hook" and have potential in both the U.S. and Canada, particularly those by high-profile experts who have excellent credentials and a strong media platform. "Please contact me by e-mail with a description of the project you are working on before sending any material. A polished proposal and excellent writing skills are essential."

The Bukowski Agency

14 Prince Arthur Avenue, Suite 202, Toronto, ON M5R 1A9

Phone: (416) 928-6728   Fax: (416) 963-9978

E-mail: assistant@thebukowskiagency.com

Web site: www.thebukowskiagency.com

Contacts: Denise Bukowski

Subject interests: General adult trade books. Prefers literary fiction and non-fiction. No genre fiction (science fiction, romance, westerns); no children's or sports books; no scriptwriters or playwrights. Specializes in projects with international potential and suitability for other media.

Comments: No unsolicited manuscripts or unpublished writers. Does not charge evaluation or other handling fees. Query first, by mail only, with writing samples and credentials. "What future projects do you have planned? Before making an investment in a little-known writer, I need to be convinced that you are not only talented but ambitious and driven as a writer." No phone or e-mail queries, please.

Canadian Speakers' & Writers' Service Limited
44 Douglas Crescent, Toronto, ON M4W 2E7
Phone: (416) 921-4443 Fax: (416) 922-9691
E-mail: pmmj@idirect.com
Contacts: Matie Molinaro, Paul Molinaro, and Julius Molinaro
   Subject interests: Non-fiction, children's subjects, and dramatic works.
   Comments: Sometimes reads unpublished writers. "If an unpublished writer presents an interesting project, we do charge an evaluation fee, as working on manuscripts and promoting new writers is becoming more and more costly." No unsolicited manuscripts.

The Characters Talent Agency
8 Elm Street, 3rd Floor, Toronto, ON M5G 1G7
Phone: (416) 964-8522 Fax: (416) 964-6349
E-mail: clib5@aol.com
Contacts: Carl Liberman
   Subject interests: Feature-film scripts and television and series pilots. "We are looking for both commercially driven (Hollywood) material and well written dramatic material."
   Comments: No unsolicited manuscripts; query by phone or e-mail. Does not read unpublished writers. No evaluation fee.

The Cooke Agency
278 Bloor Street E., Suite 305, Toronto, ON M4W 3M4
Phone: (416) 406-3390 Fax: (416) 406-3389
E-mail: agents@cookeagency.ca
Contact: Samantha North
   Subject interests: Non-fiction and literary fiction.

Comments: Accepts inquiries from unpublished writers, but no unsolicited manuscripts. No evaluation or other handling fees are charged. Requires an SASE for response.

The Core Group Talent Agency Inc.
3 Church Street, Suite 507, Toronto, ON M5E 1M2
Phone: (416) 955-0819 Fax: (416) 955-0861
E-mail: literary@coregroupta.com
Contact: Charles Northcote
Subject interests: Writing for film, theatre, and television. Deals primarily with scripts and producing and publishing them. Does not handle novels, short stories, poetry, etc.
Comments: Accepts queries from unpublished writers. No unsolicited manuscripts. No evaluation fee.

Credentials
Phone: (416) 926-1507 Fax: (416) 926-0372
E-mail: credent@rogers.com
Contact: Lynn Kinney
Subject interests: Published or unpublished material suitable for film and television.
Comments: "If a writer calls first and we determine that there may be film or television potential in a manuscript, we will ask for a 2- to 3-page synopsis of the work and proceed from there." No unsolicited manuscripts. No evaluation fee. "Most of our sales are to the U.S., but we cover Canada and Europe too."

Arnold Gosewich, Literary Agent and Consultant
40 Oaklands Avenue, Suite 207, Toronto, ON M4V 2E5
Phone: (416) 925-7836
E-mail: jackie@sympatico.com
Contact: Arnold Gosewich
Subject interests: Non-fiction, commercial fiction, and young adult novels.
Comments: No unsolicited manuscripts; send a query first. Reads unpublished writers. Charges an evaluation fee. "We prefer commercial material for North America with potential for special sales as well as television."

Great North Artists Management, Inc.

350 Dupont Street, Toronto, ON M5R 1V9
Phone: (416) 925-2051 Fax: (416) 925-3904
E-mail: gnami@gnaminc.com
Contacts: Shain Jaffe and Rena Zimmerman
   Subject interests: Film and television properties.
   Comments: No evaluation or other handling fees. No queries or
unsolicited manuscripts. By referral from industry professional.

Great Titles Inc.

18 Greenfield Drive, Etobicoke, ON M9B 1G9
Phone: (416) 231-6686 Fax: (416) 231-7913
E-mail: atsallas@allstream.net
Contact: Tina Tsallas
   Subject interests: Women's fiction and mainstream fiction with
strong characters. Also interested in mysteries and science fiction.
Children's material must be for the YA market. Non-fiction must
have broad audience appeal.
   Comments: Accepts queries from unpublished and published
writers. Submit query with first 3 chapters and a detailed synopsis
(or complete manuscript with detailed synopsis). "Know the
market for which you are writing." No reading fee. No submissions
by e-mail. Always send an SASE.

Helen Heller Agency Inc.

32 Bayhampton Court, Toronto, ON M3H 5L6
E-mail: helleragency@rogers.com
Web site: www.helenhelleragency.com
Contacts: Helen and Sarah Heller
   Subject interests: Fiction and non-fiction. "We do not handle
children's books, poetry, screenplays, science fiction, romance, or
other category fiction."
   Comments: Accepts queries from unpublished and published
writers. No unsolicited manuscripts. No fees are charged.

Lucas Talent Inc.

100 West Pender Street, 7th Floor, Vancouver, BC V6B 1R8
Phone: (604) 685-0345 Fax: (604) 685-0341

E-mail: dacia.moss@lucastalent.com
Contacts: Dacia Moss and Doreen Holmes
Subject interests: Writing for film and television only.

Comments: No inquiries or unsolicited manuscripts accepted. No unpublished writers considered. No evaluation or other handling fees are charged.

Anne McDermid & Associates Ltd.
92 Willcocks Street, Toronto, ON M5S 1C8
Phone: (416) 324-8845 Fax: (416) 324-8870
E-mail: info@mcdermidagency.com
Web site: www.mcdermidagency.com
Contact: Anne McDermid
Subject interests: Literary and commercial fiction and narrative non-fiction. No children's writing.

Comments: Accepts inquiries from unpublished writers with synopses, but no unsolicited manuscripts. No evaluation or other handling fees are charged. No telephone inquiries. Please check web site for information. No e-mailed manuscripts.

Mensour Agency Ltd.
61A York Street, Ottawa, ON KIN 5T2
Phone: (613) 241-1677 Fax: (613) 241-4360
E-mail: kate@mensour.ca
Web site: www.mensour.ca
Contact: Catherine Mensour
Subject interests: Theatre, animation, television, and film.

Comments: Does not accept unsolicited queries or manuscripts, but will sometimes read unpublished writers. No evaluation or other handling fees are charged.

Pamela Paul Agency Inc.
12 Westrose Avenue, Toronto, ON M8X 2A1
Phone: (416) 410-5395 Fax: (416) 410-4949
E-mail: agency@interlog.com
Contact: James Gordon
Subject interests: Literary fiction, children's fiction, film, theatre, television, and radio.

Comments: No queries or unsolicited manuscripts. Will read unpublished writers only with a referral.

Bella Pomer Agency Inc.
22 Shallmar Boulevard, PH2, Toronto, ON M5N 2Z8
Phone: (416) 781-8597 Fax: (416) 782-4196
Contact: Bella Pomer
   Subject interests: Quality fiction and general-interest non-fiction.
   Comments: No queries or unsolicited manuscripts. "Not taking on new clients. List is closed."

The Saint Agency
60 Pleasant Boulevard, Suite 801, Toronto, ON M4T 1K1
Phone: (416) 944-8200 Fax: (416) 944-3700
E-mail: mala@thesaintagency.com
Contact: Mala Khosla
   Subject interests: Screenplays for television and film.
   Comments: "Please call or write to enquire before sending scripts." Accepts inquiries, but no unsolicited scripts. Reads unpublished writers. No evaluation fee.

Seventh Avenue Literary Agency
1663 West 7th Avenue, Vancouver, BC V6J 1S4
Phone: (604) 734-3663 Fax: (604) 734-8906
E-mail: rmackwood@seventhavenuelit.com
Web site: www.seventhavenuelit.com
Contact: Robert Mackwood
   Subject interests: Literary and commercial fiction, and non-fiction including the following categories: popular culture, business and technology, travel, house and home, memoirs, and sports.
   Comments: Formerly Contemporary Management. "We have changed our name and launched a web site in an effort to better serve our clients and to attract new and talented writers. We are expanding our list of sub-agents and continue to try to introduce new Canadian writers to world markets." Accepts queries from unpublished writers, but see web site for submission guidelines. No unsolicited manuscripts. New clients are charged a fee for expenses.

Beverley Slopen Literary Agency

131 Bloor Street W., Suite 711, Toronto, ON M5S 1S3
Phone: (416) 964-9598 Fax: (416) 921-7726
E-mail: beverley@slopenagency.ca
Web site: www.slopenagency.ca
Contact: Beverley Slopen
  Subject interests: Narrative non-fiction and commercial fiction.
  Comments: No unsolicited manuscripts. Only occasionally reads unpublished writers if referred. Does not charge evaluation/handling fees.

P. Stathonikos Agency

146 Springbluff Heights S.W., Calgary, AB T3H 5E5
Phone: (403) 245-2087 Fax: (403) 245-2087
E-mail: pastath@telus.net
Contact: Penny Stathonikos
  Subject interests: Juvenile, young adult, and Canadiana. No academic material, science fiction, or plays.
  Comments: Accepts queries from unpublished writers, but no unsolicited manuscripts. No evaluation or editorial fees; a handling fee is charged once a writer has signed with a publisher.

Carolyn Swayze Literary Agency Ltd.

P.O. Box 39588, White Rock, BC V4B 5L6
Phone: (604) 538-3478 Fax: (604) 531-3022
E-mail: cswayze@direct.ca
Web site: www.swayzeagency.com
Contact: Carolyn Swayze
  Subject interests: Literary fiction, commercial fiction, military history, humour, strong, well-written narrative non-fiction, science, and social history.
  Comments: Accepts queries and unsolicited manuscripts of non-fiction works. For fiction, send first 50 pages. Reads work by unpublished writers. No evaluation or handling fees. "No science fiction, romances, or screenplays, please. Representing Mark Zuehlke, W. P. Kinsella, Will Ferguson, Genni Gunn, Aislinn Hunter, Miriam Toews, Karen Rivers, Bill Gaston, Alex Brett, Andrew Gray, Taras Grescoe, and Steven Galloway."

Transatlantic Literary Agency, Inc.
1603 Italy Cross Road, Petite Riviere, NS B0J 2P0
Phone: (902) 693-2026 Fax: (902) 693-2026
E-mail: wordbyword@sympatico.ca or don@tla1.com
Web site: www.lta1.com
Contact: Don Sedgwick
   Subject interests: Adult fiction and non-fiction.
   Comments: Accepts queries but no unsolicited manuscripts.
Usually not interested in unpublished writers. No evaluation or
handling fees. "We are now the second largest literary agency in
Canada, with more than 250 clients, 8 offices across Canada, offices
in 3 countries, and sub-agents around the world. Please review our
web site for further guidelines and submission information."

Westwood Creative Artists
94 Harbord Street, Toronto, ON M5S 1G6
Phone: (416) 964-3302 Fax: (416) 975-9209
Contact: Amy Tompkins
   Subject interests: General and literary fiction and non-fiction.
No poetry.
   Comments: A busy agency that responds only to inquiries of
current interest. Will consider unpublished writers. No unsolicited
manuscripts. No evaluation or handling fees.

7

WRITING AWARDS & COMPETITIONS

This chapter surveys a broad range of the literary prizes and competitions open to Canadian writers. Most of the prizes and competitions may be applied for directly. Among a number of high-profile exceptions are the Harbourfront Festival Prize, conferred each year on a celebrated writer in mid-career, and the Journey Prize, sponsored by the Writers' Trust of Canada and McClelland & Stewart, for the best short fiction from Canada's literary journals. In some cases, the judges prefer to receive submissions from publishers, but usually, as long as the application criteria are met, individual applications are also accepted.

Please note that application deadlines and details are subject to change, and that the following entries do not include full eligibility criteria or entry conditions. Many awards, for instance, require the provision of several copies of the work so that they can be circulated among the nominating jury. Applicants should always obtain full guidelines before making a submission.

Canadian writers are also eligible for a range of overseas awards, and you'll find many of these listed in standard international reference books such as *Literary Market Place*. New Canadian awards are usually advertised in the *Quill & Quire* and in some literary journals.

Acorn-Plantos Award
Jeff Seffinga, 36 Sunset Avenue, Hamilton, ON L8R 1V6
Phone: (905) 521-9196

E-mail: jeffseff@allstream.net
Deadline: June 15

A $500 prize and the People's Poet medal is awarded annually for the best full-sized volume in the People's Poetry tradition published during the previous year. Entry fee $25. May be entered by either authors or their publishers. Authors must be Canadian citizens or landed immigrants.

John Alexander Media Awards
Public Education Department, Multiple Sclerosis Society of
    Canada, 175 Bloor Street E., Suite 700, North Tower, Toronto,
    ON M4W 3R8
Phone: (416) 922-6065
E-mail: info@mssociety.ca
Web site: www.mssociety.ca
Deadline: September 30

A $500 award is given annually to the author of the best English or French newspaper or magazine article (and another $500 to the creator of the best television or radio broadcast) about some aspect of multiple sclerosis.

Arc Poetry Contests and Prizes
P.O. Box 7219, Ottawa, ON K1L 8E4
Phone: (613) 729-3550
E-mail: arc.poetry@cyberus.ca

Arc Poem of the Year Contest
Deadline: June 30

Prizes of $1,000, $750, and $500 are awarded for the best unpublished poetry not to exceed 100 lines. Entry fee $20 for up to 4 poems, which includes a 1-year subscription to *Arc*. Annual.

Diana Brebner Prize
Deadline: September 15

A $500 award for Ottawa poets who have not been published in book form. Length of poem not to exceed 30 lines. Entry fee $12 for up to 2 poems, which includes a 1-year subscription to *Arc*. Annual.

Confederation Poets Prize

Honouring Archibald Lampman, William Wilfred Campbell, and Duncan Campbell-Scott. A cash prize of $100 is awarded for the best poem published in *Arc* in the previous calendar year. All poems published in *Arc* are automatically entered. Annual.

Critic's Desk Award

Honours excellence in reviewing books of poetry. An annual prize of $100 is given annually for both a feature review and a brief review that has been published in *Arc* in the previous calendar year. Reviews are automatically entered for this award.

Archibald Lampman Award

Deadline: January 31

Named after the 19th-century Confederation poet Archibald Lampman, the $500 award recognizes an outstanding book of English-language poetry by an author living in the Ottawa area. Books must have been published between January and December of the previous year and have no fewer than 48 pages.

Atlantic Journalism Awards

Bill Skerret, Co-ordinator, 46 Swanton Drive, Dartmouth, NS
  B2W 2C5

Phone: (902) 435-9166 Fax: (902) 462-1892

E-mail: office@ajas.ca

Web site: www.ajas.ca

Deadline: January 29

Framed certificates are awarded to the winners in 28 categories. Only print and broadcast journalists working in the Atlantic region are eligible. Entry fee $40.

Atlantic Poetry Prize. *See* Writers' Federation of Nova Scotia Awards.

Atlantic Writing Competition for Unpublished Manuscripts. *See* Writers' Federation of Nova Scotia Awards.

Aurora Awards

Dennis Mullin, The Canadian Science Fiction and Fantasy

Association, 4A – 385 Fairway Road S., Suite 213, Kitchener, ON N2C 2N9

E-mail: dmullin@sentex.net

Web site: www.sentex.net/~dmullin/aurora

Deadline: dates vary (check web site)

A hand-crafted trophy by Alberta artist Frank Johnson is awarded for the best work in 3 categories of writing in English. Annual.

Best Long-Form Work in English

Awarded for the best science-fiction or fantasy novel or fiction collection by a Canadian writer released in Canada in the previous calendar year.

Best Short-Form Work in English

Awarded for the best science-fiction or fantasy novella, novelette, short story, or poem by a Canadian writer released in Canada in the previous calendar year.

Best Work in English – Other

Awarded for the best science-fiction or fantasy writing by a Canadian not encompassed by the previous 2 categories; for example, critical writing or editing, or translating into English.

Aventis Pasteur Medal for Excellence in Health Research Journalism

Canadians for Health Research, P.O. Box 126, Westmount, QC H3Z 2T1

Phone: (514) 398-7478   Fax: (514) 398-8361

E-mail: info@chrcrm.org

Web site: www.chrcrm.org

Deadline: last week in February

This annual national award recognizes the role of journalists in raising public awareness of the importance of health research in Canada. The award consists of a medal and a $2,500 bursary. The winning article must have been published in a Canadian newspaper or magazine during the previous calendar year.

Bad Moon Books Contests

Warren Layberry, Editor, 43 Saxton Private, Ottawa, ON K2H 9P3

E-mail: warren.layberry@sympatico.ca
Web site: www.badmoonbooks.ca/contests.htm

Blood & Guts Horror Story Competition
Deadline: July 31
   Winner receives $100 and publication in the form of a chapbook for Bad Moon Books for the best ghost story, horror story, tale of madness or depravation, or psychological thriller from 3,000 to 15,000 words. Entry fee $10. May submit up to 3 stories. Open to anyone writing in English.

The Cold Steel Crime & Mystery Contest
Deadline: January 31
   Winner receives $100 and publication in the form of a chapbook for Bad Moon Books for the best crime or mystery story or psychological thriller from 3,000 to 15,000 words. Entry fee $10. May submit up to 3 stories. Open to anyone writing in English.

New Cat Tattoos
Deadline: July 31
   Winner receives $100 and publication in the form of a chapbook for Bad Moon Books for the best story, from 3,000 to 15,000 words, on any topic, although a preference will be shown to stories set in Ottawa. Entry fee $10. May submit up to 3 stories. Open only to current or former residents of Ottawa.

The Alfred G. Bailey Prize. *See* Writers' Federation of New
   Brunswick Literary Competition.

Bancroft Award. *See* the Royal Society of Canada Awards.

Banff Mountain Book Competition
P.O. Box 1020, 107 Tunnel Mountain Drive, Banff, AB TIL 1H5
Phone: (403) 762-6347 Fax: (403) 762-6277
E-mail: banffmountainphotos@banffcentre.ca
Web site: www.banffmountainfestivals.ca
Deadline: August 15
   Over $5,000 will be awarded to books in the following categories: mountain literature, mountain exposition, mountain image, and

adventure travel. Presented in conjunction with the Banff Mountain Book Festival. Annual.

Bard's Ink Contests
P. J. Duane, 14984 – 96A Avenue, Surrey, BC V3R 8K5
Phone: (604) 589-5082
E-mail: pjduane@yahoo.com
Web site: www.iprimus.ca/~pjduane/contest.htm
Deadline: January 31

Short Story Contest
A prize of $50 will be awarded for the best original, unpublished short story no longer than 1,500 words. Books will be awarded to the second- and third-place winners. In addition, winners will be published on the Bard's Ink web site. Entry fee $5/story. Annual.

Poetry Contest
A prize of $25 will be awarded for the best original, unpublished poem no longer than 40 lines. Books will be awarded to the second- and third-place winners. In addition, winners will be published on the Bard's Ink web site. Entry fee $5 for up to 2 poems. Annual.

Robertine Barry Prize. *See* The Canadian Research Institute for the Advancement of Women Prizes.

Shaunt Basmajian Chapbook Award. *See* Canadian Poetry Association Awards.

B.C. Book Prizes
Bryan Pike, Executive Director, 207 West Hastings Street, Suite 902, Vancouver, BC V6B 1H7
Phone: (604) 687-2405 Fax: (604) 669-3701
E-mail: info@bcbookprizes.ca
Web site: www.bcbookprizes.ca
Deadline: December 1

Bill Duthie Booksellers' Choice Prize
A $2,000 prize is awarded annually to the originating publisher and author of the best book in terms of public appeal, initiative,

design, production, and content. The publisher must have its head office in B.C. or the Yukon, and the creative control in terms of editing, design, and production must have been within B.C. or the Yukon. The membership of the B.C. Booksellers' Association determines the winner by ballot.

Sheila A. Egoff Children's Prize

A $2,000 prize is awarded annually to the author of the best novel for juveniles and young adults, and the best non-fiction book for children (including biography) that has not been highly illustrated. The author must be a B.C. or Yukon resident or have lived in B.C. or the Yukon for 3 of the past 5 years. The book may have been published anywhere.

Hubert Evans Non-Fiction Prize

A $2,000 prize is awarded annually to the author of the best original non-fiction literary work (philosophy, belles lettres, biography, history, etc.). Quality of research and writing, insight, and originality are major considerations in the judging of this prize. The author must be a B.C. or Yukon resident or have lived in B.C. or the Yukon for 3 of the past 5 years. The book may have been published anywhere.

Roderick Haig-Brown Regional Prize

A $2,000 prize is awarded annually to the author of the book that contributes most to the enjoyment and understanding of B.C. The book may deal with any aspect of the province (people, history, geography, oceanography, etc.) and must be original. Reprints, revised editions, guide books, and how-to books are not considered. The book may have been published anywhere, and the author may reside outside B.C.

Christie Harris Prize for Illustrated Children's Books

A annual $2,000 prize is shared by the author and illustrator of the best children's picture book, picture story book, or illustrated non-fiction book. The author and/or illustrator must be a B.C. or Yukon resident or have lived in B.C. or the Yukon for 3 of the past 5 years. The book may have been published anywhere.

Lieutenant Governor's Literary Lifetime Achievement Award
A $5,000 prize is awarded annually to honour late-career authors for their entire body of work. There will also be a province-wide author tour of shortlisted writers during B.C. Book and Magazine week.

The Dorothy Livesay Poetry Prize
A $2,000 prize is awarded annually to the author of the best work of poetry. The author must be a B.C. or Yukon resident or have lived in B.C. or the Yukon for 3 of the past 5 years. No anthologies or "best of" collections. The book may have been published anywhere.

The Ethel Wilson Fiction Prize
A $2,000 prize is awarded annually to the author of the best work of fiction. The author must be a B.C. or Yukon resident or have lived in B.C. or the Yukon for 3 of the past 5 years. No anthologies.

Geoffrey Bilson Award for Historical Fiction for Young People. *See* Canadian Children's Book Centre Awards.

Earle Birney Prize for Poetry. *See* PRISM international Writing Prizes.

Blood & Guts Horror Story Competition. *See* Bad Moon Books Contests.

Carol Bolt Award. *See* Canadian Authors Association Awards.

Joseph Brant Award. *See* Ontario Historical Society Awards for Authors.

Diana Brebner Prize. *See* Arc Poetry Contests and Prizes.

Ann Connor Brimer Award
Heather MacKenzie, Halifax Regional Library, 60 Alderney Drive, Dartmouth, NS B2Y 4P8
Phone: (902) 490-5875 Fax: (902) 490-5893

E-mail: mackenh@halifaxpubliclibraries.ca
Web site: http://nsla.ns.ca/awards.html#ConnorBrimer
Deadline: October 15

A framed certificate and $1,000 prize is awarded annually to the author of a fiction or non-fiction children's book (for ages up to 15) published in the previous calendar year. The author must be a resident of Atlantic Canada. Sponsored by the Nova Scotia Library Association and awarded at the Atlantic Book Awards ceremony each year.

John Bullen Prize. *See* Canadian Historical Association Awards.

Burnaby Writers' Society Competition
Eileen Kernaghan, Burnaby Writers' Society, 6584 Deer Lake
    Avenue, Burnaby, BC V5G 3T7
Phone: (604) 421-4931
E-mail: lonewolf@portal.ca
Web site: www.bws.bc.ca
Deadline: May 31

Annual cash prizes of $200, $100, and $50 are given to the top 3 entries in the competition. Categories and themes change from year to year. Open to B.C. residents only. Entry fee $5. Write for guidelines.

Campbell River Online Story Contest
Phone: (250) 923-1857
E-mail: lou@loumilner.com
Web site: www.loumilner.com/storycontest

Two prizes of $150 and a prize gift package are awarded for the best short story (500 to 5,000 words), poem, illustration, or song (with musical accompaniment). Contest runs from January 1 to April 30. Stories must be new and follow a specific theme as outlined on the web site. Entry is free.

Canada-Japan Literary Awards
Carol Bream, Director, Endowments and Prizes, Canada Council
    for the Arts, P.O. Box 1047, 350 Albert Street, Ottawa, ON
    K1P 5V8

Phone: (613) 566-4414 or 1-800-263-5588, ext. 5041
   Fax: (613) 566-4430
E-mail: carol.bream@canadacouncil.ca
Web site: www.canadacouncil.ca
Deadline: TBA

Two cash prizes of $10,000 are usually awarded every 2 years for outstanding books of fiction, non-fiction, drama, or poetry about Japan or on Japanese themes by Canadian authors or for translations of Japanese books into French or English. Only publishers of eligible books may nominate titles for this award.

Canadian Authors Association Awards
Alec McEachern, P.O. Box 419, Campbellford, ON K0L 1L0
Phone: (705) 653-0323 Fax: (705) 653-0593
E-mail: canauth@redden.on.ca
Web site: www.CanAuthors.org

CAA Carol Bolt Award
Deadline: December 15

Winners receive $1,000 and a silver medal for the best English-language play for adults by an author who is a Canadian or a landed immigrant. All entries must have been previously published or performed in the previous year. This award is made possible by the Playwrights Guild of Canada and Playwrights Canada Press. Entry fee of $25/title. Annual.

CAA Jack Chalmers Poetry Award
Deadline: December 15

A prize of $2,500 and a sterling-silver medal is awarded in recognition of the year's outstanding book in the category of poetry by a Canadian writer. Entries should manifest "literary excellence without sacrifice of popular appeal." Nominations from author, publisher, individual, or group are eligible. Entry fee $25. Annual.

CAA Jubilee Award for Short Stories
Deadline: December 15

A prize of $2,500 and a silver medal is awarded for an outstanding collection of short stories by a Canadian author. Entry fee $25. Annual.

CAA Lela Common Award for Canadian History
Deadline: December 15
   A prize of $2,500 goes to the best work of historical non-fiction on a Canadian topic written in English by a Canadian author. Entry fee $25. Annual.

CAA MOSAID Technologies Inc. Award for Fiction
Deadline: December 15
   A prize of $2,500 and a sterling-silver medal is awarded in recognition of the year's outstanding full-length novel by a Canadian writer. Entries should manifest "literary excellence without sacrifice of popular appeal." Nominations from the author, publisher, an individual, or group are eligible. Entry fee $25. Annual.

Conference Writing Contest
Peterborough and Area Branch, CAA, P.O. Box 2412,
   Peterborough, ON K9J 7Y8
E-mail: perborocaa@yahoo.com
Deadline: January 15
   The winner of this short-fiction contest will receive $1,500 to attend the CAA annual conference. Stories to be 1,000 to 1,500 words. Open to Canadian citizens or those who have resided in Canada for more than 5 years. Annual.

Canadian Booksellers Association Libris Awards
Canadian Booksellers Association, 789 Don Mills Road, Suite
   700, Toronto, ON M3C 1T5
Phone: (416) 467-7883   Fax: (416) 467-7886
E-mail: esinkins@cbabook.org
Web site: www.cbabook.org
Contact: Emily Sinkins, general manager

Author of the Year Award
Deadline: June 1
   A trophy is awarded to the Canadian author of an outstanding literary work that contributes to Canadian culture and combines readability with strong sales. A call for nominations is sent to members of the book community. The shortlist comprises the 3 candidates with the most nominations.

Fiction Book of the Year Award
Deadline: June 1

A trophy is awarded for a Canadian work of fiction that had an outstanding impact on the Canadian bookselling industry, has created wide media attention, has brought people into bookstores, and had strong sales. A call for nominations is sent to members of the book community. The shortlist comprises the 3 candidates with the most nominations.

Non-Fiction Book of the Year Award
Deadline: June 1

A trophy is awarded for a Canadian work of non-fiction that had an outstanding impact on the Canadian bookselling industry, created wide media attention, brought people into bookstores, and had strong sales. A call for nominations is sent to members of the book community. The shortlist comprises the 3 candidates with the most nominations.

Canadian Children's Book Centre Awards
40 Orchard View Boulevard, Suite 101, Toronto, ON M4R 1B9
Phone: (416) 975-0010 Fax: (416) 975-8970
E-mail: info@bookcentre.ca
Web site: www.bookcentre.ca

Geoffrey Bilson Award for Historical Fiction for Young People
Contact: Brenda Halliday, librarian
E-mail: brenda@bookcentre.ca
Deadline: January 15

An annual prize of $1,000 is awarded to the author of an outstanding work of historical fiction for young people. The author must be Canadian. The winner is chosen by a jury appointed by the CCBC.

The Norma Fleck Award for a Canadian Children's Non-Fiction Book
Contact: Charlotte Teeple, executive director
E-mail: charlotte@bookcentre.ca
Deadline: March 30

A $10,000 prize is awarded to the author of the best children's non-fiction book. In addition, the award allocates $5,000 in marketing funds to promote the finalists, an amount that is matched by the publishers for a total of $10,000 for marketing. The text must be of exceptional quality and present the subject matter in a way that informs and excites interest. Visuals, also of an exceptional quality, should clarify, extend, and complement the text. Only books written and illustrated by Canadian citizens or landed immigrants are eligible. Annual.

Canadian Ethnic Journalists' and Writers' Club Awards

Ben Viccari, President, 22 Walmer Road, Suite 801, Toronto, ON
  M5R 2W5
Phone: (416) 944-8175 Fax: (416) 260-3586
E-mail: canscene@rogers.com
Web site: http://members.rogers.com/canscene
Deadline: March 31

Annual prizes of a plaque and free tickets to the awards event are presented for the best working journalists in ethnic print, radio, television, and Internet or a mainstream journalist writing on subjects concerning Canada's diversity. Awards are given for the best news or feature story and for the best editorial or opinion piece in 4 categories: print, radio, television, and Internet magazine. Annual.

Canadian Farm Writer's Federation Annual Writers Award

Jane Robinson, Awards Administrator, AdFarm, 150 Research
  Lane, Suite 225, Guelph, ON N1G 4T2
Phone: (519) 763-1957, ext. 228
E-mail: jane.robinson@adfarmonline.com
Web site: www.cfwf.ca
Deadline: late summer 2004 (check web site for details)

Annual award for stories from general periodicals, news releases, technical features, press features, editorials, columns, and daily, weekly, and monthly press reports. Writing must be about production agriculture. First prize $300, second $200, and third $100. Announced at annual CFWF meeting in early October.

Canadian Historical Association Awards

Joanne Mineault, 395 Wellington Street, Ottawa, ON K1A 0N3
Phone: (613) 233-7885 Fax: (613) 567-3110
E-mail: cha-shc@archives.ca
Web site: www.cha-shc.ca

John Bullen Prize
Deadline: November 30
A prize of $500 is awarded for the best doctoral dissertation written by a Canadian citizen or landed immigrant.

The Clio Awards
Deadline: December 30
Annual awards given for meritorious publications or for exceptional contributions by individuals or organizations to regional history.

The Albert B. Corey Prize
Deadline: December 31
Jointly sponsored by the Canadian Historical Association and the American Historical Association, this prize is awarded for the best book dealing with the history of Canadian-American relations or the history of both countries.

The Wallace K. Ferguson Prize
Deadline: December 2
A $1,000 prize is awarded annually to a Canadian citizen or landed immigrant who has published an outstanding scholarly book in a field of history other than Canadian history.

Sir John A. Macdonald Prize
Deadline: December 2
A prize of $1,000 is awarded in recognition of the non-fiction work of history judged to have made the most significant contribution to an understanding of the Canadian past. Annual.

The Hilda Neatby Prize in Women's History
Deadline: February 1
Awarded for an academic article (one in English and the other in French), published in a Canadian journal or book during the previous year, deemed to have made an original and scholarly contribution to the field of women's history. Annual.

Prize for Best Article on the History of Sexuality in Canada
Canadian Committee on the History of Sexuality, c/o Steven

Maynard, Department of History, Queen's University,
Kingston, ON K7L 3N6

Deadline: February 1

An award designed to recognize excellence in and encourage the growth of scholarly work in the history of sexuality in Canada. The winning article will be one that makes an original contribution in this field. Articles must be previously published and written in either English or French. Awarded every 2 years.

Canadian Jewish Book Awards

Diane Uslaner, Director of Cultural Programming, Koffler Centre
of the Arts, 4588 Bathurst Street, Toronto, ON M2R 1W6

Phone: (416) 636-1880, ext. 352 Fax: (416) 636-5813

E-mail: duslaner@bjcc.ca

Deadline: January 31

For Canadian authors, published in Canada in the previous 2 years, writing on subjects of Jewish interest in the following categories: fiction, poetry, biblical/rabbinic scholarship, history, literature for young readers, scholarship on a Canadian Jewish subject, original translation from French, Yiddish, or Hebrew, Yiddish writing, and Holocaust history or literature. Annual awards vary with donor between $500 and $1,000.

Canadian Library Association Book Awards

Brenda Shields, CLA Membership Services, 328 Frank Street,
Ottawa, ON K2P 0X8

Phone: (613) 232-9625, ext. 318 Fax: (613) 563-9895

Web site: www.cla.ca

Book of the Year for Children Award

Presented annually to the author of an outstanding book suitable for children up to the age of 14 published in Canada during the previous calendar year. Any creative work (fiction, poetry, anthologies, etc.) will be deemed eligible. Author must be a Canadian citizen or permanent resident. Nominations invited from CLA members and publishers.

Young Adult Canadian Book Award

This award recognizes the author of an outstanding English-language book written in the preceding calendar year that appeals to young adults between the ages of 13 and 18. The book must be a work of fiction published in Canada, and the author a Canadian citizen or landed immigrant. Annual.

Canadian Poetry Association Awards
P.O. Box 22571, St. George PO, Toronto, ON M5S 1V8
E-mail: info@canadianpoetryassociation.com
Web site: www.canadianpoetryassociation.com

CPA Annual Poetry Contest
Web site: www.canadianpoetryassociation.com/annual.html
Deadline: September 30
   Cash prizes of $50, $40, $30, $20, $10, and $5 are awarded annually. Any style or theme of poem is eligible. Entry fee $5/poem.

Shaunt Basmajian Chapbook Award
Web site: www.canadianpoetryassociation.com/shaunt.html
Deadline: April 30
   A cash prize of $100, publication of the winning manuscript, and 50 copies of the resulting chapbook are awarded to the winner of the best poetry manuscript of up to 24 pages (published or unpublished, in any style or tradition). Entry fee of $15 includes receipt of the winning chapbook. Annual.

Canadian Political Science Association Prizes
Canadian Political Science Association, 260 Dalhousie Street,
   Suite 204, Ottawa, ON K1N 7E4
Phone: (613) 562-1202   Fax: (613) 241-0019
E-mail: cpsa@csse.ca

C. B. Macpherson Prize
Deadline: December 2005
   A biennial award of $750 is presented to the author of the best book published in English or French in the field of political theory. No textbooks, edited texts, collections of essays, or multiple-authored works will be considered. The 2006 prize is for books published in 2004 and 2005. The author must be a Canadian citizen or permanent resident.

Donald Smiley Prize
Deadline: December 2004
An annual award of $1,000 will be given to the author of the best book, published in English or French, in a field relating to the study of government and politics in Canada. The 2005 prize is for books published in 2004. The author must be a Canadian citizen or permanent resident.

The Canadian Research Institute for the Advancement of Women Prizes
151 Slater Street, Suite 408, Ottawa, ON K1P 5H3
Phone: (613) 563-0681 Fax: (613) 563-0682
E-mail: info@criaw-icref.ca
Web site: www.criaw-icref.ca

Robertine Barry Prize
Deadline: October 15
Awarded for the best feminist article or column in the popular print media published between August of the previous year and July of the current year, inclusive. The purpose of the award is to encourage women to work for the feminist cause in this medium and to recognize their work. Articles must promote the advancement of women and exhibit excellence in analysis and literary style. Annual.

Laura Jamieson Prize
Deadline: October 15
To encourage the recognition and celebration of the growing body of feminist research in book form, the CRIAW offers an annual prize for a non-fiction feminist book by a Canadian author that advances the knowledge and/or understanding of women's experience. It may be theoretical in character, a monograph, or an edited collection; it may be drawn from any discipline. The prize is awarded for work in Canada's official languages in alternate years: in 2004 for a book written in French (published in 2002 or 2003); in 2005 for a book written in English (published in 2003 or 2004).

Marion Porter Prize
Deadline: October 15
Awarded for the most significant feminist research article from a

journal or anthology published between August of the previous year and July of the current year, inclusive. The purpose of the award is to recognize Canadian authors or articles set in a Canadian context and to publicize work that has been done. Articles will be judged on the importance of the issue to women, originality of the theme, and its academic excellence.

Canadian Writer's Journal Semi-Annual Short Fiction Contest

P.O. Box 1178, New Liskeard, ON P0J 1P0
Phone: (705) 647-5424 Fax: (705) 647-8366
E-mail: cwj@cwj.ca
Web site: www.cwj.ca/fiction.htm
Deadlines: March 31 and September 30

The writers of the best short fiction receive awards of $100, $50, and $25, a 1-year subscription to the *Canadian Writer's Journal*, publication in the journal, and inclusion in a chapbook entitled *Choice Works*. Entries must be original, unpublished stories in any genre to a maximum length of 1,200 words. Entry fee $5/story.

CBC Literary Awards

Carolyn Warren, Executive Producer, 1400 Rene Levesque E.,
    Montreal, QC H4V 1Z6
Phone: 1-877-888-6788
E-mail: literary_awards@cbc.ca
Web site: www.cbc.ca/literaryawards
Deadline: TBA

An annual writing competition, in partnership with the Canada Council for the Arts, that offers $10,000 in prizes in each of 3 categories, in English and French, for a total of $60,000. First- and second-place texts are published in *enRoute* magazine and are also produced for broadcast on CBC Radio One's *Between the Covers* and *Richardson's Roundup*. The categories are short stories, travel literature, and poetry. Entry fee $20/submission. Entry forms available on web site. You may also request an information brochure by e-mail or phone.

Jack Chalmers Poetry Award. *See* Canadian Authors Association Awards.

The Lina Chartrand Poetry Award. *See* Contemporary Verse 2 Literary Contests.

City of Edmonton Book Prize. *See* Writers Guild of Alberta Awards.

City of Toronto Book Award

Bev Kurmey, Toronto Protocol Office, 10th Floor, West Tower,
  City Hall, Toronto, ON M5H 2N2
Phone: (416) 392-8191
Deadline: end of February

Each year prize money totalling $15,000 is apportioned in recognition of works of literary merit in all genres that are evocative of Toronto. Fiction and non-fiction published in English for adults and/or children are eligible. Each shortlisted author (usually 4 to 6) receives $1,000, the balance going to the winner. No residency requirements. Reprints, textbooks, and manuscripts are not eligible.

City of Vancouver Book Award

Marnie Rice, Office of Cultural Affairs, City of Vancouver, 453
  West 12th Avenue, Vancouver, BC V5Y 1V4
Phone: (604) 873-7487 Fax: (604) 871-6048
E-mail: oca@city.vancouver.bc.ca
Web site: www.city.vancouver.bc.ca/oca
Deadline: June

An annual $2,000 cash prize is awarded in October to recognize books for their excellence and their contribution to an appreciation and understanding of Vancouver, its history, and the achievements of its residents. Entered books must be primarily set in or be about Vancouver, though the author's place of residence is not restricted, and the book may be written/published anywhere in the world. Books may be fiction, non-fiction, poetry, or drama, written for children or adults, and may deal with any aspect of the city, including its history, geography, current affairs, or the arts. Apply for guidelines.

Claremont Review Writing Contests

4980 Wesley Road, Victoria, BC V8Y 1Y9
Phone: (250) 658-5221 Fax: (250) 658-5387
Web site: www.theclaremontreview.com

Fiction Contest
Deadline: June 15
   First prize $300, second prize $200, and third prize $100 for the best work of fiction by a writer aged 13 to 19. Entry fee $15 for 1 category, $5 for each additional category entered. Each entrant receives a 1-year subscription to *The Claremont Review*.

Poetry Contest
Deadline: March 15
   First prize $300, second prize $200, and third prize $100 for the best poem by a writer aged 13 to 19. Entry fee $15 for 1 category, $5 for each additional category entered. Each entrant receives a 1-year subscription to *The Claremont Review*.

The Clio Awards. *See* Canadian Historical Association Awards.

Matt Cohen Award: In Celebration of a Writing Life. *See* the Writers' Trust of Canada Awards.

Shaughnessy Cohen Prize for Political Writing. *See* the Writers' Trust of Canada Awards.

The Cold Steel Crime & Mystery Contest. *See* Bad Moon Books Contests.

Lela Common Award for Canadian History. *See* Canadian Authors Association Awards.

Confederation Poets Prize. *See* Arc Poetry Contests and Prizes.

Contemporary Verse 2 Literary Contests

Clarise Foster, 100 Arthur Street, Suite 207, Winnipeg, MB
   R3B 1H3

Phone: (204) 949-1365 Fax: (204) 942-5754

E-mail: cv2@mb.sympatico.ca

CV2 sponsors two literary contests: the 2-Day Poem contest in November and another in the spring. Awards are $175 for first prize, $50 for second, and $25 for third. Each winner also receives a 1-year subscription to the magazine and publication as part of the prize. Guidelines and themes are available on request.

The Lina Chartrand Poetry Award

A cash prize (which varies) recognizes a distinguished contribution by an emerging female poet published by *CV2* in the previous year. Her work must reflect the dedication and values represented by Lina Chartrand, rights activist, writer, poet, publisher, dramaturge, and screenwriter. Annual.

The Albert B. Corey Prize. *See* Canadian Historical Association Awards.

Critic's Desk Award. *See* Arc Poetry Contests and Prizes.

Dafoe Book Prize

James Fergusson, Honorary Secretary, J. W. Dafoe Foundation, 359 University College, University of Manitoba, Winnipeg, MB R3T 2M8

Phone: (204) 474-6606 Fax: (204) 474-7645

E-mail: ferguss@cc.umanitoba.ca

Deadline: early December

A $10,000 prize is awarded annually for distinguished writing by a Canadian or resident of Canada that contributes to the understanding of Canada and/or its place in the world.

Dartmouth Book Awards

Jennifer Evans, Halifax Regional Library, 60 Alderney Drive, Dartmouth, NS B2Y 4P8

Phone: (902) 490-5991 Fax: (902) 490-5889

E-mail: msjel@nsh.library.ns.ca

Deadline: December

Two prizes of $1,500 each are awarded to honour the fiction and non-fiction books in any genre (except children's books) that have contributed most to the enjoyment and understanding of the cultural heritage of Nova Scotia. The winning titles best celebrate the spirit of Nova Scotia and its people. Open to any Canadian citizen or landed immigrant. Submission fee of $10. Annual.

The Donner Prize
Prize Manager, The Donner Prize, c/o Meisner Publicity and
    Promotion, 394A King Street E., Toronto, ON M5A 1K9
Phone: (416) 368-8253 Fax: (416) 363-1448
E-mail: meisnerpublicity@sympatico.ca
Deadline: November 30
    An annual award of $30,000 is awarded for the best book on Canadian public policy, with prizes of $5,000 each to the 5 finalists. The jury is looking for provocative, readable, and inspiring books on Canadian public policy that cover a broad spectrum of issues, including healthcare, social issues, educational reform, public finance, environment, regulatory and legal reform, urban affairs, youth issues, and social policy. The author must be Canadian, and the publisher of the book must be either Canadian or American.

Drainie-Taylor Biography Prize. *See* the Writers' Trust of
    Canada Awards.

Bill Duthie Booksellers' Choice Prize. *See* B.C. Book Prizes.

Sheila A. Egoff Children's Prize. *See* B.C. Book Prizes.

Arthur Ellis Awards
Cheryl Freedman, Secretary/Treasurer, Crime Writers of Canada,
    P.O. Box 113, 3007 Kingston Road, Scarborough, ON M1M 1P1
Phone: (416) 597-9938
E-mail: info@crimewriterscanada.com
Web site: www.crimewriterscanada.com
Deadline: January 15, 2005
    Established 1984 and named after the *nom de travail* of Canada's official hangman. Prizes are awarded annually for published works in the following categories in the crime genre: best crime novel, best non-fiction, best first crime novel, best crime short story, best juvenile/young adult crime book, and best crime publication in French.

Cash prizes awarded depending on availability. Open to any writer resident in Canada or any Canadian living abroad. Setting and imprint immaterial. No entry fee.

Marian Engel Award. *See* the Writers' Trust of Canada Awards.

Norma Epstein Award for Creative Writing
Eleanor Dennison, University College, 15 King's College Circle,
    Toronto, ON M5S 3H7
Phone: (416) 978-8083 Fax: (416) 971-2027
E-mail: eleanor.dennison@utoronto.ca
Deadline: May 15
Open to any student regularly enrolled in an undergraduate or graduate degree course at a Canadian university. Entry forms usually mailed to universities 4 to 5 months prior to closing date. To be placed on mailing list, please send your name and address to above address. Completed entry forms must carry the official stamp of the registrar of your college or university.

Hubert Evans Non-Fiction Prize. *See* B.C. Book Prizes.

Event Creative Non-Fiction Contest
Ian Cockfield, Assistant Editor, Event, P.O. Box 2503, New
    Westminster, BC V3L 5B2
Phone: (604) 527-5293 Fax: (604) 527-5095
E-mail: event@douglas.bc.ca
Web site: http://event.douglas.bc.ca
Deadline: April 15
Event magazine's annual contest invites good writing that explores the creative non-fiction forms of personal narrative, essay, biography, documentary, and life and travel writing. Three winners each receive $500 plus payment for publication in *Event*'s winter issue. Other manuscript entries may also be published. Accepts previously unpublished submissions up to 5,000 words. Entry fee $25/submission, which includes a 1-year subscription to *Event*.

The Wallace K. Ferguson Prize. *See* Canadian Historical
    Association Awards.

The Fiddlehead Contests
Sabine Campbell, Campus House, 11 Garland Court,
  Fredericton, NB E3B 5A3
Phone: (506) 453-3501 Fax: (506) 453-5069
E-mail: fiddlhd@unb.ca
Web site: www.lib.unb.ca/Texts/Fiddlehead
Deadline: December 15

Fiction Prize for Best Story
  A prize of $1,000 is awarded, plus publication fees, for first place, and $100 is awarded for 2 to 3 honourable mentions. Submissions to be no more than 25 pages. No previously published stories are accepted. Entry fee $24 includes a year's subscription to *The Fiddlehead*. Annual.

Ralph Gustafson Award for Best Poem
  A prize of $1,000 is awarded, plus publication fees, for first place, and $100 is awarded for 2 to 3 honourable mentions. Submissions to be no more than 5 poems. No previously published stories are accepted. Entry fee $24 includes a year's subscription to *The Fiddlehead*. Annual.

Timothy Findley Award. *See* the Writers' Trust of Canada
  Awards.

The Sheree Fitch Prize. *See* Writers' Federation of New
  Brunswick Literary Competition.

**The Norma Fleck Award for a Canadian Children's Non-
  Fiction Book**. *See* Canadian Children's Book Centre Awards.

Mavis Gallant Prize for Non-Fiction. *See* Quebec Writers'
  Federation Book Awards.

The Giller Prize
Elana Rabinovitch, c/o 40 Roxborough Avenue, Toronto, ON
  M5R 1T8
Phone: (416) 651-7066 Fax: (416) 651-9968

E-mail: elanar@sympatico.ca
Web site: www.thegillerprize.ca
Deadline: mid-August
Each year the Giller Prize awards $25,000 to the author of the best Canadian full-length novel or collection of short stories published in English, either originally or in translation, by a jury panel of 3. The author must be a Canadian citizen or permanent resident, and the book must have been published by a Canadian publisher.

John Glassco Translation Prize
Patricia Godbout, c/o 272 Heneker, Sherbrooke, QC J1J 3G4
Phone: (819) 820-1244
E-mail: patricia.godbout@courrier.usherb.ca ·
Web site: www.attlc-ltac.org/glasscoe.htm
Deadline: June 30
A $1,000 prize is awarded by the Literary Translators' Association of Canada for a translator's first book-length literary translation into English or French published in Canada during the previous year. Eligible genres include fiction, non-fiction, poetry, and children's literature. Entrants must be Canadian citizens or landed immigrants. Annual.

Danuta Gleed Literary Award. *See* the Writers' Union of Canada Awards and Competitions.

Government of Newfoundland and Labrador Arts and Letters Awards
P.O. Box 1854, St. John's, NL A1C 5P9
Phone: (709) 729-5253
Web site: www.gov.nf.ca/artsandletters
Deadline: February 13

Percy Janes First Novel Award
One prize of $1,000 is awarded for the best unpublished manuscript of at least 30,000 words. Entrants must be unpublished novelists who reside in Newfoundland and Labrador. One entry permitted per person.

Literary Arts Section Awards – Junior Division
Five prizes of $200 are awarded every year in the category of best original, unpublished poetry and best prose, including short stories, essays, and dramatic scripts (maximum 5,000 words). Entrants must be residents of Newfoundland and Labrador between 12 and 18 years of age.

Literary Arts Section Awards – Senior Division
Four prizes of $750 are awarded every year in recognition of outstanding original, unpublished poetry and short fiction (maximum 5,000 words), and 2 prizes of $750 are awarded every year for the best non-fiction prose (maximum 5,000 words) and dramatic script. Entrants must be residents of Newfoundland and Labrador. The awards are open to amateurs and professionals.

David C. Saxon Humanitarian Essay Competition
Two prizes of $750 are awarded annually for the best essay of 2,000 to 4,000 words written about a topic determined each year. Entrants must be residents of Newfoundland and Labrador.

Governor General's Literary Awards
Joanne Laroque-Poirier, Writing and Publishing Section, Canada
    Council for the Arts, P.O. Box 1047, 350 Albert Street, Ottawa,
    ON K1P 5V8
Phone: (613) 566-4414, ext. 5576, or 1-800-263-5588 Fax:
    (613) 566-4410
E-mail: joanne.laroque-poirier@canadacouncil.ca
Web site: www.canadacouncil.ca
Deadlines: March 15 and August 7
Seven annual awards of $15,000 are conferred in recognition of the best books of the year in English and in French in the following categories: fiction, literary non-fiction, poetry, drama, children's literature (text), children's literature (illustration), and translation (from French to English). In addition, the publishers of the winning titles receive a $3,000 grant for the promotion of the prize-winning books. Non-winning finalists each receive $1,000. Books must be first edition trade books and be written, translated, or illustrated by Canadian citizens or permanent residents. For translations, the

original work, written in French, must also be written by a
Canadian. Administered by the Canada Council. Write for eligibility criteria and other guidelines or consult the web site.

Grand Prix du livre de Montréal
Normand Biron, Commissioner, Grand Prix du livre de
   Montréal, Ville de Montréal service developpement culturel et
   qualité du milieu de vie, 5650 d'Iberville Street, 4th Floor,
   Montreal, QC H2G 3E4
Phone: (514) 872-1160 Fax: (514) 872-1153
E-mail: nbiron@ville.montreal.qc.ca
Web site: www.ville.montreal.qc.ca/culture/sectsout/
   gplmform.htm
Deadline: May 1
   A $15,000 award is bestowed on the author of an outstanding
book of exceptional quality and originality published in English or
French. Creative or non-fiction work and artistic or socio-historic
reference work are eligible. Open to authors living in Montreal.
Annual.

Great Blue Heron Poetry Contest
The Antigonish Review Contest, P.O. Box 5000, St. Francis
   Xavier University, Antigonish, NS B2G 2W5
Phone: (902) 8673962
E-mail: tar@stfx.ca
Web site: www.antigonishreview.com
Deadline: June 30
   A first prize of $800, second prize of $500, and third prize of $300
are awarded to the best poems on any subject matter. Prizes also
include publication in *The Antigonish Review*. Total entry not to
exceed 4 pages (maximum 150 lines), which may include 1 long
poem or several shorter ones. Entry fee $25 ($35 if outside North
America), which includes a 1-year subscription. Send only original,
unpublished material. No electronic submissions. Annual.

The Great Canadian Literary Hunt. *See* THIS Magazine
   Writing Awards.

The Griffin Poetry Prize

Ruth Smith, Manager, The Griffin Trust for Excellence in Poetry,
    6610 Edwards Boulevard, Mississauga, ON L5T 2V6
Phone: (905) 565-5993 Fax: (905) 564-3645
Web site: www.griffinpoetryprize.com
Deadline: December 31

Two prizes of $40,000 are awarded annually in the categories of international and Canadian poetry. In each category, the prize will be for the best collection of poetry in English published during the preceding year.

Ralph Gustafson Award for Best Poem. *See* the Fiddlehead
    Contests.

Hackmatack Children's Choice Book Award

3770 Kempt Road, Halifax, NS B3K 4X8
Phone: (902) 424-3774
E-mail: hackmatack@hackmatack.ca
Web site: www.hackmatack.ca
Deadline: December 31

A plaque is awarded annually for the best book in each of three categories – English fiction, English non-fiction, and French – written by a Canadian author for readers in grades 4 to 6. Books are chosen for their literary, cultural, and enjoyment factors, with an emphasis on Atlantic-authored materials. Children in reading groups vote for the nominees, who tour the region, giving readings to hundreds of children.

Roderick Haig-Brown Regional Prize. *See* B.C. Book Prizes.

Jason A. Hannah Medal. *See* the Royal Society of Canada
    Awards.

Harbourfront Festival Prize

Harbourfront Reading Series, 235 Queens Quay W., Toronto, ON
    M5J 2G8
Phone: (416) 973-4760
Web site: www.readings.org

A prize of $10,000 is awarded each year to a Canadian writer who has made a substantial contribution to Canadian letters through his or her writing and his or her efforts on behalf of other Canadian writers or writing. The winner is chosen by jury. No submissions.

Christie Harris Prize for Illustrated Children's Books. *See* B.C. Book Prizes.

Hidden Brook Press Poetry Awards
701 King Street W., Toronto, ON M5V 2W7
Phone: (416) 504-3966 Fax: (801) 751-1837
E-mail: writers@hiddenbrookpress.com
Web site: www.HiddenBrookPress.com

No Love Lost Poetry Anthology Contest
Deadline: October 30
  Ten cash prizes from $10 to $100 plus 10 honourable mentions are awarded annually. Topics eligible are love, hate, lust, desire, passion, jealousy, and ambivalence, including brotherly, sisterly, and parental love, and love of city and country. Up to 300 poems will be published. Entry fee of $15 includes purchase of the resulting book.

The Open Window Poetry Anthology Contest
Deadline: November 1
  Ten cash prizes from $10 to $100 plus 10 honourable mentions are awarded annually. Submit 5 poems, previously unpublished, of any style, theme, or length. Up to 300 poems will be published. Entry fee of $15 includes purchase of the resulting book.

Seeds International Poetry Chapbook Anthology Contest
Deadlines: April 1 and October 1
  Cash prizes and honourable mentions are awarded twice a year. Submit 3 poems of any style, theme, or length. Up to 300 poems will be published. Entry fee of $12 includes purchase of the resulting book.

The John Spencer Hill Award. *See* the Valley Writers' Guild Awards.

The Ray Burrell Hill Award. *See* the Valley Writers' Guild Awards.

The John Hirsch Award for Most Promising Manitoba Writer. *See* Manitoba Writing and Publishing Awards.

Humanist in Canada Literary Contests
Gary Bauslaugh, P.O. Box 943, Duncan, BC V9L 3Y2
Phone: (250) 746-6678 Fax: (250) 746-6672
E-mail: editor@humanistincanada.com
Web site: www.humanistincanada.com
Deadline: December 31
Annual awards of $500 for the best short story, $250 for the best poem on the theme of freedom: freedom from oppressive governments, repressive beliefs, ignorance, and superstition. Winners also have their work published in *Humanist in Canada* magazine. Stories should be less than 3,000 words, poems under 50 lines. Entries must be unpublished. Submit hard copies only. Entry fee $25 for each story (includes subscription to the magazine) and $10 for each poem (2 entries entitle writer to a 1-year subscription). Entrants must be Canadian citizens or landed immigrants.

K. M. Hunter Artists Awards
Awards Office, Ontario Arts Council, 151 Bloor Street W.,
    Toronto, ON M5S 1T6
Phone: (416) 969-7422 or 1-800-387-0058, ext. 7422 Fax:
    (416) 961-7796
E-mail: mwarren@arts.on.ca
Web site: www.arts.on.ca
Supports projects that advance an individual's career. Five awards of $8,000 each are given in the disciplines of visual arts, dance, literature, theatre, and music. Recipients are chosen from a selection of grant applications recommended by the Ontario Arts Council juries; in the case of writers, the shortlist comes from the OAC's Works in Progress program. Annual.

Innis-Gérin Medal. *See* the Royal Society of Canada Awards.

International 3-Day Novel Contest

Blue Lakes Books, 3495 Cambie Street, Suite 364, Vancouver, BC
  V5Z 4R3
E-mail: 3day@bluelakebooks.com
Web site: www.bluelakebooks.com/3day
Deadline: August 29

Research and outlines undertaken prior to the contest are permissible, but the actual writing must take place over the Labour Day weekend. Entries are judged by the editorial board of Blue Lake Books and guest writers and editors. Entry fee $50. Annual.

IODE Toronto Book Award

Education Officer, Municipal Chapter of Toronto IODE, 40 St.
  Clair Avenue E., Suite 205, Toronto, ON M4T 1M9
Phone: (416) 925-5078 Fax: (416) 925-5127
Deadline: before November 30

A $1,000 prize is conferred on the author or illustrator of the best children's book of the year written or illustrated by a resident of Toronto or the surrounding area. Annual.

Alexander Kennedy Isbister Award for Non-Fiction. *See* Manitoba Writing and Publishing Awards.

Laura Jamieson Prize. *See* the Canadian Research Institute for the Advancement of Women Prizes.

Percy Janes First Novel Award. *See* Government of Newfoundland and Labrador Arts and Letters Awards.

Jubilee Award for Short Stories. *See* Canadian Authors Association Awards.

A. M. Klein Prize for Poetry. *See* Quebec Writers' Federation Book Awards.

The Kobzar Literary Award

Ukrainian Canadian Foundation of Taras Shevchenko, 456 Main
  Street, Winnipeg, MB R3B 1B6
Phone: (204) 944-9128 or 1-866-524-5314 Fax: (204) 944-9135

E-mail: lesia@shevchenkofoundation.ca
Web site: www.shevchenkofoundation.ca
Deadline: May 13, 2005

A new $25,000 award ($20,000 to the author, $5,000 to the publisher) to recognize outstanding contribution to Canadian literature with a Ukrainian Canadian theme. Accepts literary non-fiction, fiction, children's literature, poetry, and drama in English, French, or Ukrainian. Books must have been published after May 14, 2003. Awarded every 2 years.

Gerald Lampert Memorial Award. *See* League of Canadian Poets Awards.

Herb Lampert Student Writing Award. *See* Science in Society Journalism Awards.

Archibald Lampman Award. *See* Arc Poetry Contests and Prizes.

Fred Landon Award. *See* Ontario Historical Society Awards for Authors.

Lydia Langstaff Memorial Prize
On Spec Magazine, P.O. Box 4727, Edmonton, AB T6E 5G8
Phone: (780) 413-0215 Fax: (780) 413-1538
E-mail: onspec@onspec.ca
Web site: www.onspec.ca
Deadline: January 31

A prize of $100 and a certificate are awarded to an emerging Canadian writer under the age of 30 whose work has been published in *On Spec* during the preceding calendar year. The winner is selected by the editors of the magazine.

Margaret Laurence Award for Fiction. *See* Manitoba Writing and Publishing Awards.

Lawrence House Short Story Competition
Chris Gilmour, Lawrence House Centre for the Arts, 127 Christina Street S., Sarnia, ON N7T 2M8

Phone: (519) 337-0507 Fax: (519) 337-0482
E-mail: lawrencehouse@bellnet.ca
Web site: www.lawrencehouse.ca
Deadline: May 1, 2005

A first prize of $500, second prize of $250, and third prize of $100 for the best short story. Stories must be unpublished, 2,500 words or less, and in English. Entry fee $20. Open to all Canadian citizens and landed immigrants. Annual.

Stephen Leacock Memorial Medal for Humour
Judith Rapson, Chair of the Award Committee of the Stephen
    Leacock Associates, R.R. #2, Coldwater, ON LOK 1E0
Phone: (705) 835-3218 Fax: (705) 835-5171
E-mail: drapson@bconnex.net
Deadline: December 31

A sterling-silver medal, together with a cash award of $10,000, is awarded for the year's best humorous book written by a Canadian in prose, verse, or as drama. Send 10 copies of the book, a $50 entry fee, plus author bio and photo. Annual.

League of Canadian Poets Awards
920 Yonge Street, Suite 608, Toronto, ON M4W 3C7
Phone: (416) 504-1657 Fax: (416) 504-0096
E-mail: info@poets.ca
Web site: www.poets.ca

Gerald Lampert Memorial Award
Deadline: November 1

A $1,000 cash award is given each year in recognition of the best first book of poetry written by a Canadian in the preceding year. Entry fee $15.

Pat Lowther Memorial Award
Deadline: November 1

An annual $1,000 prize recognizes the best book of poetry written by a Canadian woman and published in the preceding year. Entry fee $15.

The Poetic Licence Contest for Canadian Youth
Deadline: December 1

An annual contest for the best English and French poems in two categories: junior (grades 7 to 9) and senior (grades 10 to 12). The first-, second-, and third-place winners receive cash prizes and will get their poems published in *Re:verse*, the League of Canadian Poets' youth e-zine. No entry fee.

lichen literary journal Serial Poetry Contest

Editorial Board, 701 Rossland Road E., Suite 234, Whitby, ON
    L1N 6M7
Phone: (905) 720-2172
E-mail: info@lichenjournal.ca
Web site: www.lichenjournal.ca
Deadline: December 31

A new annual award with a prize of $500 and publication in the *lichen literary journal*. Submit 3 poems for a maximum of 75 lines total. Poems should be subtly linked or share a common thread and be unpublished and in English. Entry fee $20, which includes a 1-year subscription. Open to Canadian and international entries.

Lieutenant Governor's Literary Lifetime Achievement Award. *See* B.C. Book Prizes.

The Lieutenant-Governor's Medal for Historical Writing

Helmi Braches, Co-ordinator, Writing Competition, B.C.
    Historical Federation, P.O. Box 130, Whonnock, BC V2W 1V9
Phone: (604) 462-8942
E-mail: braches@attcanada.ca
Deadline: December 31

Awarded to the writer whose book contributes most significantly to the recorded history of British Columbia. Any new book presenting any facet of B.C. history is eligible. Judges looking for appropriate illustrations, careful proofreading, and an adequate index, table of contents, and bibliography. The prizes are $300, $200, and $100, plus a certificate of merit and an invitation to the awards banquet. Books must be submitted in their year of publication. Annual.

The Dorothy Livesay Poetry Prize. *See* B.C. Book Prizes.

Pat Lowther Memorial Award. *See* League of Canadian Poets Awards.

Lush Triumphant
sub-Terrain Magazine, P.O. Box 3008, MPO, Vancouver, BC
  V6B 3X5
Phone: (604) 876-8710 Fax: (604) 879-2667
E-mail: subter@portal.ca
Web site: www.anvilpress.com/subterrain
Deadline: May 15
  The winning entries in 3 categories – fiction, poetry, and creative non-fiction – will receive a $500 cash prize and be published in the fall issue of *sub-Terrain*. The first runner-up in each category will be published in a future issue of the magazine. Fee is $20/entry. Entrants may submit as many entries in as many categories as they wish. All work must be previously unpublished. All entrants will receive a complimentary 1-year subscription to *sub-Terrain*. Annual.

Abbyann D. Lynch Medal in Bioethics. *See* the Royal Society of Canada Awards.

Sir John A. Macdonald Prize. *See* Canadian Historical Association Awards.

The Grant MacEwan Author's Award
Alberta Community Development, 10405 Jasper Avenue, 9th
  Floor Standard Life Centre, Edmonton, AB T5J 4R7
Phone: (780) 427-6315
E-mail: paul.pearson@gov.ab.ca
Deadline: December 31
  Dr. MacEwan wrote more than 50 books on nature, folklore, agriculture, politics, the environment, literature, history, and the people of Alberta. This new award of $25,000 is presented annually to the Alberta author whose book (published the previous calendar year) best reflects Alberta and/or Dr. MacEwan's interests. Books must be original or translated works, written in either English or French.

Hugh MacLennan Prize for Fiction. *See* Quebec Writers' Federation Book Awards.

C. B. Macpherson Prize. *See* Canadian Political Science Association Prizes.

The Malahat Review Prizes
John Barton, *The Malahat Review*, University of Victoria, P.O. Box
   1700, Stn. CSC, Victoria, BC V8W 2Y2
Phone: (250) 721-8524
E-mail: malahat@uvic.ca
Web site: www.malahatreview.ca

Long Poem Prize
Deadline: March 1, 2005
   Two prizes of $400, plus payment for publication, are awarded
biennially for the best original, unpublished long poems or cycle of
poems of no more than 20 pages. Entry fee of $35 covers a sub-
scription to *The Malahat Review*.

Novella Prize
Deadline: March 1, 2004
   A prize of $500, plus payment for publication, is awarded biennially
for the best original, unpublished prose work no longer than 30,000
words. Entry fee $35 covers a subscription to *The Malahat Review*.

Manitoba Writing and Publishing Awards
Robyn Maharaj or Jamis Paulson, Manitoba Writers' Guild, 100
   Arthur Street, Suite 206, Winnipeg, MB R3B 1H3
Phone: (204) 942-6134 or 1-888-637-5802 Fax: (204) 942-5754
E-mail: mbwriter@mts.net
Web site: www.mbwriter.mb.ca

The John Hirsch Award for Most Promising Manitoba Writer
Deadline: January
   A cash prize of $2,500, donated by the estate of the late John
Hirsch, co-founder of the Manitoba Theatre Centre, is awarded
annually to the most promising Manitoba writer. Authors of poetry,
fiction, creative non-fiction, and drama are eligible.

Alexander Kennedy Isbister Award for Non-Fiction
Deadline: January

A cash prize of $3,500 is presented to the Manitoba writer whose book is judged the best book of adult non-fiction (excluding encyclopedias, textbooks, and dictionaries) written in English during the previous year. Entry fee $25. Annual.

Margaret Laurence Award for Fiction
Deadline: December

An annual cash prize of $3,500 is presented to the Manitoba writer whose book is judged the best book of adult fiction written in English and published during the previous year. Entry fee $25.

The McNally Robinson Book for Young People Award
Deadline: December

Two annual cash prizes of $2,500, donated by McNally Robinson Booksellers, are awarded for the 2 best young person's books written by a Manitoba author, one in the category of young adult and the other for children. Books of fiction, poetry, non-fiction, and drama are eligible. Entry fee $25.

The McNally Robinson Book of the Year Award
Deadline: December

An annual cash prize of $5,000, donated by McNally Robinson Booksellers, is awarded for an outstanding book in any genre (except YA or children's books) written by a Manitoba resident. The title must be non-academic and written in English. Books of fiction, poetry, creative non-fiction, non-fiction, and drama are eligible. Entry fee $25.

Eileen McTavish Sykes Award for Best First Book
Deadline: December

Presented annually to the author whose first professionally published book is judged the best written. The author receives a cash prize of $1,500, donated by Manitoba children's author Eileen McTavish Sykes through the Winnipeg Foundation. Each entry must be a non-academic title written in English. Books of fiction, poetry, non-fiction, children's and young adult literature, and drama will be considered. $25 entry fee/title.

The Mary Scorer Award for Best Book by a Manitoba Publisher
Deadline: December

Presented annually for the best book published by a Manitoba publisher written for the trade, educational, academic, or scholarly market. The author receives a cash prize of $1,000, donated by Friesens Corporation. Books judged on innovation of content, quality of editing and writing, and excellence in design and illustrations. Promotional activity and market acceptance will be considered. Entry fee $25.

The Carol Shields Winnipeg Book Award
Deadline: January

A juried annual prize of $5,000 honouring books that evoke the special character of Winnipeg, or contribute to the appreciation or understanding of the city. All genres are eligible and may be written in English or French. Entry fee $25.

McAuslan First Book Award. *See* Quebec Writers' Federation Book Awards.

The McNally Robinson Book for Young People Award. *See* Manitoba Writing and Publishing Awards.

The McNally Robinson Book of the Year Award. *See* Manitoba Writing and Publishing Awards.

Margaret McWilliams Competition
Manitoba Historical Society, 167 Lombard Avenue, Suite 470,
   Winnipeg, MB R3B 0T6
Phone: (204) 947-0559 Fax: (204) 943-1093
E-mail: info@mhs.mb.ca
Web site: www.mhs.mb.ca
Deadline: December 1

Margaret McWilliams Medals are offered each year in the following categories: scholarly book, popular book, university essay/thesis, special projects and displays, local history, audio/visual, historical fiction, and organizations/associations/institutions. The purpose of the award is to encourage the study and preservation of the history of all parts of Manitoba and of the records and memories of the pioneers who made Manitoba what it is. Awards are granted for meritorious work only and therefore are not necessarily awarded in every category each year.

Vicky Metcalf Award for Children's Literature. *See* the Writers' Trust of Canada Awards.

W. O. Mitchell Book Prize. *See* Writers Guild of Alberta Awards.

W. O. Mitchell Literary Prize. *See* the Writers' Trust of Canada Awards.

Morguard Literary Awards
Brenda Norton, Executive Assistant, Real Estate Institute of
    Canada, 5407 Eglinton Avenue W., Suite 208, Toronto, ON
    M9C 5K6
Phone: (416) 695-9000 or 1-800-542-7342   Fax: (416) 695-7230
E-mail: brenda.norton@reic.com
Deadline: April 15
    Recognizes outstanding articles or speeches relevant to the Canadian real estate industry. Sponsored by the Real Estate Institute of Canada and Morguard Investments Ltd. A $2,000 prize goes to the winner in each of 2 categories: practising industry lay writers and academic writers. Submissions must be original articles or speeches, 3,000 to 6,000 words, published or given in the past 12 months. Annual.

MOSAID Technologies Inc. Award for Fiction. *See* Canadian Authors Association Awards.

National Business Book Awards
Faye Mattachione, PricewaterhouseCoopers LLP, P.O. Box 82,
    Suite 3000, 77 King Street W., 25th Floor, Toronto, ON
    M5K 1G8
Phone: (416) 869-1130   Fax: (416) 941-8345
E-mail: faye.mattachione@ca.pwc.com
Web site: www.pwc.com/ca/nbba
Deadline: December 15
    An annual award of $10,000 recognizes excellence in business

writing for books published in Canada during the previous year. PricewaterhouseCoopers and the BMO Financial Group are co-sponsors of this award. The media sponsor is *The Globe and Mail.*

National Magazine Awards
Pat Kendall, National Magazine Awards Foundation, 109
  Vanderhoof Avenue, Suite 207, Toronto, ON M4G 2H7
Phone: (416) 422-1358 Fax: (416) 422-3762
E-mail: nmaf@bellnet.ca
Web site: www.magazine-awards.com
Deadline: January

The written categories are as follows: humour; business; science and technology and the environment; health and medicine; politics and public interest; society; investigative reporting; fiction (commissioned by the magazine); arts and entertainment; sports and recreation; columns (3 columns by the same writer in the same magazine); travel; service – health and family; service – personal finance and business; service – leisure pursuits; how-to (any article that presents practical instructional information); essays; personal journalism; profiles; editorial package (a theme issue reflecting collaboration between editors and writers); and words and pictures (an article relying for its impact on text and visuals).

Canadian staff or freelance contributors are eligible. Magazine publishers, editors, or freelancers may submit. Gold awards are $1,000 and a scroll, silver awards $250 and a scroll. As well, the President's Medal is awarded for an article considered the "Best of Show." The winner of the Alexander Ross Award for Best New Magazine Writer receives a cash prize of $1,000. Editors are encouraged to make submissions on behalf of new writers. Annual.

The Hilda Neatby Prize in Women's History. *See* Canadian
  Historical Association Awards.

New Cat Tattoos. *See* Bad Moon Books Contests.

The bpNichol Chapbook Award
The Phoenix Community Works Foundation, 316 Dupont Street,
  Toronto, ON M5R 1V9
Phone: (416) 964-7919

Web site: www.pcwf.ca
Deadline: March 30
A prize of $1,000 is offered each year for the best poetry chapbook published in English in Canada. Entry made by publisher or author. The chapbook should be between 10 and 48 pages long. Send 3 copies (not returnable) and a short C.V.

No Love Lost Poetry Anthology Contest. *See* Hidden Brook Press Poetry Awards.

North of 55 Non-Fiction Writing Contest
P.O. Box 1578, Carleton Place, ON K7H 4M3
Phone: (613) 257-5257 Fax: (613) 257-2108
E-mail: gillfoss@allstream.net
Web site: www.canauth.org and www.uphere.ca
Awarded for the best unpublished fiction about the area north of the 55th Parallel in Canada or set there. Must be no longer than 1,000 words. Co-sponsored by the Canadian Authors Association and *Up Here* magazine. The first-place winner receives $250, publication in *Up Here*, and a 1-year membership in the Canadian Authors Association. Second place receives $50 and an *Up Here* sweatshirt. Entry fee for CAA members and *Up Here* subscribers $15; all others $20. Entrants must be 18 years of age or older and Canadian citizens or landed immigrants. Annual.

**The Alden Nowlan Award for Excellence in English-
    Language Literary Arts**
Pauline Bourque, Executive Director, New Brunswick Arts Board,
    634 Queen Street, Suite 300, Fredericton, NB E3B 1C2
Phone: (506) 444-4444 Fax: (506) 444-5543
E-mail: nbabcanb@artsnb.ca
Deadline: October 1
Designed to recognize outstanding achievement and contribution to the English-language literary arts of New Brunswick, this award is presented during an annual ceremony by the lieutenant governor and includes a cash prize of $5,000. Nominees must have been born in the province or have lived there for at least 5 years. Annual.

Ontario Historical Society Awards for Authors
34 Parkview Avenue, Willowdale, ON M2N 3Y2
Phone: (416) 226-9011 Fax: (416) 226-2740
E-mail: ohs@ontariohistoricalsociety.ca
Web site: www.ontariohistoricalsociety.ca
Deadlines: end of October

An annual program that honours individuals who have contributed significantly to the preservation and promotion of Ontario's heritage. All award recipients receive recognition in publicity and a framed certificate accompanied by a copy of the citation acknowledging their contribution. Self-nominations are accepted. A book may be nominated in one award category only.

Joseph Brant Award

Honours the best book on multicultural history in Ontario. Must have been published within the past 3 years. Entry fee $10/title with 3 copies of each book.

Fred Landon Award

Honours the best book on regional history in Ontario. Must have been published within the past 3 years. Entry fee $10/title with 3 copies of each book.

Alison Prentice Award

Honours the best book on women's history. Must have been published within the past 3 years. Entry fee $10/title with 3 copies of each book.

Riddell Award

Honours the best book on Ontario's history. Must have been published within the award year. Entry fee $10/title with 3 copies of each book.

J. J. Talman Award

Honours the best book on Ontario's social, economic, political, or cultural history. Must have been published within the past 3 years. Entry fee $10/title with 3 copies of each book.

The Open Window Poetry Anthology Contest. *See* Hidden
Brook Press Poetry Awards.

Ottawa Book Awards
Faith Seltzer, Office of Cultural Affairs, 110 Laurier Avenue W.
(01-49), Ottawa, ON K1P 1J1
Phone: (613) 580-2424, ext. 27412   Fax: (613) 580-2632
E-mail: faith.seltzer@ottawa.ca
Web site: www.ottawa.ca/arts
Deadline: December 9
   A $2,500 award is presented each year to the author of a book of
literary merit in each of 4 categories: English fiction, English non-
fiction, French fiction, and French non-fiction. The author must
reside in the city of Ottawa.

Ottawa Independent Writers Travel Writing Contest
Denis St-Jean, 8 Assiniboine Drive, Ottawa, ON K2E 5R7
Phone: (613) 232-1837
E-mail: rosaleen@floral.org
Web site: www.oiw.ca
Deadline: March 12
   Prizes of $100, $75, $50, and 3 honourable mentions are awarded
for articles based on the writers' real life travel experiences. Each
article to be 1,500 words or less. Entry fee $5. Annual.

Pearson Writers' Trust Non-Fiction Prize. *See* the Writers'
Trust of Canada Awards.

Lorne Pierce Medal. *See* the Royal Society of Canada Awards.

The Poetic Licence Contest for Canadian Youth. *See* League
of Canadian Poets Awards.

Poets' Corner Award
Broken Jaw Press, P.O. Box 596, Stn. A, Fredericton, NB E3B 5A6
Phone: (506) 454-5127   Fax: (506) 454-5127
E-mail: jblades@nbnet.nb.ca
Web site: www.brokenjaw.com/poetscorner.htm

Deadline: December 31

This award is given by Broken Jaw Press and the BS Poetry Society to the author of the best poetry manuscript. Winner receives a $500 cash prize and the winning manuscript will be published. Individual poems may have been previously published in periodicals, anthologies, and chapbooks. Entry fee $20. Annual.

Marion Porter Prize. *See* the Canadian Research Institute for the Advancement of Women Prizes.

Pottersfield Portfolio Annual Compact Fiction/Short Poem Competitions

Douglas A. Brown, Managing Editor, Pottersfield Portfolio, 9879 Kempt Head Road, Ross Ferry, NS B1X 1N3

Web sites: www.magomania.com

Deadline: May 1

Winning authors receive a cash award of $250 each in two categories and have their work published in *Pottersfield Portfolio*. The work can be stories of 1,500 words or less, or poems of 20 lines or less. Entry fee $20 for first entry, $5 for each subsequent entry in the same category (includes a 1-year subscription). Canadian writers and Canadian expatriates only are eligible.

The E. J. Pratt Medal and Prize in Poetry

Rosemary Cameron, Awards Manager, Admissions and Awards, University of Toronto, 315 Bloor Street W., Toronto, ON M5S 1A3

Phone: (416) 978-2190

E-mail: ask@adm.utoronto.ca

Web site: www.adm.utoronto.ca/awd/schp_index.htm

Deadline: April 2

The E. J. Pratt Medal plus a $100 prize are awarded as a stimulus to poetic composition in the belief that good poetry is the best assurance of a vital language and a healthy culture. The competition is open to any student proceeding toward a first or a post-graduate degree at the University of Toronto. Entries should be approximately 100 lines long. No previously published compositions will be considered, except for work in campus student publications. The award will be offered annually; however, if the selection committee determines that no submission is of sufficient excellence, the award will not be given.

Alison Prentice Award. *See* Ontario Historical Society Awards for Authors.

PRISM international Writing Prizes
Creative Writing Program, University of British Columbia, Buch E-462, 1866 Main Mall, Vancouver, BC V6T 1Z1
Phone: (604) 822-2514 Fax: (604) 822-3616
E-mail: prism@interchange.ubc.ca
Web site: www.prism.arts.ubc.ca

Earle Birney Prize for Poetry
Deadline: not applicable
   One award of $500 will be won by a poet whose work has appeared in *PRISM international* during the previous year. Poets need not apply; their work is automatically considered upon publication. Annual.

Rogers Communications Literary Non-Fiction Prize
Deadline: September 30
   A $500 first prize is awarded annually to the author of an outstanding piece of literary non-fiction (up to 25 double-spaced pages). The winning entry will be published in *PRISM international*, will earn an additional payment of $20/page for publication, and receive a 1-year subscription. Works of translation are eligible. Entry fee $25 for 1 story, plus $7 for each additional piece.

PRISM international Annual Short Fiction Contest
Deadline: January 31
   A $2,000 prize is awarded for the best original, unpublished short story (up to 25 double-spaced pages). Five runner-up prizes of $200 are also conferred. All winners receive publication payment for inclusion in *PRISM international*'s Fiction Contest issue. Works of translation are eligible. Entry fee $25 for one story, plus $7 for each additional story.

Quebec Writers' Federation Book Awards

Lori Schubert, Administrative Director, Quebec Writers'
Federation, 1200 Atwater Avenue, Montreal, QC H3Z 1X4
Phone: (514) 933-0878 Fax: (514) 933-0878
E-mail: admin@qwf.org
Web site: www.qwf.org
Deadlines: May 31 and August 15 (for books published between
October 1 and September 30)

All entry fees $10. Write for criteria and entry forms. Books may
be submitted by publishers or authors.

Mavis Gallant Prize for Non-Fiction

An annual cash prize of $2,000 is awarded for the best book of
literary non-fiction written in English by a writer who has lived in
Quebec for at least 3 of the past 5 years.

A. M. Klein Prize for Poetry

An annual cash prize of $2,000 is awarded for the best work of
poetry written in English by a writer who has lived in Quebec for at
least 3 of the past 5 years.

Hugh MacLennan Prize for Fiction

An annual cash prize of $2,000 is awarded for the best work of
fiction written in English by a writer who has lived in Quebec for at
least 3 of the past 5 years.

McAuslan First Book Award

An annual cash prize of $2,000 is awarded for the best first book
written in English by a writer who has lived in Quebec for at least 3
of the past 5 years.

Translation Prize

An annual cash prize of $2,000 is awarded for the best transla-
tion. The prize alternates on an annual basis between a book translated from English to French and a book translated from French to
English, with a 2-year eligibility span for each. The two sub-
categories have very different eligibility criteria.

Thomas Head Raddall Atlantic Fiction Award. *See* Writers'
Federation of Nova Scotia Awards.

Red Cedar Book Awards
c/o B.C. Library Association, 900 Howe Street, Suite 150,
  Vancouver, BC V6Z 2M4
Phone: (604) 683-5354 Fax: (604) 609-0707
E-mail: office@bcla.bc.ca
Web site: http://redcedar.swifty.com
  Awarded to the author and/or illustrator of the best book of fiction
and non-fiction for children. No monetary value, but the prize-
winners receive engraved red cedar plaques. These are children's
choice awards, voted on by children throughout B.C. during the
program year. The authors/illustrators must be Canadian citizens or
landed immigrants who have lived in Canada for at least 2 years. The
books must have been published by a recognized publisher and be
recognized as being of general interest to students in grades 4 to 7.

Regina Book Award. *See* Saskatchewan Book Awards.

The Richards Prize. *See* Writers' Federation of New Brunswick
  Literary Competition.

Evelyn Richardson Non-Fiction Award. *See* Writers'
  Federation of Nova Scotia Awards.

Riddell Award. *See* Ontario Historical Society Awards for
  Authors.

Rogers Communications Literary Non-Fiction Prize. *See*
  PRISM international Writing Prizes.

Rogers Writers' Trust Fiction Prize. *See* the Writers' Trust of
  Canada Awards.

The Royal Society of Canada Awards
Geneviève Gouin, Publications and Awards Co-ordinator, The
  Royal Society of Canada, 283 Sparks Street, Ottawa ON
  K1R 7X9

Phone: (613) 991-5760   Fax: (613) 991-6996
E-mail: ggouin@rsc.ca
Web site: www.rsc.ca

Bancroft Award
Deadline: December 1
A presentation scroll and a prize of $2,500 is offered every 2 years if there is a suitable candidate. The award is given for publication, instruction, and research in the earth sciences that have conspicuously contributed to public understanding and appreciation of the subject. Nominations must be put forward by 3 persons, 1 of whom must be a fellow of the Royal Society of Canada.

Jason A. Hannah Medal
Deadline: March 1
A bronze medal and a prize of $1,500 is offered annually for an important Canadian publication in the history of medicine. The work must have been published in the 2 years preceding its nomination. It must be Canadian either through the citizenship or residence of the author, or through a content clearly relevant to Canadian medicine and health care.

Innis-Gérin Medal
Deadline: December 1
A bronze medal is awarded every 2 years, if there is a suitable candidate, for a distinguished and sustained contribution to the literature of the social sciences, including human geography and social psychology. Nominations must be put forward by 3 persons, 1 of whom must be a fellow of the Royal Society of Canada.

Abbyann D. Lynch Medal in Bioethics
A bronze medal and a cash award of $2,000 is offered every year, if there is a suitable nomination, for a major contribution in bioethics by a Canadian. The contribution may be a book, a report, a scholarly article, a monograph, or a series of articles that have been published in the 2 years preceding the nomination. Nominations must be put forward by 3 organizations and/or persons, 1 of whom must be a fellow of the Royal Society of Canada.

Lorne Pierce Medal
Deadline: December 1
A gold plated silver medal is awarded every 2 years, if there is a suitable candidate, for an achievement of special significance and conspicuous merit in imaginative or critical literature written in either English or French. Critical literature dealing with Canadian subjects has priority. Nominations must be put forward by 3 persons, 1 of whom must be a fellow of the Royal Society of Canada.

The George Ryga Award
c/o John Lent, English Department, Okanagan University
College, 3333 College Way, Kelowna, BC V1V 1V7
Web site: www.abcbookworld.com
An annual prize of $2,500 worth of advertising and a commemorative bust of George Ryga is awarded for the best book contributing to social awareness by a B.C. author. No entry fee.

Saskatchewan Book Awards
Joyce Wells, Saskatchewan Book Awards, 2505 – 11th Avenue,
Suite 120, Regina, SK S4P 0K6
Phone: (306) 569-1585 Fax: (306) 569-4187
E-mail: director@bookawards.sk.ca
Deadlines: July 31 (for books published between September 15 and July 31) and September 15 (for books published between August 1 and September 15)

Children's Literature Award
An award of $2,000 will be given to a Saskatchewan author for the best published book of children's or young-adult literature. Entry fee $15/title. Annual.

Fiction Award
An award of $1,500 will be given to a Saskatchewan author for the best published work of fiction (novel or short fiction). Entry fee $20/title. Annual.

First Book Award Honouring Brenda MacDonald Riches
An award of $2,000 will be given to a Saskatchewan author for

the best published first book in the following categories: children's, drama (published plays), fiction (short fiction, novellas, novels), non-fiction (not including cookbooks, how-to books, directories, or bibliographies of minimal critical content), and poetry. Entry fee $15/title. Annual.

Non-Fiction Award

An award of $2,000 will be given to a Saskatchewan author for the best published work of non-fiction. Entry fee $20/title. Annual.

Poetry Award Honouring Anne Szumigalski

An award of $2,000 will be given to a Saskatchewan author for the best published book of poetry. Entry fee $20/title. Annual.

Regina Book Award

In recognition of the vitality of the literary community of Regina, this $2,000 award is presented to a Regina writer for the best book in the following categories: children's, drama (published plays), fiction (short fiction, novellas, novels), non-fiction (not including cookbooks, how-to books, directories, or bibliographies of minimal critical content), and poetry. Entry fee $15/title. Annual.

Saskatchewan Book of the Year Award

An award of $1,500 will be given to a Saskatchewan author for the best published book in the following categories: children's, drama (published plays), fiction (short fiction, novellas, novels), non-fiction (not including cookbooks, how-to books, directories, or bibliographies of minimal critical content), and poetry. Entry fee $20/title. Annual.

Saskatoon Book Award

In recognition of the vitality of the literary community of Saskatoon, this $2,000 award is presented to a Saskatoon writer for the best book in the following categories: children's, drama (published plays), fiction (short fiction, novellas, novels), non-fiction (not including cookbooks, how-to books, directories, or bibliographies of minimal critical content), and poetry. Entry fee $20/title. Annual.

Scholarly Writing Award

An award of $2,000 will be given to a Saskatchewan author for the published work that is judged to contribute most to scholarship. His or her work must recognize or draw on specific theoretical work within a community of scholars, and participate in the creation and transmission of knowledge. The work must show potential readability by a wider audience and be accessible to those outside an academic milieu. Works in the following categories will be considered: refereed publications, reference works, and/or those published by an academic press. Entry fee $20/title. Annual.

Saskatoon Book Award. *See* Saskatchewan Book Awards.

Margaret and John Savage First Book Award. *See* Writers' Federation of Nova Scotia Awards.

David C. Saxon Humanitarian Essay Competition. *See* Government of Newfoundland and Labrador Arts and Letters Awards.

The Ruth and Sylvia Schwartz Children's Book Award
Ontario Arts Council, 151 Bloor Street W., Toronto, ON M5S 1T6
Phone: (416) 969-7438 or 1-800-387-0058, ext. 7438 Fax:
(416) 961-7796
E-mail: lfilyer@arts.on.ca
Web site: www.arts.on.ca

A panel of children's booksellers from across Canada selects 2 shortlists of 5 young adult and 5 picture books in February; 2 juries of children then select a winner in each category. There is no application process; all Canadian authored/illustrated children's trade books published in the previous year are eligible. The annual awards ($5,000 for the picture book category, shared between author and illustrator; $5,000 for the YA category) are presented by the OAC at the annual CBA convention in June or July.

Science in Society Journalism Awards
c/o Canadian Science Writers' Association, P.O. Box 1543,
Kingston, ON K7L 5C7
Phone: 1-800-796-8595

E-mail: office@sciencewriters.ca
Web site: www.sciencewriters.ca

Herb Lampert Student Writing Award
An annual cash prize of $1,000 is awarded to the student science writer of the best original material in either print or TV and radio categories. Any student writer who has a science article published in a student or other newspaper or magazine or aired on a radio or TV station in Canada is eligible.

Science Journalism Competition
Twelve cash prizes of $1,000 each are awarded to honour outstanding original contributions to science journalism in Canada in the following categories: print, radio, and television. Competitors must be Canadian citizens or residents. Write for submission criteria. Annual.

SIS Book Awards
Three $1,000 cash prizes are awarded annually to the authors of books that made outstanding contributions to science writing for the general public, for youth, and for children. Entries may address aspects of basic or applied science or technology, historical or current, in any area including health, science, environmental issues, regulatory trends, etc. Books are judged on literary excellence and scientific content. The writer must be a Canadian citizen or resident.

The Mary Scorer Award for Best Book by a Manitoba Publisher. *See* Manitoba Writing and Publishing Awards.

Seeds International Poetry Chapbook Anthology Contest. *See* Hidden Brook Press Poetry Awards.

The Carol Shields Winnipeg Book Award. *See* Manitoba Writing and Publishing Awards.

Dorothy Shoemaker Literary Awards Contest
Sheila Bauman, Events Planner, Kitchener Public Library, 85 Queen Street N., Kitchener, ON N2N 2H1

Phone: (519) 743-0271, ext. 254 Fax: (519) 579-2382
E-mail: literarycontest@kpl.org
Web site: www.skpl.org
Deadline: contest runs between June 1 and July 31

Named in honour of Dorothy Shoemaker, former chief librarian and ardent supporter of writers, and funded by her generous endowment. First, second, and third prize winners in both prose and poetry categories receive cash awards of $150, $100, and $75. Winning entries are published in the anthology *The Changing Image*. Open to residents of Ontario in 3 age categories: junior (under 12 years), intermediate (12 to 17 years), and senior (18 years and older). Submissions accepted by e-mail only for unpublished work. Commercially published writers are not eligible. No entry fee, but a limited number of submissions permitted. See web site for complete guidelines.

Short Grain Writing Contest

Business Manager, P.O. Box 67, Saskatoon, SK S7K 3K1
Phone: (306) 244-2828
E-mail: grainmag@sasktel.net
Web site: www.grainmagazine.ca
Deadline: January 31

Offers $6,000 in prizes each year for original, unpublished works in 4 categories: dramatic monologue (a self-contained speech given by a single character in 500 words or less); postcard story (a work of narrative fiction of 500 words or less); prose poem (a lyric poem written as a prose paragraph or paragraphs of 500 words or less); and Long Grain of Truth (a non-fiction creative prose piece of 5,000 words or less). Three $500 prizes are given in each category. Winners' work will be published in *Grain*. Entry fee $25 for 2 entries. Additional entries are $5 each. Entry fee includes a 1-year subscription.

The Anne Szumigalski Editors Prize

A $500 prize will be awarded each year to a poet appearing in *Grain* magazine, selected by *Grain* editors.

Donald Smiley Prize. *See* Canadian Political Science Association Prizes.

Edna Staebler Award for Creative Non-Fiction
Kathryn Wardropper, Administrator, Wilfrid Laurier University,
   75 University Avenue W., Waterloo, ON N2L 3C5
Phone: (519) 884-0710, ext. 3109 Fax: (519) 884-8202
E-mail: kwardrop@wlu.ca
Deadline: April 30
   A $3,000 prize is awarded annually for an outstanding work of
creative non-fiction, which must be written by a Canadian and have
a Canadian location and significance. To be eligible, an entry must
be the writer's first or second published book. Established to give
recognition and encouragement to new writers. Administered by
Wilfrid Laurier University.

The Dan Sullivan Memorial Poetry Contest. *See* Writers'
   Circle of Durham Region Contests.

Sunday Star Short Story Contest
Sunday Star, 1 Yonge Street, Toronto, ON M5E 1E6
Phone: (416) 367-2000
Web site: www.thestar.com
Deadline: December 31
   A first prize of $5,000 (and tuition to the Humber School for
Writers 30-week correspondence program), a second of $2,000,
and a third of $1,000 are awarded for the best original, unpublished
short stories up to 2,500 words. They will be published in *The Star*
along with 7 other stories, with those authors receiving $200 each.
Rules available on StarPhone at (416) 350-3000, ext. 2747, and on
the web site.

Eileen McTavish Sykes Award for Best First Book. *See*
   Manitoba Writing and Publishing Awards.

The Anne Szumigalski Editors Prize. *See* Short Grain Writing
   Contest.

J. J. Talman Award. *See* Ontario Historical Society Awards for
   Authors.

The Charles Taylor Prize for Literary Non-Fiction
June Dickenson, P.O. Box 301, Carlisle, ON LOR 1H0
Phone: (905) 689-0388 Fax: (905) 689-2944
E-mail: dickenson@on.aibn.com
  Commemorates Charles Taylor's pursuit of excellence in the field of literary non-fiction. Awarded every 2 years to the author whose book best combines a superb command of the English language, elegance of style, and a subtlety of thought and perception. The winner receives $25,000 and promotional support to help that and all shortlisted books stand out in the national media, bookstores, and libraries. The winning book is donated, upon request, to high school libraries across Canada. Entries must be submitted by the publisher of the work. Only Canadian authors are considered.

Terasen Lifetime Achievement Award for an Outstanding Literary Career in British Columbia
c/o B.C. BookWorld, 3516 West 13th Avenue (rear), Vancouver, BC V6R 2S3
Phone: (604) 736-4011
  A $5,000 prize is awarded annually for an exemplary literary career by a British Columbia resident. Administered by *B.C. BookWorld*.

THIS Magazine Writing Awards
c/o *This* Magazine, 401 Richmond Street W., Suite 396, Toronto, ON M5V 3A8
Phone: (416) 979-8400 Fax: (416) 979-1143
E-mail: info@thismagazine.ca
Web site: www.thismagazine.ca

The Great Canadian Literary Hunt
Deadline: July 1
  "On the trail of Canada's brightest new creative writers." Annual prizes of $750, $500, and $250 – and publication in *THIS* – are awarded in two categories: poems of up to 100 lines and short stories of up to 5,000 words. All entries must be unpublished. Entry fees are $10/piece of fiction and $10 for two poems. For regular updates on the Great Canadian Literary Hunt, send a blank e-mail to greatcanadianliteraryhunt-subscribe@yahoogroups.com.

Best New Writer Prize for Creative Non-Fiction
Deadline: March 1

In recognition of excellent literary journalism by writers early in their careers, an annual award of $250 is presented to an unpublished writer or a writer whose first publishing credit has occurred within the last 5 years.

Toronto Poetry Contest

Allena R. Litherland, Program Co-ordinator, Scarborough Arts
  Council, 1859 Kingston Road, Scarborough, ON M1N 1T3
Phone: (416) 698-7322 Fax: (416) 698-7972
E-mail: programs@scarborougharts.com
Web site: www.scarborougharts.com
Deadline: February 4

Sponsored by the Scarborough Arts Council and Arts Etobicoke. The first-prize winner of the best work of poetry receives $300, second prize is $200, and third prize is $100. In addition, the $50 Monica Ladell Prize is awarded to a Scarborough resident. Youth prizes of $100, $50, and $30 are also awarded. Only Canadian citizens or landed immigrants living in Canada are eligible to enter. Poems must not have been previously published and cannot exceed 25 lines. Annual.

The Larry Turner Award. *See* the Valley Writers' Guild Awards.

The Valley Writers' Guild Awards

Peter de Lepper, Co-ordinator, P.O. Box 534, Merrickville, ON
  K0G 1N0
Phone: (613) 269-4700
E-mail: joyhm@ripnet.com

The John Spencer Hill Award
Deadline: June 15

An annual award for short stories that are up to 2,500 words and unpublished. Entry fee $10 or 2 entries for $15. Grand prizewinner receives $500 and an engraved plaque. Secondary prizes of $200 and $100 will be awarded, plus 3 honourable mentions of $20 each. Winners will be published in and receive a 1-year subscription to the *Valley Writers' News*.

The Ray Burrell Hill Award
Deadline: November 15

An annual award for poetry in any style that is up to 60 lines and unpublished. Entry fee $5/poem. Grand prizewinner receives $500 and an engraved plaque. Secondary prizes of $200 and $100 will be awarded, plus 3 honourable mentions of $20 each. Winners will be published in and receive a 1-year subscription to the *Valley Writers' News*.

The Larry Turner Award
Deadline: March 15

An annual award for literary or personal essays, articles, memoirs, travel pieces, etc., that are up to 2,500 words and unpublished. Entry fee $10 or 2 entries for $15. Grand prizewinner receives $500 and an engraved plaque. Secondary prizes of $200 and $100 will be awarded, plus 3 honourable mentions of $20 each. Winners will be published in and receive a 1-year subscription to the *Valley Writers' News*.

VanCity Book Prize
c/o B.C. BookWorld, 3516 West 13th Avenue (rear), Vancouver, BC
   V6R 2S3
Phone: (604) 736-4011
Deadline: May 15

A $4,000 prize is awarded annually for the best British Columbia book of fiction or non-fiction pertaining to women's issues. Author should be a B.C. resident. Publishers are invited to submit eligible titles. Administered by *B.C. BookWorld*.

The Bronwen Wallace Award. *See* the Writers' Trust of Canada
   Awards.

Portia White Prize
Peter Kirby, Program Officer, Nova Scotia Department of
   Tourism, Culture and Heritage, 1800 Argyle Street, Suite 402,
   P.O. Box 456, Halifax, NS B3J 2R5
Phone: (902) 424-3422 Fax: (902) 424-0710
E-mail: kirbypc@gov.ns.ca
Web site: www.gov.ns.ca/dtc

Awarded annually by the Province of Nova Scotia to recognize artistic excellence and achievement by a Nova Scotia artist. The prize consists of a direct award of $18,000 to the recipient and a $7,000 gift to be given to the recipient's choice of either a protégé of the artist, an emerging artist that the recipient considers worthy of recognition, or a Nova Scotia arts organization that the recipient elects to support due to its value to the arts in the province.

Jon Whyte Memorial Essay Prize. *See* Writers Guild of Alberta Awards.

The Ethel Wilson Fiction Prize. *See* B.C. Book Prizes.

The Kenneth R. Wilson Awards
Alison Wood, KRW Co-ordinator, 4195 Dundas Street W., Suite 346, Toronto, ON M8X 1Y4
Phone: (416) 239-1022 Fax: (416) 239-1076
E-mail: krwawards@cbp.ca
Web site: www.cbp.ca
Deadline: March
Recognizing excellence in writing and graphic design in specialty business, professional, and farm publications and their web sites. Open to editorial or design staff, freelancers, and other contributors to such publications. Twenty categories cover editorial, marketing, retail, technology, industrial, profiles, features, news, graphic design, photography, illustration, web design, and more. Winners of gold and silver awards receive cash prizes of $1,000 and $500 respectively. Annual.

Winners' Circle Short Story Contest
Toronto Branch, Canadian Authors Association, 599-B Yonge Street, Suite 514, Toronto, ON M4Y 1Z4
Web site: www.tacob.org/winnerscircle.htm
Deadline: January 31
The best submission of a short story (of 4,000 words) receives a prize of $500, with a second prize of $200, and third prize of $100. The 3 winners and 2 honourable mentions will be published in York University's literary magazine, *existere*. Entry fee of $20/story and an SASE includes a manuscript evaluation. Annual.

Writer to Win Competition

Alberta Playwrights Network, 2633 Hochwald Avenue S.W.,
   Calgary, AB T3E 7K2
Phone: (403) 269-8564 or 1-800-268-8564 Fax: (403) 265-6773
E-mail: apn@nucleus.com
Web site: www.nucleus.com/~apn
Deadline: March 1

The longest running playwriting competition in Canada.
Winners receive $3,500 and $1,500, and get a full workshop and
staged reading at the Fresh Ink conference. Scripts must have a
running time of at least 75 minutes and have not been publicly produced. Entry fee $40. Open to all Albertans who have lived in
Alberta for at least 1 year prior to submission. Annual.

Writers' Circle of Durham Region Contests

Aprille Janes, P.O. Box 323, Ajax, ON L1S 3C5
Phone: (905) 259-6520
E-mail: info@wcdr.org
Web site: www.wcdr.org

Short Fiction Contest
Contact: Aprille Janes
Deadline: February 15

Prizes of $500, $300, and $200 are awarded for the best unpub-
lished short stories on any subject matter and of any type or style,
not exceeding 2,500 words. Entry fee $20. Open to Canadian citi-
zens and residents 18 years of age and over. Annual.

The Dan Sullivan Memorial Poetry Contest
Contact: Nancy Del Col
Deadline: February 15

Prizes are awarded in 3 categories – children (under 12), youth
(under 18), and adults – for the best poetry on any subject matter
and of any type or style, not exceeding 30 lines. Children's prizes
are $75, $50, and $25; youths' prizes are $150, $100, $75; and adults'
prizes are $300, $200, and $100. Open to Canadian residents. Entry
fee $10/submission for adults and $5/submission for children and
youth. Annual.

WCDR Online 24-Hour Non-Fiction Contest
Contacts: Dorothea and Rich Helms
Deadline: see web site for dates

Prizes of $500, $300, and $200 will be awarded for the best personal essays on the topic provided. Winners will also be published online at the WCDR web site and in *The Word Weaver*, the WCDR's newsletter. Style can be humorous, touching, dramatic, stream-of-consciousness, etc. Pre-registration is mandatory. Entry fee $10. Registration limited to the first 400. The contest page will be posted to www.wcdr.org/nonfictioncontest.html. To enter, visit the page and find out the topic and word count. You will then have 24 hours to complete your essay.

Writers' Federation of New Brunswick Literary Competition

Mary Hutchman, Writers' Federation of New Brunswick, 404
  Queen Street, P.O. Box 37, Stn. A, Fredericton, NB E3B 4Y2
Phone: (506) 459-7228 Fax: (506) 459-7228
E-mail: wfnb@nb.aibn.com
Deadline: November 11

Cash prizes (first $150, second $75, third $50) are awarded annually in the following categories: poetry, fiction, and writing for children. Manuscripts can be on any subject and should not exceed 15 pages (4,000 words) for prose, 100 lines maximum for poetry, and a maximum submission of 20,000 words for the children's category. All awards open to Canadian residents.

The Alfred G. Bailey Prize

An annual cash prize of $400 is awarded for an outstanding unpublished poetry manuscript of at least 48 pages. Some individual poems may have been previously published or accepted for publication.

The Sheree Fitch Prize

A first prize of $150, second of $75, and third of $50 are offered to young writers, aged 14 to 18 as of January 1 in the year of the contest, which alternates yearly between poetry and prose – 2004 is for prose entries, 2005 for poetry. Maximum length for poetry is 100 lines; for prose, up to 4,000 words. Work must be original and unpublished.

The Richards Prize

An annual award of $400 goes to the author of a collection of short stories, a short novel, or a substantial portion (up to 30,000 words) of a longer novel. Work must be unpublished, although some individual stories may have been published.

Writers' Federation of Nova Scotia Awards
Jane Buss, 1113 Marginal Road, Halifax, NS B3H 4P7
Phone: (902) 423-8116 Fax: (902) 422-0881
E-mail: talk@writers.ns.ca
Web site: www.writers.ns.ca

Atlantic Poetry Prize
Deadline: first Friday in December

A $1,000 prize is awarded annually for an outstanding full-length book of poetry by a native or resident of Atlantic Canada. No entry fee.

Atlantic Writing Competition for Unpublished Manuscripts
Deadline: first Friday in August

Five categories for unpublished manuscripts – novel, short story, poetry, writing for children, and essay/magazine article – receive small cash prizes of between $50 and $200 for first, second, and third places. All entries receive a brief evaluation. Atlantic Canada residents only. Annual.

Thomas Head Raddall Atlantic Fiction Award
Deadline: December 10

A $10,000 prize is awarded each year for an outstanding novel or collection of short stories, in English, by a native or resident of Atlantic Canada. Co-sponsored by the Writers' Trust of Canada. No entry fee.

Evelyn Richardson Non-Fiction Award
Deadline: first Friday in December

A $1,000 prize is awarded annually for an outstanding work of non-fiction by a native or resident of Nova Scotia. No entry fee.

Margaret and John Savage First Book Award

A prize of $1,500 is awarded to the best first book shortlisted for any of the following awards: the Dartmouth Book Award (fiction and non-fiction), the Booksellers' Choice Award, the Ann Connor Brimer Children's Literature Award, the Atlantic Book of the Year Award, the Atlantic Poetry Prize, the Thomas Head Raddall Atlantic Fiction Award, and the Evelyn Richardson Non-Fiction Award.

Writers Guild of Alberta Awards
c/o Writers Guild of Alberta, Percy Page Centre, 11759 Groat
  Road N.W., Edmonton, AB T5M 3K6
Phone: (780) 422-8174 Fax: (780) 422-2663
E-mail: mail@writersguild.ab.ca
Web site: www.writersguild.ab.ca
Deadline: December 15

A $1,000 prize is awarded annually for excellent achievement by an Alberta writer in each of the following categories: children's literature, drama, non-fiction, novel, poetry, short fiction, and best first book. Eligible books may have been published anywhere in the world. Authors must have resided in Alberta for at least 12 of the 18 months prior to December 31.

City of Edmonton Book Prize
Deadline: February 28

A $2,000 award to honour the books that contribute to the appreciation and understanding of the City of Edmonton by emphasizing its special character and/or the achievements of its residents. Subjects can include history, geography, current affairs, Edmonton's arts, or its people, or be written by an Edmonton author. Entries may be fiction, non-fiction, poetry, or drama written for adults or children in published form.

W. O. Mitchell Book Prize
Deadline: February 28

Awarded in honour of acclaimed Calgary writer W. O. Mitchell and recognizes achievement by Calgary authors. The $2,000 prize is awarded annually for an outstanding book (fiction, non-fiction, children's literature, or drama) published in the previous year. The author must be a Calgary resident on December 31 of the event year and for a minimum of 2 years prior. Sponsored by the City of Calgary, Chapters, McAra Printing Limited, and the Writers Guild of Alberta.

Jon Whyte Memorial Essay Prize
Deadline: February 28
Awarded in recognition of the best essay (no longer than 2,800 words and not previously published) submitted to this province-wide competition. First prize is $1,000, and 2 runners-up receive $500 each. Open to residents aged 18 years and older who have resided in Alberta for 12 of the past 18 months. Both beginning and established writers may apply. Entry fee $10. Co-sponsored by the Writers Guild of Alberta and the Banff Centre.

The Writers' Trust of Canada Awards
40 Wellington Street E., 3rd Floor, Toronto, ON M5E 1C7
Phone: (416) 504-8222 Fax: (416) 504-9090
E-mail: info@writerstrust.com
Web site: www.writerstrust.com

Matt Cohen Award: In Celebration of a Writing Life
An award of $20,000 is conferred on a Canadian writer whose life has been dedicated to writing as a primary pursuit to honour his or her body of distinguished work of poetry or prose in English or in French.

Shaughnessy Cohen Prize for Political Writing
A $15,000 prize is awarded annually to a Canadian author of a work of non-fiction, written in English, that enlarges our understanding of contemporary Canadian political and social issues and in the opinion of the judges shows the highest literary merit. Up to 4 runner-up prizes of $2,000 each will also be awarded.

Drainie-Taylor Biography Prize
Deadlines: July 31 and November 1, depending on publishing date
An annual award of $10,000 established in the names of 2 men who have made substantial contributions to Canadian culture and entertainment: Nathan (Nat) Taylor and John Drainie. It is given to

a Canadian author of a significant published work of biography, autobiography, or personal memoir.

Marian Engel Award

An annual award of $15,000 is conferred on a Canadian female writer in mid-career, recognizing her body of work and the promise of her future contribution to Canadian literature. Canada's premier literary award for women.

Timothy Findley Award

An annual award of $15,000 is conferred on a Canadian male writer in mid-career, recognizing his body of work and the promise of his future contribution to Canadian literature.

Vicky Metcalf Award for Children's Literature

An annual award of $15,000 is conferred on a Canadian writer of children's literature in recognition of his or her body of work that in the opinion of the judges shows the highest literary standards.

W. O. Mitchell Literary Prize

A $15,000 prize is awarded annually to a Canadian writer who has produced an outstanding body of work, has acted during his/her career as a "caring mentor" for writers, and has published a work of fiction or had a new stage play produced during the 3-year period specified for each competition.

Pearson Writers' Trust Non-Fiction Prize

Deadlines: July 31 or November 1, depending on publishing date

A $15,000 prize is awarded annually to the Canadian author of the work of non-fiction, written in English, that in the opinion of the judges shows the highest literary merit. Up to 4 runner-up prizes of $2,000 each will be awarded to the shortlisted authors.

Rogers Writers' Trust Fiction Prize

Deadlines: July 31 or November 1, depending on publishing date

A $15,000 prize is awarded to the author of the year's outstanding novel or short story collection, written in English, by a Canadian citizen or landed immigrant. Up to 4 runner-up prizes of $2,000 each will be awarded to the shortlisted authors.

The Bronwen Wallace Award

An award of $1,000 is presented, in alternate years, to a Canadian poet or a Canadian short-fiction writer under the age of 35 who is unpublished in book form but whose work has appeared in at least 1 independently edited magazine or anthology. Applicants should submit 5 to 10 pages of unpublished poetry or up to 2,500 words of unpublished prose fiction.

The Writers' Trust of Canada/McClelland & Stewart Journey Prize

McClelland & Stewart Ltd., 481 University Avenue, Suite 900, Toronto, ON M5G 2E9
Phone: (416) 598-1114 Fax: (416) 598-7764
E-mail: journeyprize@mcclelland.com
Web site: www.mcclelland.com/jpa
Deadline: January 15

The $10,000 Journey Prize is awarded annually to a new and developing writer of distinction for a short story published in a Canadian literary journal. Established in 1988, it is the most significant monetary award given in Canada to a writer at the beginning of his or her career for a short story or excerpt from a fiction work in progress. In recognition of the vital role journals play in discovering new writers, an additional $2,000 is awarded to the literary journal that originally published the winning story. The longlisted stories are selected from literary journal submissions and published annually by McClelland & Stewart as *The Journey Prize Anthology*. Only submissions from literary journals/magazines are accepted.

The Writers' Union of Canada Awards and Competitions

The Writers' Union of Canada, 40 Wellington Street E., 3rd Floor, Toronto, ON M5E 1C7
Phone: (416) 703-8982, ext. 223 Fax: (416) 504-7656
E-mail: projects@writersunion.ca
Web site: www.writersunion.ca

Danuta Gleed Literary Award
Deadline: January 31

Awarded to the best first collection of short stories in the English language, written by a Canadian citizen or landed immigrant and published in the previous calendar year. First prize $5,000; two runners-up receive $500 each. Annual.

Short Prose Competition for Developing Writers
Deadline: November 3

An annual award to discover developing writers of fiction and non-fiction. A $2,500 prize is awarded for the best piece of unpublished prose up to 2,500 words by a Canadian citizen or landed immigrant who has not previously been published in book format and does not have a contract with a publisher. The winner agrees to permit possible publication of the winning entry in a Canadian literary magazine. Entry fee $25. Apply for full entry conditions.

Postcard Story Competition
Deadline: February 14

Open to all writers. A prize of $500 will be given for any text (fiction, non-fiction, prose, poetry, verse, dialogue, etc.) up to 250 words in length. Entry fee $5/submission. Annual.

Writing for Children Competition
Deadline: April 27

A prize of $1,500 is awarded annually for the best fiction or non-fiction (up to 1,500 words) written for children. Open to Canadian citizens and landed immigrants whose work has not previously been published in book format and who do not have a contract with a publisher. The winner's and finalists' entries will be submitted to 3 publishers of children's literature. Entry fee $5/submission.

PROVINCIAL & FEDERAL WRITER SUPPORT PROGRAMS

Outlined below are the main sources of provincial and federal funding for Canadian writers. Arts council and other government grants are designed to buy the writer time to devote to his or her work for a specified period in order to support a work in progress or the completion of a particular creative project through meeting a varying combination of living, research, travel, or professional-development costs. Such financial support is most often given to the successful published author, but gifted inexperienced writers are sometimes also eligible. Several provincial initiatives are open to new as well as to established writers.

All these programs require applicants to develop detailed project proposals and budgets and to provide writing samples and other support materials.

Alberta Foundation for the Arts
10405 Jasper Avenue, 901 – Standard Life Centre, Edmonton, AB
   T5J 4R7
Phone: (780) 427-6315 Fax: (780) 422-1162
E-mail: paul.pearson@gov.ab.ca
Web site: www.affta.ab.ca
Contact: Paul Pearson, arts development consultant, Writing and
   Publishing
   Writers who have been previously published, produced, or aired

may apply to the Alberta Foundation for the Arts for the following projects:

1) Art production includes the creation of a new manuscript or work in progress that has not been published, produced, or aired. Eligible genres include fiction, drama, non-fiction, translation, adaptations, and anthologies.

2) Training and/or career development include a workshop, master class, retreat, mentorship program, or course of study in creative writing, editing, or translation. All writers regardless of experience may apply under this category.

3) Travel and/or marketing may include attending a book launch, non-academic conferences by invitation, literary festivals by invitation, acceptance of an award by invitation, promotional tours, and computer software purchase.

4) Research includes activities that support or result in the development of a writing project.

Writers who have not been published can apply for training projects only. Usually the maximum project grant under this program will not exceed $10,000 and may include up to $2,000/month subsistence allowance. Application deadlines are February 15 and September 1.

Alberta Community Development also offers the Grant MacEwan Young Writer's Scholarships. Scholarships of $2,500 each are awarded annually to 4 young Alberta writers who create a literary work between 1,000 and 5,000 words that reflects Alberta and/or Dr. MacEwan's interests. Applicants must be Alberta residents between the ages of 16 and 25. Deadline is December 31.

British Columbia Arts Council

Box 9819, Stn. Prov. Govt., Victoria, BC V8W 9W3
Phone: (250) 356-1728 Fax: (250) 387-4099
E-mail: walter.quan@gems9.gov.bc.ca
Web site: www.bcartscouncil.ca
Contact: Walter K. Quan, co-ordinator, Arts Awards Programs

Assistance is available to B.C. professional writers with at least the equivalent of 1 book previously published professionally. Awards of up to $5,000 ($10,000 for writers with 3 books or more books published professionally) may be used for specific creative projects. Eligible genres include fiction, drama, non-fiction, poetry, and juvenile. One juried competition is held annually. Application deadline September 15.

The Canada Council for the Arts

350 Albert Street, P.O. Box 1047, Ottawa, ON K1P 5V8
Phone: (613) 566-4414, ext. 5537 locally or after hours;
   or 1-800-263-5588 Fax: (613) 566-4410
E-mail: firstname.lastname@canadacouncil.ca
Web site: www.canadacouncil.ca

The Canada Council offers Canadian writers substantial financial support through a variety of programs, most notably Grants for Professional Writers – Creative Writing and Travel Grants, Literary Readings, Literary Festivals, and Author Residencies. It should be noted, however, that these grants are not available to unpublished writers. Applicants must have had at least 1 book published by a professional house or 4 major texts (short stories, excerpts from a novel, etc.) published on 2 separate occasions in recognized literary periodicals or anthologies.

Creative Writing Grants help authors working on new projects in fiction, poetry, children's literature, graphic novel, or literary non-fiction. (Literature creation projects based on the spoken word or technology may be submitted to the Spoken Word and Storytelling Program.) Grants range from $1,000 to $20,000. (Contact Andrée Laurier, ext. 5537, or Paul Seesequasis, ext. 5482.)

Travel Grants help writers with career-related travel expenses (e.g., being a keynote speaker at an international conference or festival). Grants are $500, $750, $1,000, $1,500, $2,000, and $2,500. (Contact Joanne Desroches, ext. 4088.)

The Literary Readings and Literary Festivals program provides opportunities for writers to read from their works and discuss them with the public. (Contact Mona Kiame, ext. 4016.)

Author Residencies provide financial assistance to organizations such as universities, libraries, and writers' associations to retain the services of a writer-in-residence, thus encouraging exchanges between the author and the community as well as enabling the author to work on a writing project. (Contact Mona Kiame, ext. 4016.)

The Spoken Word and Storytelling Program supports innovative literary projects not based upon conventional book or printed magazine formats through grants to creation, production, public performance, broadcast, or dissemination. This includes dub and rap poetry, poetry performance, and storytelling. Priority is given to projects that extend the boundaries of literary expression and are not just representing existing literature in a new format. (Contact Paul Seesequasis, ext. 5482.)

The Grants to Aboriginal Writers, Storytellers, and Publishers Program offers grants to Aboriginal writers and storytellers as well as Aboriginal-controlled publishers, periodicals, and collectives. (Contact Paul Seesequasis, ext. 5482.)

Please note that these programs are subject to change. Write for eligibility conditions and guidelines.

Conseil des arts et des lettres du Québec

79 René-Lévesque Boulevard E., 3rd Floor, Quebec, QC G1R 5N5
Phone: (418) 643-1707 or 1-800-897-1707 Fax: (418) 643-4558
500 Place d'Armes, 15th Floor, Montreal, QC H2Y 2W2
Phone: (514) 864-3350 or 1-800-608-3350 Fax: (514) 864-4160

Created in 1993 as a corporation under the jurisdiction of the minister of Culture and Communications. The Grant Program for Professional Artists offers several types of grants to creative writers who have published at least 1 book with a professional publisher or 4 texts in cultural periodicals, or have broadcast radio scripts. Applicants must be Canadian citizens or landed immigrants and have lived in Quebec for at least 12 months. The program is open to French and English writers.

Manitoba Arts Council

93 Lombard Avenue, Suite 525, Winnipeg, MB R3B 3B1
Phone: (204) 945-0422 or 1-866-994-2787 (toll-free in MB)
    Fax: (204) 945-5925
E-mail: jthomas@artscouncil.mb.ca
Contact: Joan Thomas, program consultant (literary)

Offers several potential sources of funding for writers: The Writers A Grant, worth up to $10,000, is designed to support concentrated work on a major writing project by professional Manitoba writers who have published 2 books and who show a high standard of work and exceptional promise. The Writers B Grant, for Manitoba writers with 1 published book, is worth up to $5,000. The

Writers C Grant, worth up to $2,000, for emerging writers with a modest publication background, is available to support a variety of developmental writing projects.

The Major Arts Grant supports personal creative projects of 6 to 10 months' duration by writers who have made a nationally or internationally recognized contribution to their discipline. Covering living and travel expenses and project costs, this grant is worth up to $25,000. Finally, published Manitoba writers can apply for a Travel and Professional Development Grant, to a maximum of $1,000, to support significant career opportunities. Write for guidelines, eligibility criteria, and application procedures. Please note that these programs are open to Manitoba residents only.

New Brunswick Arts Board
634 Queen Street, Suite 300, Fredericton, NB E3B 1C2
Phone: (506) 444-5633 Fax: (506) 444-5543
E-mail: rbarriault@artsnb.ca
Web site: www.artsnb.ca
Contact: R. Barriault, program officer
Several potential sources of funding support exist for professionals and students who are pursuing a career in the arts and full-time and short-term studies in the arts. Permanent residency in New Brunswick is required. Deadlines for applications vary according to program. Consult the NBAB web site for the available programs. Application forms can be downloaded from web site.

Newfoundland and Labrador Arts Council
P.O. Box 98, Stn. C, St. John's, NL A1C 5H5
Phone: (709) 726-2212 or 1-866-726-2212 Fax: (709) 726-0619
E-mail: nlacmail@nfld.net
Web site: www.nlac.nf.ca
Newfoundland and Labrador writers can apply to the NLAC for funding support under the Project Grant Program. Project grants are intended to help individuals carry out work in their field and may be used for living expenses and materials, study, and travel costs. Grants generally range from $500 to $2,000 or slightly higher. The amount of grant money available is based on the number of applications.

Northwest Territories Arts Council
Department of Education, Culture and Employment,
   Government of the N.W.T., P.O. Box 1320, Yellowknife, NT
   X1A 2L9
Phone: (867) 920-6370   Fax: (867) 873-0205
E-mail: boris_atamanenko@gov.nt.ca
Web site: www.pwnhc.ca
Contact: Boris Atamanenko, manager of community programs
   The mandate of the N.W.T. Arts Council is to promote the
visual, literary, and performing arts in the territories. Contributions
of up to $14,000 (10% of the total funding budget) may be applied
for. Deadline is February 28 each year. For applications and guide-
lines, call or write to the arts and culture officer.

Nova Scotia Department of Tourism, Culture and Heritage
1800 Argyle Street, Suite 402, P.O. Box 456, Halifax, NS B3J 2R5
Phone: (902) 424-3422   Fax: (902) 424-0710
E-mail: kirbypc@gov.ns.ca
Web site: www.gov.ns.ca/dtc
Contact: Peter Kirby, program officer
   The Arts Section of the Culture Division of the Department of
Tourism, Culture and Heritage is directed to support the creation
of new work by professional artists (both established and emerging)
in all disciplines, including literary, media arts (experimental film,
video, and electronic art), performing arts (music, theatre, and
dance), visual arts and craft, and multidisciplinary work. Applicants
must be Canadian citizens or landed immigrants who have lived in
Nova Scotia for at least 12 months prior to the application deadline.
   Professional Development Grants offer assistance up to $3,000
for formal study programs or to participate in other professional
development programs such as mentoring, apprenticeships, conferences, etc. Deadlines May 15 and December 15.
   Creation Grants provide assistance up to $12,000 to assist artists
in any art form by contributing toward the artist's subsistence and
the project costs. Deadlines May 15 and December 15.
   Presentation Grants offer assistance up to $5,000 to help cover
direct costs of public presentation of the artist's work. Deadlines
May 15 and December 15.

Ontario Arts Council

Literature Programs, 151 Bloor Street W., Toronto, ON M5S 1T6
Phone: (416) 969-7438 Fax: (416) 961-7796
E-mail: lfilyer@arts.on.ca
Web site: www.arts.on.ca

The Writers' Reserve program assists talented, emerging, and established writers in the creation of new work in fiction, poetry, writing for children, literary criticism, arts commentary, history, biography, or in politics/social issues. Writers' Reserve grants are awarded through designated book and periodical publishers, who recommend authors for funding support up to a maximum of $5,000.

The Works-in-Progress program offers support ($12,000) in the completion of major book-length works of literary merit in poetry or prose by published writers.

The Chalmers Program supports arts professionals for a minimum of 1 year and consists of 2 components: arts fellowships (maximum $50,000) and professional development (maximum $15,000).

Programs are open to Ontario residents only. Write to the Ontario Arts Council for detailed guidelines and application forms for these programs.

Prince Edward Island Council of the Arts

115 Richmond Street, Charlottetown, PE C1A 1H7
Phone: (902) 368-4410 Fax: (902) 368-4418

Arts assistance grants are available to support Island writers. Grant A provides assistance for individual artists. The maximum grant for a senior artist is $5,000 and the maximum for an emerging artist is $3,000. Grant B is a travel grant for a maximum of $1,000. Grant C is for professional development and/or study to a maximum of $1,000. Application deadlines are April 30 and October 30.

Saskatchewan Arts Board

2135 Broad Street, Regina, SK S4P 3V7
Phone: (306) 787-4056 or 1-800-667-7526 (SK)
   Fax: (306) 787-4199
E-mail: grants@artsboard.sk.ca
Web site: www.artsboard.sk.ca

Offered under the Individual Assistance Program: A Grants for senior artists offer up to $20,000 for creative work, up to $10,000 for professional development, or $5,000 for research. B Grants for established professionals offer up to $12,000 for creative work, $7,500 for professional development, or $3,000 for research. C Grants for emerging professionals offer up to $4,000 for creative work, $4,000 for professional development, or $1,500 for research. There are also travel grants available for A, B, and C artists that may cover up to 50% of travel costs, plus $100/day for up to 5 days of travel. Deadlines for all Individual Assistance Grants are October 1 and March 15.

The Project Assistance A Grant supports short-term specific activities or events that benefit the arts and artists in Saskatchewan and are organized and presented by groups or organizations. Maximum available is $5,000. The deadlines are October 15 and March 15.

The Artist in Residence Grant Program assists incorporated non-profit organizations in the province with the opportunity to respond to community needs for development in the arts by engaging Saskatchewan artists to work and reside in Saskatchewan communities for a period of up to 1 year. The maximum available is $35,000. Deadlines are October 15 and March 15.

Saskatchewan Arts Board grants are only available to Saskatchewan residents and organizations.

Yukon Department of Tourism and Culture
Arts Section, P.O. Box 2703, Whitehorse, YT Y1A 2C6
Phone: (867) 667-5264 Fax: (867) 393-6456
E-mail: laurel.parry@gov.yk.ca

Yukon writers may be eligible for an Advanced Artist Award of up to $5,000 for a specific project. Training support through the Cultural Industries Training Trust Fund is also available for writers who meet eligibility requirements.

9

PROFESSIONAL DEVELOPMENT

Writers at every level of experience can extend their skills and find fresh ideas through all manner of writing courses and workshops. Some believe creative writing is best fostered in the university or college environment by working with a good teacher who understands literary devices and structures and the power of language. Many skills peculiar to non-fiction writing, generally considered more a craft than an art, can be learned through courses or workshops led by experienced writers who have discovered not only how to refine ideas, but how to research them, transform them into workable structures, and, finally, market them. Some creative writers swear by the hothouse atmosphere, creative exchange of ideas, and collective reinforcement to be found in workshops led by expert facilitators.

Local branches of the Canadian Authors Association, libraries, and adult education classes offered by boards of education are some sources of writing courses and workshops. Regional writers' associations sometimes organize them, too, and are always a good source of information about what's currently available in your area.

This chapter is divided into two parts: first, a review of some of the country's most interesting writing schools, workshops, and retreats; second, a sample of the opportunities for the development of writing skills currently offered by Canadian colleges and universities. Writers' opportunities for professional development are extraordinarily diverse in Canada. Before you commit yourself, define your needs and carefully evaluate each program to see how it might meet them.

The summer courses, generally about a week long and built around small, daily workshop sessions, offer participants the chance to increase their technical skills, to submit their work to group scrutiny and critical feedback, and to enjoy, and learn from, the company of fellow writers as well as editors, agents, and other publishing professionals. Courses are sometimes streamed in order to cater to different levels of experience. Workshop facilitators are often nationally or internationally acclaimed authors, and some course participants enrol simply for the chance to work with them, but the best facilitators aren't necessarily the top literary names.

The workshop experience can be intense and demanding, and the rewards elusive. To get the most from it, bring at least one well-developed piece of writing with you and be prepared to work hard during and outside the main sessions, but also use the opportunity to rub shoulders with other seekers, to network, and to bask in that all-too-rare sense of being part of a community of writers.

For those writers harried by family and job obligations, frustrated by the distractions of city living, and with a manuscript they simply must finish, writers' retreats and colonies offer peaceful seclusion, a beautiful rural setting, and a "room of one's own" in which to work without interruption, with meals and accommodation taken care of. Note that these are not teaching situations.

The larger section of this chapter, on creative-writing and journalism courses offered at universities and colleges, surveys only some of the more significant programs, as well as a number of university-based workshops. The list is far from exhaustive. Many universities, colleges of applied arts, and community colleges offer writing courses at some level, depending on staff availability and student demand. Not all courses are taught every year, and programs can change at short notice. Continuing-education courses are open to all, but entry to credit courses is generally limited to those with specific academic prerequisites, although experienced writers can sometimes win special permission from the course convenor. Find out where you stand before developing your plans.

Creative Writing Schools, Workshops, & Retreats

The Banff Centre Writing Programs

P.O. Box 1020, Station 28, 107 Tunnel Mountain Drive, Banff, AB
   T1L 1H5
Phone: (403) 762-6180 Fax: (403) 762-6345
Office of the registrar: 1-800-565-9989
E-mail: arts_info@banffcentre.ca
Web site: www.banffcentre.ca

All the following programs provide opportunities for professional writers, who must choose the program that best serves their needs and objectives. Banff staff are happy to discuss this individually with applicants. Also contact the centre to discuss fee schedules and possible funding options.

The Banff playRites Colony
Presented through the alliance of Alberta Theatre Projects and the
   Banff Centre
May to June
Application deadline: December 1

An artist-centred program designed to meet the specific needs of each participant. Eligible submissions include works from new or established playwrights, works proposed by theatres and/or script development companies, and works from Canadian translators of Canadian or non-Canadian plays.

Creative Non-Fiction and Cultural Journalism Program
Maclean Hunter chair: Alberto Ruy-Sanchez
April to June (off-site); July to August (on-site)
Application deadline: March

Offers a small group of established non-fiction writers an opportunity to develop a major essay, memoir, or feature piece in the domain of arts and culture. Writers work with experienced and exacting faculty editors, and interact with one another, with guest speakers and with artists from other fields. Participants bring original projects to Banff in draft form (recommended length 5,000 words). The program requires completion of the projects by the end of the residency since the centre buys and exercises second rights to the material. Each participant receives a $3,000 fee for the completed essay or article.

The Leighton Studios for Independent Residencies

Web site: www.banffcentre.ca/programs/program.aspx?id=77

This year-round program offers working residencies for independent professional artists engaged in the creation of new work and provides opportunities for concentrated focus in a retreat environment. Writers, playwrights, visual artists, composers, songwriters, and performance artists are eligible. The 8 fully equipped studios are situated in a beautiful, quiet, wooded area. Applications accepted on a continuing basis. Artists can apply for discounts on the studio fee according to need.

Media and Visual Arts Division

Offers opportunities for theoretical, curatorial, and project writing residencies in media- and visual arts-related fields.

Wired Writing Studio

Deadline: June 18

The Wired Writing Studio is the online equivalent of the Banff Centre's 5-week Writing Studio. It differs by delivering part of the program online and by broadening the writer's understanding of the Internet's potential. Each participant is assigned to 1 faculty writer/editor for the length of the program.

Writing with Style

September and April

Application deadline: May 7 and January 23

A 7-day workshop for writers at all levels is led by program director Edna Alford. Resource faculty change from year to year. The program provides writers of all levels with the opportunity to work on an autobiography, a family history, a journal, unpublished stories, poetry, a mystery, or non-fiction.

Writing Studio

April to June

Application deadline: December

Offers a unique, supportive context in which writers who are already producing work of literary merit are encouraged to pursue their own visions and voices. Applicants will normally have produced a body of work (book[s], or stories/poems in magazines or anthologies) and will be working on a book-length manuscript or manuscript in progress. Writers spend 5 weeks at the Banff Centre working on their manuscripts in individual consultation with senior writers/editors. Enrolment is limited to 20 writers.

Booming Ground Writers' Community
University of B.C., 1866 Main Mall, Buch E-462, Vancouver, BC
   V6T 1Z1
Phone: (604) 822-2469 Fax: (604) 822-3616
E-mail: bg@arts.ubc.ca
Web site: www.arts.ubc.ca/bg
Contact: Andrew Gray, director
   A week-long, intensive writing conference, which takes place in early July each summer. Events include daily workshops, seminars, and public readings, all held at Green College on the campus of UBC. Workshops are available in fiction, poetry, non-fiction, and writing for children, and are led by accomplished teaching writers. Classes are offered for early-career writers, as well as mid-career, published writers. Previous instructors have included Guy Vanderhaeghe, Dionne Brand, Judith Thompson, Thomson Highway, Bonnie Burnard, Lorna Crozier, Stephanie Bolster, Gail Anderson-Dargatz, Gary Geddes, and Timothy Taylor.
   Three correspondence workshops in fiction (including writing for children) offer 1 week at Booming Ground and 16 weeks of online follow-up with the instructor and other students.
   The program cost is $695 for 1-week courses and $1,375 for correspondence courses. Some scholarships are available for students who demonstrate financial need. Nine classes will be offered in 2004, with a maximum class size of 10 students for regular classes and 7 for correspondence courses.

CANSCAIP's Packaging Your Imagination Workshop
40 Orchard View Boulevard, Suite 104, Lower Level, Toronto, ON
   M4R 1B9
Phone: (416) 515-1559 Fax: (416) 515-7022

Web site: www.canscaip.org
Contact: Lena Coakely
The Canadian Society of Children's Authors, Illustrators and Performers holds this day-long workshop on the first Saturday of November for anyone interested in writing, illustrating, or performing for young people. More than a dozen lectures, talks, and workshops are presented at Victoria College, University of Toronto, by professionals respected in their fields. Those interested should contact CANSCAIP for a brochure (available in May). Workshops are $110 with lunch, $90 without. Past speakers have included Jean Little, Sheree Fitch, Paulette Bourgeois, Barbara Reid, Brian Doyle, and Kady MacDonald Denton.

Centauri Arts Writing Courses
19 Harshaw Avenue, Toronto, ON M5S 1X9
Phone: (416) 766-7124
E-mail: directors@centauri.on.ca
Web site: www.centauriarts.com
Contact: Lena Coakely
Offers a range of creative writing and fine arts courses in a relaxing retreat setting in the Kawarthas. Courses are each 1 week long and taught by experienced professionals. The course fee (approximately $600/week) includes accommodation, excellent home-cooked meals, writing workshops, recreational activities, and access to a range of facilities within a relaxing retreat environment. Writers wishing to take time away from the rigours of life in order to learn more about the art of writing or simply to focus on their writing will find this is a perfect environment in which to do so. Courses, which are offered in July and August, include Starting to Write, Writing for Stage and Screen, the Art of Poetry, Writing Genre Fiction, the Business of Creation, Creative Non-Fiction, Writing for Children, Long Fiction, and the Art of the Short Story. Faculty, past and present, includes Stuart Ross, Beth Follett, John B. Lee, Peter Unwin, Michael Hale, and Conor Jones. Occasional workshops in fine arts are available to writers at the same facility.

Creative writing courses are also offered for ages 9 to 18 at the Centauri Summer Arts Camp in the Niagara Region. Some of the same faculty members teach at this program. For information on writing programs for young people, see the web site.

Community of Writers

Tatamagouche Centre, R.R. #3, Tatamagouche, NS B0K 1V0
Phone: 1-800-218-2220
E-mail: comwrite@supercity.ns.ca
Web site: www.tatcentre.ca (click on Community of Writers)
Contact: Gwen Davies

A week-long writing retreat that combines intensive, small-group workshops that welcome serious beginning writers and those wanting to push deeper, and a retreat program for experienced writers. Workshops are led by a professional writer and an adult educator. The aim of the week is to discover skills, push the writing, receive support, learn from other writers, and join a community that includes writers at all levels. The schedule includes daily workshop sessions, feedback on your writing, free time to write (and savour the grounds on Nova Scotia's North Shore), readings, and talks by writers.

Faculty for 2004: Poet Carole Langille leads "Poetry – Making the Invisible Visible" with poet, painter, and teacher Rose Adams. Novelist and short-story writer Bernice Morgan leads "Fiction," with editor, writer, teacher, and creator of this community Gwen Davies. Journalist, writer and broadcaster Stephen Kimber leads "Creative Non-Fiction" with photographer and educator Margot Metcalfe.

Costs for 2004 (all inclusive) are $535 for the workshops and $410 for the retreat. Dates for 2004 are July 18 to 24. Dates for 2005 are July 17 to 22.

Emma Lake Kenderdine Campus of the Arts Residency Program

117 Science Place, Room 133, Kirk Hall, University of
  Saskatchewan, Saskatoon, SK S7N 5C8
Phone: (306) 966-8675 or (306) 966-2463 Fax: (306) 966-5567
E-mail: emma.lake@usask.ca
Web site: www.emmalake.usask.ca
Contact: Kate Hobin, director

Writers, visual artists, performance artists, musicians, composers, critics, curators, arts administrators, and designers are invited to apply for the residency program during June and September. It provides work space, accommodation, and meals in a retreat environment where participants can work independently on their own projects for 1 to 3 weeks, depending on availability. The program also features an invited artist in residence whenever possible, although that artist is not required to provide formal instruction. Cost of the program is $300/week. In 2004 the residencies are from June 12 to 19, June 18 to 25, August 30 to September 6, and September 5 to 12.

Gibraltar Point Residency Program
Artscape, 60 Atlantic Avenue, Suite 111, Toronto, ON M6K 1X9
E-mail: susan@torontoartscape.on.ca
Web site: www.torontoartscape.on.ca
Contact: Susan Serran, director of arts programs and services
Located on Toronto Island, the Gibraltar Point Centre for the Arts provides 2 programs of specific interest to professional writers.

Artscape Lodge is an affordable, short-term studio and bedroom rental service for artists who want to get away from the distractions of the city and focus on their work in a beautifully situated retreat setting. Contact bookings@torontoartscape.on.ca for rates, availability, and additional information.

The Gibraltar Point International Artist Residency is an annual juried program providing 10 artists with a 30-day subsidized opportunity to live and work in a temporary community of artists during June. Open to artists working in all disciplines and usually includes at least 2 writers. Deadline for submissions is in March. See web site for details.

The Humber School for Writers
School of Creative & Performing Arts, Humber College, 3199
Lake Shore Boulevard W., Toronto, ON M8V 1K8
Phone: (416) 675-6622, ext. 3448 Fax: (416) 251-7167
E-mail: antanas.sileika.humber.ca
Web site: www.humber.ca
Contact: Antanas Sileika, artistic director

One of Canada's best schools for writers offers a week-long writing workshop in fiction, creative non-fiction, and poetry each July. A residency option is available. The workshop fee is about $950, plus approximately $325 for full board for those who wish to stay in residence. A number of scholarships are available.

Each year the school also offers a unique 30-week certificate program in creative writing by correspondence, beginning in January. This extraordinary program offers promising writers the opportunity to send their work in progress (novel, short stories, or poetry) directly to their instructor, who provides editorial feedback by mail on a continuing basis throughout the academic year. Instructors who have taught this program include the distinguished writers Bonnie Burnard, Peter Carey, Timothy Findley, Elisabeth Harvor, Isabel Huggan, Paul Quarrington, Richard Scrimger, Antanas Sileika, D. M. Thomas, and Eric Wright. The authors' pick for the best fiction manuscripts to emerge from the workshop are submitted to the Humber School for Writers Literary Agency. To date the agency has placed 10 manuscripts with publishers.

The correspondence course in creative writing is offered at the post-graduate level. Applicants must be graduates of a college or university program, or have the equivalent in life experience (Prior Learning Assessment). Applicants must also submit a 15-page writing sample along with a proposal of the work to be completed during the course. Enrolment is limited. The fee is approximately $2,300. A number of scholarships are available for those who demonstrate writing promise and financial need.

Maritime Writers' Workshop
College of Extended Learning, University of New Brunswick,
    P.O. Box 4400, Fredericton, NB E3B 5A3
Phone: (506) 453-4646 Fax: (506) 453-3572
E-mail: extend@unb.ca
Web site: www.unb.ca/extend/writers
Contact: Rhona Sawlor, co-ordinator
An annual, week-long, limited-enrolment summer program designed to help writers at all levels of experience. Offers instruction in fiction, poetry, writing for the arts, and writing for children. As well as workshops and individual tuition, the program includes lecture/discussions, public readings by instructors (all

successful published writers), and other special events. All participants are required to submit manuscript samples of their work.
Tuition fees are $395 (room and meal charges extra). Scholarships
up to the full cost of tuition and board are awarded on the basis of
need and talent.

Sage Hill Writing Experience
P.O. Box 1731, Saskatoon, SK S7K 3S1
Phone: (306) 652-7395
E-mail: sage.hill@sasktel.net
Web site: www.sagehillwriting.ca

Sage Hill's 10-day summer writing workshops are held every
August in rural Saskatchewan at St. Michael's Retreat Centre in
Lumsden, in the beautiful Qu'Appelle Valley, north of Regina. The
facility has private rooms with bath, meeting rooms, walking woods,
and home-style cooking.

The program offers workshops at introductory, intermediate,
and advanced levels in fiction, non-fiction, poetry, and playwriting
(though not all these courses are available each year). The low
writer-to-instructor ratio (usually 6 to 1) and high-quality faculty
(all established writers) help make these workshops and colloqui-
ums among the most highly valued in Canada.

Fees per course of $795 for the summer program include accom-
modation, meals, and instruction. Scholarships are available.
Enrolment is limited. Applicants should send for guidelines or
check them on the web site. Summer program registration deadline
is April 23.

Three annual Teen Writing Experiences, primarily for Saskatchewan writers aged 14 to 18, are held in July and August. For these
free, 5-day creative writing "camps," held in Saskatoon, Moose Jaw,
and Regina, out-of-towners may have to arrange their own accommodation and transportation. Application deadline is May 15.

A Fall Poetry Colloquium, held in November at St. Michael's
Retreat, Lumsden, is an intensive, 2-week manuscript-development
seminar/retreat, also open to writers from outside Saskatchewan.
This program features ample writing time, group discussions, and
one-on-one critiques by the instructor, as well as online follow-up
with the instructor. The fee of $1075 includes tuition, accommoda-
tion, and meals. Application deadline is August 30.

Saskatchewan Writers/Artists Colonies & Retreats
c/o P.O. Box 3986, Regina, SK S4P 3R9
Phone: (306) 565-8785 Fax: (306) 565-8554
E-mail: skcolony@attglobal.net
Web site: www.skwriter.com/colonies_apply.html

The colonies and retreats were established in 1979 to provide an environment where writers and artists (especially but not exclusively from Saskatchewan) can work free from distractions in serene and beautiful locations. They are not teaching situations but retreats, offering uninterrupted work time and opportunities for a stimulating exchange of ideas with fellow writers and artists after hours. All writers and artists may apply for a colony, while only Canadian residents may apply for individual retreats. Costs are subsidized by the Saskatchewan Lotteries Trust and the Saskatchewan Arts Board. St. Peter's Abbey is a Benedictine abbey near the town of Humboldt. Christopher Lake is in the forest country north of Prince Albert.

A 6-week summer colony (July to August) and a 2-week winter colony (February) are held at St. Peter's Abbey. Applicants may request as much time as they need, to a maximum of 4 weeks, but accommodation in private rooms is limited to 7 people per week. Christopher Lake hosts a 2-week summer colony in September. Participants are housed in cabins or single rooms. Individual retreats of up to 2 weeks are offered year round at St. Peter's, with no more than 3 individuals being accommodated at a time.

Fees for St. Peter's colonies and individual retreats, including meals, are $200 per week for Saskatchewan Writers Guild members and $250 per week for non-members. Fees for the Christopher Lake Colony, including meals, are $225 per week for Saskatchewan Writers Guild members and $275 per week for non-members. Applicants are required to submit a 10-page writing sample/slides of recent work, a résumé, description of the work to be done at the colony, and 2 references. Consult the web site or request a brochure for complete application information.

Deadlines May 3 and December 1 for St. Peter's, and June 25 for Christopher Lake.

University of Toronto School of Continuing Studies Creative Writing Program

Writing and Literature Program, University of Toronto School of
  Continuing Studies, 158 St. George Street, Toronto, ON
  M5S 2V8
Phone: (416) 978-6714 Fax: (416) 978-6091
E-mail: scs.writing@utoronto.ca
Web site: www.learn.utoronto.ca
Contact: Lee Gowan, program director

This is one of Canada's largest creative-writing programs and
offers the broadest curriculum of any writing program in Canada.
The courses are taught by outstanding writers and publishers, each
of whom brings a wealth of experience and accomplishment to the
classroom. Enrolment is limited to guarantee that each student
receives individual attention. The school offers a certificate in creative writing and the annual Random House of Canada Student
Award in Writing (1 prize of $1,000), open to writers who are
enrolled in the program. Winners of the prize are also published in
a chapbook produced by Random House.

The wide range of courses includes an introduction to creative
writing; writing short fiction; writing the novel; poetry, mystery and
suspense writing; romance writing; screenwriting; playwriting; creative non-fiction; prose; autobiographical writing; television
writing; script and dialogue; the individual workshop; and courses
on how to publish.

Instructors in the program include Ray Robertson, Lee Gowan,
Kim Echlin, Ken Babstock, Helen Porter, Ken Sherman, Fred
Kerner, Janis Rapoport, Michael Winter, Peter Robinson, M. T.
Kelly, David Donnell, Nalo Hopkinson, Elaine Stirling, Mike
O'Connor, Antonio D'Alfonso, Alan Zweig, Marnie Woodrow, and
Rachel Manley.

Courses are 20 hours in duration and run from October to
December, February to April, and April to June, and are priced at
$499. For more information, visit the web site or contact the SCS by
phone, fax, or e-mail and ask for a print course calendar.

Victoria School of Writing

620 View Street, Suite 306, Victoria, BC V8W 1J6

Phone: (250) 595-3000
E-mail: info@victoriaschoolofwriting.org
Web site: www.victoriaschoolofwriting.org

This summer school offers 5 days of intensive workshops in poetry, fiction/storytelling, non-fiction, and works-in-progress. Sessions are led by experienced, established Canadian authors. The 2004 faculty includes Pauline Holdstock, Rudy Wiebe, Marlene Cookshaw, Jay Ruzesky, Andrew Struthers, Ivan E. Coyote, and Harold Rhenisch. The school is held the third week of July in a residential school in Victoria, set on 22 acres of treed countryside. Registration is $575 ($525 if sent before May 1). This includes 5 lunches and a final banquet/party. Accommodation and meals are available onsite.

Weekend with an Author
111 Mount Baker Crescent, Salt Spring Island, BC V8K 2J7
Phone: (250) 538-1961 Fax: (250) 538-1963
E-mail: pluke@telus.net
Web site: www.theartsandculturalhighway.ca/pearlluke
Contacts: Pearl Luke and Robert Hilles

Each weekend from December to June, Commonweath Prize–winner Pearl Luke and Governor General's Award–winner Robert Hilles open their home to one aspiring or intermediate writer for one-on-one mentoring, tutorials, and manuscript evaluation. Instruction is flexible and suited to the individual and includes writing, process, publishing, agents, contracts, etc. Costs are $1,199/weekend, $499/one day, and $200/non-participating guest.

The Writing School at Quality of Course
38 McArthur Avenue, Suite 2951, Ottawa, ON K1L 6R2
Phone: 1-800-267-1829 Fax: (613) 749-9551
E-mail: writers@qualityofcourse.com
Web site: www.qualityofcourse.com
Contact: Alex Myers

For the last 20 years, the school has offered creative writing courses by distance. These diploma courses are designed to help the student to publish. They give starting writers a thorough and practical understanding of the needs of the marketplace, and build creative and technical skills. The courses can be completed online.

The student works with his or her tutor on a variety of assignments, each structured to improve specific skills. All tutors at the school are working writers. Assignments are tailored to reflect the individual interests and abilities of each student. Course fees are $759, which cover all costs, including books, lessons, tapes, and tutorial.

The school offers prospective students a free evaluation of their work. Call the toll-free number for a free brochure detailing course contents and methodology, and for more about the evaluation service.

Creative Writing & Journalism at Colleges & Universities

Acadia University
Wolfville, NS B0P 1X0
Phone: (902) 585-1502 Fax: (902) 585-1770
E-mail: wanda.campbell@acadiau.ca
Web site: http://ace.acadiau.ca/english/cwrite.htm
Contact: Wanda Campbell, creative writing co-ordinator

The Department of English offers the following credit courses at the undergraduate level: Exploring Creative Writing: An Introduction, Creative Writing Workshop, Advanced Creative Writing: Poetry, and Advanced Creative Writing: Fiction. There is also the option to write an honours creative writing thesis under the guidance of published authors.

University of Alberta
3 – 5 Humanities Centre, Edmonton, AB T6G 2E5
Phone: (780) 492-3258 Fax: (780) 492-8142
E-mail: english@mail.arts.ualberta.ca
Web site: www.humanities.ualberta.ca/english/
Contact: Christine Wiesenthal, Write Program co-ordinator

The Write Program of the Department of English offers Introductory Poetry, Introduction to Fiction, Introductory Non-Fiction, Intermediate Poetry, Intermediate Fiction, Intermediate Non-Fiction, Advanced Poetry, and Advanced Non-Fiction.

Algoma University College
1520 Queen Street E., Sault Ste. Marie, ON P6A 2G4

Phone: (705) 949-2301 Fax: (705) 949-6583
E-mail: jirgens@auc.ca
Web site: www.auc.on.ca
Contact: K. Jirgens, associate professor and chair, English
    Department
The English Department offers the following credit courses:
Creative Writing, Studies in Creative Writing, and Introduction to
Creative Writing.

Algonquin College
1385 Woodroffe Avenue, Nepean, ON K2G 1V8
Phone: (613) 727-4723 Fax: (613) 727-7707
E-mail: tarzwel@algonquincollege.com
Web site: www.algonquincollege.com
Contact: Lynn Tarzwell, co-ordinator
Offers a post-diploma program in scriptwriting with diploma
courses in professional writing. The School of Media and Design
offers a 2-year diploma program in print journalism.

Brandon University
270 – 18th Street, Brandon, MB R7A 6A9
Phone: (204) 727-9790 Fax: (204) 726-0473
E-mail: gasse@brandonu.ca
Web site: www.brandonu.ca
Contact: Rosanne Gasse, associate professor and chair,
    Department of English
Credit courses in creative writing, creative non-fiction, and play-
writing are offered by the English Department and the Creative
Arts Program. As well, technical-writing credit courses are available
through the Department of English, and the Department of
Business Administration offers business communications.
Publishes the e-zine *Ecclectica* and the student newspaper, *The
Quill.*

University of British Columbia
Creative Writing Program, Buchanan E462, 1866 Main Mall,
    Vancouver, BC V6T 1Z1
Phone: (604) 822-0699 Fax: (604) 822-3616

E-mail: patrose@interchange.ubc.ca
Web site: www.creativewriting.ubc.ca/crwr
Contact: Pat Rose, administrator

The Creative Writing Program offers courses of study leading to BFA and MFA degrees. A wide range of creative-writing courses are available, including writing for screen and television, the novel and novella, short fiction, stage plays, radio plays and features, non-fiction, applied creative non-fiction, writing for children, lyric and libretto, translation, and poetry. A joint MFA with the theatre program is also possible. Students may choose to take a double major in creative writing and another subject. A diploma in applied creative non-fiction is open to graduates and those with professional experience.

The literary journal *PRISM international* is edited by program graduate students.

Brock University
St. Catharines, ON L2S 3A1
Phone: (905) 688-5550, ext. 3469 Fax: (905) 688-4461
E-mail: info@brocku.ca
Web site: www.brocku.ca

The Department of English offers credit courses in reporting and news writing for mass media and creative writing courses in short fiction and poetry. A BA with a major in English and professional writing is available, as well as a minor in professional writing and a certificate in professional writing.

Cambrian College of Applied Arts & Technology
1400 Barrydowne Road, Sudbury, ON P3A 3V8
Phone: (705) 566-8101 Fax: (705) 525-2087
E-mail: info@cambrianc.on.ca
Web site: www.cambrianc.on.ca
Contact: Brenda Bouchard, manager, liaison

The School of Business, Media and Creative Arts offers a 2-year diploma program in Journalism – Print. Students gain practical experience by publishing *The Shield*, a publication in print and online. Credit courses are also available in Business Writing Strategies, Communications, Writing a Proposal, and Writing a Feasibility Report.

Continuing Education offers the following courses through Internet delivery: creative writing, poetry writing, romance writing, beginning novel writing, and writing for publication. A creative writing course is also offered in the classroom in the evenings.

University of Calgary
2500 University Drive N.W., Calgary, AB T2N 1N4
Phone: (403) 220-5470 Fax: (403) 289-1123
E-mail: engadv@ucalgary.ca
Web site: www.english.ucalgary.ca/creative
Contact: Murray McGillivray, head, English Department
Creative writing courses in prose fiction and poetry (3 levels) are offered as part of the BA program in English. Playwriting is offered through the Department of Drama. The English Department grants MA and PhD degrees in English with a creative thesis option. Theses in these programs are original manuscripts, normally poetry or fiction.

The Markin-Flanagan Distinguished Writers Program ensures an annual writer-in-residence (Natalee Caple in 2004–5), as well as short-term visits by major writers. Some writing students also participate in the poetry magazine *Dandelion.*

Camosun College
3100 Foul Bay Road, Victoria, BC V8P 5J2
Phone: (250) 370-3000
E-mail: english@camosun.bc.ca
Web site: www.camosun.bc.ca
The English Department offers credit courses in creative writing in fiction, poetry, and drama.

A variety of Continuing Education courses and programs are available in creative writing, including poetry, short fiction, and selling freelance writing.

Credit courses in writing for the print and electronic media are offered as components of the 28-month, full-time Applied Communications program. Students write and produce radio and cable television programs.

Capilano College
2055 Purcell Way, North Vancouver, BC V7J 3H5

Phone: (604) 986-1911
Web site: www.capcollege.bc.ca
Contact: Reg Johanson, co-ordinator, English
The English Department offers credit courses in creative writing for first- and second-year students.

Centennial College of Applied Arts & Technology
P.O. Box 631, Stn. A, Scarborough, ON M1K 5E9
Phone: (416) 289-5100
E-mail: thecentre@centennialcollege.ca
Web site: www.centennialcollege.ca
The Communication Arts Department offers a 3-year diploma program in print journalism (or a 2-year "fast track"), broadcasting, online writing and information design, and creative advertising. Also a 1-year diploma program in corporate communication. Programs include courses in reporting, editing, scriptwriting, broadcast journalism, production for radio and television, documentary film writing, cinematography, magazine writing, public relations, newspaper feature writing, computer graphics, and more. All programs emphasize practical skills. Various courses are also offered in the extension program. Courses are held online as well.

Concordia University
1455 de Maisonneuve W., Room LB 501, Montreal, QC H3G 1M8
Phone: (514) 848-2424, ext. 2342 Fax: (514) 848-4501
E-mail: sfrank@vox2.concordia.ca
Web site: http://artsandscience.concordia.ca/english/
Contact: Sharon Frank, assistant to the chair
The Creative Writing Program within the English Department offers workshops for credit in writing poetry, prose and drama, and scriptwriting, as well as editing and publishing, and other special-topic courses.

Concordia University College of Alberta
7128 Ada Boulevard, Edmonton, AB T5B 4E4
Phone: (780) 479-8481 Fax: (780) 474-1933
E-mail: nquerengesser@concordia.ab.ca
Web site: www.concordia.ab.ca
Contact: Neil Querengesser, English co-ordinator

The English Department offers one credit course in creative writing: Introduction to Creative Writing – Fiction.

Conestoga College of Applied Arts and Technology
299 Doon Valley Drive, Kitchener, ON N2G 4M4
Phone: (519) 748-5220 Fax: (519) 748-3534
E-mail: cjonas@conestogac.on.ca
Web site: www.conestogac.on.ca

A 3-year journalism print and broadcast diploma program prepares the graduate for employment in various fields related to news writing and news production for Internet publishers and newspapers, magazines, and radio or TV stations. Students gain practical experience working on the college newspaper, *Spoke*; the college's FM-radio station at CJIQ; and in the television studio.

Continuing Education offers a creative writing workshop.

Douglas College
P.O. Box 2503, New Westminster, BC V3L 5B2
Phone: (604) 527-5465 Fax: (604) 527-5095
Contact: Mary Burns, chair, Creative Writing Department

College credit and university transfer courses in creative writing are available. Courses include Introduction to Fiction Writing, Introduction to Playwriting, Introduction to Writing Poetry, Advanced Poetry Writing, Writing Short Fiction, Screenwriting, and Personal Narrative.

The Print Futures professional writing program is a 2-year diploma program preparing students for a professional writing career. It includes courses in writing, research, editorial and design skills, public relations writing, and writing for magazines and trade publications. For more information, contact the program coordinator at (604) 527-5292 or e-mail printfutures@douglas.bc.ca.

Publishes the literary journal *Event*.

Durham College
2000 Simcoe Street N., P.O. Box 385, Oshawa, ON L1H 7L7
Phone: (905) 721-2000 Fax: (905) 721-3195
Web site: www.durhamc.on.ca
Contacts: Blake Fitzpatrick, dean of Design and Communication

Arts; Jan Burnett, program officer, Continuous Learning
Division

Offers a Communication Arts program leading to a 2-year
diploma in journalism or advertising, or a 3-year public-relations
diploma. Graduates of other colleges and universities may qualify
for direct entry into a special 1-year program concentrating on practical subjects.

Continuous Learning offers non-credit courses in creative
writing and getting published.

Classes begin in January, May, and September, and may be
taken in class or online.

Publishes *The Chronicle*, a college newspaper that provides students with experience in writing, editing, design, layout, art, photography, and production.

En'owkin Centre Fine Arts Program
R.R. #2, Site 50, Comp. 8, Penticton, BC V2A 6J7
Phone: (250) 493-7181 Fax: (250) 493-5302
E-mail: enowkin@vip.net
Web site: www.enowkincentre.ca
Contact: Anna Lizotte, student services

Offers the following credit courses: Introduction to Creative
Writing, Writing for Children, Critical Process and World View,
Critical Process, Symbolism and Oral Tradition, Non-Fiction from
Indigenous Perspective, and Structure in Television and Cinema.

University of Guelph
Guelph, ON N1G 2W1
Phone: (519) 824-4120, ext. 56315 Fax: (519) 766-0844
E-mail: sballant@uoguelph.ca
Web site: www.uoguelph.ca/englit
Contact: S. Ballantyne, graduate secretary

The School of English and Theatre Studies offers Creative
Writing: Fiction (in fall 2004) and Creative Writing: Poetry (in
winter 2005).

Humber College of Applied Arts and Technology
205 Humber College Boulevard, Toronto, ON M9W 5L7

Phone: (416) 675-5000 Fax: (416) 675-2427
E-mail: enquiry@humber.ca
Web site: www.humber.ca
Offers a 3-year diploma program in print, broadcast, and online journalism. Business writing and technical writing courses are offered by Continuing Education. Comedy scriptwriting is available in the program Comedy: Writing and Performing.
See also Humber School for Writers, p. 399.

Lambton College
1457 London Road, Sarnia, ON N7S 6K4
Phone: (519) 542-7751 Fax: (519) 541-2408
Contact: Anne Ward, co-ordinator, English Department
Lambton offers Language and Communications, Technical Writing, Fundamentals of English, Business Correspondence, Business Reports, and Written Business Communications.

Langara College
100 West 49th Avenue, Vancouver, BC V5Y 2Z6
Phone: (604) 323-5511 Fax: (604) 323-5555
E-mail: englishdept@langara.bc.ca
Web site: www.langara.bc.ca
Contact: Dr. Megan Otton, chair, English Department
The Department of Journalism offers credit courses in the fundamentals of reporting, feature writing, advanced reporting, specialty writing, and copy editing.
A variety of writing courses are offered by the English Department, including prose fiction, stageplay, poetry, screenwriting, and non-fiction.
A wide selection of creative writing courses are offered by Continuing Studies, including novel writing, experimental short fiction, comedy writing, comic book publishing, creative non-fiction, a feature film workshop, how to get published, playwriting, travel writing, writing reviews, writing a feature film script, writing for children, writing for magazines, and writing for television.

Malaspina University-College
900 5th Street, Nanaimo, BC V9R 5S5
Phone: (250) 753-3245 Fax: (250) 740-6459

E-mail: braidk@mala.bc.ca
Web site: www.mala.bc.ca/www/crwriting
Contact: Kate Braid, chair, Department of Creative Writing and
    Journalism
Offers a comprehensive 4-year program leading to a BA major
and minor in creative writing. Includes introductory courses in journalism, poetry, fiction, and dramatic writing; second-year courses in
feature writing and newswriting, poetry, fiction, dramatic writing,
and book publishing; and senior-level courses in creative non-
fiction, feature writing, poetry, short fiction, novel and novella,
experimental and speculative fiction, documentary and historical
fiction, book publishing, writing for the stage, screenwriting, writing
for radio and television, multimedia publishing, and writing for
multimedia. These courses are offered on a rotational basis; interested students should consult the Department of Creative Writing
to determine which courses will be offered in a given semester.

Publishes a student-edited print journal, *Portal*, and an electronic journal, *Incline*.

University of Manitoba
Department of English, 625 Fletcher Argue Building, 28 Trueman
    Walk, Winnipeg, MB R3T 5V5
Phone: (204) 474-9678 Fax: (204) 474-7669
E-mail: english@umanitoba.ca
Web site: www.umanitoba.ca/faculties/arts/english
The English Department offers creative writing and advanced
creative writing.

McMaster University
Centre for Continuing Education, Downtown Centre, 50 Main
    Street E., 2nd Floor, Hamilton, ON L8S 4L8
Phone: (905) 525-9140, ext. 23128 Fax: (905) 546-1690
E-mail: conted@mcmaster.ca
Web site: www.mcmastercce.com
Contact: Todd Rich, program manager
The Centre for Continuing Education offers certificate courses
in Forms of Writing; Introduction to Writing and Publishing; the
Art of the Short Story; Techniques of Great Writers; Building a
Mystery; Newspaper and Magazine Writing and Publishing;

Writing the Novel; Writing Non-Fiction; Writing for Children; the On-Line Writing Workshop; Essay as an Art Form; Advanced Writers' Seminar; Writing Poetry; Mystery Writing Workshop; Screenwriting Rules; Freeing Your Voice; Style, Syntax and Self-Editing; the Art of Journal Writing, Advanced Poetry Writing; Creating Characters; Developing Plot; Writing "Speaking Words"; and Humour Writing.

Mohawk College

P.O. Box 2034, Hamilton, ON L8N 3T2
Phone: (905) 575-2000 Fax: (905) 575-2392
E-mail: admissions@mohawkcollege.ca
Web site: www.mohawkcollege.ca
Contact: Terry Mote, assistant registrar
The Media Studies Department offers Writing for Media, Research and Report, Broadcast Reporting, News Research, and Mass Communications. A certificate program Writing for Publication can be earned with 8 courses.

Mount Royal College

4825 Richard Road S.W., Calgary, AB T3E 6K6
Phone: (403) 440-0148 Fax: (403) 440-6563
E-mail: helliott@mtroyal.ca
Web site: www.mtroyal.ca
Contact: Hilary Elliott, director, Centre for Communication
    Studies
The Centre for Communication Studies offers a BA in Applied Communications with specializations in journalism, technical communication, public relations, and electronic publishing.
The centre also offers journalism and technical writing certificates, and a diploma in broadcasting.

University of New Brunswick

Department of English, P.O. Box 4400, Fredericton, NB E3B 5A3
Phone: (506) 453-4676 Fax: (506) 453-5069
E-mail: english@unb.ca
Web site: www.unbf.ca/english
Contact: Ross Leckie, director of Creative Writing
The English Department offers the following undergraduate

credit courses: creative writing – poetry, creative writing – short fiction, creative writing – drama, screenwriting, and writing for the new media. An MA in creative writing is also offered.

Continuing Education provides a non-credit course on the fundamentals of writing.

The university has a writer-in-residence and sponsors the Maritime Writers' Workshop in mid July each year.

Niagara College of Applied Arts and Technology

300 Woodlawn Road, Welland, ON L3C 7L3
Phone: (905) 735-2211, ext. 7753 Fax: (905) 736-6003
E-mail: pbarnatt@niagarac.on.ca
Web site: www.niagarac.on.ca
Contact: Phyllis Barnatt, program co-ordinator, Journalism Print

Offers a 2-year course in journalism. Continuing Education offers a certificate program in creative writing plus the following courses: Beginning Novel Writing, Creative Writing (beginning and intermediate levels), Grammar for Writing Professionals, Poetry Writing, Romance Writing, Writing for Publication (levels I and II), and Writing for the Web.

University of Prince Edward Island

550 University Avenue, Charlottetown, PE C1A 4P3
Phone: (902) 566-0439 Fax: (902) 566-0795
E-mail: registrar@upei.ca
Web site: www.upei.ca

The English Department offers credit courses in creative writing and advanced creative writing. The Faculty of Arts offers a 2-year Bachelors of Applied Arts in Print Journalism in partnership with Holland College, where professional training is held.

College of the Rockies

P.O. Box 8500, Cranbrook, BC V1C 5L7
Phone: (250) 489-2751 Fax: (250) 489-1790
E-mail: ask@cotr.bc.ca
Web site: www.cotr.bc.ca
Contact: G. Wakulich, instructor

The University Studies Department offers Creative Writing 101 and 102.

Ryerson Polytechnic University

350 Victoria Street, Toronto, ON M5B 2K3
Phone: (416) 979-5000 Fax: (416) 979-5277
E-mail: inquire@ryerson.ca
Web site: www.ryerson.ca

The School of Journalism offers a 4-year degree program with courses in reporting, radio broadcasting, feature writing, online journalism, TV broadcasting, and media law.

Continuing Education offers a wide range of creative-writing courses and workshops, including courses in short fiction and novel writing, poetry writing, playwriting, writing for children, writing romance, writing reviews, and writing sitcoms.

St. Jerome's University

290 Westmount Road, Waterloo, ON N2L 3G3
Phone: (519) 884-8110 Fax: (519) 884-5759
E-mail: cemcgee@uwaterloo.ca
Web site: www.sju.ca
Contact: C. E. McGee, chair, Department of English

The English Department offers a creative-writing and an arts writing course, both for credit.

University of Saskatchewan

Department of English, 9 Campus Drive, Saskatoon, SK S7N 5A5
Phone: (306) 966-5486 Fax: (306) 966-5951
E-mail: thomson@admin.usask.ca
Web site: www.usask.ca/english
Contact: Nik Thomson, administrator, Department of English

The Department of English at St. Thomas More College (affiliated) offers courses in advanced creative writing for both fiction and poetry. An introduction to creative writing is offered through the Department of English.

Sheridan College

1430 Trafalgar Road, Oakville, ON L6H 2L1
Phone: (905) 845-9430, ext. 2761 Fax: (905) 815-4010
Web site: www.sheridanc.on.ca
Contact: Joyce Wayne, professor and co-ordinator

The Journalism Department offers a 2-year diploma in print journalism, also a 1-year postgraduate program, Journalism for New Media, which includes training in digital media for broadcast and online journalism. Journalism is part of the Sheridan Centre for Animation and Emerging Technologies. Two-year-diploma students produce a weekly newspaper, *The Sheridan Sun*. Courses include newswriting for print and online publications.

Continuing Education also offers various writing courses.

Simon Fraser University
515 West Hastings Street, Suite 2300, Vancouver, BC V6B 5K3
Phone: (604) 291-5077 Fax: (604) 291-5098
E-mail: makortoff@sfu.ca
Web site: www.sfu.ca/wp
Contact: Natalie Makortoff, co-ordinator, Writing and Publishing
    Program
Creative writing classes are available through Simon Fraser's Writing and Publishing Program, the Writer's Studio, and Continuing Studies.

University of Toronto
Toronto, ON M5S 1A1
Phone: (416) 978-6662
Web site: www.utoronto.ca
Contact: Carol Robb, assistant vice-provost
Each year the English Department offers 2 courses in creative writing to selected students as well as a non-credit seminar in creative writing with the annual writer-in-residence. The undergraduate colleges also offer courses with a specialized focus: Innis College offers courses on writing, with a focus on rhetoric and professional communication; St. Michael's College offers non-credit courses in creative writing; and Victoria College offers Creative Writing: A Multicultural Approach. At the Mississauga campus, a professional writing program includes several courses on expressive writing. The Scarborough campus offers 2 courses in creative writing and has a joint journalism program with Centennial College.

The School of Continuing Studies offers a certificate in creative writing and the annual Random House of Canada Student Award in Writing ($1,000), open to writers who are enrolled in the program. They offer a broad range of courses, and the instructors are acclaimed Canadian writers.

The university has 2 campus newspapers, *The Varsity* and *The Newspaper*; individual colleges also publish their own student newspapers. Student literary magazines include *Acta Victoriana* (Victoria College), *Trinity Review* (Trinity College), *UC Review* (University College), and *Hart House Review* (Hart House).

Trent University
Peterborough, ON K9J 7B8
Phone: (705) 748-1011, ext. 1733 Fax: (705) 748-1823
E-mail: gjohnston@trentu.ca
Web site: ww.trentu.ca/english
Contact: Gordon Johnston, professor

The English Department offers a credit course entitled Introduction to Creative Writing (Poetry).

University of Victoria
Department of Writing, P.O. Box 1700, Stn. CSC, Victoria, BC
  V8W 2Y2
Phone: (250) 721-7306 Fax: (250) 721-6602
E-mail: writing@finearts.uvic.ca
Web site: www.finearts.uvic.ca/writing
Contact: Valerie Tenning

Through the Department of Writing, students can major in creative writing, choosing courses (lectures and workshops) in fiction, creative non-fiction, poetry, drama, aspects of journalism, publishing and editing, and multimedia. The department also offers the Harvey Southam diploma in writing and editing.

A course on writing children's literature is available through the continuing education program.

Publishes *This Side of West*.

University of Western Ontario
Faculty of Information & Media Studies, London, ON N6A 5B7
Phone: (519) 661-4017 Fax: (519) 661-3506
Web site: www.fims.uwo.ca/journalism

Western's 3-term (1-year) Master of Arts in Journalism is a well-rounded, professional program for candidates with an honours undergraduate degree or equivalent. The program prepares graduates for entry-level positions in newsrooms. The curriculum includes a balance of academic and practical courses, as well as a month-long internship placement, and offers a solid grounding in the basic tools and practices of print and broadcast journalism.

University of Windsor
English Language, Literature and Creative Writing, 401 Sunset,
   Windsor, ON N9B 3P4
Phone: (519) 253-3000/2289 Fax: (519) 971-3676
E-mail: dilworth@uwindsor.ca
Contact: Tom Dilworth, head, Department of English

Writing courses are available at both the general and honours level. Students may take a BA honours or an MA degree in creative writing. The BA requires completion of 5 creative-writing courses.

University of Winnipeg
515 Portage Avenue, Winnipeg, MB R3B 2E9
Phone: (204) 786-9292 Fax: (204) 774-4134
E-mail: chjalmarson@uwindsor.ca
Web site: www.uwinnipeg.ca/academic/as/english/index.html
Contact: Catherine Hjalmarson, English Department assistant

The following credit courses are offered: Introduction to Creative Writing: Developing a Portfolio; The Creative Process; Creative Writing: Poetry; and Advanced Creative Writing.

York University
210 Vanier College, 4700 Keele Street, Toronto, ON M3J 1P3
Phone: (416) 736-5910
Web site: www.yorku.ca
Contact: administrative secretary

The Creative Writing Department offers the following credit courses: Introduction to Creative Writing, Intermediate Prose Workshop, Intermediate Poetry Workshop, Senior Prose Workshop, and Senior Poetry Workshop.

10

WRITERS' ORGANIZATIONS & SUPPORT AGENCIES

Access Copyright (Canadian Copyright Licensing Agency)
1 Yonge Street, Suite 1900, Toronto, ON M5E 1E5
Phone: (416) 868-1620 or 1-800-893-5777 Fax: (416) 868-1621
E-mail: info@accesscopyright.ca
Web site: www.accesscopyright.ca

Alberta Foundation for the Arts
10405 Jasper Avenue, 901 – Standard Life Centre, Edmonton, AB
    T5J 4R7
Phone: (780) 427-6315 Fax: (780) 422-9132
Web site: www.affta.ab.ca

Alberta Playwrights' Network
2633 Hochwald Avenue S.W., Calgary, AB T3E 7K2
Phone: (403) 269-8564 or 1-800-268-8564 Fax: (403) 265-6773
E-mail: apn@nucleus.com
Web site: www.nucleus.com/~apn

Asian Canadian Writers' Workshop of Canada
P.O. Box 74174, Hillcrest RPO, Vancouver, BC V5V 5C8
Phone: (604) 322-6616
E-mail: asiancanadianwritersworkshop@shaw.ca
Web site: www.asiancanadian.net

Association of Canadian Publishers
161 Eglinton Avenue E., Suite 702, Toronto, ON M4P 1J5
Phone: (416) 487-6116 Fax: (416) 487-8815
E-mail: info@canbook.org
Web site: www.publishers.ca

Association of Canadian University Presses
10 St. Mary Street, Toronto, ON M4Y 2W8
Phone: (416) 978-2239, ext. 237 Fax: (416) 978-4738

Book and Periodical Council
192 Spadina Avenue, Suite 107, Toronto, ON M5T 2C2
Phone: (416) 975-9366 Fax: (416) 975-1839
E-mail: info@bookandperiodicalcouncil.ca
Web site: www.bookandperiodicalcouncil.ca

British Columbia Arts Council
Box 9819, Stn. Prov. Govt., Victoria, BC V8W 9W3
Phone: (250) 356-1728 Fax: (250) 387-4099
E-mail: walter.quan@gems9.gov.bc.ca
Web site: www.bcartscouncil.ca

Burnaby Writers' Society
6584 Deer Lake Avenue, Burnaby, BC V5G 3T7
E-mail: info@bws.ca
Web site: www.bws.bc.ca

The Canada Council for the Arts
350 Albert Street, P.O. Box 1047, Ottawa, ON K1P 5V8
Phone: (613) 566-4414, ext. 5537 locally or A.H.;
    or 1-800-263-5588 Fax: (613) 566-4410
Web site: www.canadacouncil.ca

Canadian Association of Journalists
Algonquin College, 1385 Woodroffe Avenue, Suite B224, Ottawa,
    ON K2G 1V8
Phone: (613) 526-8061 Fax: (613) 521-3904
E-mail: caj@igs.net
Web site: www.caj.ca

Canadian Authors Association (National Office)
P.O. Box 419, Campbellford, ON K0L 1L0
Phone: (705) 653-0323 or 1-866-216-6222 Fax: (705) 653-0593
E-mail: admin@canauthors.org
Web site: www.canauthors.org

Canadian Children's Book Centre
40 Orchard View Boulevard, Suite 101, Toronto, ON M4R 1B9
Phone: (416) 975-0010 Fax: (416) 975-8970
E-mail: info@bookcentre.ca
Web site: www.bookcentre.ca

Canadian Ethnic Journalists' and Writers' Club
22 Walmer Road, Suite 801, Toronto, ON M5R 2W5
Phone: (416) 944-8175 Fax: (416) 260-3586
E-mail: canscene@rogers.com
Web site: http://members.rogers.com/canscene

Canadian Farm Writers' Federation
c/o Clare Stanfield, 1122 – 4th Street S.W., Suite 1150, Calgary,
    AB T2R 1M1
Phone: (403) 685-0938 Fax: (403) 685-1089
E-mail: cstanfield@adculture.com
Web site: www.cfwf.ca

Canadian Intellectual Properties Office
50 Victoria Street, Room C-229, Gatineau, QC K1A 0C9
Phone: (819) 977-1936 or 1-900-565-2476 ($3 flat fee)
    Fax: (819) 953-7620 (enquiries only)
Web site: http://strategis.ic.gc.ca/sc_mrksv/cipo/cp/cp_main-e.html

Canadian Library Association
328 Frank Street, Suite 602, Ottawa, ON K2P 0X8
Phone: (613) 232-9625 Fax: (613) 563-9895
E-mail: info@cla.ca
Web site: www.cla.ca

Canadian Magazine Publishers Association
425 Adelaide Street W., Suite 700, Toronto, ON M5V 3C1

Phone: (416) 504-0274 Fax: (416) 504-0437
Web site: www.cmpa.ca

Canadian Poetry Association
P.O. Box 22571, St. George Post Office, Toronto, ON M5S 1V8
E-mail: cpa@sympatico.ca
Web site: www.canadianpoetryassociation.com

Canadian Romance Authors Network
5141 Bayfield Crescent, Burlington, ON L7L 3J5
Phone: (905) 333-4317 Fax: (905) 333-6963
E-mail: cran@getset.com
Web site: www.canadianromanceauthors.com

Canadian Science Writers' Association
P.O. Box 75, Stn. A, Toronto, ON M5W 1A2
Phone: (416) 408-4566 or 1-800-796-8595 Fax: (416) 408-1044
E-mail: office@sciencewriters.ca
Web site: www.sciencewriters.ca

Canadian Society of Children's Authors, Illustrators and Performers (CANSCAIP)
40 Orchard View Boulevard, Suite 104, Lower Level, Toronto, ON M4R 1B9
Phone: (416) 515-1559 Fax: (416) 515-7022
E-mail: office@canscaip.org
Web site: www.canscaip.org

Canadian Writers' Foundation
1 Nakota Way, Napean, ON K2J 4E9
Fax: (613) 823-0715
E-mail: smw@magma.ca
Web site: www.canauthors.org/cwf

Children's Writers & Illustrators of B.C.
3622 Point Grey Road, Vancouver, BC V6R 1A9
Phone: (604) 736-2107 Fax: (604) 736-2104
E-mail: kshoe@telus.net

Conseil des arts et des lettres du Québec

79 René-Lévesque Boulevard E., 3rd Floor, Quebec, QC G1R 5N5
Phone: (418) 643-1707 or 1-800-897-1707 Fax: (418) 643-4558
500 Place d'Armes, 15th Floor, Montreal, QC H2Y 2W2
Phone: (514) 864-3350 or 1-800-608-3350 Fax: (514) 864-4160

Crime Writers of Canada

P.O. Box 113, 3007 Kingston Road, Scarborough, ON M1M 1P1
Phone: (416) 597-9938
E-mail: info@crimewriterscanada.com
Web site: www.crimewriterscanada.com

Editors' Association of Canada (EAC)

27 Carlton Street, Suite 502, Toronto, ON M5B 1L2
Phone: (416) 975-1379 or 1-866-226-3348 Fax: (416) 975-1637
E-mail: info@editors.ca
Web site: www.editors.ca

Electronic Frontier Canada

20 Richmond Avenue, Kitchener, ON N2G 1Y9
Phone: (519) 888-4804 Fax: (519) 475-0941
E-mail: efc@efc.ca
Web site: www.efc.ca

Federation of BC Writers

P.O. Box 3887, Stn. Terminal, Vancouver, BC V6B 2Z3
Phone: (604) 683-2057 Fax: (604) 608-5522
E-mail: fedoffice@bcwriters.com
Web site: www.bcwriters.com

Island Writers Association (P.E.I.)

P.O. Box 1204, Charlottetown, PE C1A 7M8
Phone: (902) 566-9748 Fax: (902) 566-9748
E-mail: creative@peinet.pe.ca

League of Canadian Poets

920 Yonge Street, Suite 608, Toronto, ON M4W 3C7
Phone: (416) 504-1657 Fax: (416) 504-0096

E-mail: info@poets.ca
Web site: www.poets.ca

Literary Press Group of Canada
192 Spadina Avenue, Suite 501, Toronto, ON M5T 2C2
Phone: (416) 483-1321 Fax: (416) 483-2510
E-mail: info@lpg.ca
Web site: www.lpg.ca

Literary Translators' Association of Canada
1455 Maisonneuve Boulevard W., SB 335 Concordia University,
    Montreal, QC H3G 1M8
Phone: (514) 848-8702
E-mail: info@attlc-ltac.org
Web site: www.attlc-ltac.org

Manitoba Arts Council
93 Lombard Avenue, Suite 525, Winnipeg, MB R3B 3B1
Phone: (204) 945-0422 or 1-866-994-2787 (toll-free in MB)
    Fax: (204) 945-5925
E-mail: jthomas@artscouncil.mb.ca
Web site: www.artscouncil.mb.ca

Manitoba Writers' Guild
100 Arthur Street, Suite 206, Winnipeg, MB R3B 1H3
Phone: (204) 942-6134 or 1-888-637-5802 Fax: (204) 942-5754
E-mail: mbwriter@mts.net
Web site: www.mbwriter.mb.ca

New Brunswick Arts Board
634 Queen Street, Suite 300, Fredericton, NB E3B 1C2
Phone: (506) 444-5633 Fax: (506) 444-5543
E-mail: rbarriault@artsnb.ca
Web site: www.artsnb.ca

Newfoundland and Labrador Arts Council
P.O. Box 98, Stn. C, St. John's, NL A1C 5H5
Phone: (709) 726-2212 or 1-866-726-2212 Fax: (709) 726-0619

E-mail: nlacmail@nfld.net
Web site: www.nlac.nf.ca

Northwest Territories Arts Council
Department of Education, Culture and Employment, Government
   of the N.W.T., P.O. Box 1320, Yellowknife, NT X1A 2L9
Phone: (867) 920-6370 Fax: (867) 873-0205
E-mail: boris_atamanenko@gov.nt.ca
Web site: www.pwnhc.ca

Nova Scotia Department of Tourism, Culture and Heritage
1800 Argyle Street, Suite 402, P.O. Box 456, Halifax, NS B3J 2R5
Phone: (902) 424-3422 Fax: (902) 424-0710
E-mail: kirbypc@gov.ns.ca
Web site: www.gov.ns.ca/dtc

Ontario Arts Council
Literature Programs, 151 Bloor Street W., Toronto, ON M5S 1T6
Phone: (416) 969-7438 Fax: (416) 961-7796
E-mail: lfilyer@arts.on.ca
Web site: www.arts.on.ca

Ontario Ministry of Tourism, Culture & Recreation
Culture Division, 400 University Avenue, 5th Floor, Toronto, ON
   M7A 2R9
Phone: (416) 314-7265
Web site: www.culture.gov.on.ca

Ottawa Independent Writers
P.O. Box 23137, Ottawa, ON K2A 4E2
Phone: (613) 841-0572
E-mail: communications@oiw.ca
Web site: http://oiw.ca

P.E.I. Writers Guild
P.O. Box 1, 115 Richmond Street, Charlottetown, PE C1A 1H7
Fax: (902) 961-2345
E-mail: brinklow@upei.ca
Web site: www.peiwriters.ca

PEN Canada
24 Ryerson Avenue, Suite 214, Toronto, ON M5T 2P3
Phone: (416) 703-8448 Fax: (416) 703-3870
E-mail: pen@pencanada.ca
Web site: www.pencanada.ca

Periodical Writers Association of Canada
54 Wolseley Street, Suite 203, Toronto, ON M5T 1A5
Phone: (416) 504-1645 Fax: (416) 504-9079
E-mail: info@pwac.ca
Web site: www.pwac.ca

Playwrights Guild of Canada
54 Wolseley Street, 2nd Floor, Toronto, ON M5T 1A5
Phone: (416) 703-0201 Fax: (416) 703-0059
E-mail: info@playwrightsguild.ca
Web site: www.playwrightsguild.ca

Playwrights Theatre Centre
1398 Cartwright Street, Suite 201, Vancouver, BC V6H 3R8
Phone: (604) 685-6228 Fax: (604) 685-7451
E-mail: plays@playwrightsthreatre.com
Web site: www.playwrightsthreatre.com

Praxis Centre for Screenwriters
515 West Hastings Street, Suite 3120, Vancouver, BC V6B 1A5
Phone: (604) 268-7880 Fax: (604) 268-7882
E-mail: praxis@sfu.ca
Web site: www.praxisfilm.com

Prince Edward Island Council of the Arts
115 Richmond Street, Charlottetown, PE C1A 1H7
Phone: (902) 368-4410 Fax: (902) 368-4418
E-mail: artscouncil@pei.aibn.com

Public Lending Right Commission
P.O. Box 1047, 350 Albert Street, Ottawa, ON K1P 5V8
Phone: (613) 566-4378 or 1-800-521-5721 Fax: (613) 566-4418

E-mail: plr@canadacouncil.ca
Web site: www.plr-dpp.ca

Quebec Writers' Federation
1200 Atwater Avenue, Suite 3, Montreal, QC H3Z 1X4
Phone: (514) 933-0878 Fax: (514) 934-2485
E-mail: admin@qwf.org
Web site: www.qwf.org

Saskatchewan Arts Board
2135 Broad Street, Regina, SK S4P 3V7
Phone: (306) 787-4056 or 1-800-667-7526 (SK)
    Fax: (306) 787-4199
E-mail: grants@artsboard.sk.ca
Web site: www.artsboard.sk.ca

Saskatchewan Writers Guild
P.O. Box 3986, Regina, SK S4P 3R9
Phone: (306) 757-6310 Fax: (306) 565-8554
E-mail: swg@sasktel.net
Web site: www.skwriter.com

Scarborough Arts Council
1859 Kingston Road, Scarborough, ON M1N 1T3
Phone: (416) 698-7322 Fax: (416) 698-7972
E-mail: sac@scarborougharts.com
Web site: www.scarborougharts.com

SF Canada
106 Cocksfield Avenue, Toronto, ON M3H 3T2
E-mail: micigold@sympatico.ca
Web site: www.sfcanada.ca

Storytellers of Canada
R.R. #2, Lanark, ON K0G 1K0
Phone: (613) 256-0353 Fax: (613) 489-5640
E-mail: membership@sc-cc.com
Web site: www.sc-cc.com

Territorial Writers Association
Aurora Arts Society, P.O. Box 1042, Yellowknife, NT XIA 2N7
E-mail: madpete@ssimicro.com

Toronto Arts Council
141 Bathurst Street, Toronto, ON M5V 2R2
Phone: (416) 392-6800 Fax: (416) 392-6920
E-mail: mail@torontoartscouncil.org
Web site: www.torontoartscouncil.org

Vancouver Children's Literature Roundtable
Ron Jobe, Department of Language and Literacy, Faculty of
    Education, 2125 Main Mall, University of B.C., Vancouver, BC
    V6T 1Z4
Phone: (604) 683-1808 Fax: (604) 822-3154
E-mail: ron.jobe@ubc.ca
Web site: www.library.ubc.ca/edlib/rdtable.html

Vancouver Office of Cultural Affairs
453 West 12th Avenue, Vancouver, BC V5Y 1V4
Phone: (604) 873-7487 Fax: (604) 871-6048
E-mail: oca@city.vancouver.bc.ca
Web site: www.city.vancouver.bc.ca/commsvcs/oca

Victoria Children's Literature Roundtable
Colleen Stewart, Youth Department, Greater Victoria Public
    Library, 735 Broughton Street, Victoria, BC V8W 3H2
Phone: (250) 382-7241 Fax: (250) 382-7125
E-mail: cstewart@gvpl.victoria.bc.ca
Web site: www.library.ubc.ca/edlib/victoria.html

The Word Guild
P.O. Box 487, Markham, ON L3P 3R1
Phone: (905) 294-6482
E-mail: info@thewordguild.com
Web site: www.thewordguild.com

Writers' Alliance of Newfoundland and Labrador
P.O. Box 2681, St. John's, NL A1C 5M5
Phone: (709) 739-5215 Fax: (709) 739-5931
E-mail: wanl@nfld.com
Web site: www.writersalliance.nf.ca

The Writers' Circle of Durham Region
P.O. Box 323, Ajax, ON L1S 3C5
Phone: (905) 259-6520
E-mail: info@wcdr.org
Web site: www.wcdr.org

Writers' Federation of New Brunswick
P.O. Box 37, Stn. A, Fredericton, NB E3B 4Y2
Phone: (506) 459-7228
E-mail: wfnb@nb.aibn.com
Web site:
    www.sjfn.nb.ca/community_hall/W/Writers_Federation_nb

Writers' Federation of Nova Scotia
1113 Marginal Road, Halifax, NS B3H 4P7
Phone: (902) 423-8116 Fax: (902) 422-0881
E-mail: talk@writers.ns.ca
Web site: www.writers.ns.ca

Writers Guild of Alberta
11759 Groat Road, Edmonton, AB T5M 3K6
Phone: (780) 422-8174 or 1-800-665-5354 Fax: (780) 422-2663
E-mail: mail@writersguild.ab.ca
Web site: www.writersguild.ab.ca

Writers Guild of Canada
366 Adelaide Street W., Suite 401, Toronto, ON M5V 1R9
Phone: (416) 979-7907 or 1-800-567-9974 Fax: (416) 979-9273
E-mail: info@wgc.ca
Web site: www.writersguildofcanada.com

Writers in Electronic Residence
317 Adelaide Street W., Suite 300, Toronto, ON M5V 1P9
Phone: (416) 504-4490   Fax: (416) 591-5345
E-mail: wier@wier.ca
Web site: www.wier.ca

The Writers' Trust of Canada
40 Wellington Street E., Suite 300, Toronto, ON M5E 1C7
Phone: (416) 504-8222   Fax: (416) 504-9090
E-mail: info@writerstrust.com
Web site: www.writerstrust.com

The Writers' Union of Canada
40 Wellington Street E., 3rd Floor, Toronto, ON M5E 1C7
Phone: (416) 703-8982   Fax: (416) 504-7656
E-mail: info@writersunion.ca
Web site: www.writersunion.ca

Young Alberta Book Society
11759 Groat Road, Edmonton, AB T5M 3K6
Phone: (780) 422-8232   Fax: (780) 422-8239
E-mail: info@yabs.ab.ca
Web site: www.yabs.ab.ca

Yukon Department of Tourism and Culture
Arts Section, P.O. Box 2703, Whitehorse, YT Y1A 2C6
Phone: (867) 667-5264   Fax: (867) 393-6456
E-mail: laurel.parry@gov.yk.ca

11

RESOURCES

For those seeking practical advice and inspiration about their craft, there is a cornucopia of writers' resource books on the market: style guides, practical handbooks, personal meditations, marketing primers, as well as more advanced "workshops" on the narrative and descriptive arts. In addition, there are increasing numbers of writers' web sites that offer everything from dictionaries to articles on how to deal with rejection.

With a growing industry in writing about writing, it is possible to offer only a short selection of resources here. As you'll see, the following listing includes books from the United States and Britain, as well as from Canada. Most are available here in good bookstores; a few are out of print but may still be held in libraries.

Stylebooks, Handbooks, & Guides

Appelbaum, Judith. *How to Get Happily Published* (5th ed.), Harper Perennial, New York, 1998.
Aslett, Don, and Carol Cartaino. *Get Organized, Get Published: 225 Ways to Make Time for Success,* Writer's Digest Books, Cincinnati, 2001.
Bacia, Jennifer. *Chapter One: Everything You Want to Know About Starting Your Novel,* Allen & Unwin, St. Leonards, Australia, 1999.

432

Baker, Edward. *A Writer's Guide to Overcoming Rejection*, Summersdale Publishers, Chichester, U.K., 1998.

Ballon, Rachel Friedman. *Breathing Life into Your Characters*, Writer's Digest Books, Cincinnati, 2003.

Barker-Sandbrook, Judith. *Thinking through Your Writing Process*, McGraw-Hill Ryerson, Toronto, 1989.

Bates, Jefferson D. *Writing with Precision*, Penguin Books, New York, 2000.

Bell, Julia, and Paul Magrs (eds.). *The Creative Writing Coursebook*, Macmillan, London, 2001.

Bernstein, Theodore M. *Miss Thistlebottom's Hobgoblins: The Careful Writer's Guide to the Taboos, Bugbears and Outmoded Rules of English Usage*, Simon & Schuster, New York, 1971.

Berton, Pierre. *The Joy of Writing*, Anchor Canada, Toronto, 2003.

Birkett, Julian. *Word Power: A Guide to Creative Writing*, A. & C. Black, London, 1993.

Blackburn, Bob. *Words Fail Us: Good English and Other Lost Causes*, McClelland & Stewart, Toronto, 1993.

Blamires, Harry. *The Penguin Guide to Plain English*, Penguin Books, London, 2000.

Block, Lawrence. *Telling Lies for Fun and Profit: A Manual for Fiction Writers*, William Morrow, New York, 1994.

Blundell, William E. *The Art and Craft of Feature Writing*, Plume, New York, 1988.

Bly, Carol. *Beyond the Writers' Workshop: New Ways to Write Creative Nonfiction*, Anchor Books, New York, 2001.

Bly, Robert W. *Secrets of a Freelance Writer* (2nd rev. ed.), Owl, New York, 1997.

Braine, John. *Writing a Novel*, Methuen, London, 1974.

Brandeis, Gayle. *Fruitflesh: Seeds of Inspiration for Women Who Write*, Harper San Francisco, 2002.

Burgett, Gordon. *How to Sell More Than 75% of Your Freelance Writing*, Prima, Rocklin, CA, 1995.

———. *The Travel Writer's Guide* (2nd ed.), Prima, Rocklin, CA, 1992.

Camenson, Blythe, and Marshall J. Cook. *Your Novel Proposal: From Creation to Contract*, Writer's Digest Books, Cincinnati, 1999.

The Canadian Writer's Guide: Official Handbook of the Canadian Authors Association (13th ed.). Fitzhenry & Whiteside, Toronto, 2003.

Checkoway, Julie. *Creating Fiction*, Story Press, Cincinnati, 1999.

Cheney, Theodore A. Rees. *Getting the Words Right: How to Rewrite, Edit and Revise*, Writer's Digest Books, Cincinnati, 1983.

The Chicago Manual of Style (15th ed.). University of Chicago Press, Chicago, 2003.

Clayton, Joan. *Journalism for Beginners: How to Get into Print and Get Paid for It*, Piatkus, London, 2000.

———. *Writing Science Fiction and Fantasy*, Self-Counsel Press, North Vancouver, 1998.

Cropp, Richard, Barbara Braidwood, and Susan M. Boyce. *Writing Travel Books and Articles*, Self-Counsel Press, Vancouver, 1997.

Davies, Richard. *The Canadian Writer's Handbook*, Gage, Vancouver, 2000.

Derricourt, Robin. *An Author's Guide to Scholarly Publishing*, Princeton University Press, Princeton, NJ, 1996.

Dick, Jill. *Writing for Magazines* (2nd ed.), A. and C. Black, London, 1996.

Dufresne, John. *The Lie That Tells a Truth*, W. W. Norton & Co., New York, 2003.

Editing Canadian English (2nd ed.), Editors' Association of Canada, Macfarlane Walter & Ross, Toronto, 2000.

Embree, Mary. *The Author's Toolkit*, Allworth Press, New York, 2003.

Fee, Margery, and Janice McAlpine. *Guide to Canadian English*, Oxford University Press, Toronto, 1997.

Forché, Carolyn, and Philip Gerard. *Writing Creative Nonfiction*, Story Press, Cincinnati, 2001.

Formichelli, Linda, and Diana Burrell. *The Renegade Writer*, Marion Street Press, Oak Park, IL, 2003.

Frank, Thaisa, and Dorothy Wall. *Finding Your Writer's Voice: A Guide to Creative Fiction*, St. Martin's Press, New York, 1994.

Frey, James N. *How to Write a Damn Good Mystery*, St. Martin's Press, New York, 2004.

Frank, Steven, *The Pen Commandments*, Pantheon Books, New York, 2003.

Gage, Diane, and Marcia Coppess. *Get Published: Editors from the Nation's Top Magazines Tell You What They Want*, Henry Holt, New York, 1994.

Gardner, John. *The Art of Fiction: Notes on Craft for Young Writers*, Vintage, New York, 1983.

———. *On Writers and Writing*, Addison-Wesley, New York, 1994.

Gerard, Philip. *Writing a Book That Makes a Difference*, Writer's Digest Books, Cincinnati, 2000.

Gibaldi, Joseph. *MLA Style Manual and Guide to Scholarly Publishing* (2nd ed.), The Modern Language Association of America, New York, 1998.

Giltrow, Janet. *Academic Writing* (2nd ed.), Broadview, Peterborough, ON, 1994.

Goldberg, Natalie. *Thunder and Lightning: Cracking Open the Writer's Craft*, Bantam Books, New York, 2001.

———. *Wild Mind: Living the Writer's Life*, Bantam Books, New York, 1990.

———. *Writing Down the Bones: Freeing the Writer Within*, Shambhala, Boston and London, 1986.

Grant, Vanessa. *Writing Romance*, Self-Counsel Press, Vancouver, 1997.

Grobel, Lawrence. *Endangered Species: Writers Talk About Their Craft, Their Visions, Their Lives*, Da Capo Press, Cambridge, MA, 2001.

Gutkind, Lee. *The Art of Creative Nonfiction*, John Wiley and Sons, New York and Toronto, 1997.

Harper, Timothy (ed.). *The ASJA Guide to Freelance Writing*, St. Martin's Press, New York, 2003.

Heffron, Jack. *The Writer's Idea Workshop*, Writer's Digest Books, Cincinnati, 2003.

Hemley, Robin. *Turning Life into Fiction*, Story Press, Cincinnati, 1994.

Herman, Jeff, and Deborah Levine Herman. *Write the Perfect Book Proposal*, John Wiley & Sons, New York, 2001.

Hicks, Wynford. *English for Journalists* (2nd ed.), Routledge, London, 1998.

Hodgins, Jack. *A Passion for Narrative: A Guide for Writing Fiction*, McClelland & Stewart, Toronto, 1993.

Jacobi, Peter P. *The Magazine Article: How to Think It, Plan It, Write It*, Indiana University Press, Bloomington, IN, 1991.

Kane, Thomas S., and Karen C. Ogden. *The Canadian Oxford Guide to Writing*, Oxford University Press, Toronto, 1993.

Karl, Jean E. *How to Write and Sell Children's Picture Books*, Writer's Digest Books, Cincinnati, 1994.

Kelton, Nancy Davidoff. *Writing From Personal Experience: How to Turn Your Life into Salable Prose*, Writer's Digest Books, Cincinnati, 1997.

Kercheval, Jesse Lee. *Building Fiction: How to Develop Plot and Structure*, Story Press, Cincinnati, 1997.

Kilian, Crawford. *Writing for the Web*, Self-Counsel Press, North Vancouver, 2000.

Konner, Linda. *How to Be Successfully Published in Magazines*, St. Martin's Press, New York, 1990.

Kress, Nancy. *Dynamic Characters: How to Create Personalities That Keep Readers Captivated*, Writer's Digest Books, Cincinnati, 1998.

LaRocque, Paula. *The Book on Writing*, Marion Street Press, Oak Park, IL, 2003.

Larson, Michael. *How to Write a Book Proposal* (2nd ed.), Writer's Digest Books, Cincinnati, 1997.

Lavasseur, Jennifer, and Kevin Rabalais (eds.). *Novel Voices*, Writer's Digest Books, Cincinnati, 2003.

Leland, Christopher T. *The Art of Compelling Fiction: How to Write a Page-Turner*, Story Press, Cincinnati, 1998.

Lerner, Betsy. *The Forest for the Trees: An Editor's Advice to Writers*, Riverhead Books, New York, 2001.

Levin, Donna. *Get That Novel Written: From Initial Idea to Final Edit*, Writer's Digest Books, Cincinnati, 1996.

Levin, Martin P. *Be Your Own Literary Agent: The Ultimate Insider's Guide to Getting Published*, Ten Speed Press, Berkeley, CA, 2002.

Levinson, Jay Conrad, Rick Frishman, and Michael Larsen. *Guerrilla Marketing for Writers: 100 Weapons for Selling Your Work*, Writer's Digest Books, Cincinnati, 2001.

Lunsford, Andrea, Robert Connors, and Judy Z. Segal. *The St. Martin's Handbook for Canadians*, Nelson Canada, Toronto, 1995.

Mandell, Judy. *Book Editors Talk to Writers*, John Wiley and Sons, New York, 1996.

Marshall, Evan. *The Marshall Plan for Getting Your Novel Published*, Writer's Digest Books, Cincinnati, 2003.

Mayer, Bob. *The Novel Writer's Toolkit*, Writer's Digest Books, Cincinnati, 2003.

McFarlane, J. A., and Warren Clements. *The Globe and Mail Style Book* (9th ed.), McClelland & Stewart, Toronto, 2003.

McKeown, Thomas W., and Carol M. Cram. *Better Business Writing*, Clear Communications Press, Vancouver, 1990.

McKercher, Catherine, and Carman Cumming. *The Canadian Reporter: News Writing and Reporting*, Harcourt Brace Canada, Toronto, 1998.

Mencher, Melvin. *News Reporting and Writing* (8th ed.), McGraw-Hill Ryerson, Toronto, 2000.

Mettee, Stephen Blake. *The Portable Writers' Conference: Your Guide to Getting and Staying Published*, Quill Driver Books, Fresno, CA, 1997.

Miller, Casey, and Kate Swift. *The Handbook of Nonsexist Writing* (2nd ed.), Harper & Row, New York, 1988.

Miller, Peter. *Get Published! Get Produced!* Lone Eagle Publishing, Los Angeles, 1998.

Novakovich, Josip. *Fiction Writer's Workshop*, Story Press, Cincinnati, 1995.

Oxford Style Manual, Oxford University Press, Oxford, 2003.

Perkins, Lori. *The Insider's Guide to Getting an Agent*, Writer's Digest Books, Cincinnati, 1999.

Peterson, Franklynn, and Judi Kesselman-Turkel. *The Magazine Writer's Handbook*, Prentice-Hall, Englewood Cliffs, NJ, 1982.

Pfeiffer, William S., and Jan Boogerd. *Technical Writing: A Practical Approach*, Prentice-Hall Canada, Toronto, 1997.

Rivers, Dyanne. *The Business of Writing: The Canadian Guide for Writers and Editors*, McGraw-Hill Ryerson, Toronto, 1994.

Roth, Martin. *The Writer's Partner: 1001 Breakthrough Ideas to Stimulate Your Imagination*, Michael Wiese Productions, Studio City, CA, 2001.

Rubens, Philip (ed.). *Science and Technical Writing: A Manual of Style*, Routledge, New York, 2001.

Rubie, Peter. *The Everything Get Published Book*, Adams Media Corp., Avon, MA, 2000.

Seidman, Michael. *The Complete Guide to Editing Your Fiction*, Writer's Digest Books, Cincinnati, 2000.

Staw, Jane Anne. *Unstuck: A Supportive and Practical Guide to Working through Writer's Block*, St. Martin's Press, New York, 2003.

Stevens, Mark A. *Merriam Webster's Manual for Writers and Editors*, Merriam-Webster, Springfield, MA, 1998.

Strunk, William, Jr., and E. B. White. *The Elements of Style* (4th ed.), Allyn and Bacon, Boston, 2000.

Sutcliffe, Andrea J. (ed.). *The New York Library Writer's Guide to Style and Usage*, HarperCollins Publishers, New York, 1994.

Tasko, Patti (ed.). *The Canadian Press Stylebook* (12th ed.), The Canadian Press, Toronto, 2002.

Waller, Adrian. *Writing! An Informal, Anecdotal Guide to the Secrets of Crafting and Selling Non-Fiction*, McClelland & Stewart, Toronto, 1987.

Williams, Malcolm (ed.). *The Canadian Style: A Guide to Writing and Editing*, Dundurn Press, Toronto, 1997.

Words into Type (3rd ed. rev.). Prentice-Hall, Englewood Cliffs, NJ, 1974.

Zinsser, William. *On Writing Well: The Classic Guide to Writing Nonfiction* (6th ed.), HarperCollins, New York, 1998.

Dictionaries & Thesauruses

The Canadian Oxford Dictionary, ed. Katherine Barber, Oxford University Press, Toronto, 2001.

Canadian Thesaurus, ed. J. K. Chambers, Fitzhenry & Whiteside, Markham, ON, 2001.

Collins Concise Dictionary (5th ed.), ed. J. M. Sinclair, HarperCollins, Glasgow, 2001.

The Concise Oxford English Dictionary (10th ed.), Oxford University Press, Oxford, 2002.

Gage Canadian Dictionary, Gage Educational Publishing Co., Toronto, 2000.

Gage Canadian Thesaurus, ed. T. K. Pratt, Gage Learning Corp., Toronto, 1998.

Merriam-Webster's Collegiate Dictionary (11th ed.), ed. Frederick C. Mish, Merriam-Webster, Springfield, MA, 2003.

Microsoft Encarta College Dictionary, ed. Anne H. Soukhanov, St. Martin's Press, New York, 2001.

Nelson Canadian Dictionary of the English Language, ITP Nelson, Toronto, 1998.

The New Fowler's Modern English Usage (3rd ed. rev.), ed. R. W. Birchfield. Oxford University Press, Oxford, 2000.

The Oxford Compact Thesaurus (2nd ed.), ed. Maurice Waite, Oxford University Press, Oxford, 2001.

The Oxford Writers' Dictionary, ed. R. E. Allen, Oxford University Press, Oxford, 1990.

The Penguin English Dictionary, ed. Robert Allen, Penguin Books, London, 2003.

Random House Webster's Unabridged Dictionary (2nd ed.), ed. Wendalyn R. Nichols, Random House, New York, 2001.

Roget's Thesaurus of English Words and Phrases, ed. Betty Kirkpatrick, Penguin Books, London, 1998.

Webster's New World Roget's A to Z Thesaurus, ed. Charlton Laird, Macmillan, New York, 1999.

Yearbooks, Almanacs, & Other Regularly Published Reference Sources

The Book Trade in Canada (annual), *Quill & Quire*, Toronto.

Canadian Almanac & Directory (annual), Micromedia, Toronto.

The Canadian Global Almanac, Global Press, Toronto, 2004.

CARD (Canadian Advertising Rates & Data) (monthly), Rogers Media, Toronto.

Canadian Publishers Directory (biannual), supplement to Quill & Quire magazine.

Guide to Literary Agents (annual), Writer's Digest Books, Cincinnati.

Literary Market Place (annual), R. R. Bowker, New York.

Matthews Media Directory (quarterly), Syd Matthews & Partners, Meaford, ON.

Novel and Short Story Writer's Market (annual), Writer's Digest Books, Cincinnati.

Poet's Market (annual), Writer's Digest Books, Cincinnati.

Publication Profiles, published annually with the May issue of *CARD* (see above), Rogers Media, Toronto.

Scott's Canadian Sourcebook (annual), Southam, Toronto.
Writers' & Artists' Yearbook (annual), A. & C. Black, London.
Writer's Market and *Writer's Market Online* (annual), Writer's
Digest Books, Cincinnati.

Some Major Canadian Magazine Publishers

Annex Publishing and Printing Inc., 222 Argyle Avenue, Delhi,
ON N4B 2Y2 Phone: (519) 582-2513 Fax: (519) 582-4040
Web site: www.annexweb.com (trade)

Bowes Publishers Ltd., P.O. Box 7400, London, ON N5Y 4X3
Phone: (519) 471-8320 Fax: (519) 471-8320 E-mail:
bowes@bowesnet.com Web site: www.bowesnet.com (business,
farm)

Business Information Group, 1450 Don Mills Road, Don Mills,
ON M3B 2X7 Phone: (416) 442-2212 Fax: (416) 442-2214
(business)

Canada Wide Magazines Ltd., 4180 Lougheed Highway, 4th
Floor, Burnaby, BC V5C 6A7 Phone: (604) 299-7311 Fax: (604)
299-9188 E-mail: cwm@canadawide.com Web site:
www.canadawide.com (business, consumer, trade)

CLB Media Inc., 240 Edward Street, Aurora, ON L4G 3S9 Phone:
(905) 727-0077 Fax: (905) 727-0017 Web site: www.action-
com.com (trade)

Craig Kelman& Associates Ltd., 2020 Portage Avenue, Suite 3C,
Winnipeg, MB R3J 1K4 Phone: (204) 985-9780 Fax: (204)
985-9795 E-mail: info@kelman.mb.ca (trade)

Family Communications Inc., 37 Hanna Avenue, Suite 1, Toronto,
ON M6K 1W9 Phone: (416) 537-2604 Fax: (416) 538-1794
E-mail: family@interlog.com Web site: www.todaysbride.ca
(consumer)

Farm Business Communications, 201 Portage Avenue, 25th Floor,
P.O. Box 6600, Winnipeg, MB R3C 3A7 Phone: (204) 944-5753
Fax: (204) 942-8463 Web site: www.agcanada.com (farm)

Koocanusa Publications Inc., 1510 – 2nd Street N., Suite 200,
Cranbrook, BC V1C 3L2 Phone: (250) 426-7253 Fax: (250)
426-4125 E-mail: info@kpimedia.com Web site:
www.koocanusapublications.com (business, consumer)

Metroland Printing, Publishing & Distributing Ltd., 10 Tempo
   Avenue, Willowdale, ON M2H 2N8 Phone: 416) 493-1300
   Fax: (416) 493-0623 E-mail: result@metroland.com Web site:
   www.metroland.com (business, consumer)
Norris-Whitney Communications Inc., 23 Hannover Drive, Unit
   7, St. Catharines, ON L2W 1A3 Phone: (905) 641-3471 Fax:
   (905) 641-1648 Web site: www.nor.com/nwc (consumer, trade)
Rogers Media Publishing, 1 Mount Pleasant Road, Toronto, ON
   M4Y 2Y5 Phone: (416) 764-2000 Fax: (416) 764-3943 Web site:
   www.rogersmedia.com (business, consumer, trade)
Trajan Publishing, 103 Lakeshore Road, Suite 202, St.
   Catharines, ON L2N 2T6 Phone: (905) 646-7744 Fax: (905)
   646-0995 Web site: www.trajan.ca (consumer)
Transcontinental Publications, 1 Place Ville Marie, Suite 3315,
   Montreal, QC H3B 3N2 Phone: (514) 954-4000 Fax: (514)
   954-4016 Web site: www.transcontinental.com (consumer)
Tribute Publishing Inc., 71 Barber Greene Road, Toronto, ON
   M3C 2A2 Phone: (416) 445-0544. Fax: (416) 445-2894
   (consumer)

Online Resources

The following list of online resources is by no means exhaustive.
Rather, it is intended to give the writer a starting point from which
to begin his or her investigation into what sites are available on the
Internet.

Authorlink
http://authorlink.com
   An American site where writers have the opportunity to get a literary agent and sell their work to publishers throughout the
English-speaking world. Fees apply.

The Bible Gateway
http://bible.gospelcom.net/bible?
   Allows you to look up any verse or phrase in many versions of
the Bible.

CanadaInfo
www.craigmarlatt.com/canada
 A source of facts about Canada and its people.

Canadian Authors Association
www.canauthors.org
 News about the organization, literary awards, and extensive links of interest to writers.

The Canadian Encyclopedia
www.thecanadianencyclopedia.com
 A convenient site on which to research Canadian topics.

Canadian Studies: A Guide to the Sources
www.iccs-ciec.ca/blackwell.html
 Provides links to many Canadian sites of interest to researchers.

Canadian Who's Who
www.utpress.utoronto.ca/cgi-bin/cw2w3.cgi
 The 1997 edition of *Canadian Who's Who*.

Chicago Manual of Style Queries
www.press.uchicago.edu/Misc/Chicago/cmosfaq/cmosfaq.html
 Queries about the 15th edition of *The Chicago Manual of Style*.

CopyrightLaws.com
www.copyrightlaws.com
 Canadian media and copyright lawyer Lesley Ellen Harris provides information on Canadian, U.S., and international copyright law.

Creative Freelancers
www.freelancers.com
 Includes classified ads for American jobs for freelance writers.

The Eclectic Writer
http://eclectics.com/writing/writing.html
 Articles on all aspects of writing with lots of links.

The Elements of Style
www.bartleby.com/141/index.html
 Contains rules of usage, principles of composition, and commonly misused and misspelled words.

Encyclopedia.com
www.encyclopedia.com
 Provides access to 57,000 updated articles from the *Columbia Encyclopedia*, and you can subscribe to their eLibrary of 28 million documents.

Encyclopedia Britannica
www.eb.com
 Subscribers have access to the 32 volumes of the *Encyclopedia Britannica*, plus thousands of newly added articles, graphics, and related Internet links.

Familiar Quotations
www.bartleby.com/100
 Searches Bartlett's, Columbia, and Simpson's Quotations.

Freelance Writing
www.freelancewriting.com
 Includes a reading room, career centre, and freelance jobs.

John Hewitt's Writer's Resource Center
www.poewar.com
 Contains job listings, book reviews, and articles and exercises about all aspects of writing.

Literary Market Place
www.literarymarketplace.com
 Lists Canadian, U.S., and other international publishers, as well as literary agents.

Literati Club
www.emeraldinsight.com/literaticlub
 Offers guidance on every step of writing an article.

Magomania
www.magomania.com

Provides contact information for and descriptions of hundreds of Canadian magazines, plus links to their web sites. Administered by the Canadian Magazine Publishers Association.

MediaFinder
www.mediafinder.com

Subscribers can access the most comprehensive database of print media in Canada and the U.S.

Merriam-Webster OnLine
www.m-w.com

Subscribers have access to either the *Merriam-Webster Collegiate* or *Unabridged* dictionaries, with a thesaurus and other reference material included. Premium members also have access to the *Encyclopedia Britannica*.

Novel Advice
www.noveladvice.com

Contains a long resource list and a message board where you can post your work.

Oxford English Dictionary
www.oed.com

Access to the 2nd edition of the *Oxford English Dictionary* for subscribers.

Publishers' Catalogues
www.lights.com/publisher

Provides links to the catalogues and news of Canadian publishers, as well as of publishers from around the world.

Purple Crayon
www.underdown.org/articles.htm

Articles on writing and illustrating children's books and getting them published.

The Query Guild
www.queryguild.ca
A site where your book and screenplay queries can be viewed by agents, publishers, and film producers.

Rosedog Books
www.rosedog.com
Subscribers can post their manuscripts for viewing by agents and publishers.

Shaw Guides
www.shawguides.com
Provides information about writers' conferences and workshops worldwide.

Thesaurus.com
www.thesaurus.com
Contains a thesaurus, dictionary, and guides to grammar and style.

The Vocabula Review
www.vocabula.com
A monthly e-zine that seeks to promote the richness and correct use of the English language.

What You Need to Know about Freelance Writers
www.freelancewrite.about.com
Includes job postings, articles, newsletters, and forums.

Writer Alerts
www.nwu.org/alerts/alrthome.htm
Provides warnings about book publishers, organizations, and magazines.

Writer Beware
www.sfwa.org/beware
Lists agents and publishers that writers should be wary of.

Writers Guild of Canada

www.writersguildofcanada.com

Lists of literary agents and lawyers, and links of interest to writers and screenwriters.

Writer's Market

www.writersmarket.com

Subscribers have access to listings of agents and publishers, plus advice and daily industry updates.

Writers Write

http://writerswrite.com

Includes *The Internet Writing Journal* with articles about writing and writers.

Writing Basics

www.scalar.com/mw/pages/articles.shtml

Tips on writing fiction and non-fiction, motivation and inspiration, editing, style, and usage. Includes a writers' marketplace with information on marketing your work, writing book proposals, what editors want, and how to deal with rejection.

Writing for Dollars

www.writingfordollars.com

Provides markets and a newsletter covering the business side of writing.

Writing-World.com

www.writing-world.com

Offers features and columns on all aspects of writing, lists of classes and contests, and job listings.

www.dictionary.reference.com

As well as an English dictionary, this site includes *Roget's Thesaurus* and dictionaries in French, German, Greek, Latin, Spanish, and more.

Your Dictionary

www.yourdictionary.com

Access to general dictionaries in many languages and specialty dictionaries.

Zuzu's Petals Literary Resource

www.zuzu.com

Has links to a wide range of writers' resources for all types of writing, publishers, contests, copyright information, and more.

INDEX OF CONSUMER, LITERARY, & SCHOLARLY MAGAZINES